JUDY
A Dog in a Million

JUDY
A Dog in a Million

Damien Lewis

Quercus

First published in Great Britain in 2014 by
Quercus Editions Ltd
55 Baker Street
Seventh Floor, South Block
London
W1U 8EW

A CIP catalogue record for this book is available from the
British Library

HB ISBN 978 1 84866 536 1
EBOOK ISBN 978 1 84866 537 8
TPB ISBN 978 1 84866 542 2

10 9 8 7 6 5 4 3 2 1

Typeset by IDSUK (DataConnection) Ltd
Plates designed by Rich Carr
Printed and bound in Great Britain by Clays Ltd, Elcograf S.p.A.

(HB only) Endpaper illustrations taken from the collection of
Museum The Hague.

Minitus acuminae – 'Protected with a sting'
Motto of the Yangtze River Gunboat, HMS *Gnat*

'. . . even the mosquito was sick of the taste of blood'
Alice Renshaw, pupil at Pensby High School for
Girls, on the Japanese POW camps of the Second
World War.

Acknowledgements

Special thanks are due to the following for their help in bringing this book to fruition. My literary agent, Annabel Merullo, her assistant, Laura Williams, and all the team at PFD, including but not limited to Rachel Mills and Alexandra Cliff. My film agent, Luke Speed. Richard Milner and Josh Ireland, my editors at Quercus, plus the entire team there – including but not limited to David North, Patrick Carpenter, Jane Harris, Caroline Proud, Dave Murphy and Ron Beard. Heartfelt thanks to you all. Thanks also to Simon Fowler, for your expert and tenacious research capabilities, and to Tean Roberts for reaching out as you did to survivors and their families.

Special thanks are due to the following who gave freely of their time, their expertise and/or their life experiences to enable me to bring this story to life on these pages. First and foremost Rouse Voisey, who shared his incredible life story with me. Rouse, I am hugely and forever in your debt. Captain George W. Duffy, for sharing your incredible life story, for your fantastic written work, and for the on-going assistance and encouragement. Peter Fyans and Fergus Anckhorn, author and subject of the book *The Conjuror on the Kwai*, which tells the story of Fergus's life and his extraordinary survival as a Japanese prisoner of war. Thank you for your time, your memories and your help. You were and remain an enormous inspiration to me. Lizzie Oliver, for your inspiration and enthusiasm and for your grandfather's sketches and memories, and for reading various drafts. Meg Parkes, for your peerless expertise and your father's diaries, and for your continuing assistance unto the very end. Phillip Wearne, for reaching out to some of the key people on my behalf, which proved invaluable. Adrienne Howell, of the Mere Literary Festival, for the generous introductions to those who were able to be of so much help in the writing of this book. David Tett, for the excellent volumes of postcards and correspondence from the POW camps. Henk Hovinga, for your persistence in getting your book to me and your steadfast help and advice. Les Parsons, for sharing some of your great uncle's experiences as a prisoner of war of the Japanese. Imogen Holmes, for sharing some of your father's experiences as a prisoner of war of the Japanese. Tony Spero, also for sharing some of your father's experiences as a prisoner of war of the Japanese. Tyson Milne, for sharing some of your grandfather's experiences as a prisoner of war of the Japanese. Amanda Farrell and Jonathan Moffatt for your assistance in the research and for providing invaluable contacts. My thanks are also due to those others who were of assistance to me, but preferred to remain unacknowledged.

Finally, special thanks to my wife, Eva, and to David, Damien Jnr, and Sianna-Sarah, for putting up with Dad's grumpy hours spent locked away in his study writing. Again.

Author's Note

During the Second World War and the years leading up to it, Judy, the dog whose story is told in these pages, adopted many human companions. However, there are sadly few if any survivors from those years. Throughout the period of the research for and the writing of this book I have endeavoured to contact as many of Judy's adopted human companions as possible, plus surviving family members of those who have passed away. If there are further witnesses to her incredible story who are inclined to come forward, please do get in touch with me. I may be able to include further recollections of this wonderful dog in future editions.

Particularly when dealing with the prisoner-of-war years there are few written accounts of what took place. So many people remember Judy, her companions and their adventures: so few documented those memories. This is understandable. The time spent by Allied servicemen as prisoners of war of the Japanese was terribly traumatic, and many did not want to speak about it. Many chose to take their stories to their graves. I am very grateful to those few still living who felt able to speak to me. Moreover, memories tend to differ, and apparently none more so than those from an environment like the Far East prisoner-of-war camps, in which so many days felt like a repeat of the hellish days that went before. There were so few milestones with which to mark the passing of time, or to anchor the memories.

The passage of the decades has also served to further obscure memory. The few written accounts that do exist also tend to differ in matters of detail. Locations and timescale are often somewhat uncertain. That being said, I have done my best to provide a comprehensible sense of place, chronology and narrative to the story as told in these pages. In the POW years in particular the methodology I have used to reconstruct where and when events took place is the 'most likely' scenario. If two or more testimonies or sources point to a particular time or place, I have opted to use that account as most likely. Where necessary I have recreated small sections of dialogue to aid the story's flow.

The above notwithstanding, any mistakes herein are entirely of my own making, and I would be happy to correct any in future editions. Likewise, while I have endeavoured to locate the copyright holders of the photos, sketches and other images used in this book, again this has not always been straightforward or easy. I would be happy to correct any mistakes in future editions.

For all at Sunninghill.

A little slice of paradise.

For giving
David, Damien Jnr and Sianna
the chance to be who they can be.

Preface

Only one animal ever achieved the dubious accolade of being made an official prisoner of war of the Japanese in World War Two. It was a dog. She was a beautiful and regal-looking English Pointer, and perhaps one of the most extraordinary of our canine companions ever to grace this earth.

In September 1942 she was given Japanese prisoner-of-war number '81A-Medan'.

Her real name was Judy, or 'Judy of Sussex' as her shipmates came to call her – for she spent most of her service life as the mascot of the Royal Navy gunboats the *Gnat* and the *Grasshopper*. But Judy of Sussex was much, much more than just a ship's dog. The way in which I came across her story drew me to it, inexorably, convincing me that this was a tale that absolutely had to be told.

In the spring of 2013 I wrote a book called *War Dog* (although I prefer the title my American publishers gave it, *The Dog Who Could Fly*). It tells the story of Ant, the extraordinary German Shepherd puppy rescued from no-man's-land who went on to fly numerous sorties with the RAF in the Second World War. In recognition of his heroic wartime exploits Ant – or Antis as he was renamed – was awarded the Dickin Medal, more commonly known as The Animal VC.

Ant's master was the Czech – later British – airman Robert Bozdech, with whom he flew into battle with RAF Bomber Command, was wounded, crash-landed and faced death countless times. In among the photos of the post-war Dickin Medal ceremonies, I found one that appeared to show Antis receiving his medal along with two other dogs. The animal to the right of the photo was a striking-looking liver-and-white English Pointer.

There was something compelling about that image and the animal it portrayed – a sense somehow of the dog's extraordinary courage and spirit that spoke across the decades. When next I met the Bozdech family – Robert Bozdech's surviving children – I showed them the photo, and asked who the mystery dog might be. We were at Pip's – the eldest sister's – lovely Devon farmhouse, having a family get-together to celebrate the publication of the book telling their father and Antis's story.

Pip took a look at the photo. 'I think that must be Judy. Yes, it's got to be her. Isn't she lovely? She's another Dickin Medal winner and she has the most wonderful story . . .'

Pip told me the little she knew of Judy's wartime exploits. Indeed, it did sound quite remarkable. My curiosity piqued, I made a promise to myself to try to find out more about the dog – but I was working on another book at the time, and any thoughts of looking into Judy's history fell by the wayside. That was until a second chance happening.

Some months later I was giving a talk at the fantastic Mere literary festival, in green and leafy Somerset. At some stage after the talk I happened to mention to the festival organizer, the delightful Adrienne Howell, my interest in the story of the only animal ever to become a prisoner of war of the Japanese. She threw me a shrewd look, as if trying to assess just how much she should reveal to me.

'Well, you know, Mere has a long history associated with the prisoners of the Japanese in the Far East,' she remarked. Adrienne paused for moment, then went on: 'In fact, my uncle was one . . . And there are any number of other POW families in the area. But the man you should really speak to is Phillip Wearne. His father, the Reverend Wearne, was a prisoner along with my uncle. He buried my uncle and brought the news of his death back to my grandparents.'

Adrienne very kindly offered to put me in touch with Philip Wearne, who she explained was very active in the FEPOW (Far East Prisoner of War) community.

'Of course,' she added, 'we've all heard of Judy's story. She was simply a wonderful dog. Extraordinary. What she did on the ships and in the POW camps – well, there's nothing quite like it.'

Two chance conversations; two people telling me the same thing – *this dog was absolutely out of the ordinary*. My appetite for the story quickened. As Adrienne had predicted, Phillip Wearne was most forthcoming and helpful. He advised me that, among others, I really needed to talk to one Lizzie Oliver. Her grandfather, Stanley Russell, was in the same camp as Judy; one of her many POW companions. And while it almost beggars belief, he'd somehow managed to keep a secret diary of his time in the camps, which, had it been discovered, could well have cost him his life at the hands of the Japanese and Korean guards.

Lizzie and I duly met at the Frontline Club, a London venue for those who write about, report on or otherwise deal with the field of the frontline and war. In the refined quiet of the wood-panelled clubroom, Lizzie explained to me that she was in the final stages of completing her PhD on the Far East POW camps, much of which was inspired by her grandfather's diaries.

Her next comment to me was this: 'Whenever you mention the Sumatran railway or the camps, everyone says: *Oh, you mean the railway with the dog? Judy, wasn't it?* It's amazing: absolutely everyone you talk to remembers her with such affection.' She laughs. 'There were *people* suffering there also, as well as a dog, but she seems more famous than the railway or the camps! That gives you a sense of just how much she was loved by all who came across her.'

Lizzie had a point. After serving for several wild, war-torn years as a ship's dog on the Royal Navy's Yangtze River gunboats, Judy had been bombed and shipwrecked repeatedly, before ending up in the POW camps of north Sumatra, part of modern-day Indonesia. She and her fellow POWs had been forced to work on the so-called hell railway – driving a single-track railway through impossible jungle and knife-cut mountains in the centre of what was then a land of utter wilderness, a veritable world lost in time.

This wasn't the Thai–Burma Death Railway, which is relatively well known today – the one immortalized in the 1957 film *The Bridge on the River Kwai*, and more recently in the movie *The Railway Man*, starring Colin Firth. This was the *other* death railway – one built over 2,000 kilometres away, in Sumatra, by the Japanese, using Allied POWs and locals as slave-labour.

If anything its story is even darker. Today, few if any have heard of Sumatra's hell railway, or the terrible horrors endured there. But people might just have heard of the camp's dog – Judy!

With some reverence, Lizzie produced from her bag a large and heavy, bound book – her grandfather's diary. 'There's something I want to show you.' She opened the diary at a place that she'd bookmarked. 'There.' She pointed at the page, proudly. 'Recognize it? So, who d'you think that is? It's unmistakably Judy. What other dog would ever look like that?'

Taking up half of one page was a hand-drawn sketch of a beautiful liver-and-white English Pointer. She was snuffling about in the tropical undergrowth, seemingly searching for a rat to catch among one of the bamboo huts in which the prisoners were forced to live, packed in there like sardines.

'It's something that's almost never been written about,' Lizzie explained. 'There's so much told about the horrors of the camps: the brutality, the unspeakable things that were done to the POWs. But those are the things they were forced to suffer. They had no choice, of course. That wasn't how they survived. In part they survived by the choices they made – and keeping a dog or another pet was something that helped keep them going. It was a thread that pulled them back to a little piece of normality. It was something extra to keep alive for during a hard day's labour, and to come back to at the end of the day. It offered a hint of home life; of family; of domesticated pets in the home.'

Lizzie told me I really had to go and see Rouse Voisey, a ninety-two-year-old veteran of the Japanese prison camps. As far as she knew he was the last living British survivor of the Sumatran railway, and no one would be better qualified to add layers of richness and texture to the story of the forgotten death railway and its celebrated dog. But before doing so I should meet Meg Parkes, she said. Meg's father had been a Japanese POW and again, in a way that almost stretches credulity, her father had managed to keep incredibly detailed diaries of his time in the camps.

The way in which a handful of POWs managed to keep these diaries is a gripping story in itself. More often than not they used scraps of paper, scribbled on in the dead of night, then secreted in old jars or tins, which they buried in the camp graveyard. The two things the Japanese guards seemed utterly fearful of were insanity and death. Those POWs who had lost their minds were shunned by the Japanese, and anything to do with death was also to be avoided. It was their extreme necro-phobia – their fear of death and dead bodies – that made the graveyard such a perfect hiding place for the illicit diaries.

In due course I did meet with Meg and she very kindly gave me a copy of her father's diaries, writings that spoke of the extraordinary relationship he had with a pet cat in the camps, among other animals. Meg echoed Lizzie's sentiments – that the whole history of how the POWs relied upon animals to help get them through their hellish ordeal had never really been written about. There were even camps wherein the POWs tamed and then trained pigeons to carry messages to and from the outside world, either to secure news or let the world know they were still alive.

Simply extraordinary.

Meg was involved in a fantastic schools project, with Pensby High School for Girls, in Yorkshire. Tom Boardman, then a ninety-two-year-old survivor of the POW camps, had come to the school to talk about his experiences. The eleven- and twelve-year-olds were asked to write short poems, imagining themselves to be an animal – any animal – in the camps. Meg gave me a copy of the booklet they'd produced with snippets of their poems. They were incredibly poignant.

'And the cat said . . . the prisoners stroke me and think of home. I like it, but I am afraid of the hunger in their eyes.' Elena Davies

'And the dog barked . . . why are we here? And why do some of us disappear?' Sophie Burns

'And the pigeon said . . . I'll carry their sad messages. I am their family and they are mine.' Alice Renshaw

But there was no story to rival Judy's, Meg added. She was truly a dog in a million. Meg, like Lizzie, advised me that the one person I really did need to meet was Rouse Voisey. In due course I drove up to rural Norfolk to meet the man himself. My satnav took me to a pretty bungalow that looks out over wild woods and rolling fields lying to one side of the neat row of houses in which he has his home.

Rouse had clearly been awaiting my arrival. He greeted me on the garden steps – an incredibly sprightly and sharp-looking ninety-two-year-old. We shook hands. He scrutinized me with a quick, piercing look, as if trying to appraise the calibre of the 'young man' who had driven such a long way to come and speak to him about events that lay some seven decades in the past.

He glanced at the scenery, which was lit by a bleak winter's midday sun. 'You know, on some days the birdsong is so loud that I can't hear myself greet my neighbours across the fence.' He smiled. 'I love it here. You're very welcome.' He gestured to his half-open door. 'Please, come in, come in.'

Rouse was a remarkable man, to put it mildly. Not only was he a survivor of Sumatra's railway hell, he'd also lived through what by his own admission was a 'worse' slave-labour project under the Japanese. He was among a group of Allied POWs who were forced to clear the coral island of Haruku of its jungle, in order to hack out a landing strip from the bare rock – in preparation for Imperial Japan's planned invasion of Australia, something that of course never happened. Haruku is an island in the Moluccas – the so-called 'Spice Islands' – but under the blistering sun, and in the scorching heat and dust, building that runway had all but killed Rouse, and so many of his fellows had died.

If that wasn't enough, he had then been loaded aboard one of Imperial Japan's so-called hell ships – rusting death traps used to transport POWs like slaves of old from one forced labour project to another – for a journey which he feared would be his last. So ill was he that he could remember little of the voyage, prior to the sinking of the ship, the *Junyo Maru*, by a British submarine. It was, at the time, the worst maritime disaster of history in terms of confirmed loss of life: some 5,600 Allied prisoners of war plus local slave-labourers perished at sea.

Somehow Rouse survived the shipwreck. In doing so he made it to Sumatra, to join the many hundreds of POWs slaving in that living hell. It was then that he first heard about Judy, the de facto mascot of the trans-Sumatran railway. As with all those who'd spoken before him, Rouse was unable to mention Judy's name or recall her memory without a warm smile. He glanced at a photo of his own dog – now deceased – hanging on the living room wall.

'That was my dog, Shona. She was a tri-colour English Setter. She was the most loving, wonderful companion you could ever wish for. I used to take her to the office where I worked – she'd sleep under my desk. She had the most lovely nature. I put the leg of my chair on her ear once by accident. She didn't snarl or bark at me. She just rolled her eyes and whined, as if to say – *hey, that really hurts, you know.* I never got another dog after Shona. I couldn't – not after her. And Judy – she was exactly that kind of a dog. There wasn't another like her.'

Rouse went on to share with me stories from his time in the prison camps, with his fellows and their camp dog – ones that perhaps he'd never discussed with anyone before, not even his recently deceased wife. He ended our chat with this.

'I was amazed that a dog could survive it all. That Judy outlived the hell of that place – it was incredible. The Korean camp guards in particular – they used to eat dogs. And they had the power of life or death over us all. It makes you wonder how anyone got away with it – keeping a dog like Judy. It's all part of the wonder of her story.'

I left Rouse's little bungalow with a box heaped full of yellowing newspaper articles, dog-eared books, photos and reports from the POW camp survivors – much of the 'library' that Rouse had built up over the years.

'Yes, yes – take it all,' he reassured me, as I asked again if he really was happy with me borrowing his 'library' for a while. 'I've got little use for it at my age. And if you need to come and talk to me again, please do. I'm here on my own with nothing much to do other that watch the box – and there's never anything on but repeats these days!'

I loaded the precious container onto the back seat of my car, but as I went to say a last goodbye Rouse held out a hand to restrain me. 'You know, there's one question you never asked which people always tend to: *After what happened, do you hate the Japanese?* I rather like it that you felt you didn't need to ask that of me.'

Rouse shook his head, his eyes lost in memories of the past. 'No, no – I don't hate the Japanese. How can you hate an entire people? I hate the guards who did those unspeakable things to us. But I could never hate an entire people. I think the hate would eat you up. It would consume you.' He laughed. 'So that's probably how I've lived to such a ripe old age!'

After visiting Rouse I spent time with other survivors of the POW camps, and their relatives and families, learning more about the story that was beginning to captivate me. Fergus Anckhorn, the irrepressibly youthful ninety-five-year-old who survived the POW camps due to his use of magic – he was once the youngest and is now the oldest member of the legendary Magic Circle – told me about his own incredible relationships with pets in the POW camps, including a dog, monkeys and even a chameleon! The chameleon would lie on his chest at night while he was sleeping, and flick out its tongue to catch mosquitoes. It was his de facto mosquito net!

'Those pets – they kept us sane, you know. They were a little tiny slice of the familiar, of what we knew – of home. And somehow, you knew you had to stay alive and return at the end of a day's hard labour to look after your dog or monkey, or whatever was waiting faithfully for you! You had to stay alive for *them*.'

Fergus told me about the value of those pets in sustaining the prisoners' morale – or more accurately, their will to live. In many cases, individuals opted to share some of their meagre ration with their pet animal, rather than allowing another living being to starve to death. Fergus loved dogs. He had a relationship with them that went very deep and was incredibly enduring. He was a cat-lover too.

'Once I spotted a tiny bird like a sparrow on a bush,' he told me, a rare sadness creeping into his mischievous, fun-filled eyes. 'I stalked up to that bird on hands and knees. On the other side of the bush was an emaciated cat. It was a race between the two of us. I saw the cat spring, the bird took off to escape and – pow! – I caught the tiny bundle of feathers in mid-air. I cooked that little bird and ate it that very evening. But when I looked at the pile of bones afterwards, I felt so guilty that I'd left the cat to starve. I never could forget it, or forgive myself.'

Like Rouse, Fergus believed that those POWs who hated the Japanese were eventually consumed by their hatred. Those who forgave lived longer and happier lives. And Fergus was one of many who'd go on to explain to me the vital role that pets played as the unsung heroes of the prison camps. It was a story that few had told, and one that Judy epitomized more than any other animal that had made it through the hell of the prison camp years.

This, then, is Judy's tale. It opens in Shanghai several years before the start of the war, when British gunboats still cruised the mighty Yangtze River, guarding British interest far into the heart of China. It commences with a tiny bundle of curiosity who ran away from home and ended up serving as the mascot of the doughty Royal Navy gunboat the *Gnat*. It follows Judy and her fellows' extraordinary adventures over the years – from the Yangtze River to the Sumatran hell railway, and everything in between.

People often say that truth is stranger than fiction. Undoubtedly, Judy of Sussex's story is one that anyone would find distinctly challenging to make up.

It is certainly one that I feel privileged to have been able to tell.

Damien Lewis,
Cork, Ireland, December 2013

Chapter One

The tiny puppy wiggled her nose a little further under the wire.

Blessed with a gundog's excellent peripheral vision she was keeping one eye on those to her rear – her fellow siblings, plus the kennel staff, who would little appreciate yet another escape attempt. Ahead of her, just a breath away, lay the outside world – the teeming hustle and bustle of life that lay all about, but which she and her fellow pups were seemingly forever forbidden from experiencing.

It was all just so tantalizingly close.

The English-run Shanghai Dog Kennels had bred the beautiful liver-and-white English Pointer puppies to serve as gundogs for various English gentlemen then resident in Shanghai. But this one pup, it seemed, had other ideas. The Kennels were like an island of calm amid the sea of chaos that was 1936 Shanghai – chaos to which the puppy poised halfway under the wire felt irresistibly drawn.

Before her very nose rickshaws – ancient-looking wooden carts pulled by human bearers – tore back and forth as they weaved through the dusty streets, carrying the better-off Shanghai residents trussed up in formal-looking top hats and dress-coats. Those rickety carriages fought for space with trams and buses, chugging their ponderous way past roadside stalls selling freshly fried and spiced delicacies. And everywhere bright red cloth banners hung from the shopfronts, advertising their wares in exotic-looking Mandarin and Wu calligraphy.

Why it was only she of her siblings who felt this insatiable urge to see, to smell and to taste the wider world – *to escape* – she didn't know. But ever since birth, curiosity had seemed to get the better of this still nameless puppy. And now here she was, glistening nose thrust under the wire and twitching at the bewitching smells that assaulted it, round and chubby backside still within the safe confines of the kennel, but with only a few more wriggles and a final squeeze required to break free.

Doubtless, one voice inside the pup's head was telling her: *don't do it!* But another, equally strident voice was urging – *go for it, girl!* In that moment of indecision as she peered beneath the wire the little puppy heard a yell of alarm from behind. *She'd been spotted!* It was the cry of Lee Ming, the local Chinese girl whose mother lived and worked at the kennels, raising the alarm. Lee Ming was quick and nimble and would be on her like a flash unless she got a move on.

Tiny forepaws thrashed and scrabbled at the dirt, as she fought to squeeze her way under the wire. The wrinkly folds of puppy fat rolled and gave beneath her, as she got her belly down even lower and wriggled like a fat fish stuck on an angler's hook. The bare stub of a tail, sticking out behind her like a long and rigid finger, twitched to and fro as she strove with all her might to break free.

Behind her Lee Ming came to a sudden halt and reached to grab the disobedient puppy, but as she did so the tiny ball of irrepressible energy gave one last Herculean effort and she was through. An instant and a scamper later and – *pouf!* – the diminutive four-legged figure was gone, paws flying as she was swallowed up into the noise and dust and utter disorder of downtown Shanghai.

For a horrible moment Lee Ming stared after the puppy that had disappeared, in complete dismay. There were so many dangers stalking those city streets that she didn't have the heart to imagine the half of them. If there was one thing the little puppy wasn't, it was streetwise. In her headlong confusion she might be run over by a rickshaw. In her fright she might tumble into one of the city's myriad open sewers. But worst of all, a roly-poly puppy like her would offer a tantalizing meal to those partial to dog meat – which included the large majority of the city's native population.

In 1936 Shanghai the flesh of man's best friend was much sought after, being seen as something of a 'sweet'-tasting delicacy. A young and tender dog that no one seemed to own or to care for would be fair game. Lee Ming turned back towards the large, colonial-style house that lay in the centre of the kennel compound. She headed for reception to report the bad news, and to help raise whatever search party they would send after the wayward pup. But her heart was heavy and a dark foreboding lay upon her.

She feared very much that was the last they'd ever see of the puppy that had run away.

The Shanghai that the puppy had made a break for was no place for any defenceless being, let alone an English Pointer barely a few weeks old. Then a city of some three million inhabitants,

Shanghai – a port city lying in the very centre of China's coastline – was a bustling metropolis red in tooth and claw. Positioned at the mouth of the mighty Yangtze River – Asia's longest, and a vital conduit for trade and commerce into China's vast interior – the great powers of Britain, America and France had long-established trading settlements in the city.

For decades, Shanghai had been known as 'The Paris of the East', but in recent years she had become a city beset by troubles. Weak leadership and infighting among the Chinese government had allowed vicious gangs of bandits to thrive. Warlords had taken control of large tracts of the nation's interior. Increasingly, Britain, America and France had been forced to send gunboats far into the interior on the Yangtze, in an effort to dissuade these lawless elements from disrupting their lucrative trade in silk, cotton, tea and other valuable commodities.

Recently, trouble had piled upon trouble, in particular with the resurgence of China's age-old enemy – Japan. In an escalating series of bloody skirmishes the Japanese Navy had bombarded Shanghai. As they had with the British and the other 'great powers', the Chinese were forced to sign a treaty with Imperial Japan, allowing the Japanese to establish a permanent presence in the 'treaty port' of Shanghai. Imperial Japan made little secret of her desire to conquer and subjugate the entire Chinese nation, and Shanghai was the gateway to China's then capital city, Nanking.

This then was Shanghai, the city that the escapee from the kennels had absconded to – one menaced by gangland banditry, and whose streets were increasingly plagued by soldiers from Imperial Japan, who showed ill-disguised contempt for the local inhabitants. So it was something of a miracle that several weeks after her dramatic breakout, the puppy who had run away was still very much alive and breathing.

The silky chubbiness was long gone, of course. Instead, adolescent ribs poked through a liver-and-white coat that had lost much of its shine and lustre. Her nose was dry and cracked, a sure sign that she was in a dreadful condition. Only her eyes seemed to demonstrate their signature brightness, betraying a strength of character that had distinguished her from birth, and perhaps led to her present, unenviable predicament. They shone with a burning curiosity and a zest for life, despite all that she had suffered since her ill-fated 'escape'. But there was something else now in her gaze – uncertainty and vulnerability, a sense that the young dog had realized to her cost that not every human was her natural friend and ally.

How stupid she had been, she now recognized, to run away. She had traded the comfort and luxury of the kennels for a battered old cardboard box lying in a smelly, fly-blown Shanghai alleyway. She'd traded the companionship and playfulness of her brother and sister puppies for the loneliness of life on the streets. And in place of the English kennel owner's natural love for and protection over her dogs, she'd faced cruelty and abuse at every turn in this overcrowded human zoo of a city.

All apart from one individual – Soo. For whatever reason, Soo the Chinese trader was an unreconstructed lover of dogs. Her shabby box-cum-home lay to the rear of his store, and ever since the puppy had found her way to it Soo had taken it upon himself to deliver titbits of food to her, of an evening when his long day's work was done. It was hardly the kind of diet she'd grown accustomed to at the kennels, but at least it had served to keep her alive.

Like many Chinese, it wasn't in Soo's nature or family tradition to keep a dog at home as a pet. In the China of 1936 dogs had to earn their keep as working animals, or they were invariably for the pot. In fact, the eating of dog meat in China had a history stretching back thousands of years, the meat being thought to possess mystical medicinal properties. There were even some breeds of dog that were kept specifically for human consumption, especially in times of seasonal hunger.

Fortunately, Soo wasn't one of those who were partial to having dog on the menu, and the lost puppy from the Shanghai Dog Kennels was lucky indeed to have fallen by chance under his protection.

But tonight, all of that was about to change.

With a sixth sense that was to become her absolute trademark, the lonely pup detected the danger before it was audible or visible to any human ear or eye, Soo's included. A Japanese gunboat had docked in the port of Shanghai, and the sailors of His Japanese Imperial Majesty's Ship were making their noisy way along the very road upon which Soo's shop was situated, no doubt in search of alcohol and some locals on which to vent their aggression. It was late evening, but the hard-working Soo was still there, his being one of the few stores on the street remaining open.

That alone offered enough of an excuse for the gunboat crew to pounce.

As the Japanese sailors started verbally abusing Soo and helping themselves to his wares, he of course protested. Voices were raised in anger, but the Japanese sailors didn't stop there. Within minutes Soo's shop had been plundered, its rickety wooden shelves torn down and smashed to pieces. As for Soo, he was set upon by the Japanese sailors, who were working themselves up into a towering rage.

Hearing her one protector in the world being so cruelly assaulted, the adolescent pup had stolen out of her alleyway and sneaked around the corner to see if there was anything she could do to save him. Inching forward on her belly, she alternately whimpered in fright and tried to muster her most threatening growl, as the strange figures in their baggy trousers over knee-high black boots kicked and punched her protector.

Then one of the aggressors spotted the cowering dog. He stepped away from Soo and took a few paces towards her. Moments later one of those perfectly polished boots was swinging towards the adolescent puppy's midriff. The powerful blow lifted her from the cobbles and flung her across the street into a pile of rubbish on the far side. There she lay, whimpering and in agony, and hoping beyond hope that these cruel men in their strange uniforms wouldn't come for her again.

By the time their oppressors had departed, Soo had been beaten so badly that he had to be helped away from the scene. The dog that had until now viewed him as her protector was forced to take refuge in the empty shadows of a nearby doorway. Into it she crawled, body sore from the kicking, belly sore from that and the ravening hunger, and her spirit numbed by the trauma and the cold of the long night that lay ahead.

Even though the Japanese sailors were long gone, the lonely puppy sensed that tonight her dream of escape from the Shanghai Kennels had descended into the blackest of nightmares – but as is so often the case, the darkest moment is just before the dawn.

As the sun crept above the city's grand, colonial-style skyline, a familiar figure began to pad her way along the street on which the young dog lay. The lone puppy was shivering and crying to herself and lost in misery – so much so that she almost didn't notice the pitter-patter of footsteps come to a halt, or to hear the words uttered in amazement in her direction.

'Shudi? Shudi? Oh, Shudi! What happened? Where have you been?'

The long tail of the Pointer – now stained off-white with the dirt and soot from her street-side existence – almost failed to wag in any sign of recognition. But the young dog *had* recognized the soft tones of the voice, just as surely as the little girl from the kennels had recognized the distraught puppy. Her distinctive markings – a sleek liver-brown head, a similarly-coloured saddle-like marking thrown across her shoulders, plus the large formless splodge of colour splashed across her rear right flank – had been instantly recognizable to Lee Ming.

No doubt about it – this was the one that had run away!

In a sprawling city of some three million inhabitants the girl from the Shanghai Kennels had, by chance, chosen to walk that morning past the very door where the lost and injured dog was sheltering. Lee Ming bent, scooped the puppy up and thrust her deep inside her jacket. With that she ran and skipped through the largely deserted streets, eager to announce her find to the English lady who ran the kennels.

By the time she had reached the big house that lay inside the compound and unzipped her jacket, the puppy had fallen fast asleep.

'Look! Look! I find Shudi!' the little girl announced ecstatically.

The Englishwoman peered doubtfully over the high desk behind which she sat. Spying the puppy, she reached out uncertainly and took the little dog from the girl's outstretched arms. She pulled her closer, stroked her and fondled her just behind the ears, as she studied the markings and tried to compare them to those in her memory. The puppy opened one lazy eye, saw where she was, seemed to smile exhaustedly, then slipped back into a sweet sleep.

It was the turn of the Englishwoman to smile. '*It is her*. It really is the one who ran away.' She glanced at Lee Ming, who was beaming with happiness. 'So, I think it's time you gave her a good bath and a dinner, don't you?'

Lee Ming nodded enthusiastically. There was nothing she'd like more than to feed and comfort the wayward pup. She held out her arms so 'Shudi' could be returned to her and she could whisk her off for some much-needed tender loving care.

The woman handed the pup across. She glanced at Lee Ming curiously. 'But tell me, why do you call her Shudi?'

Lee Ming placed the warm but exhausted bundle back inside her jacket. 'I always call this one Shudi,' she replied shyly. 'Shudi means peaceful. Peaceful is how she looks, yes?'

The woman reached out and caressed Lee Ming's face. 'She does. Yes she does. And Lee Ming – that shall be her name from now on: *Judy*.'

So it was that the puppy who had run away and come back again against all odds was given a name perhaps most ill-suited to her nature: the Mandarin word for the peaceful one – *shudi* – or rendered into 'Judy' for whichever lucky Englishman might be her future master.

As the little girl carried Shudi – Judy – off for a good pamper, little did she realize how a dog with such inauspicious beginnings would go on to distinguish herself in the coming bloody and all-consuming conflict . . .

Lee Ming could have no idea how famous the English Pointer from the Shanghai Kennels would become, once the Second World War drew to a close.

Chapter Two

Even in the summer of 1936, four years prior to the start of the war, the signs of Japanese Imperial aggression were sweeping through the streets of Shanghai and across wider China.

Using her military might Imperial Japan would strike a hammer blow through Shanghai and into the Chinese capital, Nanking – a name that would become synonymous with unspeakable terrors and brutality. But for now such dark horrors lay far in the future, and much of the city of Shanghai and the Yangtze River remained under the stewardship of the British and Allied gunboat fleets.

The British gunboats were of the Insect Class, a name that belied their true purpose, which was to patrol the shallow seas and rivers across the more war-torn reaches of the British Empire. Built by the Lobnitz shipyard on the Clyde, the Insect Class ships had initially seen active service during the First World War, in what was then Mesopotamia (modern-day Iraq), patrolling the Tigris and Euphrates rivers.

By 1936 they were two decades old, and were by no means state-of-the-art warships. But they remained relatively fast, nimble and well armed. With their flat bottom and shallow draught, they were designed specifically to operate in rapid-flowing rivers like the Yangtze. Known colloquially as the 'large

China gunboats', they boasted two Yarrow engines and boilers, each driving a separate propeller set in a shaft sunk into the hull, to minimize the chance of snagging in the river shallows.

As Shudi – Judy – settled into the blissful comfort of kennel life once again, one of those British gunboats was just completing her annual refit at Shanghai docks. She was preparing to return to patrol duties, deterring piracy and banditry on the lower reaches of the Yangtze – covering a length of river stretching almost one thousand miles inland.

HMS *Gnat* had not been a particularly happy ship of late, and much of the crew's angst centred around two key aspects of ship's life that were in distinctly short supply right now. The first was the ship's stocks of beer. The China gunboats were unique in the Royal Navy in that they carried with them a stock of beer from which, when on operations, every crew member got a daily allowance. But as the Captain of the *Gnat*, Lieutenant Commander Waldegrave, had commented in the ship's log, there was only a few weeks' supply of the precious brew remaining, even with strict rationing in force.

Recently a United States Navy gunboat had docked alongside the *Gnat*. The officers and crew had been invited to share in the British gunboat's hospitality – chiefly her beer – but only once a week on Saturday nights, in an effort to preserve stocks. In exchange, the officers and crew of the *Gnat* had been invited to the thrice-weekly movie screenings held in the American ship's cinema.

The second problem was unique to the *Gnat* among the British gunboat flotilla then on the Yangtze: she lacked a ship's mascot, which if anything was even more unthinkable than running out of beer. On her sister ships HMS *Cricket, Cicada, Ladybird*, and the flagship, the *Bee*, there were variously cats, dogs and even a ship's monkey. But the crew of the *Gnat* possessed no furry, four-legged or even a feathered friend, and so it was that the ship's Captain set his junior officers the task of finding one.

The junior officers had in turn called upon the resources of the *Gnat*'s Canteen Committee in an effort to decide which would be the most suitable species of bird, mammal or reptile to grace the vessel's deck. The nominations had flooded in, but many – Chinese soft-backed river turtles, giant pandas and alligators included – were judged as being somewhat impractical and inappropriate, if good for the laughs.

The Canteen Committee decided that any mascot for the *Gnat* had to possess three essential qualities. Firstly, as the ship's officers and crew could really do with some female company she would have to be distinctly feminine. Second, she would have to be easy on the eye. And thirdly, for practical reasons she would need to be able to earn her keep. So it was that on an early November afternoon in 1943 a delegation of junior officers left the *Gnat* to pay a visit to the Shanghai Kennels.

Like most 'gundogs', English Pointers are blessed – or cursed – with a surfeit of energy. They have been bred to be powerful, alert and absolutely tireless no matter what extent of terrain they are tasked to cover. Such are the qualities required of a dog whose purpose is to locate, chase after, flush out and – very often – retrieve game. Essentially a hunting dog, Pointers should be always at the ready to let fly.

Judy had certainly proved herself ready to let fly when she'd squirmed under the kennel wire and run away. Even for an extremely high-energy breed like Pointers, she'd shown herself to have an extraordinary abundance of get-up-and-go. On first consideration, these weren't perhaps the ideal qualities for a ship's mascot – one that was going to be constrained to the confines of a vessel that measured 237 feet from stem to stern and 36 feet across. But as soon as they'd spotted her, the junior officers of the *Gnat* seemed oddly convinced that Judy was the one for them.

By now she was approaching six months old, and had fully recovered from her stint as a Shanghai street dog. She was striking-looking, holding herself with a poise that seemed to mark her out as a true aristocrat of the breed. She carried her head high on a graceful but powerful neck, and her dark eyes – like glistening coals – were set well back from her long, sweeping muzzle. She gazed at these strange men in their smart uniforms who had come to inspect her, displaying the shy reserve natural to a female of the breed.

To the delegation from the *Gnat*, blissfully unaware of Judy's epic escape and long sojourn in the back alleyways of Shanghai, she seemed like the perfect lady. As an added bonus she was a gundog, which would mean that any shooting parties sent ashore to secure meat for the galley would have a dog to root out and retrieve game. Though not specifically bred as retrievers, Pointers can be trained to chase down and gather anything that has been shot – *or at least, that's the theory*.

Back at the *Gnat* the last of the ship's stores and ammunition were being stowed away below decks, in preparation for

14

pending departure – including supplies of bread, beef, fuel (petrol and kerosene), plus coal. The last licks of paint were being applied to cover the odd patches of rust on the superstructure. The Chinese mess-boys – locals employed to help cook and make tea in the galley – had returned from their shore leave, and they were preparing the first brews back aboard ship.

A gaggle of seamen were milling about on the mess-deck, situated in the ship's bows, preparing to change into fresh white uniforms for one of their final nights ashore. It was then that the head of the Coxswain – the officer in charge both of steering the vessel and of managing the ship's crew – appeared through the open hatch from the main deck above and made an announcement.

'All hands on deck in ten minutes!'

As the sailors pulled on their uniforms, they wondered what on earth might be up. Surely, not something that would prevent them from having one of their last nights ashore? In keeping with her wild and exotic reputation Shanghai was a party town par excellence, and no one wanted to be kept from the bars where the beer flowed freely – as opposed to the dwindling supplies aboard the *Gnat*.

The men gathered anxiously on the foredeck, forming two ranks beneath the long canvas awning that stretched practically from one end of the ship to the other. It lent the vessel a somewhat odd appearance, the lengthy covering resembling almost a roof, and making the *Gnat* seem from a distance like an elongated tramcar at sea. But the awning had proved hugely useful during long patrols up the Yangtze, providing shade to the main deck and shelter from the monsoon rains that would sweep the length of the great river.

'Atten-shun!' the ship's Coxswain called, once all were present. 'Ship's company mustered, sir,' he reported to a figure standing close by.

The *Gnat*'s First Lieutenant, R. Haines, stepped forward and mounted an empty wooden ammunition crate, one that would normally carry rounds for the ship's .303 calibre Maxim machine guns. Three of these light machine guns – a weapon that had become synonymous with the projection of Great Britain's colonial power – were positioned on either side of the boat, giving her impressive all-around firepower. But right now it was far less war-like matters that the First Lieutenant had on his mind. Having given the order to 'stand easy', he began to address the men, the faint suggestion of a smile flickering across his normally inscrutable features.

'A few weeks back the Canteen Committee, with myself as chairman, passed a resolution to the effect that we would have a ship's pet.' He paused, as if checking a sheet of paper in his hand, then continued, the smile creeping further into his eyes. 'To remind you, we decided on having some female compan-ionship; a lady, who would be attractive and could earn her keep. I have studied your very interesting suggestions, most of which I regrettably had to discard.'

The First Lieutenant eyed the men ranged before him. 'On the *Bee* they have two cats,' he continued. 'The *Cricket* has a dog – of sorts. The *Cicada* has a monkey – heaven help them!' A long, weighty pause. 'As for the *Gnat*, from this moment onwards no shooting party will be able to return to ship claiming to have shot twenty-three quail, but that only one could be found.'

He turned and let out a cry: 'Quartermaster!'

A figure emerged from the door behind him, one that led into the ship's superstructure and up to the bridge. A few paces to his rear a head appeared at knee level, peering curiously around the doorframe. As the Quartermaster – the ship's store-man – pulled gently on a lead, the rest of the figure stepped into the light. It was a four-legged creature – a white English Pointer, with dramatic liver-coloured markings across her head and body.

The Quartermaster moved to where everyone could see. All eyes were on the dog. Not yet fully grown, she had an odd, endearing, floppy kind of a walk, as she padded across the deck on paws that still seemed too big for her body. Man and dog came to a halt between the First Lieutenant and the phalanx of ship's crew ranged before him. Judy proceeded to plonk herself down, her well-bred, ladylike air evaporating as a large floppy pink tongue lolled out from what appeared to be a decidedly goofy grin.

It was as much as the men could do not to dissolve into laughter.

The First Lieutenant swept his arm theatrically across the dog now squatted before him. 'Here she is, then, gentlemen. Meet the first lady of the gunboats. Meet Judy – RN!'

Judy was given a right royal welcome by the crew of the *Gnat*. They picked the nickname 'Judy of Sussex' for her, in keeping with her purebred, aristocratic kind of attitude. Sussex was chosen for no other reason than it was a very long way from

Shanghai, and because several of the ship's crew hailed from that part of England.

The natural choice for the important post of 'Keeper of the Ship's Dog' fell to Able Seaman Jan 'Tankey' Cooper. Tankey was in charge of the ship's food stores and fresh water, but more importantly he was also the ship's butcher, which meant he was able to lay his hands on a regular supply of bones.

Via Tankey, Judy was allotted an open-topped box – an empty ammunition crate – positioned near the ship's bridge, plus a ship's blanket as her sleeping quarters. But in the coming weeks and months she would be found as often as not elsewhere, so much preferable was it to be curled up fast asleep with one of the ship's crew.

Judy was even given an official ship's book number. Every man serving in the Royal Navy had a unique set of letters and numerals assigned to him – for example, JX125001. It identified him as serving in one of four pay grades: 1. Seaman and Communicators; 2. Stokers; 3. Officers, Cooks and Stewards; 4. All others. Judy's number identified her with the 'MX' prefix, meaning she was an 'All others', and that she had joined the service after 1925, before which a different system of numbering and lettering was in place.

Judy's ship's number didn't confer any wage-earning status on her, for it hadn't been formally logged with the Admiralty yet. But had the officers of the *Gnat* so desired, they could doubtless have got away with it, for the ship's number system was famously confused and confusing. Many a Royal Navy sailor had the same number as another, only one letter in the prefix differentiating the two.

But in any case, Judy would have little need of money now she was aboard the *Gnat*. Life as a ship's dog was going to prove as fine an approximation to doggie paradise as any – or at least in the early months it would. On the *Gnat*, Judy of Sussex was going to have everything she could wish for or that money could buy, including a surfeit of food, good company, warmth and companionship.

Being a gundog and one intended to 'earn her keep', Judy was supposed to be kept away from the crew, in the officers' quarters positioned – unusually – towards the front of the ship. Indeed, it was the ship's Captain, Lieutenant Colonel Waldegrave, plus the Chief Petty Officer, Charles Jefferey, who had forked out the money to buy her on behalf of the ship's company. As such, they reckoned they had every right to keep her to their quarters, and to train her 'for the gun' – to act as a ship's officers' gundog.

Pointers are bred to do just as their name suggests – to point out prey. A Pointer is supposed to adopt a rigid pose whenever a game animal is scented. Though it can differ from dog to dog, classically speaking an English Pointer is supposed to adopt the following pose: head lowered, tail held horizontal in line with the head, one leg raised and bent at the wrist, paw pointing to guide the hunter to the target.

But as the officer's mess-boy aboard the *Gnat* was among the first to point out, in Judy's case there seemed to be a fatal flaw in her 'pointing' abilities. In her first forty-eight hours aboard ship she only seemed to go rigid or to point at one thing: whenever she could smell the delicious aroma of dinner wafting around the *Gnat*, she'd point unerringly at the ship's galley!

No problem, the ships' officers argued. They'd train her to point at the right kind of thing – chiefly the duck, quail, antelope and gazelle that they were keen to hunt along the Yangtze. But there just seemed to be no way of controlling where this taut bundle of energy would be found next aboard ship. Her inquisitive nose took her to just about every nook and cranny, and it was only ever from one quarter – the Chinese mess-boys and cooks – that she seemed to receive anything other than a rapturous welcome.

No matter what the officers' intentions, from the very start the ship's company treated Judy as a much-favoured pet. It was as if she was everybody's companion – which, indeed, as ship's dog arguably she was supposed to be. Owned by nobody, she was everyone's dog, and therein lay the impediment to any serious attempts to train her for the gun. Likewise, Tankey Cooper's strict efforts to regulate her meals proved equally frustrating. Whenever his back was turned squares of chocolate and even the odd glass of beer were slipped in the young dog's direction.

By the time HMS *Gnat* was ready for departure from Shanghai, in the second week of November 1936, the ship's Captain and Chief Petty Officer – those who had originally procured the dog – had accepted Judy's shortcomings with reluctant good grace. She was first and foremost a ship's dog and not a gundog, and in that she was proving herself wildly successful. Not a man among the *Gnat*'s crew hadn't warmed to her, and Judy's presence aboard ship had proved a much-needed boost to morale.

Having survived the menacing streets of Shanghai, Judy appeared to be set for a long and happy career aboard HMS *Gnat*, gallant ship of the Royal Navy's Yangtze gunboat fleet. But as chance would have it, Judy's next close encounter with mortal danger was but a few turns of the ship's screw away.

And once again, it was curiosity that would almost prove the death of her.

Chapter Three

For decades the scientific study of dogs – and much of the theory around their training – has relied upon the example provided by their ancient ancestor, the wolf. Unlikely as it may seem, all modern-day dogs – from Pekinese to Great Danes – are descendants of one species, *Canis lupus*, the grey wolf. Dogs share 99.96 percent of their DNA with the wolf.

But those genetics have been overlain with up to 30,000 years of selective breeding and, more importantly, domestication. Many millennia ago humans and dogs began what was to be the most long-lived and enduring man-and-animal partnership of all. The dog was the first animal that we domesticated, and today they possess an ability to bond with and relate to humans that no other being can match.

The belief that dogs would revert to behaving like wolves in the absence of human influence long ruled the way we trained our canine companions. Studies suggested that wolves were pack animals, with two dominant adults – one male, one female – threatening violence or expulsion to subjugate those under them. Using the argument that dogs are essentially wolves, humans were thought to have to dominate their canine pets, to prove they were 'the master of the pack'.

In recent years much of this thinking has been turned on its head. Most studies of wolf packs were carried out in captivity, generally in zoos. Captive 'packs' were made up of a discordant group of animals thrown together arbitrarily, and with little relevance to the wild. Recent studies of wolf 'packs' as they occur in nature prove them to be nothing more menacing than extended family units.

In nature the wolf pack usually consists of one breeding pair, plus their adolescent offspring who help the adults to bring up new cubs. The pack can turn violent, but only against another pack that tries to encroach upon its territory. Wolves, then, are naturally sociable, family-oriented animals. Within the family unit – the so-called pack – they exhibit cooperation, kindness and care towards each other.

Likewise, most dogs simply want to feel part of the family and to enjoy family life, as others in the family unit – whether human or canine – do. Viewed in this context, training dogs by employing dominant behaviour, threats and even physical punishment is about as appropriate as doing so with a child. What dogs respond to best is love, reward and play – and crucially, being made to feel an integral part of the family. And luckily for Judy, she'd just fallen into the biggest, most playful and fun-loving family she ever could have wished for.

Life aboard a Yangtze gunboat was by necessity close-knit and familial. With a crew numbering in the fifties – Chinese cooks and kitchen boys not included – the *Gnat*'s company wasn't a great deal bigger than your average wolf pack. Most such packs are happy family units, wherein disagreements do happen but are usually resolved harmoniously. Cooperation, not coercion, is the rule.

While Judy had yet to find her two-legged 'master' aboard the *Gnat* – someone with whom to bond absolutely – within the first few days of coming aboard she was at one with the close-knit band of the ship's crew. She was at home with them all. And by the time the *Gnat* was ready to set sail Judy of Sussex appeared to have grown well accustomed to life aboard ship. She seemed to be finding her sea legs, and to be more than ready for the long voyage into the country's interior.

At 0800 hours on 10 November 1936 the *Gnat*'s crew began stowing away the last of the stores, in preparation for the departure. At 0900 hours the special sea-duty crewmen and cable parties prepared to cast off. Like all dogs, Judy had an uncanny ability to read human body language and actions. She dashed about the *Gnat*, sniffing excitedly as cables were slipped and fenders hauled aboard.

Ten minutes later the *Gnat* had slipped anchor, the throb of the twin engines beginning to shake and vibrate the deck. Twenty minutes after that the ship pulled into shore again, and tied up alongside the Asiatic Petroleum Company's wharf where 68.1 tonnes of fuel oil were to be pumped aboard. Judy had just endured her first short voyage 'at sea', and all aboard were mightily impressed by how she had behaved. But all of this had been in the comparatively sheltered waters of the Shanghai port. The word Shanghai itself means 'on the ocean', and the city sits at the confluence of the Yangtze River and the East China Sea.

Fuel oil pumped aboard, the vessel did an about turn, and at 1220 hours she began to steam to a new wharf, where she would load ammunition supplies. In addition to her six Maxim machine guns mounted aft of the bridge, the *Gnat* boasted a 12-pounder anti-aircraft gun, and a pair of 6-inch Mark VII guns, which were able to fire a 45-kilogram shell over a ten-kilometre range. The 6-inch guns were the largest calibre of any gunboat then serving on the Yangtze, lending the Insect Class boats a punch that belied their name.

Life aboard the Yangtze gunboats was colourful, but it was also fraught with danger. Hostile vessels menaced the river waters. The Yangtze was wild and unpredictable in places, and ships could easily be driven ashore or dashed to pieces on the rocky sides of the gorges through which they passed. The constant tension and danger took an inevitable toll, and young sailors needed quality downtime in which to destress and unwind. Shanghai, with its wild bars and subterranean clubs, offered them ample opportunity to do so.

But as always was the case when young sailors went partying, there were some at least who were loath to leave the joys of the shore behind them. In the past few days Captain Waldegrave had been forced to send two of the *Gnat*'s crew to the Military Detention Quarters, in Shanghai, for thirty days' punishment. No doubt the sailors in question had found the beer supplies aboard the *Gnat* somewhat wanting, or perhaps they had baulked at leaving a local girl behind them.

But at the same time, the Captain had also found cause to issue a number of good conduct badges to his crew, and he had written up at least one for a Good Conduct Medal. Overall, the seamen were pulling together admirably, and the Captain put that down in part to the newest arrival among them. But while she'd brought them great joy and a renewed sense of purpose, Judy was about to prove that she could also bring them a great deal of trouble.

It was on the morning of 14 November when the *Gnat* finally slipped her mooring for the long voyage upriver. She steamed eastwards at first, heading out to sea, before turning west into the churning maw that forms the vast expanse of the Yangtze River delta. Taking full advantage of her fourteen-knot speed and triple rudders – which gave her a tight turning circle, crucial for operating in the narrow confines of the river's higher reaches – the *Gnat* began to battle against the ten-knot current that was sweeping this massive expanse of fresh water out to sea.

Here, where the mighty Yangtze drains into the East China Sea, the delta is over twenty miles wide: around the same width as the English Channel at its narrowest. Gazing out over the grey November water both man and dog would need to remind themselves that this was a river, and not an ocean. Wild eddies and currents swept beneath the flat bottom of the *Gnat*'s hull; powerful waves and swells the size of ocean rollers rumbled past her sides. The cold, muddy, grey-yellow water was heavy with silt, and every now and again a swirling whirlpool spun across their path, sucking nameless debris into its depths.

As the port city faded into the distance, land was barely visible. Instead of the steady hustle and bustle of Shanghai harbour life, a new sound filled the crew's ears. It was the unearthly, hollow rushing of the river as the *Gnat* fought her way upstream, passing over the sandbanks and mudflats that litter the Yangtze's final approach to the sea. The noise rose to a deafening roar each time the flat-bottomed vessel clawed over the narrowest of shallows, where the depth decreased to a matter of feet, then died down again as the riverbed plunged to some 100 feet or more in depth.

During the weeks that she'd spent living on the streets of Shanghai, Judy had become accustomed to the roar of the city – the ceaseless cacophony of engines, voices, industry and human endeavour. But this was something entirely different. This was the throaty bellow of a wild waterway – the third longest river in the world – tantalizingly close and at its most awe-inspiring. This was the breathtaking power of nature distilled into a surging mass of water, and the wild, untamed strangeness of it all drew Judy to it . . . like a moth to the prover-bial candle flame.

Chief Petty Officer Jefferey was the first to realize the danger. He was moving aft when he caught sight of the dog that he had half-paid-for nosing about by the ship's rail. As he yelled out a cry of warning, he saw her slip beneath the rail, until she was poised on the polished steel plates of the outboard – the narrow outer edge of the deck. Judy gazed at the frothing water below, seemingly as unheeding of Jefferey's cries of alarm as she had been of Lee Ming's, a few months earlier at the Shanghai Kennels.

She danced from paw to paw, uttering excited yelps and barks at the deafening grey monster that churned and roared a few dozen feet beneath her outstretched forelegs. But a moment later Judy lost her footing completely, and with a despairing yelp she plunged out of view. Whoever said it was curiosity that killed the cat had clearly never met the ship's dog of HMS *Gnat*!

An ashen-faced Jefferey turned and yelled to the bridge, screaming at the top of his voice in an effort to make himself heard.

'Dog overboard! Dog overboard! *DOG OVERBOARD!*'

The cry of *man overboard* is one of the last any sailor ever wants to hear at sea – but even less so on a waterway like the Yangtze. The combined speed of the river's flow and the *Gnat*'s forward progress meant that the ship's mascot was now being carried astern at something like fourteen knots, or a little over sixteen miles an hour. Jefferey's cry of 'dog overboard' was equally unwelcome to those who caught it, among a ship's crew who were growing to love and cherish their canine companion.

Fortunately, the Captain was one of those who had heard and he took immediate action. 'Stop, and full astern! Stop, and full astern!'

Captain Waldegrave knew for certain what would happen if his ship didn't rapidly reverse its course. There wasn't the slightest chance he could turn the gunboat around in time. The climate in east-central China is similar to that in continental Europe: it is temperate, with warm springs, hot summers, cool autumns and bitter winters. The Yangtze in November would be icy cold, conditions that would quickly sap the reserves of even the toughest dog, as she fought against the vicious currents and eddies. By the time he'd turned his ship around, Judy would have been swept far downstream in the chilly waters, and lost.

She had fallen a little more than a dozen feet from the ship's rail, but even so she would have gone under, and fresh water has far less buoyancy than seawater, providing less chance of bringing a body back to the surface. All the Captain could hope for was that Judy was a strong swimmer, one blessed with a gundog's natural instinct to fight for her survival – at least until they could come to her aid. Even so, he didn't rate her chances very highly. Either they got to her in the next few minutes, or Judy of Sussex was going to a cold and watery grave.

By the time the Captain had brought his vessel to a stop, man of action Leading Seaman Vic Oliver had readied the *Gnat's* launch. Oliver would be on the tiller, with a colleague to operate the engine, and he had a somewhat reluctant Chinese boat boy called Wugle perched in the prow, charged with grabbing the errant dog. The diminutive craft was swung overboard and lowered over the side, but by the time she was in the water Oliver had lost all sight of the missing dog.

The last he'd seen of her was a distant black speck coursing downriver. He'd tried to fix her location in his mind, so he could steer the launch in the general direction. Unsighted as they now were he set off on the best bearing he could muster, the speed of the launch combining with the current to propel the boat downriver like a cork fired from a champagne bottle.

The little vessel slammed and bucked her way across the choppy water, which close up appeared like a viscous orange soup as it foamed and boiled around her prow. Oliver figured that by the time they'd got the boat into the water Judy was maybe half a mile astern of the *Gnat*. At the speed the launch was motoring he reckoned they'd overhaul her within two minutes – *if* he had them on the correct bearing.

He knew full well that if he'd got it wrong, they wouldn't get a second chance. Many a man had gone to their deaths in the Yangtze, and a fall into the river this far from land very often spelled the end. Oliver dreaded to think what the chances were for a not yet fully grown dog.

Time dragged horribly. The boat fought its way across the river's surface for what seemed like an age. Then, quite suddenly they crested a wave and sped past a black speck just visible off the port side. The men in the launch had caught the flash of white forepaws thrashing about frantically, eyes wide with fear as Judy fought to prevent herself from being dragged under. She was keeping her head above the turbid waters, but only just.

Yelling out snatched words of encouragement, Oliver threw the launch into a tight turn. This time they came back towards her on an interception bearing and motoring upstream. The boat's progress was far slower and more controlled, as she fought the powerful current, and Oliver presumed that this time they had Judy within their grasp. But as they slowed for the pick-up and Wugle leaned over the side to grab her collar, the boat pitched on a wave crest and suddenly he was in the water too.

Boat boy and ship's dog went under and nothing more could be seen of them. Oliver sent the launch around in a second speeding turn. They returned to the spot, but both Wugle and Judy were nowhere to be seen. Finally, a pair of desperate figures broke the surface, and Oliver used the boat hook to drag them closer in. Then all hands were reaching over the side . . . and a sodden ship's boy and half-drowned ship's dog were dragged aboard by the scruff of their necks.

A ragged volley of cheers echoed across the water from the deck of the *Gnat*, where what seemed like the entire ship's company had gathered to watch the drama. Acknowledging them with a wave, Oliver got the launch underway once more, heading back towards the *Gnat*. Something of a natural-born showman, he gripped the tiller between his knees and sent a short message of confirmation, using the boat's semaphore – a system of flags held at arm's length in various positions, each corresponding to a letter of the alphabet – to do so.

'CHRISTENING COMPLETE,' was the short but entirely appropriate message transmitted.

Bedraggled and with thick Yangtze river mud in hair, eyes and ears, Judy and Wugle were the first to be lifted back aboard the ship. They were rushed below for a good hot bath. The scrubbing that Judy received was at the hands of Chief Petty Officer Jefferey himself, who was fast becoming one of her foremost protectors. The bath was laced with disinfectant, on the orders of the ship's surgeon, for the Yangtze wasn't just laden with silt and mud – it was also thick with sewage from the many towns and cities that lined her banks.

Jefferey rubbed Judy dry with his own towel, before deciding to give her a walk around the vessel, pointing out all the obvious dangers. It was like learning to ride a horse, being aboard ship: if you fell off – or overboard – you just had to get right back on again. At first Judy was noticeably scared to be out on deck. She shivered with fright and gave the ship's rails the widest berth possible. As the *Gnat* steamed ahead she was reluctant even to take a peek at the frothing water surging past to either side of the hull.

At that Jefferey allowed himself a small smile of satisfaction. At least she seemed to have learned her lesson.

Captain Waldegrave recorded their near-loss in the ship's log at 1800 hours that day: *a man accidentally overboard and retrieved by the lifeboat crew*. The fact that Judy's 'accident' was officially recorded as happening to a *human* crewmember reflected just how those aboard the *Gnat* had begun to view their ship's dog. But while the crew were growing to cherish their newest shipmate, many had begun to question if she really would satisfy the third quality they had demanded of her – that of *usefulness*.

The night of the 'accident' a shaken Judy *did* sleep in the officers' quarters, lying close by Jefferey's bunk for extra comfort. Usually in life a man will choose his dog. Just occasionally a dog gets to choose her man. After her near-death experience in the Yangtze Judy was in need of real comfort. But she remained the kind of dog who'd make her own choice of master – or better still life companion – very much in her own good time. There were plenty of ready candidates aboard the *Gnat*: the ship's Captain, CPO Jefferey and Tankey Cooper to name but a few. Yet as far as Judy of Sussex was concerned, Mr Right hadn't stepped onto her deck just yet.

Thankfully, tonight was a night of comparative quiet aboard the *Gnat*, devoid of the roar of tortured water rushing past the hull, or ship's screws thrashing, or engines thumping away below decks. As with all Yangtze gunboats, the *Gnat* steamed only during the hours of daylight, when her crew could see properly to defend themselves against the dangers that lurked along the river's length. Come nightfall, she'd either anchor in the shallows, or pull into one of the many wharfs and jetties that dotted the river's course.

By any standards the Yangtze was a busy thoroughfare, and most of the local sampans and junks that plied her waters – traditional wooden-hulled sailing ships – did so all hours of day and night. Few if any carried any warning lamps – customarily a red light to port and a green to starboard – as vessels are supposed to during hours of darkness. The dangers of having a collision with an unseen craft were legion.

But there were other, more malevolent forces that menaced the waters during the night hours – which is why the Yangtze gunboat captains always preferred to find a riverside dock come sundown. Even there danger still lurked. Armed bandits roamed the fertile lands of the Yangtze River delta, a vast maze of waterways, marshlands and rice paddies that it would take the *Gnat* a week or more to navigate. Further inland the plains, valleys and lake-lands would eventually give way to the dramatic mountains and rugged forests of the interior, all of which were plagued by warlords and the ruthless gangs under their control.

Even when moored up at night, the crew of the *Gnat* had to be ready to rouse themselves in an instant. The piercing blow of the ship's whistle and the yelled order of *Repel boarders! Repel boarders!* would mean trouble was at hand. China's nationalist government of Chiang Kai-shek was locked in a struggle with a relatively new adversary – the Soviet-backed Chinese commu-nist revolutionaries. Parts of the country were in a state of virtual civil war, and amid the conflict and insecurity warlords and banditry thrived.

The communist rebels resented the foreign 'imperialist' powers that plied the Yangtze, and they were yet another force to be reckoned with. At the order of *Repel boarders*, carbines would be broken out of the ship's armoury, and the Maxim machine guns brought to bear, as men lined whichever side of the ship the threat was coming from. But the first line of defence was to use the ship's steam hose – the scalding hot water being a non-lethal means to drive back any aggressors.

As with all British gunboats, the Captain of the *Gnat* was under orders to minimize casualties wherever possible. China was a powder keg waiting to blow, and a massacre of locals could prove the spark that would light the fuse. If there was an 'incident' – and there were always incidents when out on the Yangtze – Lieutenant Commander Waldegrave was to avoid deaths wherever possible, unless Her Majesty's subjects or property were directly threatened.

Thankfully, the night of Judy's shock christening in the Yangtze proved entirely peaceful, which was just what she needed to aid her recovery. At the crack of dawn – the start of day two of their journey upriver – the ship's bugler blew a sharp blast to awaken the crew. It was 0600 hours, and time to ready the vessel for another day's journey up the Yangtze.

In the officers' quarters, set in the bows forward of the galley and the ship's bridge, Chief Petty Officer Jefferey was woken by one of the Chinese boat boys, bringing him a mug of tea. Sharing a little of the hot, sweet brew with the handsome beast curled up at his side, Jefferey wondered what the day might bring. There would, he hoped, be no further misadventures by one thoroughly irrepressible ship's dog.

As soon as he opened his cabin door a crack Judy pushed through and scampered onto the deck, head down and nose sniffing as she caught the scent of food from the galley. *Ah, eggs. Scrambled to perfection, just as I like them.*

She padded past the caged chickens, giving them a good long sniff as she went. Jefferey hoped that Judy's keen interest in the ship's poultry – taken aboard at Shanghai, to provide some fresh meat for the journey – reflected the natural affinity she had for game and the performance of her duties as a gundog in the weeks ahead.

Tankey Cooper, Official Keeper of the Ship's Dog, took early morning custody of Judy, so he could serve her breakfast. Like Jefferey, Tankey was a keen huntsman, and once Judy was fed he decided to give her hunting prowess its first real test. Getting down to eye level with the lithe dog, he proceeded to explain to her in great detail and with seemingly boundless patience what was required of an English Pointer when out on the hunt.

Gazing into her eyes – which under the dawn light filtering through the canvas awning seemed less coal-like, and more a-sparkle with eager fire – he felt as if she understood his every word. With her long, floppy ears framing her face, there seemed to be something slightly mournful and intensely serious about her expression – and then she'd ruin it all by curling one lip in a lopsided smile, or flopping out that long pink tongue of hers for a goofy bout of panting.

Still, she wasn't yet fully grown, and Tankey reckoned she had plenty of time to prove her worth as a gundog. Deciding a spot of practical demonstration was in order, he proceeded to 'point' at the caged chickens, which were the nearest thing to game aboard the *Gnat*.

Judy stared at him for a long second, head cocked quizzically to one side. She knew from Tankey's body language that he was up to something of real import, but she couldn't for the life of her imagine what. Tankey held the pose for as long as he could – *see, like this* – before Judy gave a rigorous shake of her head, blew a snort through her nostrils seemingly in derision, and turned her nose towards the tantalizing smells wafting from the ship's galley. Her meaning was crystal clear: *message neither received nor understood!*

Undeterred, Tankey resolved to repeat the demonstration every morning after breakfast until Judy got it. But part of him wondered whether Judy hadn't been having a good laugh at his expense, as he swayed about on one leg trying to show an English Pointer how to point.

Once things were ship-shape, the *Gnat* was untied from her mooring and she pulled into the main flow of the river. The pitch of her engines rose to their familiar throb as she got underway. Making sure to keep well back from the rail, Judy stood on the ship's raised prow, nose into the wind. They had barely made a mile's progress, but already the mascot of the *Gnat* could smell trouble on the river up ahead.

Just after midday – at 1203 hours to be precise – the *Gnat* passed by a gunboat of the Imperial Japanese Navy steaming in the opposite direction. Just an hour later, the French gunboat *Francis Garnier* followed, also bound for Shanghai. And shortly a third foreign warship, the French gunboat *Balny*, passed the *Gnat*, but this time heading upriver into the Chinese interior. No doubt about it, the Yangtze was getting busy as rival world powers vied for control over the rich trade plied along these waters.

But right now the *Gnat* was about to be menaced by another threat entirely. From her position upfront Judy was first to give voice to the danger. She raised her head, took an extra long sniff and began barking into the far distance. A vessel could just about be made out drifting lazily downriver. Twin-masted, with grey- and dun-coloured square-cut sails set over a high prow, the wooden junk looked like a throwback to the Dark Ages compared to the modern, steel-hulled gunboats.

This was the kind of vessel that the *Gnat's* crew had seen hauled up the worst of the Yangtze's rapids by gangs of human 'coolies'. Using dozens of ropes slung from the banks and attached to the hull of the ship, bare-chested men would bend to the strain as they waded through the shallows, dragging the boat behind them step by exhausting step – and all to the rhythmic cry of the gangmaster who hired his men out to passing vessels. The *Gnat's* crew had grown used to such archaic scenes, but the boat ahead of them had a look that none of them liked very much.

The ancient-looking wooden vessel was lying low in the water, which meant it was laden with some seriously heavy cargo. None of the crew could be sure, but as Judy pranced about on the *Gnat's* prow and barked excitedly, they knew something untoward was bearing down on them. Their dog had never behaved like this before, not even after tumbling into the cold and churning maw of the Yangtze. Something about that vessel had her spooked.

Straining his eyes to get a proper look at the distant ship, Captain Waldegrave turned to his Chief Petty Officer. He had a curl to his lips that betrayed just the slightest hint of repulsion. Jefferey whipped out a pair of binoculars to take a closer look. Through the 8x magnification he could make out the distant boat in more detail. It had a dark hold lying open to the elements, and Jefferey was ninety per cent certain what lay inside.

Approaching the *Gnat* was one of the dreaded 'cess ships', and Judy seemed to have sensed it long before any of the crew had the slightest inkling what was coming. The ship's Captain altered course, orders were relayed from the bridge to batten down all hatches, close all portholes and make the ship as airtight as possible – after which all crewmembers were to get themselves below decks as quickly as possible.

The Yangtze River cess ships carried human waste – invariably well decomposed and stinking to high heaven – down the great river, to where it could be dumped away from the major towns and cities. More often than not it was used to fertilize the verdant green rice paddies that lay to either side of the river. The *Gnat* was approaching the riverside city of Zhanjiang, and no doubt the vessel full of rotting human ordure emanated from there.

Thanks to Judy's barking, by the time the sickening stench was upon them most crewmembers were sealed inside the vessel – including one ship's dog who'd just demonstrated her unexpected usefulness. The cess ships were a constant hazard on the lower reaches of the Yangtze. If the stench got inside the vessel it would linger in hair, clothes and furnishings for days. Judy had just proved herself to be the *Gnat*'s on-board early warning system.

She'd done so using her extraordinary sense of smell. A dog's world, unlike a human's, is almost entirely defined by odour. Their scent-detecting powers are so superior to our own, it's almost as if they experience an entirely different dimension – a world defined by innumerable layers of scent.

While humans possess 5 million scent detectors, a gundog like Judy has approaching 300 million. Such a dog can differentiate between over a million different aromas, as opposed to our mere thousand, and can do so at far tinier concentrations. With her wet muzzle – caused by tear ducts that run all the way to the tip of the nose – Judy could feel the way the wind was blowing, so isolating the direction from which the smell was coming. Moisture on the nose would then dissolve the tiny scent molecules, so receptor cells could identify them.

But Judy's powers of scent-detection were even more advanced than that. Because humans navigate largely by sight, we have a large element of the brain for processing visual information. In dogs, the olfactory (smell) centre in the brain is forty times more developed than in humans. Scents are even picked up by a dog's whiskers, which channel them to the brain. Plus dogs have a scent-detecting organ – the voremonasal, situated in the roof of the mouth – which is completely lacking in humans, and one that we as yet little understand.

To Judy, smell was her universe, the first sense by which she interpreted the world around her. Out here on the Yangtze, her nose was the filter via which she would sift all the scent-related information coming to her, to better understand and deal with this new and exotic – and sometimes life-threatening – environment. Detecting a cess ship on the Yangtze at a mile's distance was no trouble to a dog equipped with such acute powers of smell.

This time, Judy's canine senses had saved the ship's crew from nothing more than a few hours' sickening and suffocating stench.

But the time was fast approaching when Judy would need to use her incredible canine powers to save the lives of all aboard the *Gnat*.

Chapter Four

Continuing upriver the *Gnat* steamed past four Japanese warships, each trailing the distinctive bright-red rising-sun flag in her wake. It was ominous, the way in which Imperial Japan, China's age-old adversary, was making her presence increasingly felt this far inland. It was clear that trouble was brewing. The crew of the *Gnat* could feel it in their bones.

On 20 November the British gunboat reached Nanking, then China's sprawling capital, pausing only to pick up a sailor who was able to rejoin the ship, having been treated for an ailment in hospital in Shanghai. That done, the *Gnat* pressed onwards until she reached the smaller settlement of Wuhu, where she rendezvoused with her sister ship, the *Ladybird*.

The *Gnat* pulled in to moor alongside her – the two gunboats with their tall, twin funnels and long canvas awnings running from stem to stern resembling a mirror image of one another. They were also remarkably similar in another key respect: both the *Ladybird* and now the *Gnat* had a dog serving as their mascot.

Officers and men from the *Ladybird* were invited aboard the *Gnat*, as ship's rum was served and intelligence swapped between the two parties. This was an ideal opportunity for the Captain of the *Gnat* to glean information about any dangers that might lie ahead, for *Ladybird* was en route to Shanghai after a long sojourn upriver.

But one member of the *Ladybird*'s crew was decidedly not welcome. Bonzo, their ship's dog, had started acting very strangely just as soon as the *Gnat* had steamed onto the horizon. A large Boxer-Terrier cross, Bonzo had started to dash about the deck like a mad thing, tearing back and forth ceaselessly. With Bonzo's nose glued to the *Gnat*, it didn't take the brains of an archbishop to work out what was up. He had sensed the presence of a beautiful and glamorous young lady-dog aboard their sister ship and had amorous designs upon her.

On being alerted to the threat, Captain Waldegrave ordered Tankey, as Keeper of the Ship's Dog, to maintain Judy under strict lock and key. The last thing they wanted right now was a brood of Boxer-Terrier-English-Pointer crosses. Judy of Sussex wasn't particularly happy at being so constrained. She'd always enjoyed free run of the ship, but little did she know it was being done for her own good. She remained safely locked away until the *Ladybird* departed down-river, and Bonzo's dishonourable intentions towards her had been well and truly thwarted.

With Bonzo gone, Judy was free to join the *Gnat*'s crew on expeditions ashore. There was a Navy canteen located on the Wuhu docks where – joy of joys – the beer flowed freely. For some reason the place also seemed to have an inexhaustible supply of something that Judy proved very partial to – ice-cream. As soon as the ship's crew entered the canteen Judy would adopt a suitably regal pose, nose pointed directly at the trunk that contained the delicious treat.

One evening the men forgot to provide her with her customary plateful. Finally losing her patience, she sneaked behind the canteen bar, grabbed the handle of the ice-cream trunk in her jaws, and dragged it out into the centre of the room. She turned to the astonished drinkers, barked once in command, and demanded that her ice-cream be duly served.

Above Wuhu the Yangtze narrows considerably, as the flatlands of the delta give way to a series of dramatic, sweeping valleys. Three chokepoints – the Xling, Wu and Qutang gorges – funnel the river waters through towering rock-faces and knife-cut cliffs that rear up hundreds of feet to either side. Such terrain offered the perfect territory for the kind of piracy for which the Yangtze was infamous – although the *Ladybird* had been able to give no specific warnings of any such threats lying ahead.

Two days out from Wuhu the *Gnat* entered the steep-sided, echoing Xling Gorge, sparsely vegetated slopes sweeping down into the fast-flowing water. With dusk approaching the Captain decided to anchor for the night. As thick smoke from the *Gnat*'s funnels drifted across this valley that dwarfed the ship, he manoeuvred his vessel into shallower water, before ordering the anchor dropped.

With the *Gnat* safely moored Captain Waldegrave declared, 'Ship secure – hands to tea.' It was time for a refreshing brew after a long day's steaming on the Yangtze.

This being wilder, less-populated terrain, the crew was instinctively more alert. But as the slash of sky above them turned a velvety purple with the setting sun, there was little sign of any danger lurking out there on the darkening river. All was apparently peaceful until around 0300 hours, when Judy sat bolt upright in her box-cum-bed on the *Gnat*'s bridge. Throwing aside her ship's blanket, she pricked up her ears. Moments later she'd leaped onto her four paws and made a mad dash for the open wing of the bridge.

Barely pausing to fix the direction of the approaching threat, she began to bark wildly at a point somewhere in the darkness. For a moment the officer on watch wondered whether it mightn't be another stinking cess ship that had dragged Judy out of her slumber, but it was quickly clear that her attitude and demeanour were entirely different this time. There was an aggression and ferocity in her barking the likes of which he'd never heard before.

The crew of the *Gnat* were learning by now to pay all due attention to their dog. The officer on watch took immediate action. He grabbed the nearest Aldis lamp – a powerful, hand-held light more normally used for signalling from ship to ship – switched it on, and turned it towards the point at which Judy was directing her fury. Immediately the reason for her behaviour became apparent: two large junks were drifting silently towards the *Gnat* – though not quietly enough to have avoided detection via a dog's hyper-sensitive hearing.

Wasting not a second, the officer on watch drew his pistol and fired a single shot into the dark sky, the hollow crack of the low-velocity bullet reverberating around the sleeping ship and bringing the crew instantly awake. From all directions pyjama-clad men tumbled out of hatches and doorways, rifles, pistols and an assortment of other weapons held at the ready, as they hurried to their pre-determined stations to repel boarders.

The watch officer, meanwhile, had ordered Judy to be quiet. Now they knew what threat they faced, her early warning had given the ship's crew a perfect opportunity to get one over on their foremost adversaries – two large vessels packed full of fearsome Yangtze River pirates.

The pirates were making their attack approach in typical fashion – a pair of junks drifting silently abreast with a thick bamboo hawser slung between them. Once the rope snagged on the *Gnat*'s bows it would pull the pirate ships in towards her, and upon contact the waiting men would leap aboard the still-sleeping vessel, decimate the crew and loot to their hearts' content. At least, that had been their intention until Judy had caught wind of their coming on the chill night air.

The tension aboard the *Gnat* was palpable as the seconds ticked by. Then there was a faint, barely audible thunk as the bamboo rope made contact with the *Gnat*'s prow. By now Captain Waldegrave was directing operations with gusto from the bridge. As the two pirate vessels swung in towards his ship, the river gurgling under their bulging wooden hulls, he had his men positioned at the ready. One of them, a Stoker, only had time to don his scarlet pyjama top before grabbing a fire axe with which to set about the approaching threat.

Before the first vessel had even made contact with the *Gnat*, the Captain ordered those manning the Maxim machine guns, mounted on a platform to the rear of the twin funnels, to open fire. They let rip with ten-second bursts, raking the flanks of the pirate vessels, splinters of wood being blasted into the river. The Maxims were mounted three to each side of the ship,

44

chiefly for anti-aircraft use, but they were also the perfect weapons with which to signal the *Gnat*'s intent.

The river pirates knew for sure now that their target was forewarned, not to mention heavily armed, but there was no stopping the drift of their vessels as the rope dragged them in. The first craft bumped alongside. Shadowy figures reared up and attempted to board the *Gnat*. But they were met with a fusillade of gunfire – plus one roaring Stoker with his manhood on show swinging an axe above his head, and one ship's dog barking and snarling furiously.

Battle had most surely been joined.

Two of the *Gnat*'s crew were stationed in the prow and they were chopping furiously at the pirate's hawser. As the final strands of the bamboo rope were sliced through, the pair of junks were dragged free by the current and they slipped into the darkness. The last of the pirates turned tail and took a leap into the void in a desperate effort to rejoin their fast-disappearing ships.

Those who failed to make that jump faced a long swim in the rough waters churning through the Xling Gorge – a christening far more fraught with risk than the one suffered by Judy of Sussex a few days previously. As the pirate junks drifted away into the murk, triumphant cheers rang out from the deck of the *Gnat*. The feeling aboard was unanimous: it was the early warning provided by their intrepid ship's dog that had enabled them to vanquish their enemy so comprehensively.

Whether Judy would be of any use on the hunt no one yet knew, but tonight she had proved her worth ten times over – for her actions had been truly those of a lifesaver.

*

Prior to domestication dogs used their acute sense of hearing to track both prey and predators in the wild. They can hear a far greater range of frequencies than humans, they can do so over far greater distances and they can pinpoint accurately the direction the sound is coming from – just as Judy had done. In fact, a dog's hearing is ten times more effective than ours: a sound a human might hear at twenty metres they can hear at two hundred. Had there been a mouse living aboard the *Gnat*, Judy would have been able to hear it squeak from many metres away.

Using their large, movable ears they can pinpoint the source of a sound pretty much instantaneously – in one-six-hundredth of a second – hence Judy's rapid-fire actions aboard the *Gnat*, which had allowed the ship's crew to repel the river pirates without injury or loss of life. In the fight of the Xling Gorge, Judy's canine senses truly had saved the day.

Over the coming week the diminutive British warship – the gunboats were among the smallest vessels in the Royal Navy's fleet – pushed onwards through the Wu and Qutang gorges, and moved into the complex system of lakes, marshes and tributaries of the Hunan province beyond. Prior to reaching her first major stopover and possible turn-around point – the bustling treaty port of Hankow (now Wuhan), some 900 kilometres inland – the *Gnat* was set to rendezvous with the flagship of the British gunboat flotilla, the *Bee*.

Being the flagship of the fleet, the *Bee* had lost some of her main guns so that more space could be given over to officers' accommodation. In spite of this, on several patrols the illustrious *Bee* had pushed as far inland on the Yangtze as Yichang in the west and Changsha in the south, both approaching 1,500 kilometres from Shanghai and the sea. Those had been truly voyages into the wild and the unknown.

Unusually for Royal Navy ships, the Yangtze gunboats tended to sail – and to fight – as lone operators, cruising the river many days or weeks apart. Mostly, their commanders and crew had few if any senior officers watching over them. This tended to lead to a tight-knit, familial atmosphere aboard ship, and to a degree of independence of action rarely seen in the Royal Navy.

But without firmly enforced procedures to keep the gunboats ship-shape, long weeks spent in isolation upriver could render such busy, crowded vessels decidedly unpleasant places to be. As with all gunboat commanders, Captain Waldegrave had a strict routine in place for keeping the *Gnat* spick and span. Hands were ordered daily to clean – sluicing down the decks, polishing brass, making good the paintwork, generally clearing up the decks, stowing gear, refreshing brightworks (the polished metal parts of the vessel), and servicing the Maxim machine guns.

As the Captain of the *Gnat* knew well, a biannual Admiralty Inspection could be sprung on any Yangtze gunboat at any time. Rear Admiral Reginald Holt, the Senior Naval Officer (SNO) Yangtze Fleet, happened to be aboard the *Bee* when the *Gnat* docked alongside her, and he must have decided there was no time like the present to put the newly arrived gunboat through her paces. Needless to say this would be the *Gnat*'s first such formal ship's inspection with her new crewmember, Judy of Sussex, aboard.

It was the crack of dawn when the Rear Admiral came aboard the *Gnat*, complete with his aide, to announce the surprise inspection. The ship's officers and crew knew instantly what they were in for. The Rear Admiral would scour the vessel from stem to stern for the slightest infraction of ship's rules. He'd put every man and ship's department through their paces, to ensure the *Gnat* was operating at peak performance, and ready to wage war should such be necessary.

Or as Judy's keeper, Tankey Cooper put it – he'd come aboard to put them through 'the works'!

First off came the inspection of the crew. The men were lined up on the main deck in two ranks, at so-called 'Divisions'. The Rear Admiral proceeded to check over their kit and bedding, all of which was supposed to be neatly laid out, each item labeled with the owner's name. In due course he came to the newest crewmember . . . Judy. She was positioned between Tankey Cooper and her ammunition box of a bed, ship's blanket neatly folded before her.

The Rear Admiral stared down at the seated dog with a gimlet eye. She in turn gazed up at him tongue lolling, and with the signature silly grin that she seemed to reserve for any formal occasion aboard ship. At her feet were coiled two spare leads, plus an extra collar displaying her name clearly – *Judy*. All appeared to be present and correct, so without a word or a twitch in his deadpan expression the Rear Admiral moved on, shadowed by his aide.

Similar inspections followed all over the ship, as mess-decks, storerooms, stores, engine rooms, galley and all were given the once over. Finally seeming to be satisfied, the Rear Admiral and his aide returned to where they had started – the ship's bridge. From there he began to order the men through every drill known to the Yangtze gunboat flotilla, plus some seemingly yet to be invented.

To the casual observer the ship would have appeared a mass of chaos, but to Captain Waldegrave this was strictly ordered chaos in action. Every man knew his place and his duties, as block and tackle groaned and pulleys whirred and the ship was 'dressed' – involving a 'washing line' of brightly-coloured flags being raised from stem to stern – then the topmast lowered, the ship's generator stripped down and reassembled, and so on and so forth.

That done the Rear Admiral gave the order to 'land armed guard', and the launch was manned, lowered and it motored away from the *Gnat*. No sooner had it left, than he announced a 'man overboard' – which left the crew in some confusion as to how they were to rescue the fictitious victim, with the launch already half-way to storming some unseen adversary ashore.

'He'll just 'ave to swim until the ruddy boat gets back!' one of the sweating seamen muttered, as he ran to a new task.

In quick succession came orders to 'action stations', then 'fire all guns' – with quite spectacular results – and 'away kedge anchor', the kedge anchor being a light secondary anchor used to help a ship manoeuvre in narrow estuaries or rivers. The *Gnat*'s crew was becoming more than a little exasperated when Judy decided it was time for her to do something. As would prove to be the case many times over in future, whenever Judy sensed that her 'family' was in distress she'd find some means to come to their aid.

Without warning she raised her fine head to the skies above the bridge and began to bark. *Aruuf-ruuf-ruuf-ruuf-ruuf.* The barking was continuous and insistent, and the ship's crew recognized it instantly for what it was – *a warning.* As the barking grew to a fierce crescendo, they felt certain they were facing some kind of imminent danger – though no pirate ships were likely to attack two British gunboats in broad daylight, and the threat appeared to be *coming from the skies.*

As for the Rear Admiral, the orders he'd been issuing had been drowned out by a madly barking dog, and he was turning a noticeable shade of puce. Just as it seemed he was about to lose control and vent his anger on Judy, the cause of her distress became clear. All of a sudden a Japanese warplane swooped out of the seemingly empty heavens and dived towards the British warships. It swooped low over the *Gnat*, flew across the *Bee* at little more than mast-height, then pulled up into a steep climb and was gone.

No Japanese warplane had yet engaged a British or Allied ship on the Yangtze, but the meaning of the 'buzzing' was all too clear. Had they wanted to, the Japanese aircrew could have bombed or strafed the British gunboat pretty much at will. Japan had more or less total air-superiority in the skies above China. The Chinese Air Force was pitifully ill-equipped and manned, and no Allied aircraft were able to patrol this far into her territory.

Judy only ceased her barking once the Japanese plane had dwindled into an invisible speck on the horizon. Next, she did a very odd thing. She started to whirl around on the spot as if madly chasing her own tail, and once she was certain she'd completely monopolized the Rear Admiral's attentions, she proceeded to curl up on the floor at his feet.

The Rear Admiral stared at her for several seconds. She was wrapped comfortably around his gleaming toecaps, seemingly sound asleep after all the barking and whirling. He glanced at the rigid face of Captain Waldegrave, and raised one bristly eyebrow.

'Remarkable ship's dog you have here. Sound vibrations, presumably. That's how she did it.' A weighty pause. 'But the time is coming, I fear, when we all may need a dog like this stationed on the ship's bridge.'

The Rear Admiral must have realized that he had nothing in his repertoire to compete with Judy's early-warning demonstration, and the Admiralty Inspection was promptly declared over. The officers and crew of the *Gnat* had passed with flying colours – all of them, including one very remarkable ship's dog seemingly gifted with a miraculous form of canine radar.

Dogs possess eighteen separate muscles with which to raise, lower or swivel about their ears, ensuring they can pin down exactly which direction a sound is coming from. In detecting that Japanese warplane, Judy had demonstrated just how effectively those muscle-driven ears can be used to track distant sounds. But Judy's ability to detect that aircraft – and the threat it embodied – went far deeper than purely physical attributes.

Somehow, Judy had also sensed that this thunderous noise in the sky equated to danger, and since she'd yet to suffer any air attacks there was no obvious reason for her to do so. As with the pirate ships, she seemed able to sense *danger itself* – and it

was that which had so impressed itself upon the Rear Admiral
... not to mention all of her fellow crewmates.

A few days after she'd passed her Admiralty Inspection the
Gnat steamed into Hankow harbour, with no more pirates, or
Japanese warplanes – or even cess ships! – having menaced her
onward passage up the Yangtze. Here she joined the many other
British, American, French and Japanese gunboats floating at
their moorings, plus the odd Italian and German ship that also
patrolled these waters.

At Hankow the Captain's orders were simple. He was to show
a presence and fly the flag, looking efficient and war-like so as
to deter any trouble in this vitally important riverside city. Over
the eight decades that the Yangtze had been patrolled by the
foreign powers, Hankow had grown into the key treaty port
and gunboat hub, largely due to its strategic location in the
centre of the navigable stretch of the great river. As a result, the
city offered all the luxuries lacking aboard a ship like the *Gnat*.

The officers' mess on an Insect Class boat was fairly well
appointed for a vessel her size. The *Gnat* even had a wardroom,
set in the forward part of the hull, squeezed between the
Captain's quarters and the oil fuel tanks. The wardroom was
designed to resemble a miniature version of an English gentle-
man's club, complete with comfortable armchairs draped in
pristine cloth, yellowing copies of *The Times* newspaper on
side-tables, and white-coated Chinese stewards poised to top
up the pink gins when required.

But in spite of such on-board comforts, Hankow promised
the officers and men of the *Gnat* an exceptionally good time

ashore. Hankow resembled a classic European city of the time, both in terms of its grand, colonial-style architecture, its layout and atmosphere. The fashionable Hankow Club offered excellent dining and drinking, cabaret, bridge parties, tennis, plus good hunting in the surrounding bush. Hankow even boasted a race club, one that resembled Royal Ascot as much as ever it could here in deepest darkest China.

The Hankow Bund – the riverside harbour area where the *Gnat* was tied up – was designed to appear like a waterside promenade at any fashionable European port city. It was dominated by the Chinese Customs House clock tower and the splendid white colonnades of the Hong Kong and Shanghai Bank. The ground floor of the bank had been converted into a wet bar and clubroom, complete with billiard table and English-speaking Chinese bar boys.

Once a fortnight the wet room would host a Navy Opera, to which the assorted Royal Navy crews would invite the public for a singsong, one that was lubricated by copious quantities of a local beer called EWO Pilsner. Produced by the EWO brewery in Shanghai, the beer seemed to give off a peculiar pong of onions and it was unusually potent.

The wet room had been nicknamed the Strong Toppers Club, after the powerful, onion-scented beer quaffed in there. New members could only gain access to the club after an exacting initiation ritual. The newbie had to stand before a panel of three, while undergoing the Yangtze River variation of the popular drinking game 'Cardinal Puff'.

Holding his beer in his left hand, he'd announce a toast 'to the health of Cardinal Puff', strike the table once with his right hand, stamp both feet, tap the glass on the table, then drain his beer. The sequence had to be repeated with a fresh beer, only now he had to drink to the health of 'Cardinal Puff Puff', and repeat all the actions two times over. A third successful rendition – only now doing all actions three times over – and he was duly admitted to the club. But any mistake – reciting the lines wrong, getting the actions wrong, or drinking with the wrong hand – would be met with noisy jeers and jibes from the crowd. The unfortunate initiate would have failed and he'd have to start all over again.

During the long voyage upriver Judy had grown somewhat partial to her beer. As she was by now a fully fledged member of the ship's crew – she had even had the *de rigueur* christening in the Yangtze – her presence was required at such convivial evenings. Hence Tankey Cooper put together his own version of the Strong Toppers Club initiation ritual, especially for her. Before the assembled throng Judy had to bark once, twice, then three times in succession, each outburst of yelping punctuated by a noisy bout of lapping from someone's glass.

That completed, Judy of Sussex was declared in. She was now free to wander regally from face to familiar face, here and there taking a nibble from a handful of peanuts and a lap from a glass of onion-scented beer. Such riotous evenings ended in the traditional rendition of the Yangtze Anthem, to which Judy proved able to provide a remarkably soulful accompaniment, as she threw back her head and howled along to the verses.

Strong Toppers are we
On the dirty Yangtze

'Gunboats' or 'Cruisers'
We're here for a spree.

The Strong Toppers Club was largely a male environment, and Judy was one of the few ladies permitted access. And in her own peculiar way, she seemed to understand what this signified, in terms of her acceptance into the bosom of the all-male family that was the crew of the *Gnat*. She'd come a long way from that lonely back alleyway behind Soo's shop on the tough streets of Shanghai, and in singing along with the ship's company in the Strong Toppers Club Judy had truly found her tribe.

Chief Petty Officer Jefferey, by now Judy's closest companion, believed their ship's dog was developing a 'human brain', or at least a means with which to view the world of the Yangtze River gunboats pretty much as the sailors did. She appeared to understand every word spoken to her, read every gesture and expression, and she seemed to have adapted to the nuances of gunboat life as easily as any human crewmember had before her.

Early one morning Jefferey took Judy for a walk in the grounds of a smart Hankow hotel, a favourite with visiting Europeans. Man and dog strolled for a mile or so along the approach road, with dense jungle stretching away to their left. All of a sudden Judy darted off into the bush. Jefferey presumed she'd scented some game animal – most likely a deer, for he'd spotted their tracks already that morning.

Moments later he heard a yelp of alarm from somewhere within the bush. He knew instantly that it was Judy. He called her, and shortly she shot forth from the undergrowth. But she was clearly very alarmed, for she was trembling from head to toe. Jefferey had never seen her acting like this before, not even after her near-death experience in the Yangtze. He called the dog to him, but instead she bounded ahead on the road, making towards the hotel and forcing him to hurry after.

As he rushed along some sixth sense made him glance over his shoulder. There in the fringes of the bush was a large forest leopard. The thought flashed through his mind instantly – *so that's what spooked Judy*. It was only when he reached the safety of the hotel that Jefferey allowed himself to imagine another scenario – that Judy had picked up the big cat's scent and gone into the forest deliberately to distract its attention, for the leopard had in fact been stalking him!

Jefferey would never know for sure which it was. But one thing was certain – whenever she sensed that her extended family was in danger, Judy was proving herself willing to risk all to protect them.

Unperturbed by his close encounter with the leopard, Chief Petty Officer Jefferey decided to make full use of their Hankow stop-over to put Judy through her paces as a supposed gundog. By now she was approaching eight months old, and she'd grown into a fine-looking animal – muscular, sleek and fit, with a glistening coat, and always ready for a run around.

In fact, Hankow had offered her many a chance to hone her fitness, for the various crews were forever holding inter-ship football, rugby or hockey matches. With both football and rugby the ball proved a little too large for Judy to master, but she had become an absolute demon at hockey. She'd grab the ball in her mouth and streak for whichever goal was the nearest, paying little heed to whichever side she was supposedly playing for. This made for an utterly impartial player, though not one who could be counted upon to boost the *Gnat*'s score-line.

With serious gundog business in mind, CPO Jefferey organized a dawn hunting expedition. After an early breakfast aboard ship the crew – consisting of Jefferey, Tankey Cooper, plus four other keen hunters – set off, with Judy taking up the proud lead. Beyond Hankow in the open bush there was an abundance of King Quail – a game bird in the same family as the pheasant – and that was what the hunting party were after.

At the first sign of the distinctive birds taking to the air – a flash of iridescent blue plumage above bright orange feet – the guns roared. As quail were hit and tumbled from the sky Judy looked on impassively, making no move either to point or to fetch. The men took turns using the guns, while others acted as 'retrievers' to gather up the fallen birds, and still Judy didn't seem to take the hint or make any moves to join them.

Finally, Tankey Cooper decided enough was enough. He bent to Judy's eye level and gave her a little talking to, explaining what they wanted her to do.

Then he pointed in the direction of a freshly shot bird: 'Good girl! Fetch! Fetch!'

Seeming at last to understand what was expected of her Judy gave an excited wag of her hindquarters, dropped her head and dashed off into the bush. Now and again her long white tail popped up into view over the undergrowth, or there was a flash of liver-and-white as she bounded over the thick scrub. For a while she seemed to be making good progress, and then all sight and sound of her was lost. The watching party waited several minutes before weapons were made safe, and Tankey volunteered to go and find her.

Barely had he set off when he heard an anguished howl echo forth from the terrain up ahead. He knew instantly that it was Judy, although he'd never heard her utter anything like the tortured cries she was now making. As further heartrending yowls rent the air, he dashed forward, fearing the very worst. Was their ship's dog caught in some kind of animal trap, he wondered, or worse still crushed in the hungry jaws of a forest leopard?

Tankey crashed through the tall grass desperate to get to Judy, using his ears as his guide. Moments later he'd stumbled right upon her. At his feet lay some kind of pool, and somehow Judy had tumbled in. Worse still, the pond seemed to be full of a thick cloying mud from which the poor dog seemed unable to escape. As she eyed him desperately, imploring him to help, Tankey didn't for one moment hesitate – he plunged right in.

Landing on his feet he began to wade through the waist-deep mess. It was only then, and as the thick crust that covered the pond's surface was further torn asunder, that his senses were hit by an unbelievable stench. As the crisp, sun-baked skin broke apart so the ripe contents below were exposed to the air, along with their telltale odour. What Judy and now Tankey had leapt into here was an open cesspit.

Paralysed almost from the shock and the overpowering, suffocating stench – that of human faeces cooked for months under the strong Hankow sun – Tankey stood there for an instant and did as Judy was doing, howling out his distress. And then the realization hit him: while he was able to stand waist-deep in the sickening mess, poor Judy was having to doggy-paddle – in effect, treading water in a pool full of unspeakable torment.

Forcing his brain and body to function – dragging his mind out of the horror of the moment – he grabbed Judy by her collar, threw her onto the bank and hauled himself out behind her. There Tankey stood on the cesspit's edge, his legs, the lower half of his torso, and his arms covered in a revolting slick of ordure. The gunk was all over his hands even, from where he'd grabbed Judy's collar, plus he could feel it squelching evilly inside his boots.

But Judy was in an even worse condition: only her head had escaped immersion in the devilish pit. Using thick clumps of grass Tankey tried as best he could to scrub off the worst of the mess. Having done what he could for himself, he turned to Judy and used the same technique to try to rub her down. But even though Pointers have relatively short hair, still Judy's coat had soaked up enough of the thick black horror that it proved all but impossible to clean her.

There was nothing for it: they would have to make haste to the *Gnat*, where hot baths laced with disinfectant were very much in order. With a hangdog expression on both man and dog's features they hurried over to the hunting party – but none of their companions would come within twenty feet of them. Too disgruntled and disgusted to care much, Tankey led Judy back towards the harbour, a thick cloud of voracious flies marking their progress through the bush.

Long before they reached the *Gnat* Tankey heard the clanging of the ship's bell. One of those on the hunting party had clearly got back to their vessel before them. A voice drifted across to him as they hurried along the Hankow Bund. It was the Quartermaster, calling out the sonorous chant: 'Unclean! Unclean! Unclean!'

Above the ship the yellow 'Q' flag had been raised – denoting quarantine – but neither man nor dog had it in them to find much to laugh at in their present predicament.

After Judy's second bath laced with disinfectant in as many months, most of the terrible smell seemed to be gone. Even so, it was several days before she was considered done with her quarantine, and fit to be allowed back into the bosom of the ship's family. As for Tankey, he'd spent hours scrubbing himself lobster-pink, in a desperate effort to be rid of the last vestiges of the unspeakable ordure. During the process he'd made a momentous decision: there would be no more forcing Judy to be a gundog, that was for sure.

As the *Gnat's* early warning system, Judy had proved herself to have no equal. But as far as classic pointing duties went, Tankey Cooper had concluded that she was very much a round peg in a square hole. She might have helped the *Gnat* avoid the cess ship on the Yangtze, but here in Hankow she'd led Tankey Cooper into the heart of a cesspit without rival!

The *Gnat's* crew saw out that Christmas and the New Year in Hankow, after which the *Bee* sailed into port to relieve her of her duties. So it was that in the icy months of early 1937 the *Gnat* turned her prow eastwards, to start the return voyage downriver to Shanghai.

Unbeknown to her crew, the *Gnat* was sailing into bloody trouble – as was the entire British gunboat fleet on the Yangtze. The conflict that was almost upon them would eclipse the spot of bother that the *Gnat*'s crew had experienced at the hands of the Yangtze River pirates, or indeed anything that had ever gone before.

Shortly, Judy of Sussex would be called upon to save their lives many times over.

Chapter Five

Late in the spring of 1937 the Japanese Imperial Armed Forces made their move. In the north-east of the country, around Peking (now Beijing), the Japanese military began manoeuvres involving large numbers of ground troops. Tensions mounted inexorably as the Chinese military commanders watched what was unfolding, and shadowed the Japanese soldiers' every move.

Finally, during a night exercise by Japanese forces around the strategically important Marco Polo Bridge – an ancient granite span lined with fantastic carved dragons that crosses the Yongding River, providing a crucial access point into Peking – shots were exchanged. What began as confused, sporadic exchanges of fire rapidly escalated into full-scale fighting, with soldiers hit and wounded on both sides.

This was the excuse that Imperial Japan had been waiting for. Japan demanded that all Chinese troops withdraw from the area – in effect, ordering the Chinese military to vacate its own sovereign territory. When the ultimatum wasn't met the Japanese military launched an all-out offensive, bombarding Peking's port city of Tientsin (now Tianjin). Under fierce air and land attack both Tientsin and then Peking itself fell to Japanese forces in late June 1937.

So began what was to become known as the Second Sino-Japanese War. Age-old belligerents, the two nations had first resorted to all-out conflict in 1894. During a year of intense fighting the Japanese had scored a string of victories, and China's Qing Dynasty had been forced to sue for peace. Now, barely four decades later conflict had again engulfed these two ancient adversaries.

China's nationalist leader, Chiang Kai-shek, was quick to retaliate against the Japanese aggression. He directed the army and Air Force to counter-attack against those Japanese forces based at the mouth of the Yangtze River in Shanghai. It was 13 August 1937 when war erupted in the port city – and the Paris of the East was engulfed in fire. Months of intense conflict lay ahead, during which 200,000 Japanese troops, backed by air and sea power, would do fierce battle with the ill-equipped but spirited Chinese defenders.

If Shanghai fell, it would open up the entire length of the Yangtze to the Japanese, and the Chinese commanders knew full well what their next target would be – their capital city, Nanking, about 300 kilometres inland. Desperate to save Nanking, the Chinese strung a boom across the mighty Yangtze, one made up of what few warships they possessed, interspersed with junks transformed into makeshift gunboats and with thick bamboo hawsers strung between them.

The aim of the boom was to block any Japanese warships from moving upriver, but in placing it the Chinese had unwittingly cut off thirteen British gunboats from the sea, plus six American and two French vessels. Among them was the *Gnat*, complete with her crew and ship's dog. None of the gunboats had any way of escaping the warfare that had erupted at the mouth of the great river that they had for decades patrolled with such freedom.

After weeks of bloody street-to-street fighting Shanghai fell. Though beaten back from the city, Chinese forces had won a propaganda victory of sorts. Imperial Japan had openly boasted that it could take Shanghai in three days, and all of China in as many months. In reality, it had taken them three months of intense fighting – with heavy casualties on both sides – to seize the city at the mouth of the Yangtze.

As Chinese forces fell back from Shanghai, so the Japanese were able to break through the boom across the Yangtze. But there was little relief for the crew of the *Gnat*, or for those of the other gunboats. At a point halfway to Nanking a second boom was thrown across the river, and once more the Allied gunboats were trapped within a bloody conflict not of their making. Thus far none of the ships or their crew had fallen victim to the bloodshed, but they were hostages to fortune and few believed they could avoid its predations for ever.

With the Japanese pushing inland, Rear Admiral Reginald Holt, the Commander of the British gunboat fleet, tried to negotiate safe passage for his flotilla through the boom and out to sea, but to no avail. Japanese land forces were moving to encircle Nanking, and a massive aerial bombardment of the city had begun. By now it was early October 1937, and the Allied gunboats – the *Gnat* included – resorted to painting large national flags on their upper sides, in an effort to avoid getting pounced upon by marauding Japanese warplanes, which daily swept the lower reaches of the Yangtze, seeking targets.

At the same time that Japanese troops closed in on the Chinese capital, reports of terrible atrocities reached the gunboats. Civilians were being tortured, raped and massacred in their thousands. In the face of diehard Chinese resistance, the Japanese Army had been ordered to implement the 'Three Alls' policy – kill all; loot all; destroy all. With the noose tightening around Nanking, the Three Alls were about to be put into practice, with terrifying consequences.

The British and Americans – the two closest of allies, united by a common language, ancestry and culture – often performed joint patrols on the Yangtze, including anti-piracy taskings, bandit sweeps or rescue missions. Increasingly, the two fleets reacted to the mounting danger by grouping river traffic into convoys, each protected by as many British and American warships as could be mustered.

In the process, the crew of the *Gnat* struck up a fine friendship with the crew of an American gunboat, the USS *Panay*. One evening during a break in the patrols, the ship's crews rendezvoused at a riverside canteen. The beer began to flow and the sailors' voices raised the roof in song. The American sailors took a real shine to Judy, especially when she threw back her head and yowled along to their sea shanties, making herself the centre of attention.

But by the time Tankey Cooper had navigated his inebriated way back to the *Gnat*, he'd realized that Judy was no longer with him. The ship's dog being missing, he sobered up quick enough. Sailors searched the *Gnat* from stem to stern, but there was zero sign of her. They flashed a signal from their bridge, via the Aldis lamp, asking their fellows aboard the *Panay* if they had seen her. The reply that was signalled back was: 'Sorry, no trace of her here.'

Tankey was not the only member of the ship's crew who got precious little sleep that night. He blamed himself for not keeping his watch over Judy, but in truth she was the ship's dog and every man among them should have kept a proper eye out. But the following morning all seemed to be much brighter, if a little more sinister at the same time. The *Gnat*'s Chinese boat boys had heard a rumour that Judy was safe and sound – and hidden aboard the American gunboat!

'So that's how they want to play it,' Tankey had growled, upon learning the news.

He and his fellows spent the day plotting revenge. When darkness fell that evening a sampan stole alongside the USS *Panay*. Two fleeting figures crept aboard, and when they judged the coast was clear they seized their chance. Their business being done, they slipped back into the shadows of the sampan, and it pulled away from the American gunboat, heading for the *Gnat*.

Shortly after dawn a signal was telegraphed from the USS *Panay* to the British gunboat: 'To *Gnat*: boarded at night by pirates. Ship's bell stolen.'

The reply from the *Gnat* read as follows: '*Gnat* to *Panay*: we also pirated – of Judy. Will swop one bell belonging to USS *Panay* for one Lady named Judy property of officers and ship's company of HMS *Gnat*.'

Within the hour Judy was back aboard the British ship, and the quarter-deck of the USS *Panay* was once again graced by the ship's bell. No one – not even the US Navy – was about to part the gallant seamen of the Royal Navy from their ship's dog. But such high-spirited japes belied the extent of the threat now menacing the Yangtze. Shortly, the gunboats were to fall victim to the rising Japanese aggression – the USS *Panay* foremost among them.

On 11 December Japanese land forces unleashed their ire against their first Allied target – the British gunboat and sister ship to the *Gnat*, HMS *Ladybird*, plus the vessels she was protecting. *Ladybird* was anchored off Wuhu, watching over several British steamships. Without the slightest warning and under zero provocation, Japanese warplanes streaked out of the skies and unleashed their bombs, returning for a second time to strafe with machine guns.

One British steamer was sunk and another badly damaged. The radio message that *Ladybird* sent to the flagship, the *Bee*, anchored upriver near Hankow, left no doubt as to the serious-ness of the situation. Immediately the *Bee* set sail to come to her aid, but she was too late to prevent the *Ladybird* from being fired upon by Japanese shore-based guns at little more than point-blank range.

HMS *Ladybird* was hit repeatedly, and the onslaught only ended when she was able to steam far enough downriver so as to put herself out of reach of their fire. But the damage was done. Sick Berth Attendant Terence Lonergan had been killed outright, and not an officer aboard the *Ladybird* had escaped without injury. By the time the *Bee* reached Wuhu she too came under attack, and was only able to escape serious damage by repeatedly dodging Japanese shellfire.

Meanwhile, lying off besieged Nanking the sister gunboats HMS *Scarab* and *Cricket* were guarding a fleet of British cargo ships when yet more Japanese warplanes appeared from out of the sky towards the east. By now *Ladybird's* timely warning had been transmitted to all British and Allied shipping on the Yangtze: *the Japanese were on the warpath and all vessels were to be on high alert for hostile acts*. The British gunboats were primed and ready.

As the aircraft dived to attack they were met by a fierce barrage of fire put up by a dozen Maxim machine guns, plus four heavier guns threading lines of vicious flak across the sky. The warplanes were forced to abort their sortie, dropping their bombs at random along the river as they raced for the safety of the clouds. But the attacks along the Yangtze were far from over, and the Japanese would turn their aggression next against their foremost future enemy – the Americans.

The crew of the gunboat USS *Panay* – Judy's erstwhile kidnappers – had just finished evacuating all remaining US citizens from the besieged capital, Nanking. As a result, the little ship had become the de facto American Embassy in China: she had aboard her five officers, fifty-four crew, plus four Embassy staff and a dozen-odd related civilians. She was escorting three other ships – the Standard Oil tankers *Mei Ping*, *Mei An* and *Mei Hsai*, which were in the process of evacuating Standard Oil employees from Nanking.

It was early afternoon when a flight of twelve Japanese naval aircraft swooped for a surprise attack. The carrier-based warplanes – two Nakajima A4N fighters, escorting a flight of Yokosuka B4Y bombers – dropped a total of eighteen

60-kilogram bombs, and strafed the river flotilla with 7.7mm machine-gun fire. The *Panay* was hit by two bombs, and repeatedly raked by gunfire. The gunboat sank rapidly, going down in the shallows.

As the stricken gunboat settled onto the river bottom, so the three Standard Oil tankers were hit and set aflame. Many aboard were killed, and the *Panay* had herself suffered numerous casualties. Two of the *Panay*'s crew had been killed, an Italian journalist aboard was also dead, and there were forty-eight wounded and injured.

A pair of American news cameramen aboard the *Panay* had been able to film the early stages of the attack, plus the sinking of the ship once they had reached shore. When their news footage was aired around the world, the scenes of the unprovoked assault would cause widespread outrage. But for now the *Panay* was lost, and news of her sinking had yet to reach the American high command.

Admiral Yarnell, then Commander-in-Chief of the US Asiatic Fleet, was the man tasked with keeping watch over the unfolding troubles facing US forces along the Yangtze. Unable to raise the *Panay* by wireless, the Admiral put a radio call through to the *Bee*, asking the Commander of the British fleet to try to locate the missing American ship – last known location just north of Nanking.

The *Bee* was busy escorting the heavily damaged British gunboat the *Ladybird*, but she responded to the American request and steamed down-river to investigate. Rear Admiral Holt soon discovered why the USS *Panay* had fallen silent. Among the still smouldering wreckage that lined the riverbank he discovered the battered but unmistakable superstructure of the American gunboat lying proud above the waters.

The officers and crew of the *Bee* surveyed a scene of smoke-laden ruin, and at first there appeared to be no survivors. Then a pair of Americans emerged from the bush and began shouting and waving at the British warship. The remaining survivors, many seriously wounded, had been moved inland to the nearest Chinese village. The *Bee* landed a shore party of twenty-five men, and the survivors, including all the injured, were taken aboard the British warship.

When the Rear Admiral radioed his American colleague with news of what had transpired, it would shock the world. Reactions from the American and British governments were swift in coming. They demanded that the unprovoked attacks along the Yangtze cease forthwith, that the Japanese officer commanding those forces that had bombed the British and American warships be removed from his post, and that compensation be paid for the loss and damage caused.

The Japanese response was to claim that the attacks on the British ships, plus the sinking of the USS *Panay*, had been cases of 'mistaken identity'. Their pilots hadn't seen the flags painted on the vessels' superstructure, and had mistaken them for Chinese warships. But they paid the compensation demanded, removed from his post the Air Force Colonel who had overseen the attacks, and promised that there would be no further such incidents.

Just twenty-four hours after the sinking of the USS *Panay*, Nanking itself fell, and what became known as the 'Rape of Nanking' ensued. As many as 300,000 Chinese were killed in the most horrific of ways. This was still an undeclared war: Japan had yet to formally declare hostilities with China. But with news of the Nanking Massacre reaching foreign ears, strong diplomatic protests were lodged – first and foremost by those governments that still had gunboats on the Yangtze, and who were receiving eyewitness accounts of the terrible happenings.

In light of the nightmare unfolding ashore the British and American gunboats continued with their river patrols as best they could, but always in the face of mounting Japanese aggression, particularly against the locals. By March 1938 the *Gnat* found herself in Kiukiang, 400 kilometres upriver from Shanghai. She was there to find out which British residents were willing to evacuate in light of the relentless march of Japanese forces inland.

Typically, a somewhat exasperated Captain Waldegrave reported in his March letter to Rear Admiral Holt that the British residents in Kiukiang were intending to remain where they were 'throughout all hostilities'. Mr and Mrs Porteous, Miss Rugg and Miss Luton, all Christian missionaries of the China Inland Mission, were intent on maintaining a very British stiff upper lip in the face of the Japanese invaders.

Of course, the Captain of the *Gnat* was unable to force any British citizens to evacuate. All he could do was have a word with the local British Safety Committee – a Home Guard-like set-up formed by the handful of British citizens resident in the area – in an effort to put some procedures in place should the Japanese turn against British nationals when they overran Kiukiang, as they surely would in the next few days.

The sympathies of the British gunboat crews in this unfolding conflict – plus their animal mascots – lay fully with the Chinese. They had Chinese crewmen serving on their ships; they had befriended many locals along the river during the long years spent on duty there; and there were any number of British sailors who had fallen in love with a local girl and stayed behind to raise a family with her.

In fact, the crew of the *Gnat* – Judy included – had officiated over one such marriage recently, during a stop-over in Shanghai. Chief Petty Officer Charles Goodyear served on the *Bee*, but he was a close friend of both Vic Oliver, the man who had rescued Judy from the Yangtze, and of the dog herself. It was only right that both were invited to his wedding – proof of how love could flourish in the midst of war.

CPO Goodyear's chosen bride was a Russian barmaid – and widow – then serving in the Pig and Whistle bar in Shanghai. After the wedding the crew of both the *Bee* and the *Gnat* had retired to the Pig and Whistle, to celebrate the nuptials. An aged Chinese soothsayer with the ability to read a person's future was persuaded to examine the palms of a number of the sailors. Of course, the groom had to be among them. But when the soothsayer had scrutinized Goodyear's palm, he'd blanched visibly and refused to say a word.

Most of those present had teased Goodyear remorselessly, but not Vic Oliver. He'd felt a strange conviction that the soothsayer *was* able to tell the future, and that Goodyear and his bride would have little time together, in a world about to be torn apart by war. Certainly, if their Yangtze campaign was anything to go by, the forces of Japanese aggression were going to prove nigh-on unstoppable.

The gunboat-men were powerless to act as the Japanese drove the Chinese resistance relentlessly backwards. Japanese soldiers took Kiukiang, from which the British residents had doggedly refused to evacuate. With barely a pause they pushed onwards towards Hankow – the Yangtze gunboats' 'home city', the headquarters of the Strong Toppers Club and the place where only months earlier Judy had dragged the unfortunate Tankey Cooper into the cesspit.

In the face of the bloody conflict, all aboard the *Gnat* had to strive to remain neutral – including a ship's dog who had as a young puppy herself fallen victim to the cruelty of the Japanese military. Judy seemed to have been blessed with an unfailing instinct for detecting which of her two-legged fellows were dog-lovers, and which were inclined to view her either as a potential tasty meal, or as the enemy. And it was to be in Hankow that she would next come face to face with her tormentors. But first there were old acquaintances to renew, plus some sad and heartfelt farewells to be dealt with.

It was early April 1938 when the *Gnat* found herself again based at Hankow. Hankow being her homeport away from home, there was the inevitable local fixer and master of all trades here, one who had made it his business to tend to the crew's every need. In Portsmouth, the *Gnat*'s British homeport, there had been 'Tubby' Greenburgh, a rotund and jolly naval tailor from whom the men could always borrow ten shillings on 'blank' days – those immediately prior to payday – interest-free and sealed with nothing more than a handshake.

Here in Hankow, 'Tubby' Greenburgh's equivalent was Sung. For reasons lost in the mists of time Sung was better known to all who sailed the Yangtze as 'Joe Binks'. A huge bear of a man, Joe Binks would beam with undisguised good humour as the men poured forth from the *Gnat* intent on some quality shore-time, but he reserved an especially warm welcome for the *Gnat's* ship's dog.

Joe Binks was the *Gnat's* official Hankow comprador – the man charged with supplying the ship with all the food and other stores she might require. He often brought his wife and four young children with him when doing business aboard the British gunboat, and the children in particular delighted in Judy's company. In spite of being bred for the hunt, English Pointers generally display an instinctive love of children, and Judy adored being in the presence of the Sung youngsters.

Dashing about the ship, hiding in her favourite cubbyholes, and challenging the kids to find her – these were some of Judy's happiest moments amid all the tension and chaos of the war-torn lower Yangtze. Cries of delight from the children indicated that they'd discovered her, but Judy would rapidly turn the tables by dancing excitedly from paw to paw, then going rigid and seeming to 'point' at the children's bulging pockets – for the Sung youngsters always came bearings tasty gifts for *Shudi*, the peaceful one.

Judy's next-best friend among the locals was known to all simply as 'Sew-sew'. The reason for the nickname was self-evident: she was tasked with carrying out any sewing or other repairs required to clothing or furnishings aboard the *Gnat*. Sew-sew would spend her time perched on a stool on the open

74

deck, needle and thread flashing in the sunlight as she attached a new white tape to the collar of a formal mess jacket, all the while talking in her soft, sing-song voice to her chief companion – an enraptured Judy.

But perhaps Judy's foremost 'family of friends' among the locals were the Amah brood. Amah herself was a woman of fierce repute along the Hankow Bund. Her entire family lived in a small, rattan-covered sampan that was tied up on the dock-side. Contracted to the British Admiralty, Amah had fought for and won the right for her boat to be used as the British gunboats' 'general use' vessel. She and her children spent their day ferrying men and materiel from ship to shore and back again, or if there was no demand for her ferry services she'd busy herself touching up the paintwork on a gunboat's hull.

Judy had grown to adore Amah and more specifically her children. Whenever she got the chance she'd leap from the *Gnat* into the sampan, and standing proud on the bow she'd oversee operations as Amah ferried a group of sailors to shore. But by far her favourite moment was when she was able to dart beneath the boat's rattan covering, whereupon delighted squeals and shrieks would reveal that she was having a fine rough-and-tumble with Amah's children.

Such were Judy's special friends at Hankow, and via her local family she was doubtless able to get in touch with her feminine side. But on the troubled lower Yangtze in 1938 it was perhaps inevitable that few such extended families would remain intact for very long, not even those aboard the gunboats.

Inevitably, there was a 'churn' among the British crews, as those who had completed their two-and-a-half years 'foreign service' were rotated back to the UK. Many were reluctant returnees. Especially in the midst of a conflict like that presently unfolding, the life of a gunboat-man was exciting and fraught with danger, which made it strangely compelling. By contrast, England in 1938 remained a land of stability and of peace, offering none of the young sailors the buzz they could expect when patrolling the Yangtze.

But as with all good things, every crewman's gunboat posting had to come to an end. Sadly for Judy, it was now the turn of her foremost shipmates to be rotated back to England. Vic Oliver, who'd plucked her out of the Yangtze; Tankey Cooper, who'd plucked her out of the Hankow cesspit; and Chief Petty Officer Jefferey, who'd plucked her out of the Shanghai Kennels and chosen her as ship's dog – all were going home. In light of the loss of so many of her close family, perhaps it was serendipitous that Judy was about to start a family of her own . . .

After heartfelt goodbyes between those who were departing and the dog they were leaving behind, replacement crewmen came aboard the *Gnat*. Among them Judy seemed to take an instant liking to two very distinctive individuals. One was an easygoing giant of a man, Leading Seaman Law. The other, Able Seaman Boniface, better known to all as 'Bonny', was a real joker and was to become the character of the ship. It was to be Bonny and Law who'd perform the pivotal role in Judy's forthcoming motherhood.

A French gunboat, the *Francis Garnier*, had docked opposite the *Gnat*, with an American vessel, the USS *Tutuila*, pulling in alongside. At first the arrival of the two Allied gunboats was seen as being a good excuse for some fine-spirited hospitality.

The crew of the USS *Tutuila* were invited aboard the British ship for *limited* use of the ship's canteen – in other words, her stock of beer. The beer was expected to last only until 26 April, before rationing would again be required.

Following a fine evening's Anglo-American carousing, the crew of the *Gnat* challenged their Yankee fellows to a rifle match. It was a close-run thing: the British sailors won by one point. But from the *Francis Garnier*, the *Gnat*'s crew was about to receive an altogether more unexpected challenge – and very much more than ever they had bargained for.

It was Bonny who first noticed Judy's odd behaviour. He was seated in the crew's mess, in the bows of the ship, trying to concentrate on the letter he was writing to his sweetheart back in Portsmouth. But whenever he seemed to get the words he was composing in his head just about right, Judy would get to her feet, whine insistently, wander about unhappily, then flop back down again.

Finally, she padded across to the ladder leading to the main deck and fresh air, and stared upwards with a fixed expression on her features. Then she turned imploringly to Bonny, with the most heart-melting look in her eyes that he had ever seen.

Bonny put down his pen and stared right back at her. 'How d'you expect me to persuade the barmaid in the Air Balloon that it's all right for me to take her on holiday without her mum, if you keep moaning and fidgeting?'

Judy flicked her gaze back to the ladder, then pinned Bonny once more with that pleading look.

Bonny got to his feet. 'What's up with you? You want to go for a little walk, is that it? Go on then – up we go!'

Judy had become a dab hand at navigating the ladder, which was set at a thirty-degree angle with wide steel rungs like steps. Bonny followed, and together man and dog mooched about on deck for a good few minutes. It was then that Judy took the initiative and led them down the gangway to the *Gnat's* mooring, which was next to an old hulk of a merchant ship with all her masts and riggings removed.

Expecting Judy to want a run-around and have a good play, Bonny was more than a little surprised when all she seemed interested in doing was parading up and down the bare deck of the hulk. Head held at a proud slant, tail up and flying like a signal flag, she sauntered back and forth in a most uncharacteristic fashion. It was odd. Very odd. Bonny was at a loss to understand what she was about.

Then he happened to glance across to the far side of the hulk, where the *Francis Garnier* was tied up. Suddenly the penny dropped. On the French ship's bridge was a very distinctive looking four-legged crewmember, whose eyes were glued to Judy of Sussex's every regal move. But what struck Bonny most was this: though slightly taller and broader of chest than Judy, the *Francis Garnier's* ship's dog could have been her brother.

He was an uncannily similar liver-and-white English Pointer.

Chapter Six

Bonny stared at the *Francis Garnier*'s dog in surprise. As for Judy, she seemed to think that her work here was done. With a jaunty shake of her rear quarters she proceeded to turn tail on the French gunboat and her smitten admirer, and saunter back up the gangway of the *Gnat*.

Bonny shook his head in amazement. 'So that's what it's all about, then. But how like a typical female! She must have known he was there, yet she didn't so much as look at him. Just showed herself off, then disappeared!'

In no time the courtship became the stuff of legend. In contrast to Judy, Paul, the *Francis Garnier*'s dog, made no attempt to disguise the fact that he had fallen head over heels in love. Now that he knew the object of his desire lay so tantalizingly close he was forever breaking free and careering down the French vessel's gangway, ending up spreadeagled on the hulk in his haste to get close to her.

Unperturbed, he'd bound back and forth across the open deck like a medieval knight in a heavy suit of armour, unaware that Judy would be watching in disdain with bared teeth and curled lip. Finally, in a desperate effort to gain her attention and curry her favour, Paul hammered along the entire length of the hulk at top speed, legs thrashing in a super-canine show of male prowess. Unfortunately, he'd miscalculated his stopping power on the smooth deck.

With a despairing wail the French ship's dog sailed off the bow and ended up in the harbour, with a loud splash. Ironically, it was now that Judy finally showed her true feelings. She sprang to the *Gnat*'s rail, barking in alarm as her beau beat a path through the water towards her. Sensing that he couldn't scale the sheer side of the British gunboat, Judy raced down the gangway with Bonny close behind. With Judy peering over the edge and continuing to bark urgently, Bonny reached down, grabbed Paul's thick collar and hauled him out of the water.

The French dog was soaked from head to toe. But his ducking and his near-humiliation would prove more than worth it in the end – for in making himself a laughing stock Paul had managed to break Judy's icy English reserve. Without any further dissembling on her part she proceeded to lick his face dry, nuzzle against his wet body and paw him all over.

Bonny stared at the two of them in amazement. From being a total no-hoper, via his exuberant misfortune Paul had gone in an instant to being the first love of Judy's life. All of a sudden this had the promise of a match made in heaven. In which case, Bonny decided, the men of the *Gnat* needed to give their ship's dog a good talking-to.

By now Judy was approaching two years old – the equivalent of her early twenties in human years. Bonny figured she was as ready as she'd ever be to have a litter, and with the *Francis Garnier*'s dog being on hand they had a golden opportunity both to strengthen the *entente cordiale* and to breed a fine line of Franco–English pointers. But that didn't mean that any nuptials could be entered into without Judy being fully acquainted with the facts of life, not to mention her responsibilities.

On the afternoon of Paul's tumble into the harbour, five chosen men of the *Gnat* sat around the mess table, on which was perched a carefully groomed Judy of Sussex dressed in her smartest collar.

Bonny eyed her with a serious expression. 'We feel that the time has come when we need a proper talk. We are so to speak your legal guardians, and we naturally want to do the best for your happiness. But you'll understand that everything must be done properly and in accordance with the rules.'

He paused to let his words sink in. Judy cocked her head to one side, quizzically. It was as if she was saying: *come on – get on with it!* At the same time she flicked out her tongue to lick Bonny's hand, as if to reassure him that she was glued to his every utterance.

Bonny nodded, happy she was paying proper attention. 'Now, Paul is doubtless a very nice dog, with a pedigree too. Plus they are a very nice bunch on the *Francis Garnier*. So we've decided you can get engaged today and if all goes well you'll be married tomorrow. But only on one condition – that you name your first pup Bonny.'

Judy appeared to nod her agreement, and so one of the ship's engineers proceeded to lift her left paw and slip over it an anklet designed for this very occasion.

'That,' he announced, as he closed it more tightly around her ankle, 'is your engagement ring.'

Judy stared at the loop of silver for a long moment. She knew from the tone and demeanour of the men gathered around her that something of great import was afoot, but she perhaps didn't quite yet understand what all of this signified.

The very next day Judy and Paul were to be married. They were led forth onto the centre of the hulk, so both crews could watch the ceremony. Bonny officiated, together with his opposite number from the French ship. As the men of both vessels cheered and clapped enthusiastically – and a group of perplexed locals gathered to scratch and shake their heads – Bonny proceeded to pat both dogs on the head and rounded off the ceremony as appropriately as he could.

'And so, with no further ado I am pleased to pronounce you . . ?' He struggled for a moment to find the right words. 'Dog and bitch?' He glanced around the crowd hoping for some inspiration. 'Paul and Judy?'

Then a heavily accented voice called out from the bridge of the *Francis Garnier*. It was their First Lieutenant. 'One!' he cried. 'Pronounce zem one!'

'Perfect – I pronounce you one!' Bonny confirmed.

And so Judy of Sussex and Paul of Paris – Paris because it sounded classy and thoroughly romantic – were duly married.

Paul was permitted onto the *Gnat*, where a special love nest had been constructed for the two dogs. After three days in doggie heaven he was returned to the *Francis Garnier* complaining loudly, but all were deaf to his protestations.

As was perhaps fitting, Judy would bring new life into the world just as death and destruction threatened to engulf all around her. During the weeks since her romantic liaison with Paul she had grown plumper and plumper, her eyes shining with anticipation of her soon to be realized responsibilities. But at the same time Japanese warplanes had started hitting the heart of the Chinese resistance hard, targeting the city of Hankow first and foremost.

As the war along the Yangtze intensified, so the Japanese Imperial Air Force deployed their modern, twin-engined Mitsubishi G3M medium bomber, operating from land bases in Japan. Specialist units were formed to fly missions across the East China Sea, carrying out mass bombing raids over China's key cities. The Mitsubishi G3M carried 800 kilograms of bombs – many times the payload of the carrier-based biplanes that had previously attacked the Yangtze gunboats – and boasted a 4,400-kilometre flight range.

None of these warplanes had yet targeted the gunboats tied up at the Hankow Bund. But each time they roared over the city Judy would curl herself around her distended stomach, as if in an effort to safeguard her unborn litter, and snarl defensively at the skies. She was learning to hate these giant angry birds that pounced from the heavens, unleashing death and destruction and threatening to snuff out the lives she was carrying before they could even be realized.

But the morning duly came when – as yet another wave of Japanese bombers thundered through the skies above Hankow – there was the miracle of birth aboard the *Gnat*. A tired and unshaven Bonny (the *Gnat's* self-appointed midwife) tumbled down the steps to the mess-deck.

'They're here!' he yelled, triumphantly. 'All thirteen of them!'

There was a rush for the ladder, as the crew jostled each other to be first to see the new arrivals, not to mention their proud mother. Sure enough, squeezed into a ship's basket that seemed barely able to contain them were thirteen tiny replicas of Judy – each liver-coloured from the neck up just like their mother, but with several also exhibiting their father's distinguishing white streak running from forehead to nose.

Of the thirteen pups three of the weakest quickly perished, leaving ten to grow fat on their mother's milk. Lying protectively with her brood, Judy appeared to be the perfect mum, and not even the constant stream of well-wishers who poured aboard the *Gnat* appeared able to disturb or discomfit her.

She seemed happy to show off her babies to all and sundry – Sew-sew, the Sung family, and Amah the boat-lady's children included. But the one individual prevented from seeing them was the pups' father, Paul. Now that he'd done his business Judy seemed to have forgotten her French beau almost as if he'd never existed.

In no time at all everywhere there were unsteady puppies tumbling about the *Gnat*, chubby little legs flailing as they tried to escape from the ship's crew, who were equally intent on ushering them back to their nest. They got into every conceivable corner, chewed anything even remotely chewable and everywhere they left spreading puddles of puppy mess.

Only when they were old enough so that each could be taken on a lead for a walk did Paul finally get to see his offspring. He sniffed at them curiously, as if trying to work out if they were really his doing, before they were ushered back aboard the *Gnat*. No one wanted to be out in the open for very long. With

Japanese warplanes menacing the skies, any outing around Hankow spelled danger.

One afternoon shortly after the puppies' first foray off ship, a squadron of Japanese bombers flew in to attack Hankow, using the river valley to mask their approach until the final moment. But Judy heard them coming. By now the attacks were so commonplace that she rarely had time or opportunity to issue her customary warning. Yet today she seemed to sense that this was different, and that the enemy in the air was coming for her family – both her four-legged and two-legged ones.

Whining frantically, she called her pups to her, and as the bombers roared in to attack she attempted to wrap herself protectively around them, yelping out a desperate last-minute warning to the ship's crew. Seconds later the lead aircraft swooped over the *Gnat*, releasing its bombs. Like evil black demons they plummeted towards the vessel, but at the last instant their trajectory proved slightly off and they overshot the ship.

They hit the river ahead of the *Gnat* and detonated, throwing up huge plumes of tortured white water. The reverberations of the explosions punched through the ship's hull, as a protective mother curled closer around her cowering brood, and blasted river water rained down all around. Taken by surprise – so far, the Japanese had kept their promise, made after sinking the USS *Panay*, not to attack any neutral ships – the crew of the *Gnat* raced for their battle stations.

Behind the lead bomber the rest of the squadron thundered in. But as the *Gnat*'s gunners swung the Maxim machine guns onto their target, a new sound rent the skies above the Hankow Bund – the howl of Pratt & Whitney 'Wasp' radial engines.

Judy couldn't know it, and her fear for her brood was doubtless redoubled under the aerial onslaught, but a flight of ace fighters had flown to the rescue, and by the looks of things just in the nick of time.

A ragged volley of cheers went up from the deck of the ship, as the distinctive snub-nosed forms of eight Boeing P-26 'Peashooters' dived to attack. The P-26 was the first American all-metal fighter aircraft ever built, and the Chinese Air Force operated several flights of the redoubtable warplane. The Japanese had already felt the wrath of the Peashooter's Browning machine guns, with a score of Mitsubishi G3M bombers having been shot down over Nanking.

In an instant the bombers targeting the Hankow Bund broke formation, and jettisoned their bombs in an effort to lighten their load and escape. But some proved too slow. The Boeing P-26s were flown by Chinese pilots, aided by a handful of ace British, American and other volunteer aircrew. They had swooped from where they'd been flying a holding pattern at altitude and they tore into the Japanese warplanes.

Two bombers were raked from nose to tail by the Peashooter's 7.62mm machine guns. The Mitsubishi G3Ms shuddered under the onslaught, before smoke and fire bloomed along the fuselage, and first one and then the other fell from the sky into the waiting Yangtze. The *Gnat* – and Judy and her brood with her – had been saved from what had seemed like almost certain annihilation, but the narrow escape only served to reinforce the urgent need to get the puppies out of danger.

Homes would need to be found for the ten pups, and quickly.

*

Unbeknown to any aboard the gunboat's crew, the timely appearance of those Boeing P-26 fighters wasn't quite as miraculous as it might have seemed. There was in place a secret early-warning system that signalled to the Chinese Air Force the impending arrival of enemy warplanes, and it was happening right under the very noses of the Japanese. Unwittingly, the British gunboat the *Gnat* had played a pivotal role in getting that early warning system up and running.

Some months earlier Stanley Cotterrall, the *Gnat's* telegraphist – her Morse code operator – had been landed at Wuhu, to undergo an urgent medical operation at the American Mission Hospital. During his recuperation the hospital had need to send a signal to the Wuhu docks, to secure the help of a doctor who was serving aboard a ship moored there. Cotterrall had offered to send one using Morse code, which he duly did using a mirror from the hospital roof, employing flashes of sunlight to alert the ship.

In due course the hospital sister asked Cotterrall to teach some of them Morse, so they could do the same for themselves in future. One or two of the Chinese staff proved to be particularly enthusiastic pupils. They very quietly went on to learn radio-operation as well, and under a cloak of absolute secrecy they proceeded to install a radio on the hospital roof.

Whenever a flight of Japanese warplanes flew over Wuhu, using the Yangtze to navigate inland to their target, those Chinese medics would sneak onto the roof to send a radio warning in Morse code. Thus Hankow was forewarned, and the P-26 Peashooters were able to appear as if by magic to blast the Japanese aircraft out of the sky. Eventually the Japanese would discover that the radio messages were being sent, but were never able to locate the transmitter hidden on the roof of the American Mission Hospital.

As far as possible, the giving away of Judy's puppies was a gradual process, so as to soften the blow. First choice went naturally to the officers and men of the *Francis Garnier*. Next in line was the Hankow Race Club, which made an offer that the ship's Captain felt unable to refuse: one Lewis light machine gun and four magazines of ammunition, in exchange for the puppy. Further pups went to diplomatic staff based in Hankow, and one of the last was gifted to the American gunboat the USS *Guam*.

The tenth and final puppy went to a Scottish Engineer who served aboard one of the steamers still operating on the Yangtze. Once more Judy was reduced to the company of her two-legged family, on a diminutive British warship increasingly feeling the wrath of the Japanese. And in the coming days the steel of the gunboat crew was about to be tested as never before.

Towards the end of the summer of 1938, with Japanese troops poised to take Hankow, a Chinese Customs ship, the *Chianghsing*, was out on the river moving marker buoys, in an effort to make it more difficult for Japanese warships to navigate into the city's harbour. Spotted from the air, the *Chianghsing* was pounced on by Japanese aircraft and strafed and bombed.

With his ship sinking and on fire, Captain Crowley, the *Chianghsing*'s British Commander, rammed her into the riverbank in an effort to allow the crew to escape. But in the process of getting his men onto land, Captain Crowley, his First Officer and his engineer were machine-gunned by the Japanese warplanes. All three were killed. Several of the crew were wounded, and the Japanese aircraft loitered in the skies seeking out survivors.

The *Gnat* was the nearest British warship that could go to their aid. She steamed out onto the Yangtze, needing only the thick black pall of oily smoke to guide her to the crippled vessel. With her men at action stations and her guns at the ready – plus one dog barking furious warnings about the danger in the skies – she sailed under the circling warplanes and lowered both her boats. The *Gnat*'s crewmen were able to reach the survivors and evacuate them, along with the bodies of the dead, and for whatever reason the Japanese aircraft failed to interfere.

Shortly afterwards, the *Gnat* received a gift of two footballs from the Hankow Customs House. With them was a hand-written letter of thanks from those of the staff most closely connected with the sinking of the *Chianghsing*. It summed up the wonderful *esprit de corps* exhibited by all aboard the *Gnat* – both man and dog.

You British Navy men, whatever your rank, are invariably and cheerfully ready to go to the help of anyone whoever they may be. Although you regarded this trip as just part of the day's work, your attempt to pass off a very gallant act as a mere bit of routine work does not diminish in the least the feelings of respect and gratitude with which we civilians regard you.

But no amount of such selfless gallantry could prevent the Japanese from overrunning the city of the gunboats.

With the coming of the winter monsoon fierce winds blew the Japanese invaders into Hankow. In the final moments the Chinese resistance had decided that it was better to melt into the bush, and to live to fight another day rather than launch a last-ditch defence of the city. As Japanese warplanes buzzed overhead, and Japanese warships steamed into dock at the Hankow Bund, heavily armed Japanese sentries were posted all across this, the newest Chinese city to fall under their dominion.

Aboard the *Gnat*, moored at her customary resting place beside the hulk, the chill wind of an approaching enmity blew across the decks and along the corridors. In her ammo-box-cum-bed on the ship's bridge, Judy lifted her fine head and sensed the changed atmosphere that had descended upon her surroundings. The homely clatter and chatter of Chinese port life had been replaced by the low murmur of a people under an occupation of unprecedented savagery.

Judy's first confrontation with the invaders was not long in coming. Just a few days after the fall of Hankow, Bonny – her erstwhile midwife – and Leading Seaman Law – her giant of a protector – took her for her customary early morning walk around the Bund. The trio had completed their usual circuit without incident and were returning to the *Gnat* when trouble stepped onto the riverfront before them, in the form of one of the dozens of Japanese sentries posted there.

Judy, in her customary fashion, trotted over and took a sniff of his knee-length boots. The sentry's reaction was as unexpected as it was inept, and bound to cause trouble. Within seconds his voice had risen to a screaming frenzy, as he berated the ship's dog and her two fellow crewmembers. With flecks of spittle at his thin lips, the enraged guard gestured for the dog – and her sailor companions – to get the hell out of there.

Judy stood her ground. She raised her head from his boots, and no doubt with early memories coursing through her head of Soo, her Shanghai protector, and the beating he had endured, she curled her lips into a silent snarl. The sentry took a step backwards, his face puce with rage. His hand went to his rifle, he unslung it, and the sharp *clatch-clatch* of steel on steel rang out across the largely deserted dock as he chambered a round.

The sentry went to level his gun, but this was no ordinary dog that he intended to shoot here: this was a dog of the Royal Navy, the mascot of the gunboat HMS *Gnat*, and a fully fledged veteran member of her crew. Leading Seaman Law didn't so much as hesitate. The massive form of the crewman barrelled forwards, shoved Judy aside, lifted the diminutive sentry into the air, and with him screaming unintelligible abuse Law turfed both man and rifle over the dockside.

There was a despairing scream truncated by a splash, and the sentry was no more. Bonny, Law and Judy made haste for their ship. Knowing how many of the Japanese soldiers were hopeless swimmers the trio paused only long enough to see the bedraggled sentry crawl ashore, before hurrying aboard to report the incident. The first reactions from the Japanese weren't long in coming.

Following an exchange of terse messages, a stiff-legged officer from the Imperial Japanese Army was piped aboard the *Gnat*, complete with a sword that threatened to trip him over. Of necessity, the British gunboat captains had learned to be consummate diplomats. During the past year of hostilities superhuman efforts at diplomacy had been required to navigate the Yangtze. Accordingly, Judy had been well hidden, and by the time the Japanese visitor had departed he'd been mollified via a combination of soothing verbal exchanges and lashings of ship's rum.

There were several further such visits, as the Japanese commanders tried to ascertain how and why one of the 'glorious liberators' had been treated with such disrespect, and who exactly was responsible for *the dog*. But the stocks of wardroom rum obviously held out, for nothing more was ever said to Bonny and Law about the incident. Yet one signal change was afoot: Judy of Sussex was henceforth confined to the ship.

Any further close encounters between Judy and the Japanese might well prove the death of her.

Chapter Seven

By the turn of the year the gunboats of the British fleet were becoming decidedly old ships. Launched in 1916, they'd first seen service during the First World War and were approaching a quarter of a century in age. For some time now the Admiralty had been intending to replace them with more capable, modern warships.

In the early months of 1939 the first of those new vessels, HMS *Scorpion, Grasshopper* and *Dragonfly*, sailed from Britain to take over duties from the veteran gunboats HMS *Bee, Ladybird* and *Gnat*. The first vessel, HMS *Scorpion*, the new flagship of the fleet, had been built at a cost of £168,000. She was the model design for her sister ships.

Slightly shorter and narrower in the beam than the *Bee*, HMS *Scorpion* nevertheless boasted greater speed, armaments and protection than her predecessor, plus more powerful communications and targeting facilities. Bulletproof plating was fixed around her pair of 4-inch guns, her eight .50-calibre machine guns, wheelhouse, wireless office and vulnerable machinery housings.

But ironically, these new and more potent warships would hit the waters of the Yangtze just as the rule of the gunboats was all but over.

*

In June 1939 the crew of the *Gnat* – ship's dog included – transferred to their gleaming new home, HMS *Grasshopper*. Much was different aboard the vessel. She came with a new captain, one Lieutenant-Commander Edward Neville, which meant that by now both of those who had purchased Judy from the Shanghai Kennels – Chief Petty Officer Jefferey and Commander Waldegrave – were no longer at her side.

HMS *Grasshopper* also had a crew of seventy-five, meaning that the atmosphere aboard ship was somewhat less tight-knit and convivial than it had been on the *Gnat*. Sadly, Judy would have to make do without even the companionship of Bonny and Law, for they were remaining with the *Gnat* as part of her skeleton crew. Yet it was now, just when all the certainties of the previous years were being taken from her, that Judy would face the greatest challenges of her life so far.

Hardly had the ship's crew got used to their new vessel when Britain declared war on a belligerent Germany. Japan had still to enter into the hostilities, yet few doubted upon whose side she would fight when this truly became the second conflict of the twentieth century to menace the entire world. The *Grasshopper* had barely had the chance to enjoy a few good turns of her screw up the Yangtze, when she was ordered by the Admiralty to set sail for open seas.

The *Grasshopper* would accompany the *Scorpion* and the *Dragonfly* steaming via Hong Kong and Macau to the British island stronghold of Singapore. The route would take her some 3,000 kilometres, arguably in the right direction – *away from Japan* – but for Judy this would be the very first time she'd left the Yangtze River valley and headed onto the wide ocean.

Forced to leave her offspring and most of her friends, Judy planted her brave paws on the shifting deck as the *Grasshopper* pulled away from Shanghai, setting a course for the waters of the South China Sea. Behind her, the *Gnat* and many of the other gunboats were preparing to sail to Singapore with skeleton crews. The Yangtze had been the *Gnat's* home for two and a half years, and Judy's for three, but neither ship nor ship's dog would ever grace her waters again.

Designed as a river gunboat, HMS *Grasshopper* only had a six-foot-six-inch draught. As a result, she rolled, slewed and heaved her away into the ocean swell, pushing ahead at close to her maximum speed of seventeen knots. At first Judy was violently seasick. In spite of all the cajoling of those who knew her, she refused to eat or to leave her ammunition-box bed. But finally the crew got her out on deck doing regular exercise, in an effort to aid her recovery. By the time the *Grasshopper* was approaching Hong Kong, Judy had found her sea legs and was eating like the proverbial horse. She would never suffer from seasickness again.

Sandwiched between modern-day Malaysia and Indonesia, Singapore was supposedly Britain's unassailable fortress in the Far East, one that would halt Japanese forces in their tracks should she declare war. Known as 'the Gibraltar of the East', this island citadel was protected by massive 15-inch guns dug into apparently impregnable coastal batteries.

Should Japan enter the war, everyone up to Winston Churchill himself expected Singapore to hold out for three months at least, buying time for reinforcements to reach the island fortress and drive back the attackers. Unfortunately, there were several flaws in this assumption. One, the Japanese had air superiority. The British warplanes based at Singapore were few and obsolete, and they were no match for a Japanese Air Force equipped with the Mitsubishi A6M2 – the dreaded 'Zero'.

Moreover, the defenders of Singapore possessed few if any tanks, and all of the coastal guns were set on the seaward side of the island. There were none positioned to defend Singapore if an invasion were to come from overland. As an added drawback, though Singapore was well garrisoned, practically none of the troops stationed there had any training in what they were about to face – jungle warfare, a discipline in which the Japanese military were to excel.

But with Japan yet to declare hostilities, the *Grasshopper* and her sister ships arrived in Singapore when it was still a place that lived up to its early wartime reputation of 'business – *and pleasure* – as usual'. As the conflict raged across Europe and British and Allied troops were driven out of France, Singapore remained seemingly remote and untouched by the entire conflict.

As for Judy, gradually she was settling into this strange new life aboard a warship that no longer cruised the waters of the mighty Yangtze River. Compared to the months she had spent aboard a gunboat on active duty patrolling China's waterways, Singapore proved remarkably uneventful – but it would only remain that way for so long.

Judy had made a new set of special friends aboard ship, most notably Petty Officer George White, whom she had first met in the strangest of ways. The morning Coxswain White joined the *Grasshopper* at Singapore's Keppel Harbour he strode up the gangway to report for duty, little expecting what was coming. He stepped aboard and threw up a smart salute, only to be half knocked over by something that cannoned into his shoulders, and seemed to cling there – before whipping off his sailor's cap!

Coxswain White's attacker was himself a relatively new arrival aboard the ship – Mickey the monkey. The crew of the *Grasshopper* had agreed to look after Mickey temporarily, while his ship and crew were away on duties in the Persian Gulf. Judy hated the monkey, but she watched with a peculiar fascination that morning as Coxswain White was assaulted. The man proved more than a match for the monkey. Quick as a flash he grabbed Mickey before he could escape, reclaimed his cap, and dumped the little animal unceremoniously on the deck.

Screeching with rage Mickey tried to reclaim his prize, but Coxswain White was having none of it. He replaced the cap firmly on his head, and it was then that he spied Judy. Head cocked to one side in amusement, she was sitting well out of range of Mickey, who was attached by a leash to a length of wire running the length of the ship. Coxswain White would have been struck by how beautiful she was, if it hadn't been for the fact that she was watching him almost as if she'd set him up.

'She's laughing her silly head off,' he muttered, suspecting that ship's dog and monkey had colluded in the attack.

Very quickly White would learn that there was no love lost between the two animals. The first time that Judy had run into

Mickey had been perhaps her most ignominious since her plunge into the Hankow cesspit. Unbeknown to her, Mickey had just been installed aboard the ship, the wire being strung up with a sliding metal ring so he could shimmy back and forth. Judy had stepped into range, unaware of the threat, and Mickey had proceeded to vault onto her back.

The entire crew appeared to be watching as Judy leapt, bucked, sprung and cavorted like a rodeo horse, but Mickey had clung on with both hands and would not be thrown. Eventually, confused and defeated, Judy did the same as she'd done when trapped in the Hankow cesspit – she cried out for help at the top of her lungs. Seemingly realizing the distress he was causing, Mickey had dismounted. He went to try to put a comforting arm around his steed's neck, but Judy was having none of it.

She backed away slowly, keeping her eyes on the little brute until she was able to dart down the mess steps – all to a loud round of applause from the ship's crew. From then on Judy tolerated Mickey, but that was about all. Whenever he succeeded in leaping onto her back she'd carry him to wherever she was going, suffering in dignified silence. But she was determined to get some enjoyment out of the little devil's presence, which she'd just had in watching him ambush Coxswain White.

A second new arrival joined the gunboat flotilla that day, and like Coxswain White he was fresh out of England. Upon reporting for duty, Leading Stoker Les Searle managed to dodge the cheeky monkey, but very quickly he would be drawn to Judy – a ship's dog who had started to gain legendary status as the staunchest of defenders of the gunboats, a reputation that was about to be tested to the limits and beyond.

Driven by a hunger for natural resources – Japan possessed few of her own – and with the war going badly for Britain and her allies in Europe, Imperial Japan decided now was the time to strike. The chief aim of her carefully coordinated series of surprise attacks was to seize the rich oil and coal reserves of modern-day Malaysia, Indonesia, Brunei and the Philippines. With Singapore lying right in the centre of the territory that she coveted, the island fortress would have to be pounded into oblivion for the Japanese plan to succeed.

Several thousand miles across the ocean in the mid-Pacific, the American base of Pearl Harbor would also have to be reduced to a burning ruin, if Imperial Japan was to prevent US forces coming to the aid of their allies. American bases on the Philippines – also within easy striking distance of Malaysia and Indonesia – would also have to be bombed into submission.

So it was that at 0400 hours on the morning of 8 December 1941 – although it was still 7 December across the international dateline in Hawaii – the first waves of Japanese bombers swept in to hit an unsuspecting Singapore. Simultaneously, flights of Japanese carrier-based warplanes launched a savage attack against Pearl Harbor. Striking with complete surprise, they caused considerable damage to the United States Pacific Fleet. Further Japanese air attacks struck bases in the Philippines, as ships landed troops in Malaysia for the overland push on Singapore.

With waves of Japanese warplanes bombing Britain's island fortress, the British warships HMS *Repulse* and *Prince of Wales* set sail from Jamaica to come to her aid. Part of the so-called 'Force Z', the battleship and battlecruiser had four destroyers as escorts, but no protecting shield of air cover. En route they had the misfortune of being spotted by a Japanese submarine, the I–56, which was able to vector the first of the warplanes onto them.

Successive waves of Japanese Mitsubishi G3M bombers – the same as had bombed the gunboats along the Yangtze – hit the warships with torpedoes and bombs. At 12.35 on 11 December the *Repulse* was the first to go down, with the *Prince of Wales* sinking less than an hour later. Just four enemy warplanes had been lost.

The news that both ships had been sunk was received with utter shock in Britain. Churchill's initial response was one of disbelief. 'Are you sure it's true?' he asked. It was a crushing blow for those forces tasked to defend Singapore and to halt the Japanese in their tracks.

Unbelievably, the three Yangtze River gunboats that had ended up in Singapore were now some of the largest warships available to the defenders. In the days that followed Japanese forces rolled onwards, pushing ever southwards through Malaya (now Malaysia) towards Singapore. The defenders fought valiantly, but they were outgunned, outmanoeuvred and menaced everywhere from the air.

The *Grasshopper* and *Dragonfly*, plus their sister ship, HMS *Scorpion*, were in action repeatedly, although they could move only at night due to the threat from the skies. They bombarded enemy forces, they lifted retreating troops out of the jungle in daring rescue operations, and everywhere they relied upon Judy's ferocious barking as an early warning system, enabling them to hide from any marauding Japanese warplanes.

In one daring operation the three gunboats evacuated 1,500 British troops from under the very noses of the Japanese, bringing them safely to Singapore. During another mission Leading Stoker Les Searle – who'd only just recently joined the gunboats in Singapore – was put ashore as one of a party of five, to try to locate and rescue Allied troops. Instead, his tiny force ran into the enemy in the darkness and Searle was shot in the leg.

The Leading Stoker and his fellows made it back to their ship, and he was taken to the Naval Hospital in Singapore. Since the opening of hostilities Judy had made a habit of accompanying the *Grasshopper*'s Sick Berth Attendant during his visits to sick and injured crewmen ashore. She seemed to sense that her presence among the wounded offered them great comfort.

Les Searle knew all about the *Grasshopper*'s miracle dog, but the time convalescing with his leg wound was his first real chance to get to know her. As he ran his fingers through her fine, glossy coat, his mind would drift to thoughts of home. That was the beauty of having a dog like Judy aboard ship – or visiting the sick, as she was now. It took minds away from the savagery of the war to thoughts of gentler times, ones that sadly seemed to be fading into a distant past.

There was a deep and instinctive connection between Les Searle the wounded seaman and Judy the ship's mascot. Theirs would prove to be a long-lived and life-affirming friendship in the bloody months and years that lay ahead.

It was 11 February 1942 when the fleet of little ships remaining in Singapore was finally given permission to evacuate. Over the preceding eight weeks the island fortress had been pounded into near-ruin from the air. The port's huge oil storage tanks were burning fiercely, casting a thick pall of choking, toxic smoke across the harbour, which mingled with that from the fires burning all across the city.

Hoping for another Miracle of Dunkirk, many believed the flotilla would somehow evacuate all to safety – disregarding the near-total Japanese superiority in the air and at sea. The gunboat HMS *Scorpion*, already badly damaged by Japanese bombing, was one of the first of the little ships to leave. Packed with civilians fleeing the besieged island, she reached as far as the Berhala Straits, some 300 kilometres south of Singapore, before running into the vanguard of the Japanese invasion fleet – the light cruiser *Yura*, and two destroyer escorts *Fubuki* and *Asagiri*.

Though her guns barked defiance the diminutive gunboat stood little chance. Blazing from stem to stern and out of control, there were only twenty survivors by the time the ship went down, all of whom were picked up by the Japanese. One of those who perished was Chief Petty Officer Charles Goodyear, whose marriage to the Russian barmaid had been so ominously received by the Chinese soothsayer back in Shanghai. Many more of Judy's treasured friends would lose their lives before the week was out.

On 13 February the final evacuation of Singapore got underway, with some fifty little ships preparing to evacuate the besieged island city. Priority was given to women and children. As the crew of the *Grasshopper* carried frightened infants aboard and comforted bewildered mothers, they were trying to work out how on earth they were going to accommodate the hordes of extra passengers.

Judy of Sussex didn't have to worry herself with such niceties: she was everywhere that day, dashing from one new arrival to the next, tail wagging ceaselessly and nose nuzzling into the hands of those who were the most tearful and distressed. She seemed to sense somehow the gravity of the situation, and to know how the presence of a dog, a symbol of normality and of home, would comfort the evacuees, many of whom had been forced to leave behind their own much-loved pets.

She was especially fantastic with the children. Judy led them around the ship, showed them the finest hiding places, and played her favourite games with those who still possessed the spirit to play. But there was precious little room for any fun, for the *Grasshopper* was becoming a very crowded ship indeed. Her normal complement of seventy-five had been swollen four-fold, as some 200 extra bodies crowded her decks.

Petty Officer White – recently the victim of Mickey the monkey's assault – was Coxswain of the ship, which meant it was his job to see to the chief needs of all evacuees. Somehow, in war-ravaged Singapore he had to find enough water and food for 200 extra souls, and satisfy all their special needs like baby milk, soap, toilet-paper, and the odd piece of chocolate for the children, if such could be found.

Since the previous September the *Grasshopper* had had a new Captain. Together with his senior officers Commander Jack Hoffman was busy on the bridge studying possible escape routes – though none seemed to offer them much of a chance of making a getaway. News had just reached him that three of the little ships crammed with escapees – local vessels the *Redang, Siang Wo* and *Giang Bee* – had been intercepted and sunk that very day.

At nine o'clock that night the *Grasshopper* threw off her moorings and headed for the open sea. She was in the company of her sister ship, the *Dragonfly*, plus a dockyard tugboat and two double-decker pleasure steamers. All five vessels were packed from stem to stern with evacuees. To the rear of the crowded *Grasshopper* Judy had found her special place. She was curled up with those who were most in need – the children who were being evacuated from the besieged island, which was being pounded into fiery oblivion even as they steamed out of Keppel Harbour.

As the *Grasshopper* headed for the comparative safety of the darkened seas, so the banshee howl of diving Japanese warplanes rent the air. The spine-chilling sound was punctuated by the scream of falling bombs, and the earth-shaking roar as they exploded among the port facilities. The occasional searchlight punched through the smoke-laden darkness, as the defenders sought to nail a Japanese bomber in its light, and put up some answering fire. But to those sailing away from Singapore the fate of the island fortress was plain to see.

Come sunrise the flotilla was heading for the Berhala Strait. *Dragonfly*, under the captaincy of Commander Alfred Sprott, was leading. The sea was flat calm and the sky a cloudless blue, offering zero cover to hide from Japanese warplanes. To the south and east lay a myriad of tropical islands, and the ships' commanders were hoping to find some respite from the Japanese naval forces by hiding among them.

But the first developments that day proved darkly ominous. At around 0900 hours the distinctive form of a Japanese four-engined flying boat – a Kawanishi H8K, Allied codename *Emily* – appeared seemingly from out of nowhere. Powering along at her top speed of 465 kph, the otherwise graceful warplane dived to attack the lead ship. Two bombs were dropped on *Dragonfly*, but both fell wide of the mark, after which the flying boat was driven off by machine-gun fire.

Chiefly a maritime patrol aircraft, the H8K could carry around 1,000 kilograms of bombs, so it was good to have got rid of it. But no one doubted what this signified.

They had to presume that their exact coordinates had been radioed through to the nearest Japanese forces, whether warships or warplanes.

Chapter Eight

Barely minutes after the flying boat had disappeared a series of deep explosions echoed across the seas, as the first vessels to be attacked that morning were hit. Three little ships – *Kuala, Kung Wo* and *Tien Kwang* – had come under attack.

A group of small islands lay between their location and that of the *Dragonfly* and *Grasshopper*, so no one aboard the British gunboats could see exactly what was happening. But they could hear that vessels were being set upon by Japanese warplanes, and that they were being bombed and strafed from the air.

Earlier that morning *Kuala, Kung Wo* and *Tien Kwang* had pulled into the cover of the nearby Pombong Island, so luckily some of the crew had gone ashore, searching for material with which to camouflage their vessels. They at least would survive the bombing and sinking of the three ships. One of those survivors was a young Royal Air Force technician called Frank Williams. Unbeknown to him his fate was tied up inextricably with a very special crewmember aboard the *Grasshopper* – a ship's dog that was even now comforting the children as the terrifying sound of explosions and gunfire echoed across the early morning seas.

The *Grasshopper* and her sister ships were following a 'safe channel' leading south, one that was supposed to have been swept clear of mines. That channel extended through the Berhala and Banka straits, leading into the more open waters of the Java Sea beyond. Unfortunately, it was exactly via this route that the Japanese invasion fleet had chosen to approach the doomed island of Singapore.

Ahead of the *Grasshopper* and *Dragonfly* the first vessel to encounter the oncoming armada was the tiny gunboat HMS *Li Wo*, commanded by Royal Navy Lieutenant Wilkinson. The *Li Wo* found herself sandwiched between a massive Japanese naval force – two rows of transport vessels, each led by a cruiser and tailed by a destroyer.

Undaunted, the Captain ordered his ship to close to within 2,000 yards of the nearest enemy transport ship and open fire. The third salvo from the *Li Wo*'s single 4-inch gun hit just below the bridge and set the enemy vessel on fire, but by now the Japanese had very much woken up to the attack.

With the damaged ship now very close at hand Lieutenant Wilkinson ordered his vessel to ram her. This she did, hitting at top speed amidships and the two craft became locked in their death throes. Battle commenced at close quarters. It was brutal and ferocious, as each crew raked the other's vessel with machine-gun fire. The British gunners finally silenced their rivals, forcing the Japanese to abandon their ship, which was burning fiercely.

The *Li Wo* backed out of the hole she'd torn in the side of the vessel, but by now she had a Japanese cruiser in hot pursuit. Facing a barrage of fire from her 6-inch guns, the *Li Wo* kept zigzagging to avoid being hit. But after the ninth salvo had raked her with shrapnel the order was given to abandon ship.

Shortly thereafter the aft magazine must have been hit, causing a cataclysmic explosion.

The *Li Wo* went down with the Captain, Lieutenant Wilkinson, still on the bridge, and there would be few if any survivors. For his heroic actions in command of his tiny vessel – outnumbered and outgunned, but defiant to the last – Lieutenant Wilkinson would be posthumously awarded the Victoria Cross.

Less than a mile away another of the little ships, the *Vyner Brooke*, commanded by Royal Navy Lieutenant Burton, was the next to be attacked. After two direct hits she too was sent beneath the waves. Scores of survivors, including several dozen Australian nurses, managed to reach the safety of nearby Banka Island, only to be captured by a Japanese shore patrol. The men were marched out of sight of the nurses and bayoneted to death in the jungle, or beheaded. The women were very likely raped, before being driven into the sea and machine-gunned in the water.

Several dozen miles to the north of Banka Island, the *Grasshopper* and the *Dragonfly* were heading towards this bloody, tortured patch of ocean, along with three little ships packed with civilian evacuees – the two pleasure steamers and the tugboat. And it would be Judy who would first realize that the enemy was all but upon them.

The first hint of the approaching danger came via the *Grasshopper*'s informal early warning system. All of a sudden Judy sat bolt-upright. One moment she had been larking around with the children, the next her ears were pricked forward and she was frozen as only a Pointer can be – limbs tense, her eyes glued to the distant horizon, mind totally focused on her sense of hearing.

Seconds later she had abandoned her position and was making a mad dash for the ship's bridge. She was barking out a warning even as she flew up the iron steps, arriving at the feet of the ship's Captain, Commander Hoffman, breathless and panting. The Captain was about to order her below again, but he and Petty Officer White – Mickey the monkey's erstwhile nemesis – watched with a growing sense of alarm as Judy's all-too-familiar actions began to unfold.

She set her sleek muzzle to skies to the north and let out a long series of fierce barks, and there was zero sign of her stopping. Knowing what this must signify the Captain ordered his men to battle stations. Sure enough, as Judy's barking rose to a frenzied and staccato *ruff-ruff-ruff-ruff-ruff*, so the first tiny speck appeared on the distant burning blue. Still inaudible to the human ear, it was only the sunlight glinting off distant wings that revealed it to be not a seabird, but a warplane.

This was no lone flying-boat reconnaissance aircraft. As the air armada bore down on them, those on the *Grasshopper*'s bridge counted well over 100 bombers flying in five separate formations. During the long weeks spent under bombardment first on the Yangtze, and more recently in Singapore, the ship's crew had grown used to the sight of mass waves of enemy aircraft roaring through the skies. But to encounter them here in the open ocean, and with hundreds of civilian passengers under their protection, was an entirely more daunting proposition.

The Japanese warplanes were sleek, twin-engined Mitsubishi Ki-21 heavy bombers, each carrying over 1,000 kilograms of bombs. It was approaching midday on 14 February 1942 when the first of those aircraft thundered in across the ocean to attack.

The lead bombers swooped onto the flotilla's flagship, HMS *Dragonfly*. As her machine guns and cannon sparked fiery defiance, the first of the bombs fell all around her like rain. The Captain had his vessel going at full speed and circling in avoiding action, as his guns unleashed hell, and for long moments the warplanes seemed unable to hit her. But while the *Grasshopper* likewise had all guns blazing, she wasn't to be so lucky.

The first direct hit on the *Grasshopper* sent shrapnel pinging off her thick armoured plating and ricocheting all around her superstructure, the explosion raking the bridge with burning hot shards of steel. Commander Hoffman was himself injured in the blast, suffering a deep gouge to his leg, while Petty Officer White's right arm and hand was peppered with flying splinters of blasted metal.

A fire had been sparked by the bomb, but the ship's crew soon managed to get it under control. Yet even as they were doing so more Ki-21s howled in, their bombs plummeting towards the ship with banshee wails that sent a shiver up the spine. Towering gouts of white were thrown up all around the *Grasshopper* as she ploughed onwards through the firestorm. At times the vessel was all but invisible due to the wall of water churned up by the explosions.

Grasshopper's guns continued to spit defiance, even though the gunners were half-blinded by the plumes of spray. The tugboat and the two double-decker pleasure steamers were entirely defenceless – apart from the fire put up by the gunboats. Within minutes both pleasure steamers had come to a stop and were burning fiercely. The tugboat, which had taken a direct hit, had disappeared completely.

For several minutes the *Dragonfly* seemed to lead a charmed life, as none of the bombers appeared able to score a direct hit. Then a bomb must have exploded in her aft magazine – the ammunition store, set just to the rear of the bridge – or on the depth charges stored on deck. Even from over a half a mile away, which was the distance now separating the *Dragonfly* and the *Grasshopper*, the explosion seemed devastating.

There was the blinding flash of the blast and a roar like thunder rolled across the sea towards the *Grasshopper*. A massive plume of smoke and debris punched above the *Dragonfly* aft of the bridge. When visibility finally cleared all that remained of the back half of the British warship was a mass of twisted and scorched metal. Any evacuees who'd been sheltering in the rear half of the vessel would have been killed instantly. The stern of the *Dragonfly* seemed to have been torn clean away, the engines had stopped, and the ship looked doomed.

As those in the *Grasshopper* watched aghast the *Dragonfly* began to sink, stern-first. Within a matter of minutes she was half-submerged. The survivors launched a whaler, plus some circular Carley survival rafts, and the injured who could be rescued were hauled aboard. It was then that Commander Sprott gave the final order to 'abandon ship', and all those who were able to dived overboard and swam away from the fast-sinking vessel.

Just as she was going under two tiny figures jumped from the bridge, ran along her side, slid down the ship's bottom and into the sea. Commander Sprott and his First Lieutenant had made it off the *Dragonfly* in the nick of time. Within seconds she was all but gone, just a few feet of her prow remaining prone above the waves. It was no more than five minutes since the cataclysmic explosion had torn her apart – and HMS *Dragonfly* was no more.

The few dozen survivors were clinging onto Carley floats, or were packed into the lone lifeboat. They were a dozen miles or more from the nearest land and crammed into hopelessly over-crowded vessels. On the bridge of the *Grasshopper*, Commander Hoffman made the only decision that he could. He turned his vessel towards the point where the *Dragonfly* had gone down and with the engines at full throttle he set a course for rescue. If he could also go to the aid of the survivors from the two pleasure steamers, so much the better.

But the circling warplanes were far from finished yet. As Judy pranced about barking maniacally at the thundering skies, some sixty-odd enemy aircraft turned in formation and began to bear down on the lone surviving gunboat. They separated into flights each of six aircraft and dropped down to 2,000 feet, wave after wave lining up for a low-level attack designed to finish the stubborn British gunboat once and for all.

For the umpteenth time that morning Commander Hoffman ordered his gunners to open fire, and *Grasshopper*'s six .303-inch machine guns spat defiance into the face of the attacking bombers. By now Judy had got used to the sound of the ship's guns. She clearly didn't like it, but as her hackles rose and she bared her fangs at the skies above the ship, it was clear that she knew from where the real danger emanated.

From the *Grasshopper*'s bridge the scene appeared almost unreal. Judy's barking mingled with the cries of the women and children crowded onto the decks, the distant jungle-clad 'paradise' islands adding a surreal edge to the scene. If anything, the first few minutes of the onslaught proved even more surreal: repeated waves of Ki-21s screamed overhead, as the *Grasshopper* charged onwards at 17 knots churning up the seas in a series of tight circles, yet each time their bombs somehow seemed to miss her.

With each revolution that his ship cut through the water, Commander Hoffman was bringing her ever closer to the nearest landfall. If she was hit, as he feared she was going to be, he wanted to be close to land, so as to have a chance of saving his crew and those civilians who were crouched in terror on his decks.

It was then that one of the Japanese warplanes must have got lucky. A sleek black object seemed to plummet in slow motion directly towards the bridge. At the last moment it overshot, and slammed into the rear mess-deck, just aft of the ship's superstructure. It exploded in the bowels of the vessel, wreaking havoc in the after mess-deck, the blast shaking the ship like a dog with a bone.

The *Grasshopper* shuddered from stem to stern, but so far the damage didn't appear terminal. It was only when angry gouts of flame burst forth from the ship's hold adjacent to the rear magazine – the ship's ammunition store – that Commander Hoffman knew they were in trouble. With the fire burning furiously, the crew struggled to flood the magazine with seawater to prevent it exploding, but it proved impossible. Word was sent to the bridge that nothing could be done to stop the flames from reaching the ammunition, which could blow at any time.

Commander Hoffman knew now that he had to get everyone off his ship and fast. If the fire reached the ammunition store they would suffer a similar fate to that of the *Dragonfly* – the rear of their vessel would be blasted asunder. Injured though he was, Captain Hoffman was still very much in charge of his ship. With her bows pointed directly at the pristine white sands of the nearby tropical island, he demanded one final burst of power from her twin engines.

Her bow cleaving the water like a knife, *Grasshopper* made her final, desperate run. There was little time for any finesse here: with further waves of Japanese warplanes thundering into attack, Commander Hoffman planned to ram his ship into the shallows and beach her. As the engine room began to flood, the stokers coaxed the last remaining power from her boilers. Turbines throbbed, the deck thrummed and *Grasshopper*'s twin propellers thrashed the seas, as a long plume of oily smoke streamed out into the skies behind her, acting like a marker signal to the approaching Ki-21 warplanes.

Twice more they dropped their bombs all around the stricken gunboat, as she steamed hell for leather for land. Miraculously, none of those munitions found their mark. Finally, there was a tearing, juddering impact from the bowels of the vessel, and the *Grasshopper* came to a halt, stuck fast on the bottom. The pristine white sands were barely a hundred yards distant, which should have made it easy enough to ferry the wounded and the survivors – both human and canine – to shore.

The Captain gave the order to abandon ship. As the *Grasshopper*'s crew dashed about manically, launching Carey floats and lifeboats, and hurrying the terrified women and children into them, the one consolation seemed to be that the skies above them had fallen mercifully silent. As quickly as it had materialized the Japanese air armada had disappeared: most likely they were all out of bombs. But even now a new and terrible drama was about to unfold around the wreckage of their sister ship, the *Dragonfly*.

The *Dragonfly*'s one lifeboat was hopelessly overcrowded – so much so that those aboard had had to refuse to take any more survivors. The Carey floats were likewise swamped, and those small groups still in the sea had no option but to start the long swim to land. But some thirty minutes after the last of the Japanese warplanes had disappeared, a new threat hove into view. Flying in from the east and at very low level was a second wave of warplanes.

There were fewer Ki-21s this time, but there was also less 'work' to be done. They broke into formations of three flying in line abreast, and thundered in at close to naught feet above the waves. The first trio bore down on the *Dragonfly*'s single lifeboat and opened fire. Machine-gun rounds tore into the little vessel. A second and third formation roared across the sea, likewise pounding the lifeboat mercilessly. With the tiny wooden craft having been riddled with gunfire, the Ki-21s turned their attentions to those clinging to the Carley floats, plus any they could find in the water.

Having shot up the survivors from the *Dragonfly*, the warplanes turned towards their one remaining target – the *Grasshopper*. By now the wounded and the women and children had been loaded aboard the ship's lifeboat. Most of the crew were gathered around the Carley floats, or had set off in groups swimming the short distance to shore. But Captain Hoffman and Petty Officer White remained on the bridge with vital work to do – directing the fire of the ship's guns.

Beached, broken and burning she might be, but the *Grasshopper* still had fight in her. And it was vital that her six .303-inch machine guns kept firing until those making for the island had got into the cover of the thick jungle. With a sickening sense of anger and disgust, the crew of the *Grasshopper*, who had seen what those Japanese bombers had done to the survivors of the *Dragonfly*, were poised to meet murderous fire with fire.

Though marooned and doomed, the *Grasshopper* still made an excellent and stable fire platform – or at least she would do until her aft magazine was caught by the flames, and blew. Sure enough, under the protective hail of bullets thrown up from the stricken ship, the lifeboat and the Carley floats made landfall pretty much unharmed.

When the signal was finally given that all had made shore safely, the *Grasshopper*'s guns fell silent. Those few remaining aboard ship – in the gun positions and on the bridge – made a dash for the sea and the short swim to the shallows. But as Petty Officer White cast a final look around the stricken ship he was unable to find one very special crewmember – Judy. Amid the hell of battle, the *Grasshopper's* dog and ever-faithful mascot seemed to have disappeared.

Presuming Judy must have made her own way to land, White launched himself into the sea and swam ashore.

Chapter Nine

Even as the last of the *Grasshopper*'s crew dived into the warm sea, the final moments of Britain's 'island fortress' were playing out. Within hours Singapore would fall, in the largest surrender of a British-led military force in history. Some 80,000 British, Australian, Indian and other Allied service personnel would be taken as Japanese prisoners of war, in what Churchill would describe as the 'worst disaster' in British military history.

Just as 15 February 1942 was one of Britain's darkest hours, so too the fate of the survivors of the *Grasshopper* was proving decidedly bleak. Five of the crew were reported dead, four were severely wounded, and there were several, both military and civilians, reported missing. Many of the survivors were in shock. Their situation on this unknown island appeared dire indeed. They had few possessions, no medical supplies, little food and no visible sign of fresh water.

At the same time it was obvious that Japanese forces were swarming all around these islands. The first priority was to get the wounded into proper cover, where they could be hidden from view and whatever treatment possible might be given them. Commander Hoffman might have lost his ship, but he was still in charge of his crew, and he did a rapid assessment of who and what he had available to him.

In addition to some fifty-odd ship's crew, he had a handful of Australian nurses: they should prove useful caring for the wounded. There were six Royal Marines in his company, themselves survivors of the recent sinking of the British warships *Repulse* and *Prince of Wales*. He set the Marines the task most suited to them – to scour the length and breadth of the island, searching for fresh water, any local inhabitants, or survivors from the other ships.

He also had any number of women and children somehow to comfort and care for. One of the women was blind, and she was constantly being tended to by her daughter. The welfare of the civilians had to be one of his first priorities, after the wounded. Commander Hoffman set the ship's crew the task of clearing a camp where the beach met the jungle. Rough stretchers were lashed together from tree branches, and the wounded were lain in the shade on those. Next, graves were dug in the sandy soil, and the dead, such as they'd been able to bring ashore, were buried.

Later that afternoon the Marines returned from their search with bleak news. As far as they could tell the island was uninhabited. They'd found little evidence of any other survivors, and worse still there was no sign of any drinking water. This was now Commander Hoffman's chief concern. On the open beach the sun was blistering, and even under the shade of the trees it was suffocating and humid. They desperately needed water, especially if the wounded were to rehydrate after losing so much blood.

Commander Hoffman turned his gaze towards the *Grasshopper*. The tide was further out now, leaving the beached ship lying high and at an odd angle to the sea. Smoke still roiled about her aft deck from the fire. The odd explosion echoed across the water, as the flames caught on something more inflammable. There was no knowing what risks anyone would be exposed to if they returned to the ship, but unless they did, many of those in his company would surely die.

Hoffman glanced at a figure beside him – Petty Officer White, the *Grasshopper*'s hardy Coxswain. He gave a nod towards the ship. 'Cox'n, when the lifeboat returns I want you to get back aboard the *Grasshopper*. Take some hands with you and see what if anything can be salvaged. Priority has to be water, medical supplies, food, clothes and some bedding.'

It was White's turn to eye the ship. The lifeboat had been sent off to circumnavigate the island, doing a more thorough search for any survivors. It could be any amount of time before it returned – time that the wounded could ill-afford.

'Permission to go now, sir,' White volunteered. 'It's only a short swim and I can knock up a raft once aboard.'

'Very well, Cox'n. As soon as you like.'

The Captain of the *Grasshopper* hadn't been the slightest bit surprised at Coxswain White's suggestion. He would have been more shocked if White hadn't volunteered to go. But at the same time he didn't doubt the man's bravery. In addition to the dangers of returning to the burning ship, sharks had been sighted circling the wreck, no doubt drawn to it by the bodies that had ended up in the water.

Undaunted, White strode purposefully into the sea and set out for the vessel. He was doing all he could to keep his mind focused on the task ahead of him, but his thoughts kept drifting to what might be lurking *under* the water. Did sharks always swim with their dorsal fin poking out when approaching their prey? Or might they sneak in unseen at depth, and strike from below, going for the legs?

By the time he'd reached the ship, he was sure that he'd broken the world record for the fifty yards dash! He hauled himself up one side of the vessel, which had heeled over considerably as the tide receded. His first task now was to construct a raft, so he could use it to ferry any salvage to shore. Both the bridge and the wheelhouse had a 'deck grating' – a tough wooden lattice-work that lay across the floor – and those should make the perfect platform for a raft.

He dragged them into the open air, lashed them together one on top of the other, then manhandled them over the ship's side. He now had a usable floating platform, which he lashed to the ship's rail with a length of rope. That done, White eased himself into what had once been the officers' quarters, set forward of the ship. This was still mostly above water and dry. He grabbed bedding, pots and pans and as much tinned food as he could lay his hands on. Each item was pushed up through the hatch and piled on the deck above. As an extra bonus he found an unbroken bottle of whisky.

'For medicinal purposes only,' he told himself, as he placed it with the growing pile of salvage.

He moved further towards the ship's main mess-deck. White was careful going down the steel rungs of the ladder, for the sea had flooded into this part of the vessel and the water was soon up to his waist. He inched into the gloom, nudging his way past tables and chairs that bobbed about in the oily darkness, searching with his hands for anything that might prove useful.

The further into the far corners he went, the darker it became, until he was finding his way about largely by feel alone. It was then that he froze. Faintly, he'd caught the most unexpected and worrying of sounds. At first White told himself that his ears had to be playing tricks on him, but as he strained to hear he caught the noise again. From ahead of him in the eerie murk came the distinct and uncanny suggestion of groaning.

It was such an unexpected noise to have detected down here, in the bowels of a ghost ship run aground at sea. There it was again – part groan and part whine. It sounded almost like a young child crying. It sent shivers up his spine. It was almost as if someone – some being – had been left behind here in the flooded mess-deck, somehow trapped and in great distress. Or was it maybe the spirits of those who had died down here, come to haunt the doomed ship already?

White turned around in the sloshing water, his ears straining to track the ghostly noise. As far as he could tell it seemed to be coming from beneath an overturned set of metal lockers. Using the bulkhead as his guide, he traced his way around with his hands held out before him, his heart beating like a machine gun inside his chest. He caught himself holding his breath: *Who – or what – could it be?*

White approached the chaos of the overturned lockers, water bumping against their hollow sides as he moved closer. *Thump, thump, thump* – the water beat against the steel drawers like a drum. The whining kept growing in intensity – almost as if someone was calling to him. There was no doubt in his mind now: behind those upturned lockers was a living presence, one that was somehow still alive amid the darkness and the flooded chaos.

White felt a rush of fear mixed with adrenalin, similar to that which he'd experienced as he'd made his mad dash through the shark-infested waters to get to the ship. He inched closer, his bone-white hand reaching ahead to feel behind the upturned lockers. He stretched further into the darkness. For an instant he could feel nothing – certainly no living being – and then his fingertips made contact with . . . a clump of wet and soggy hair.

But this wasn't like any human hair he'd ever felt before. An instant later a cold and damp nose had found his hand, and White knew in a flash who he had discovered here.

'Judy! Judy!' he exclaimed, joyously. 'You silly bitch! Why didn't you bark for me?'

Amid all the confusion and shock of the attack and the escape, the officers and crew of the *Grasshopper* had lost track of their dog. White had presumed she was off scouring the island with the search party, or maybe in the lifeboat looking further afield. It had never occurred to him that their beloved ship's dog might be still aboard the stricken vessel, and trapped. Had the Captain not ordered White to search for salvage, this would surely have proved to be her watery grave.

With murmured words of comfort he lifted the first of the heavy lockers off her, and shortly Judy was free. Fearing the worst, he gathered the sodden dog in his arms and waded towards the steps, all the while muttering words of remonstration – *why didn't you bark for us?* – plus words of reassurance, in her ear. Once on the deck he laid her down carefully, so he could go about assessing her injuries.

Holding her still with the one hand, he felt all along her legs and body for breakages. As he did so, Judy seemed to be giving him this look out of the corner of her eye – *thanks for the rescue, but what on earth are you up to now?* Finally, he allowed her to go free. He watched worriedly as she climbed to her feet. He was half-expecting her to stumble painfully, as a broken foot or leg gave way.

Instead, Judy proceeded to shake herself from head to tail, a dog-shower of seawater raining down across her rescuer. And then she took one stiff-legged leap to the left and one to the right, with her head down as if ready for play!

The next moment she had plonked herself down at White's feet and was licking his hand. He shook his head in amazement. Not knowing quite whether to laugh or to curse, he opted to do both, before yelling out the good news towards the shore.

'Judy! I've found Judy! She's here on the ship!'

With Judy's help he scoured the remainder of the vessel. By the end of their search they had a large pile of all types of swag heaped up on the deck. White took several minutes loading as much as he could aboard the floating platform, and last of all he lifted the ship's dog onto the rickety craft. It proved heavy and unwieldy, and unsurprisingly it took all of his seamanship to steer the overloaded raft away from the ship.

Judy meanwhile was up on four paws, peering over the edge. Something in the water had her transfixed. Moments later she began to bark wildly, as if she was warning of a new flight of Japanese warplanes in-bound – only now she had her eyes fixed on something deep below. Then, with an extra powerful yelp of warning, Judy launched herself off the raft and into the sea.

White didn't have much of a clue what she was up to, and in any case he needed all of his concentration to guide the low-lying craft towards the beach. Judy meanwhile was swimming strongly, doing laps of the raft as if she was circling it protectively. Only once strong hands had joined White in guiding the clumsy craft into the shallows, did Judy stop what she was doing and haul herself onto dry land.

Then she did her second shake of the morning – head to tail, and showering all her friends with seawater – before unleashing one last protective round of barks towards the sea. White hadn't liked to dwell on it too much as he'd made his way across the water, but he suspected very much that Judy's extraordinary sense for danger had detected a shark in the water. Just as she'd gone into action at Hankow to safeguard Chief Petty Officer Jefferey from a forest leopard, so she'd dived into the waters off this tropical island to distract a shark from its intended human prey.

Having recruited further hands to help pilot the raft and fend off any marauding sharks, White began to ferry the rest of the salvage from ship to shore. As the pile of stores grew, so the immediate issue of food had been resolved. The chief problem now remained water, for the little they'd managed to salvage off the *Grasshopper* wouldn't last long. The ship's crew had scoured the island from end to end, but not the smallest stream nor spring seemed to grace this otherwise picture-perfect tropical paradise setting.

As the ship's crew continued to poke around, digging shallow holes in the dankest parts of the forest and otherwise investigating anywhere that seemed to possess even the vaguest promise of water, Judy joined them. She had a general sniff about. She trotted from figure to figure, tail wagging busily, and tongue hanging out as she endeavoured to cool herself in the late afternoon swelter.

But much as everyone tried to explain to her what they were doing – *we're looking for water, see* – Judy didn't quite seem to get it. She kept lolloping her way back to the sea, where she'd have a good splash and a roll in the surf. Like her human companions, Judy was doubtless feeling hot and bothered, not to mention thirsty, and a good dip was as good a way as any to cool off. The ship's crew kept calling her back to help in the search for water, but she seemed fixated on this one stretch of shoreline.

The rough, makeshift camp that had been hewn out of the jungle was already starting to resemble some kind of front-line field hospital. Using the medical supplies salvaged from the *Grasshopper* the Australian nurses were tending to the wounded as best they could – bandaging up breaks, cleaning and disinfecting wounds, and doling out the precious pain-killers. But without water there was a limit to what they could achieve.

Where the camp met the beach the Marines were busy constructing a bush stove – one with which they would be able to cook, but without the telltale smoke that an open fire gives off. One of the Marines was struck by how Judy kept returning to the exact same patch of sand, right beside the water. She'd make her way there, whine and paw at the ground, then bark excitedly – as if trying to attract the attention of her human companions.

The Marine called over to a member of the *Grasshopper*'s crew. 'What's up with your dog, chief? Can she see something down there we can't?'

The sailor wandered over to join Judy. There was no doubt about it – her behaviour was curious. He knelt beside her, giving her a good scratch behind the ears where he knew she liked it best.

'What's up then, old girl?'

In answer, Judy gave an eager whine and then she began to dig. With her forepaws flying she scooped away at the wet sand, which went blasting out behind her. Caught up in the dog's apparent enthusiasm the mystified sailor joined her in her excavations. All of a sudden, there was a gurgling at the bottom of the hole and a stream of clear water bubbled up from below.

It looked for all the world like a spring.

The sailor couldn't believe it. He bent, scooped with an eager hand and drank. It was fresh and sweet. He turned and yelled up the beach.

'Water! Water! Judy's found water!'

What Judy had demonstrated here were two of the most unique and extraordinary aspects of canine behaviour. One is 'intelligent disobedience' – the ability to hear a human's command or request and to ignore it, because the dog knows better. Judy had heard the *Grasshopper*'s crew urging her to join the hunt for water in the forest, but she had other – and as it turned out better – ideas. The second is the dog's sixth sense.

So often – as Judy had just demonstrated – dogs appear able to read our minds. They seem to have the gift of anticipating our next move and guess how we are feeling. In the most extreme cases, they've been known to foresee earthquakes, the approach of a violent storm, or even the death of a human companion. The most sensitive canine noses – like a Pointer's – can detect human pheromones, and so they may well be able to 'smell' our moods.

Had Judy read the body language of the ship's crew – which to her meant digging for something of vital importance – combined that with smelling their thirsty urgency, and set off to find what they were so desperately seeking? It certainly looked that way. Most likely she had heard the spring running beneath the sand, or smelled the fresh water. Either way, her sixth sense had led her to understand what her human family needed and then to go and find it.

With the problem of food and now – thanks to their wonder dog – water being solved, the most pressing issue had become the wounded. The lifeboat from the *Dragonfly* had reached them, guided to the makeshift camp by the burning wreck of *Grasshopper*. It was riddled with bullet holes from where the Japanese warplanes had strafed it, and few of those aboard had escaped injury. Only those seated at the very front of the vessel – the opposite end from the direction in which the aircraft had attacked – had avoided being hit.

The dead had been put overboard, for the badly holed boat had been barely able to carry those still living. Leading Stoker Les Searle – wounded already in the battle for Singapore, and comforted by Judy in that island fortress's hospital – was one of the most senior surviving ranks aboard the *Dragonfly*'s lifeboat. He gave an account as best he could to Commander Hoffman of all that had happened, including that the Dragonfly's Captain,

Commander Sprott and his First Lieutenant were most likely dead.

'We were hit by two bombs, sir, and sank almost immediately,' Les Searle reported. 'Most of the wounded are still on the next island, with ERA Williams in charge. No officer survived, sir. The last, Lieutenant Shellard, died there on the island.'

As far as Les Searle was able to report, the highest surviving rank from the *Dragonfly* was an Engine Room Artificer (ERA), one Leonard Walter Williams, the senior operator of all the vessel's mechanical plant. All those above him in rank – from the Engineer Officer all the way up to the ship's Captain – had lost their lives in the sinking of the *Dragonfly*, and the strafing of the survivors in the water.

'Thank you, Searle,' Commander Hoffman replied. 'See my Cox'n and have your chaps all moved over here with us. We'll be better off together. We'll have another talk later on.'

Commander Hoffman received the dire news with barely a flicker of emotion passing across his granite features. To command in a situation such as this required nerves of steel, and a rock-solid demeanour to boot. The good spirits of all of those under him – servicemen, women and civilians alike – depended upon it. But just about their biggest ever morale booster right now would prove to be Judy, their irrepressible ship's dog.

Perhaps unsurprisingly, the 'paradise island' that they had landed upon was proving a little less than idyllic at close quarters. Defiant yelps from Judy signalled that she'd found yet another jungle creature with which to wage war. Clearing the makeshift camp had forced hordes of snakes out of hiding, not to mention gruesome spiders as big as your hand. Judy of Sussex was proving to be the critter-catcher extraordinaire.

She sprang stiff-legged around an unidentified serpent that she'd managed to corner. For its part, the snake had doubtless never set eyes before on such an adversary – a liver-and-white English Pointer. Judy feigned an attack, the snake darted its head forward to strike, and she sprang in the other direction, seeking the perfect time to strike. When it came she darted in lightning fast, attacking with paws and jaws until the battle was very much won.

Then she'd grab the limp form of the serpent in her mouth and carry it proudly to the feet of the chosen one – more often than not a very fortunate Petty Officer White. But with sundown on their first day on Shipwreck Island, Petty Officer White was to have other, more urgent matters to deal with. A new and pressing drama was about to unfold on the island sands.

It was the daughter of the blind evacuee who delivered the news. There were two Dutch ladies in their party and they were heavily pregnant. It seemed that both were about to give birth. White's first thoughts were that the Australian nurses should come to the women's aid, but they were busy tending to the *Dragonfly*'s wounded. He could expect no help from that quarter. And so it was that the Petty Officer of the *Grasshopper*, aided by a tireless ship's dog, prepared to deliver two babies on an unknown tropical island in the east Java Sea.

Fortunately, White had some prior experience as a makeshift midwife. It was during the 1936–9 Spanish Civil War that he'd first lent a hand in bringing new life into the world. His then vessel, the destroyer HMS *Grenville*, had been docked in

Barcelona harbour, and White had been press-ganged into acting as 'assistant midwife' during an unexpected birth aboard ship. How much more difficult could it be, he reasoned, with two births pending and his midwifery suite to be here on Shipwreck Island?

With the blind lady's daughter helping on one side, and Judy lending a sympathetic ear on the other, two baby boys were brought into the world. Around midnight White cut the umbilical cords using what he had to hand – his bowie knife. In due course the babies would be baptized in the sea, with Judy cavorting in the waters around them. And Petty Officer George Leonard White would glow with pride as the newborns were named George and Leonard after him.

But the hour was fast approaching when George Leonard White would leave this war-torn patch of territory, and not in the company of the dog that he had saved from the *Grasshopper*'s flooded hold – a dog that was growing to love him.

Just when Judy needed her nearest and dearest most, fate would conspire to tear them apart.

Chapter Ten

The five days the survivors spent on Shipwreck Island were ones of permanent battle. They waged war against the heat, mosquitoes, sand-lice, ravenous ants, plus the venomous scorpions and spiders that seemed to get everywhere they weren't wanted. With food supplies dwindling and medicines fast running out, the surprise appearance of a wooden sailing ship making directly for their position was greeted with real relief – as long as it would prove friendly.

It was clearly a local vessel. The island was part of what was then known as the Dutch East Indies (now Indonesia), at that time under the control of a Dutch colonial government – so the ship was very likely crewed by those friendly to the Dutch, which meant on the side of the Allies. The *tongkang* – a traditional trading boat, with twin masts, battered sails and a 'put-put' motor – steered part the wreckage of the *Grasshopper* and into the shallows. She dropped anchor and a party came ashore.

The local Dutch administrator – he would become known to the many Allied escapees that he helped simply as 'Dutchy' – had sent the ship from the nearby island of Singkep, to investigate if there were any survivors that needed rescuing. Via the tongkang the crew of the gunboats – plus the Royal Marines, the Australian nurses, the women and children, two newborn babies, the surviving wounded and one ship's dog – were ferried across to Dutchy's headquarters, in the small settlement of Dabo, on Singkep.

In spite of the obvious risks – if, or more likely *when*, the Japanese caught up with him, he knew full well what his likely reward would be – Dutchy had started an escape pipeline, providing food, water, boats and guidance to all who were passing through 'his' islands. The advice he offered to Commander Hoffman was this: his party should follow the route of those who had gone before, making for the nearby landmass of Sumatra and from there by ship either west to Ceylon (now Sri Lanka), off the coast of British-held India, or south to Australia.

Singkep Island lay a little more than 100 kilometres from Sumatra's east coast. Dutchy would be able to provide a large tongkang for the voyage. The beauty of the shallow-draught wooden craft was that they were equally suited to navigating the many rivers that crisscross the islands of this region – for their onward escape route would involve journeying up one such waterway.

The intended destination, Sumatra, is the sixth largest island in the world. A landmass of 473,481 square kilometres and some 1,790 kilometres in length, it consists of dense jungle and soaring mountain ranges cut through with turbulent rivers. Dutchy's tongkang would take them first to their east coast landfall on Sumatra, from where they would need to traverse the entire breadth of the island – some 350 kilometres of river, mountain and jungle – to reach the port city of Padang on the far side. From there Allied ships were reportedly taking off evacuees, for Sumatra had yet to fall to the Japanese.

The journey that lay before the escapees was a daunting one, to put it mildly. But the only alternative if they stayed put was to be taken prisoner by the enemy. After what the Yangtze River veterans had witnessed of Japanese atrocities in China, and what all had heard and seen since during the fall of Singapore, anything was preferable to being taken captive. Most took heed of Dutchy's advice and prepared for the long journey that lay ahead.

But Petty Officer White, along with two others of the *Grasshopper*'s crew – Engineer Thompson and Able Seaman Lee – decided otherwise. White figured that with the Japanese having taken Singapore they would turn their attentions to the next big prize in the region: Sumatra. The massive island had stupendous reserves of natural resources, most notably rich deposits of gold, coal and oil. In the time it would take the escapees to reach her west coast, White feared Sumatra would have been overrun by the enemy.

Though none of them could know it yet, White's suspicions were well founded. The day after the fall of Singapore the Japanese had dropped paratroopers on the strategically important city of Palembang, south Sumatra's capital. In seizing Palembang they had taken a key airport, to which the RAF had withdrawn many of its aircraft just prior to the fall of Singapore. Palembang offered the Japanese a staging post from which to occupy every major town and city across Sumatra. Already, Japanese troop transports had set sail for the island's coast, seeking to sweep westwards and overrun the entire territory.

A seaman through and through, White argued that the only possible route to safety lay by whatever boat they could get their hands on, sailing west towards India. It was a seemingly impossible sea journey of some 2,680 miles, but better that than get cut off by the advancing Japanese forces as they took Sumatra, with nowhere left to run or to hide. Few cared to join him, and so it was that White and his two fellows parted company with the main body of survivors – Judy included.

Much that it tortured him to leave Judy, it was inconceivable that White might take her with him. The *Dragonfly* and *Grasshopper* might have been sunk and shipwrecked, their sailors left bereft of any ship, but Judy remained very much a Royal Navy ship's dog. The ship's crew remained her family, and she their mascot and guide. Judy would be going with them overland to Sumatra's west coast, and hopefully a sea-going passage to safety.

When the moment of departure came – the Sumatra-bound party was the first to leave Singkep – White felt overwhelmed with sadness. But oddly, Judy appeared to understand all that was going on around her and she didn't seem particularly troubled. She sat before White, dark head held high, nose pointed very much at his, her calm eyes locked with his gaze. She had on her face a serene and untroubled look. It was as if she had always known when their hour of parting would be at hand, and why.

White had yet to find a boat with which he and his fellows might try to make good their escape. Dutchy had promised to secure one, but they were in acutely short supply. Everyone wanted an escape-boat right now. For a moment he wondered whether he wouldn't be better joining the main party, heading west to Sumatra. But he felt in his bones that journey would not go well. Somehow, he sensed that Judy knew that too, but that she would go to her fate with her family regardless, and loyal to the last.

With a final lick of White's hand – her signature gesture of love, and now of farewell – Judy turned away to board the waiting tongkang.

During the short and largely uneventful sea voyage to Sumatra, Judy settled into the company of an old friend, Les Searle. Searle had formed the nucleus of a tight-knit group that included Jock Devani, a typically tough Glaswegian seaman who seemed to fear nothing on this earth. Jock was a blagger and scrounger without rival, skills that would come to the fore in the bitter months ahead. As for Judy, she appeared like an aristocrat among their rough and ready company, but strangely she seemed to fit in well with this group of born survivors.

The tongkang on which they were embarked was under a Chinese Captain and crew, so those like Judy who were veterans of the Yangtze were back with the countrymen they knew so well. The interior of the ancient ship was lit by only one lantern, which swung gently to and fro. The hold was clearly designed for carrying cargo, as opposed to human – or canine – passengers. It consisted of an empty and echoing shell that ran the entire length of the ship, but at least there was room enough on the bare wooden boards for all to lie down.

It was dark, airless and evil-smelling, the odour of unwashed bodies and recent trauma mixing with the scent of tar and rotting timbers. Fear and shock have their own smells, ones that Judy was becoming ever more acquainted with, as her family's fortunes became ever more dire. Dogs rely chiefly on the emotional part of their brains. As a result they can read human emotions extraordinarily well and probably better than we read each other. From our body language and the smells we give off, they pick up on our emotional state very quickly.

The state of mind of those crammed aboard that tongkang below decks – defeated, shipwrecked, shocked and on the run – was very clear to Judy. But there was also a new scent on the dank air in that vessel's hold – one of a faint yet carefully nurtured hope. At least the escapees were on the move again, and even better they were hidden by the ship's main deck from any marauding Japanese warplanes.

Even the giant cockroaches that scuttled across the wooden boards were preferable to the ravenous ants of Shipwreck Island, or their night-time brothers-in-arms, the swarms of dive-bombing mosquitoes. Hope springs eternal in the human heart and in that of our canine soulmates, and with each puff of wind in the tongkang's sails those sheltering in her hold dared to indulge a dream of escape and of home.

The tongkang reached the gaping mouth of the Indragiri River without mishap. Unlike the Yangtze, which is a vital transport artery for much of the Chinese interior, Sumatra's Indragiri River is a waterway of far lesser size or importance. Its situation is also unlike that of the temperate climes of China's mighty waterway. Lying on the very equator, which cuts Sumatra in two, the Indragiri is baking hot, sluggish and torpid, especially on its lower reaches.

As the tongkang pushed inland, there was the flash of a white belly and a splash to left and right, as huge crocodiles slid off the mudflats that litter the river and into the muddy brown waters. It would be well-nigh impossible for an inexperienced crew to navigate the Indragiri, which is plagued by shallows and strong currents. Luckily, the Chinese Captain was a veteran trader, and he and his crew had sailed this way many times before.

Amid the stifling heat and the windless calm of the jungle that crowded in from either bank, the boatload of escapees chugged upriver, every turn of the ship's engine taking them closer to their end-destination – the port of Padang and the Allied ships waiting to carry them to safety. To either side lay dense forest inhabited by any number of exotic species – the Sumatran tiger, Sumatran orangutan, Sumatran rhinoceros, Sumatran elephant, the Malayan sun bear and more.

Clearly, any journey overland would present its own, daunting challenges to those aboard the tongkang. The Indragiri rises into a fast-flowing and angry torrent at its source in the towering Barisan Mountains, which form the backbone of the island of Sumatra. As the tongkang hit the lower reaches of this highland waterway, so navigation became ever more challenging. Eventually they reached the tiny settlement of Rengar, near where the Ombilin and Sinamar rivers converge to swell the Indragiri's waters, and from here no boat of any real size could go any further.

Judy, Les Searle and Jock Devani – plus other assorted gunboat-men, soldiers, civilians and the wounded that were able to travel – duly put ashore. The advice from the locals in Rengar was simple: from here on the journey west could only be continued by land. Sticking to the course of the river, the travellers should be able to make it through the mountains – which at their dizzying heights rose to 3,800-metre peaks – to a railhead that rose at Sawaluento, on the far side. From there it would be an easy, 80-kilometre train-ride into Padang, the port from where they hoped to sail to safety.

But the locals also had worrying news. Even as far inland as this isolated riverside settlement, one besieged by impenetrable jungle on all sides, reports of the war were filtering through. Japanese forces had landed in the south, and were already marching inexorably northwards. In effect, the escapees had a race on their hands to see who would be the first to reach their goal – themselves, or the forces of the Japanese Imperial Army.

There was clearly no time to waste. Fashioning makeshift stretchers from branches cut from the nearest trees, the party set off north along the river, with Judy of Sussex naturally taking up the lead. In their desperation to reach Padang ahead of the enemy, few preparations could be made for the journey. As they pushed deeper into the jungle that lined the beaten track, all signs of civilization were quickly lost behind them. The forest crowded around – thick, claustrophobic and brooding.

From the deck of the tongkang there had been something wholly exotic and noble about the dramatic, jungle-clad slopes. From within, and with some 200 kilometres of such terrain lying ahead of them, it was an entirely different story. Massive, wall-like roots of the tropical giants – so-called buttress-roots, which anchor the tree in the thin soil – blocked their path. Stumbling into one in heavy military boots sent an eerie noise like a hollow drumbeat echoing through the dark jungle.

At the head of the ragged column of humanity Les Searle felt as if the very trees had eyes and were watching. He was more than glad to have Judy in the vanguard, ears perked up and alert for any danger. Where she led, the rest followed, as she tried to pick a navigable path through the sodden terrain. The only clear route was the track running by the river, but much of the ground this close to the thundering waterway was boggy and waterlogged. Bright-green vegetation gave way unexpectedly, revealing the quagmire that lurked below.

Having four paws was a massive advantage right now. The soft pads on Judy's feet helped spread her weight, and having four points of hold on the ground lent her far greater agility than her two-footed companions. No doubt about it, in such terrain a dog made an invaluable pathfinder.

Blessed with speed, power and a fine sense of balance, Judy could shift her body weight about rapidly, to avoid being sucked under or trapped. Her powerful hindquarters, which in canines are equipped with large and long muscles, could deliver fast movement – forward jumps, springs to the side, even backward flips – almost instantly. Storing energy in muscles and tendons, and with the hind knees flexed most of the time, a dog can use its limbs like springs, so propelling it out of trouble.

As Judy forged a route ahead, quartering back and forth to check for any dangers, she appeared convinced that the entire party was in her care. She also seemed suffused with a sense of urgency. Every now and again she'd pause and glance back at Les Searle and Jock Devani, a look of laser-like intensity on her features, as she signalled them onwards. *Come on. Hurry. The route's clear. No time to waste.*

Back at their point of disembarkation on the river, Jock Devani had somehow managed to find and 'liberate' the distinctive, gold-braided cap of an officer of the Royal Navy. He had it perched at a jaunty angle on his head, which somewhat belied the desperate straits the party found themselves in. That distinctive golden cap acted like a visual marker for Judy whenever she got ahead of herself, and felt the need to check if her two-legged fellows were still following her.

Night fell almost instantly. The sun sank into the west – the direction of their travel – but the sunset went unseen by those struggling through the ranks of towering trees. With the sun gone, little if any starlight filtered through the jungle canopy. The moon remained a fleeting sliver of brightness, glimpsed only occasionally among the skein of branches stretched high overhead. What before had been shadowed now was invisible. A thick darkness black as ink blanketed all.

The party set camp. At times they'd found themselves trudging through thick and stinking riverside mud. It had proven home to a legion of leeches. The leeches latched on to passers-by, crawled up the legs and made for the groin area. It was damp, warm and moist in there, and replete with blood. After an hour's sucking a wriggly, black worm-like sack barely the width of a pencil would be swollen to more than an inch across.

The leeches weren't overly keen to abandon their human hosts. Pulling them off might leave the 'head' embedded in the flesh, which would result in infections and horrible tropical ulcers. The only way to be rid of them safely was to burn then off with a lighted cigarette. It was also a great excuse to smoke, not that many felt they needed an excuse after the trials and tribulations of the day. And watching the horrible black balloons of blood writhe in pain under the heat of a glowing butt-end proved peculiarly heartening.

The morning of the second day Judy came up against her first major obstacle on the march. It was large and obstinate and it came equipped with an armoured skin, scales and snapping jaws. But if anything Judy was even more stubborn and unwilling to back down than the beast she faced. They came head to head at the riverside – the massive Sumatran crocodile completely blocking the way. It lay in a narrow clearing and was most likely sunning itself. Had Judy allowed it time to back away gracefully, no doubt it might have done so.

Instead, she went for it as if it were a snake on Shipwreck Island. But this was no shy and retiring serpent. Barking furiously, Judy tried the same tactics as she'd used on those critters – darting from side to side, ducking low, then dancing ahead as if to strike. The croc sat there unmoving, seemingly asleep . . . but very much watching from behind slitted eyes. As Judy pranced ever closer, her confidence got the better of her and in an instant the reptile struck.

Moving with lightning speed for its size the croc's body jackknifed, propelling it forwards, jaws opening and slashing shut, rows of knife-like teeth slicing down across each other. At the last moment Judy had sprung backwards, whipping her head away. The flashing maw missed her by inches, but not the claw that the sly croc whipped around to slash her on the flank.

Judy let out a yelp of pain and staggered backwards in surprise. Snake, spider, leopard, *human* – never before had any adversary managed to get the better of her. But already, a row of deep slash marks were showing red and bloody, high on her shoulder where the croc had mauled her.

Still she wouldn't back off. But this was crocodile territory, and no way was Mr Smile about to run away from a fight that he'd already started to win. It was most probably the rush of human reinforcements that saved Judy. Hearing her yowl of agony, Jock Devani and Les Searle were on the scene in seconds, yelling abuse at the crocodile and with guns and bowie knives at the ready.

Sensing perhaps that discretion had become the better part of valour, the croc thrashed its tail a few times and wriggled back into the river. With a final angry and muddy plop it was gone. But the damage was done. Judy was hurt. Their pathfinder and guardian was able to put her weight on the injured shoulder only with some difficulty. More importantly, they'd have to properly clean and sterilize the wound, for in the intense, suffocating heat and humidity it would quickly fester.

A few miles further on they came across an abandoned rubber factory – natural rubber is made from the sap of trees that grow in the tropics – where they could rest up and clean the wound. Oddly enough, it was the rough and ready Jock Devani who took charge, demonstrating an uncharacteristically gentle touch when tending to Judy's injuries. As for Judy she seemed to have little idea how close she'd come to losing her head in the jaws of Mr Smile.

Once her injuries were patched up she had a good drink and a rest, after which she seemed full of energy and raring to go once more. Jock took her for a wander around the factory, just to check if she really was fit and able to continue. There was another reason for having a quick nose around. Jock hoped there might be something here that they could scavenge, to sustain them on their travels.

It was in a back room that he stumbled upon a most unexpected find. The first signs of the discovery were a wild Glaswegian whoop of joy, and a Naval Officer's cap being thrown high into the air. They say you either love it or hate it, and Jock was clearly of the former opinion. Bizarrely, what he'd found in the shadowy recesses of an abandoned Sumatran rubber factory was a large stock of the British nation's favourite spread – Marmite.

They were a little short of white sliced toast to spread it over, complete with lashings of butter. But while being careful not to rouse Mr Smile, water was fetched from the river and boiled over an open fire. Laced with the wondrous black stuff, it made for a nourishing and refreshing hot drink.

The rest of the unopened jars were packed away carefully, fuel for the epic journey ahead.

Chapter Eleven

It took five mud-, sweat- and blood-soaked weeks to reach their journey's end. On average, they made less than six kilometres a day. No doubt the able-bodied and their dog could have made it in a fraction of the time, but not the children and the wounded. They were everywhere hampered by the stretcher-cases, as they marched over streams, through bogs, via savage thorn thickets and across highlands swept by freezing tropical rainstorms seemingly without end.

Had the able-bodied forged ahead they might well have saved themselves much of the coming years of torment, but it wasn't in the nature of the ship's company – *the family* – to so much as entertain such a thought. And so they reached their final destination, the railhead at Sawaluento, with clothes in rags, faces heavily bearded, sweat-soaked and mud-stained from head to toe, but still very much two gunboats' ships' companies, plus some.

As for Judy, she seemed to have learned her lesson well from Mr Smile. Whenever she'd stumbled across any more of the all-powerful denizens of the jungle, she had afforded them due seniority. In the days since her close encounter, her shoulder wound had healed remarkably well. Only those who had seen her take on the croc would ever believe that at the start of their trek she had been so badly mauled.

The welcome from the Dutch running the Sawaluento railway station was heartfelt. A hot meal was served and space was made in the rail buildings so the party could bed down for the night. A train was scheduled to leave for Padang the following morning; all was looking well. That train would be packed with those fleeing the advance of the Japanese: in addition to Judy's party, there were soldiers, sailors and airmen hailing from across an Allied war machine then in desperate retreat, plus the civilians who accompanied them.

When that locomotive puffed into the port city of Padang the following morning, it should have felt like a triumphant entry, especially for those who had made such a seemingly impossible journey largely on foot. But oddly it did not. As this rag-tag army of the dispossessed tumbled off the train, one of the first things that the Dutch officials did was to order any remaining weapons to be handed over forthwith. It was a strange way to receive what were supposedly allies retreating before a common enemy.

Those in Judy's party who still had their rifles or pistols were likewise ordered to hand them in. Exhausted from their nerve-racking journey, weak from exertion and lack of proper food or shelter, but also elated at having made it – few saw any need to resist the order, or any sense in doing so. They would come to bitterly regret that decision.

Weapons handed in, the assembled party – human and animal – had to march through the city streets under the pounding heat of the midday sun. They were making for a deserted Dutch school, where they were to be billeted. It seemed odd to be making for a billet, when all they wanted was to head for the docks, board a ship and sail away to safety, but once again there seemed little sense in questioning things. After all, freedom was just one small step away.

What should have been a proud procession through the streets of Padang for those who had made it against all odds, became something very different. There was an odd, frenetic, almost angry and distrustful air about the city. The battered army soon fell silent as they made their ragged way. Gradually it became clear that many of the Dutch in Sumatra blamed them – for Singapore's downfall had opened the way for the Japanese to march into Sumatra and beyond. By the time the escapees had reached their schoolhouse billet many were feeling bitter and let down. Les Searle and Jock Devani, with Judy at their side, felt as if they'd just undergone some kind of degrading funeral procession or death march, their penance for ignoble defeat at Singapore.

But there was worse – *much worse* – to come.

It was only when they reached the schoolhouse – dispossessed of their arms as they were – that the Dutch officials revealed the bitter truth to those who had spent the best part of two months fighting, and then fleeing from the marauding Japanese.

They had reached Padang twenty-four hours too late.

The last ships taking escapees away from the city had sailed the day before. And while there was just the vaguest chance that another might dock at the city's port, no one really expected the British to risk sending in further vessels under the very noses of the Japanese. For that's how close the enemy were now. They were expected in Padang at any moment, at which point the Dutch administrators intended to hand the city over uncontested.

There was to be no attempt made to fight, or to defend Padang, the Dutch official explained. And while the 'escapees' weren't exactly prisoners as such, no one was allowed to leave their billet. But the very worst was this: anyone caught trying to get anywhere near the few remaining boats that were tied up at the city dock was to be shot on sight. The Dutch colonial administrators had made it forbidden on pain of death for anyone to make any further escape attempts.

After all that they had been through Les Searle and Jock Devani were in a murderous mood. They decided the Dutch Administrator with his 'pro-Jap' prescriptions could go to hell. *Bugger staying locked up in the schoolhouse, waiting for the enemy to ride into town.*

They made their way directly to the docks with Judy at their side, cursing with every footstep that they'd handed over their weapons so willingly. If the British seamen had still had their arms they could have taken a boat by force if needed, and to hell with the Dutch authorities. And sure enough, the Dutch had placed armed guards all around the port area to prevent any such attempt. The Brits felt as if they had been let down, deceived and betrayed.

In truth the Dutch alone were not to blame for the appalling state of affairs in Padang. The British authorities had to shoulder their share of responsibility. Earlier that day the British Consul in Padang had heard a radio broadcast announcing the surrender of Sumatra to the Japanese, and that the forces of occupation were already moving into the city. Believing it to be true, he had rushed to carry out his orders – burning all of his secret papers, including his radio codebooks.

The broadcast was in fact false. But by the time he had realized this, his precious codebooks had been reduced to a pile of ashes. Even if there were British or Allied warships steaming off the coast of Sumatra, he now had no way to make contact with them and let them know that the city was still unoccupied, and that there were many hundreds who were desperately awaiting evacuation.

The full extent of his blunder was brought home when a British Naval reconnaissance aircraft circled the city that afternoon. It hailed from a British warship steaming off the coast, but without the codebooks no communications could be made, or instructions received. If contact could have been made, a rendezvous with the vessel might have been possible north of the city, away from Dutch control and the advancing Japanese. As it was, that was rendered impossible.

That evening, the enemy reached Padang. It was Judy who first alerted her fellows to their arrival. She was lying in the centre of the small classroom where they were billeted. Her head was resting on her forepaws, her eyes fixed unerringly on the door. Les Searle had his gaze on Judy, but his mind was lost in angry, bitter thoughts of an escape that had been so needlessly and senselessly thwarted.

It was then that Judy rose to her feet. For a few seconds she stood there – tense, taut like a coiled spring, her senses totally focused on something outside. Just as the distant, throaty roar of a motorcycle became audible to the human ear, so her lips curled into a silent snarl. The tone of the engine noise changed as the rider slowed, and there was the noise of other vehicles following. They came to a halt outside the school-house building.

After Judy's warning, not a man doubted what had happened: the Japanese were here.

The schoolhouse was filled with the sounds of shouted commands. Harsh orders echoed along the corridors. They were given in a high-pitched, unintelligible tongue – one that had to be Japanese. It sent a shiver down the spines of all those waiting inside.

Les Searle reached for Judy. Rarely if ever was she put on a lead. She had had the freedom of the ship's company ever since she'd first set paw among them, some five years earlier. But now he reached for her and threaded a length of cloth through her collar. Keeping a firm grip on that he held her protectively by his side.

A figure strode in, closely followed by three of his acolytes. Had the situation not been so utterly dark it would have been a moment of great hilarity. The Japanese officer – a Colonel as it transpired – was short and squat, and he stared at the thwarted escapees through thick-rimmed glasses like jam-jars. Even more bizarrely, he carried an enormous sword at his side over polished jackboots, which seemed equally over-sized. The sword was so obviously too big for him that each time he took a step it half tripped him over.

Face to face at last. This, then, was the victorious enemy.

The Colonel ran his eyes along the line of ragged, defeated men. His pudgy face broke into a gleaming, gold-toothed smile.

He barked some orders at his fellows and they let out a chorus of brays. *Haw-haw-haw*. Dutiful laughter for their esteemed officer.

All of a sudden the Colonel's flashing smile evaporated. His arm shot out, finger stabbing toward the mascot of the late lamented HMS *Grasshopper* – at Judy. A series of short, sharp sentences erupted from his lips, each ending in a peculiarly squeaky high note. His number two stood stiffly to attention, head lowered in silence and shoulders beating time to his commanding officer's utterances. The Colonel's torrent rose in a final crescendo, before he turned on his over-large heel and stormed out of the room, sword clanking after him.

Judy, it seemed, had not been a hit with the Japanese Colonel. His deputies followed in his wake, but not before each had thrown a disparaging look at one very distrustful ship's dog. The Japanese were gone for now, or at least from the immediate environs, but no one missed the armed sentries posted at the school gates.

That night the subject of escape was on many a man's lips. It would be easy enough to scale the school wall and slip into the night, avoiding the sentries. But then what? Any escapee would be marooned on a jungle-clad island, with no way off but via a journey of a thousand leagues or more at sea. The Japanese would have secured the docks by now, and the chances of grabbing a boat to make a getaway were reduced to near zero.

Yet if escape was out of the question, then what was the alternative? All had heard the rumours. The Japanese raped and tortured the womenfolk of their vanquished enemies; and they couldn't be bothered much with keeping prisoners of war. Few slept that night. Les Searle and Jock Devani had added worries keeping them awake. Their ever-faithful dog – she who had saved the lives of the ship's crew so many times before – was clearly no favourite of the Japanese Colonel, the man whom they had to presume had the power of life or death over the lot of them now.

The following morning it became clear that they weren't about to be executed, or at least not immediately. Instead, the men were separated from the woman and children – which in itself was worry enough – and each party was sent to a different 'prisoner camp' in town. The crewmen of the vanquished *Dragonfly* and *Grasshopper* were being sent to a Dutch Army barracks, and Judy – despite her being of the fairer sex – was going with them.

This march across Padang from the Dutch school to the Dutch barracks would be etched for ever in the minds of those who survived the war years. It started ignominiously enough – a rag-tag hodgepodge of sailors, soldiers and airmen of various units and nationalities trudging through the early morning streets. The ground underfoot was dusty, and the locals seemed to have gathered to stare at their passing. Under escort from heavily armed Japanese soldiers, every man was aware of how dirty and unkempt he must look, beside their smart, disciplined, polished conquerors.

But gradually the spirit of that procession began to change. Allied servicemen marching on foot, they began to find a collective rhythm. Their defeat and humiliation goaded many – the gunboat crews first and foremost – to lift their heads, expand their chests and to carry themselves like fighting men. Arms swinging in time to their stomping feet, the march became an opportunity to show the enemy – and the goggle-eyed locals – that their spirit was far from broken. Struggling against their pain, even the walking wounded fought to maintain their poise and their place in the line of march.

Stepping out at their side, Judy sensed the change in mood – for emotions run up leash and down again, and Les Searle still had her fastened to her makeshift lead. The English Pointer – lithe, beautiful and in tip-top condition, despite her long sojourn in the jungle and her close encounter with Mr Smile – lifted her head and scented the air. The Japanese were everywhere in this town. Judy knew them to be the enemy not only of herself, but of her entire family. She could smell the aggression and enmity emanating from them, and she could read fear and defeat in the body language of her fellows.

But as the marchers swung in step through the streets of this defeated city, she also sensed something new. None of those with whom she had shared so many wild and bloody adventures had been cowed, bowed or beaten – not yet, anyway.

The Dutch Army barracks turned out to be a benign kind of a place of incarceration, at least compared to the hellish camps that were to come. It consisted of four large, one-storey blocks, forming a quadrangle, with a fair-sized football pitch in the centre. Upon arrival the men were broken down into four groups, each of which was assigned a barracks: British, Australian, Dutch and all officers (regardless of nationality). There were separate smaller buildings for the Japanese guards, plus a storeroom.

To the east of the camp lay a range of rugged mountains – the same that the escapees had slugged their way through for weeks on end, on the journey from the Indragiri River to Padang. It served as a stark and bitter reminder of all they had suffered in the name of escape, and for naught. Those thrown into this camp dreamed of an avenging army – most likely the Americans – storming across those peaks, or across the Indian Ocean, to liberate the many thousands taken captive.

Among the prisoners it was always 'the Americans' who were talked about as the liberators. In those first few days it was always the hope of the avenging Yanks that crossed people's lips. Subconsciously perhaps, the British in particular had lost faith in their own countrymen. Bruised by the shock of spectacular defeat – in particular, the mass capitulation of 80,000 troops at Singapore – it was the hope of another nation and its fighting men that buoyed their spirits.

There were many who really did believe that the Yanks were coming any day now, and that the ascendancy of the Japanese would be rapidly cut short. When one officer wisely suggested that they should ask the Japanese guards for vegetable seeds and start digging a garden, in order to supplement their meagre rations, he was laughed at. *What's the use of digging a garden?* many asked scornfully. *We'll be out of this place before the seedlings have time to break the surface. Why, the Yanks will be coming any day now.*

Such hopeful – but ultimately misguided – sentiments were soon overtaken by one overriding priority: the daily struggle to get enough nourishment to keep body and soul alive. Each prison block had its own 'honcho' – a leader appointed by the

Japanese to ensure their rules were adhered to. By far the greatest challenge for the honcho was to secure enough to eat for those in his domain. But for no prisoner was the food situation anything like as bad as it was for Judy.

Les Searle had done everything in his power to try to convince the Japanese Camp Commandant that the *Grasshopper*'s ship's dog was as much a member of the Royal Navy as any serving sailor. But his arguments had fallen upon deaf ears. Except for the odd savage kick from the guards – which Judy somehow always managed to evade at the last moment – for now at least she was largely being ignored.

But only an official prisoner with a POW number warranted a food ration, and Judy's state of non-existence meant she got nothing. Les Searle, Jock Devani and the others in her immediate circle did their best for her. They each set aside a few grains of boiled rice for their beloved dog. But it was now of necessity that Judy's survival instincts would come to the fore. She stalked and killed anything that moved and was even vaguely edible: lizards, rats, snakes and small birds; even flies caught on the wing were snapped down hungrily.

Following Jock Devani's lead, she also became a first-class scrounger from the more affluent prisoners: the Dutch, who tended to have far more material possessions than the others. Many of the Dutch hailed from Padang itself, and they had come to the camp complete with everything but the kitchen sink. Laden down with mattresses, blankets and suitcases full of possessions salvaged from their homes – including cash – they had much with which to barter or buy extra food from the locals.

But in spite of her endeavours, Judy began to experience for the first time in her life what all the Brits and Aussies were starting to feel – a dull ache in the pit of the stomach which comes from not having had enough to eat; the perpetual pang of hunger. It drove men to steal from the camp food store, such that the Japanese had to station a round-the-clock guard at the door. It was hunger that drove the British prisoners to scavenge in the rubbish bins that lay outside the Dutchmen's hut, seeking any edible scraps of discarded food.

It was hunger that led many to start to resent the Dutch prisoners – those who had resources and hence food for the simple reason that they had not lost everything in ship-wreck and struggle, or in bloody battle against the enemy. Many of the Brits and Aussies had only the clothes they stood up in. The Dutchmen were able sit on the veranda of their hut smoking cigars and supping coffee. By contrast, the British and Australian prisoners were forced to roll a smoke from the Dutchmen's butt-ends, in an effort to puff away the pangs of hunger.

Between supposed allies an enmity began to fester. It was born from the betrayal, as many saw it, of the would-be escapees upon their arrival in Padang, and it was nurtured by the gulf between their welfare and circumstances once they had been taken as prisoners of war. The daily ration consisted of nothing more substantial than two tiny bread buns, two bananas and one cup of steamed rice. It was far from enough for Englishman, Australian – or Dutchman, for that matter – to subsist on, and in the former's gradual starvation an enmity of the latter was nurtured.

Those with few material possessions or little money – among whom were the shipwrecked crew of the gunboats – were forced to fall back on their wits to survive. Along with one or two other co-conspirators, Les Searle, Jock Devani and Judy formed a group of the most desperate, yet resourceful. With nothing whatsoever to barter, they resorted to the time-honoured tradition of expropriating whatever they could from those who were able to spare it.

Operation Snatch was their chief brainchild. On one day each week the Japanese allowed local traders to set up stalls in the camp, selling the bare necessities: chiefly food, soap and a few scraps of bedding and clothing. Market day soon became *Operation Snatch* day for the team from the gunboats. Success meant relatively full bellies, but failure meant a savage beating or worse. Still, no one – Jock Devani first and foremost – baulked at the risks.

Op Snatch would commence with Les Searle acting as if he had something with which to barter. With the stallholder's attention distracted, Jock Devani would nudge a few things from the stall. In an instant Judy would be there, whipping them up in her jaws and making a mad dash for safety. A fourth conspirator would be waiting in the wings somewhere unobserved, so Judy could make her way to him and deliver whatever swag she had helped pilfer, at which moment it would be swiftly hidden away.

Few stallholders were able to follow the rat-runs that Judy used, or trace their wares, or catch the culprits. But by far the greatest *Operation Snatch* success was scored against the Japanese themselves. There were two goats kept on the camp, for the purpose of supplying milk to the Commandant. Using banana skins as bait, one of those goats was coaxed to the window of the British hut. As it nibbled at the fragrant skins, a noose fashioned from electrical wire was slipped around its neck, and with a savage tug the animal was hoisted off its feet and hauled through the window.

There was little sleep had in the British hut that night, either by the human prisoners or by one very contented dog. Come morning, worried Japanese guards searched high and low for any sign of the missing goat. It had disappeared off the face of the earth: not a scrap of skin or hoof or horn or bone could be found. And much that they might cast accusing glances at the bulging bellies of the British prisoners – and their accursed dog – there was zero evidence to prove what might have happened.

Of course, the forbidden fruits of the goat-feast only put the gnawing pangs of hunger at bay for a few days. It was hunger that first drove Judy to leave her family's side, and venture out alone in search of sustenance. During the long, dragging hours of daylight, Les Searle and the others kept her always by their side. They knew what the guards would do if they got so much as half a chance – they would shoot Judy and they would eat her. Any number had made that clear by the gestures they made whenever they laid eyes on the dog.

But at night when all were asleep Judy started to venture forth secretly in search of food. Her dark forays were only discovered when she jumped in through the half-open window of the hut and landed on the chest of a sleeping prisoner – one Petty Officer 'Punch' Puncheon. He jumped out of his skin, only to find a familiar figure before him – Judy, looking equally startled, and with a half-eaten chicken clamped in her jaws.

Unbeknown to all, she had been sneaking under the wire mesh fence of the camp – rather as she had done as a little puppy, in Shanghai – and heading out to scour the town for food. From then on Judy had to be tied up at night. She clearly didn't like it, but Punch Puncheon did his best to explain to her why it was so necessary.

'It's not as a punishment,' he told her. 'It's because we don't want *you* to get eaten!'

The days slipped by, each largely the same as the one that went before. There was little news of the outside world or of the fortunes of the wider war. It was almost as if they were in a world lost from time. Then rumour built upon rumour, and it became clear that the men were about to be moved from the camp. Spirits soared. Surely, anything had to be better than the perpetual, dull boredom of their existence, not to mention the hunger?

In fact, Padang was a virtual paradise compared to where they were heading. Men – and dog – were hungry, certainly, but none had started to die. Yet hope springs eternal in the heart of man: many of those who heard the news of their impending departure allowed themselves to dream of a better future.

In truth, these men – and their much-loved dog – had begun a journey into a place very close to hell.

Chapter Twelve

At long last the warning to move was given. 'By order of the Imperial Japanese Commander,' the head guard announced, speaking via an interpreter, 'five hundred men will leave tomorrow for Belawan, a port on the north-east Sumatran coast. From there they will embark for an unknown destination.'

Five hundred men constituted half the number presently in the camp. Les Searle, Jock Devani, Punch Puncheon and a score of other gunboat regulars were among those listed to leave. Of course, though her name wasn't on any roster, Judy of Sussex was going with them. The prisoners boarded a convoy of waiting transport trucks. When no one was looking, Punch Puncheon lifted Judy up to the group of waiting figures, and after a few reassuring pats she was hidden from view beneath some rice sacks.

This journey was to be the first of many where Judy's ability to understand absolutely what was required of her, and why, would serve to save her life. Somehow she knew that she had to lie quietly in the back of that truck for the long journey ahead, so that she could materialize at their new destination seemingly miraculously, and almost as if she had always been there.

As the long line of vehicles moved out of the Padang camp, there were cheerful shouts and waves from many aboard. The prisoners were ragged, somewhat emaciated and unshaven, but at least something was happening at last. Change was afoot, and with it hopes were raised.

'We'll see you in Blighty for Christmas!' some even shouted.

It was the autumn of 1942, and none of those aboard those trucks were destined to see a Christmas at home for another three terrible years.

After a crunching of gears the convoy of twenty-odd vehicles got up speed, and the streets of Padang were left behind in a cloud of dust. From the open rear of their truck Les Searle and his fellows could see just what kind of terrain lay to the north of the city. If anything it was even more remote and rugged than that which they had passed through on foot some six months earlier. The road to Belawan ran 500 kilometres or more northwards, threading its way along the spine of the dramatic Barisan mountain range.

The road had been carved out of dense jungle, plunging crevasses and towering rock faces, forming a series of crazy hairpin bends around which the convoy flew at speed. But despite the questionable driving skills of the Japanese soldiers at the wheel, the men's spirits rose. They had the wind in their faces, and they were speeding through breathtaking scenery. When you weren't tasked to march through them on foot, the Sumatran highlands were stunningly beautiful.

On the afternoon of the fourth day the convoy reached the high plateau around Lake Toba, a place of unique loveliness that had long been a hill station and a holiday destination for the Dutch residents of Sumatra. The Japanese guards decided this was a good place to stop the vehicles. An early lunch – the same scanty rice ration as always – was served by the roadside, from where all could admire the view over the shimmering expanse of water and into the majestic pine-clad hills beyond.

Lake Toba was magical and uplifting. No one could fail to be stirred. Even the Japanese guards seemed moved to soften their attitude. With apparently reassuring smiles and gestures they handed around bunches of bananas – but in retrospect, this would only serve to exaggerate the contrast between the beauty of this place and the darkness and drudgery that was to follow.

The final destination of the convoy was the village of Gloegoer, a clutch of native houses clustered around a street lined with Chinese shops. Along a side-road lay a former Dutch Army barracks, with beyond that a lunatic asylum. These were to become known as 'Gloegoer One' and 'Gloegoer Two' respectively, and they were to be forced-labour camps for Imperial Japan's prisoners of war.

The men were herded off the trucks and into Gloegoer One, the former barracks. Hopes that had been buoyed by the long and invigorating journey were ebbing fast. Gloegoer One was far smaller and more dismal than their former camp had been. One thousand men were herded together in an area not much larger than a football field. It consisted of a serried rank of long barrack blocks, separated by thin stretches of grass.

Once again the men were divided by nationality, with one hut reserved for the officers. Accommodation was basic. Wooden boards had been laid across steel girders to form shelves running along either wall of the huts – the prisoners' sleeping platforms. Between them ran a central gangway about eight feet wide – a bare concrete floor. Above, the tiled roof was infested with ferocious banana-eating rats.

There were unglazed windows lining the walls, complete with steel bars and wooden shutters. Each prisoner was allocated a slot on a sleeping platform around two-and-a-half feet wide and six long. This tiny space constituted his home. There he would eat, sleep, and pass the dragging hours, and it would be his sick bay when he fell ill with malaria, or the numerous other debilitating diseases that would plague Gloegoer One. Here, there was to be no privacy for any man but in his own thoughts.

That Gloegoer One would prove a sorry sequel to Padang was confirmed when the first food rations were handed out. The camp's central kitchen served two meals a day. It would rarely if ever vary: a cup of watery rice known as 'pap'; a thin, tasteless soup with a few leaves floating around in it; plus an unidentifiable gooey mess which was actually flour boiled into a stodgy porridge. If at Padang they had been on hunger rations, Gloegoer One's looked set to starve them.

At first the men were kept locked in the barracks all day long. There was no relief from the stultifying boredom and inactivity, not to mention the airless heat. Many wished they were back in the relative liberty and luxury of Padang. Some drifted into hopelessness and apathy. But after three weeks of enforced captivity, Colonel Banno, the Japanese Camp Commandant, announced that the prisoners had now completed their 'punishment for fighting the Imperial Japanese Forces', and from now on would be treated 'properly' as prisoners of war.

Colonel Banno was an enigmatic figure: a tall, somewhat distinguished-looking former farmer, on first impression he gave the appearance of being a relatively reasonable, fair-minded Japanese officer. But beneath his apparently benevolent air there lurked a darker heart – one that viewed enforced imprisonment for weeks on end as being perfectly reasonable retribution against those who had dared stand against Imperial Japan.

None of the prisoners had had the slightest idea that they were being 'punished' by being locked up, but just to be allowed out of the huts during daylight felt like blessed release. Further changes were afoot, Colonel Banno announced. Work parties were to be sent out of the camp, so the prisoners could labour on various projects that the Japanese had initiated in the area. Local traders were also going to be allowed to set up stalls twice weekly, selling such 'luxuries' as fruit, eggs, tobacco, soap and even pencils and paper.

With news of such 'improvements' morale lifted a little at Gloegoer, but only for so long. It was via the presence of the local traders around the camp that the prisoners were first to witness the unspeakable savagery that the Japanese were wont to unleash on anyone who dared cross them.

Gloegoer One was staffed both by Japanese guards and their Korean underlings. The Koreans wore Japanese Army uniforms but were seen as being inferior by the Japanese. There was a rigid pecking order. The Japanese officers looked down upon and regularly abused and beat their own troops. The regular soldiers looked down upon and abused and beat the Korean guards. The Korean guards in turn would take it out on anyone 'under' them – chiefly the locals, and in time, the POWs.

The first sign of the savagery this 'system' engendered came when a local trader was caught trying to smuggle some money into camp. One of the POWs must have offered something to sell – a watch maybe, or perhaps a precious gold ring. But such barter was forbidden under the camp rules – POWs could only exchange money for goods with the locals.

First, the POW was beaten unconscious by the Guard Commander himself, the most senior rank having the honour of delivering the first blows. After that, the entire guard force was free to set upon the unconscious figure. Each tried to outdo the other in the enthusiasm with which he rained down blows from rifle butt or boot upon the prostrate form. Finally the victim was revived by having a bucket of cold water thrown over him, after which he was lashed to the flagpole by his hands and left there to hang under a burning sun.

But if anything the punishment meted out to a Chinese trader – the Chinese being Imperial Japan's age-old enemy – was even worse. Accused of theft, he was strung up with a notice hung above his head, on which was written the one word: 'THIEF'. A noose was slung around his neck, attached to a large canvas bag. All passers-by – POWs included – were encouraged to place a stone in the bag, so that the noose would slowly tighten with the weight . . . and strangle him.

Those who witnessed these sadistic acts were sickened, but they also saw in these very public 'punishments' a warning as to what would befall any POWs who fell foul of the camp rules. And in Gloegoer, the rules were sacrosanct. First and foremost, all POWs had to bow whenever they were in the presence of a Japanese or Korean guard. They had to do so from the waist, leaning as far forward as possible, preferably to touch their toes. The lower the kowtow, the less likely it was to trigger a vicious beating for not showing 'proper respect' to the victors.

Learning when to kowtow wasn't easy, but most of necessity learned fast. Even if a Japanese or Korean guard was within sight they had to be bowed to. Failure to spot the guard was no excuse not to have bowed, and it was sure to unleash a paroxysm of verbal abuse and violence, whereupon the culprit had to stand to attention while the guard rained punches on his chin and kicked his shins. It was crucial to stand and take the 'punishment', and not to go down – for then the guard would put the boot in, and literally kick the victim's head in.

Les Searle, Jock Devani, Punch Puncheon and the others in 'Judy's gang' watched such acts of casual savagery with deep revulsion and concern – as much for their dog as for themselves. In her own way Judy seemed to have learned to kowtow. She lolloped around the Gloegoer camp with her eyes downcast, her head low and doing her utmost to avoid the guards. But she couldn't hide her hatred of them completely. Whenever one was nearby, her lips would curl into a silent snarl. More than once she went for one of the worst of the guards, and she seemed to be the only prisoner incapable of not speaking her mind.

Such obvious hostility from a 'lowly dog' put Judy's life in constant danger. This was especially so with the Korean guards who were very partial to eating dog, as were the locals. In this part of Sumatra any dogs that weren't strictly under someone's protection were hunted, shot and placed in the pot. And in

Korea dog meat was viewed as a particular delicacy. There were any number in and around Gloegoer who wanted to get their teeth into the Royal Navy's mascot.

With camp rations in Gloegoer being so meagre, and with Judy's protectors having little or nothing to trade with the locals, there just wasn't enough food to go around. Once again Judy started to sneak out of camp in search of food. She'd return with a snake or a chicken clutched in her jaws, darting past the angry gate-guards, and making a mad dash for the British hut and her 'family'.

Not once did she release her hold on her prize until she'd found them, and she was able to drop it triumphantly at their feet. In time Judy would return from one of her expeditions outside the wire having got much more than she had bargained for – but for now it was worry enough that she was running the gauntlet of getting seen, shot and eaten.

With the lock-down being over in the camp, the forced labour began. Groups of men were formed into 'work parties', and marched out daily to their allotted tasks. One of the earliest for Les Searle, Judy and their fellows was to fetch sand from the nearby river for construction work at the Medan aerodrome. The Japanese were intent on lengthening the runway, so it could host their heavy bomber squadrons. Digging out and carrying the sand in wicker baskets was hot and exhausting work, and it was only the opportunity to cool off in the river that made it half-bearable – for man and dog alike.

Knowing the capability of America's long-range Liberator bombers to strike even this far afield, the Japanese ordered tracks to be cleared into the jungle so concealed fuel and ammo dumps could be built. This was hard, intensely physical labour, but it offered its own compensations to those for whom hunger had become a constant companion.

Felling the massive tropical giants with hand axes took considerable skill – even more so to get one to crash down in the direction of the Japanese or Korean guards, so forcing them to flee in headlong panic. At the yell of 'Timber!' the tree – some over 100 feet in height – would fall, dragging other, smaller boughs and branches with it.

The second the tangle of vegetation hit the floor, scores of figures dressed in rags would swarm across it, searching for their quarry. The jungle was full of wildlife, and much of it – snakes, birds, lizards, small mammals – proved edible to those who were as desperate as the inmates of Gloegoer One. And there was never a prisoner that was quicker off the mark in seizing her prey than Judy of Sussex.

The forced-labour projects began to multiply, as the Japanese set about industrializing their rape of Sumatra's natural resources. Ships docked at the nearby port of Balawan carrying cement, barbed wire and ammunition, all of which needed unloading by the POWs. Among the supplies were drums of oil and petrol, which needed loading onto waiting railway trucks. With their will and their spirit of resistance far from broken, the human pack animals – Les Searle and Jock Devani among them – saw an opportunity here for a little sabotage.

They stacked the drums on the flatbed carriages with their bungs facing downwards. The bungs were loosened when the guard's back was turned. The hope was that the bumpy ride inland would shake the bungs free, so that the drums would empty themselves of their contents along the way. But more often than not the attempted sabotage was discovered, where-upon the guards would fly into a volcanic rage, seizing the first prisoner they could lay hands upon.

After the compulsory savage beating, a new and unspeakable punishment was instituted for any prisoner who had the temerity to try anything so audacious as sabotage. It was Colonel Banno, the Camp Commandant, who instigated the dreaded solitary confinement cell. At Gloegoer One there was a tiny dark hovel of a hut, one that had once been used to store animal manure. The place still reeked to high heaven.

The only light or air came via the one door, which had thick wooden bars. It had a movable section at the bottom, which could be slid aside to allow a prisoner to be shoved and kicked inside. On the Colonel's orders any would-be saboteur would be thrown inside the hovel for a period of 'punishment' lasting days, weeks or even months at a time.

But it wasn't the cell itself that betrayed the Colonel's full sadistic bent – it was the accompanying torture. For the long hours of daylight the prisoner wasn't allowed either to sit, or to lean against the cell walls. The agony of having to stand for twelve or thirteen hours without a rest was unbearable. But if the man broke and slumped against the walls, he'd get a savage beating from the watching guards. He was allowed nothing to sleep on but the hard stone of the floor – not even a blanket with which to try to fend off the swarms of mosquitoes. And in Gloegoer, the nights were thick with clouds of such blood-sucking, disease-ridden pests.

No sentence in the cell came without starvation – most usually one sparse meal every third day. The only relief from the gnawing hunger and the ache of limbs locked into one position in an effort to remain standing, was to gaze through the wooden bars. But even that brought its own kind of torture. The kitchen lay to one side of the cell, and at mealtimes the work parties would pass close by carrying the cauldrons of rice and soup en route to the barrack blocks.

The punishment cell reduced some to tears, others to sheer madness. Occasionally, it moved the Japanese sentry placed on guard to pity, and he'd slip a banana or a piece of Japanese chocolate through the bars. Those who did so revealed their human side. They weren't all monsters. They were also taking a massive risk, for if a superior saw one of his men showing pity to a prisoner – especially one singled out by Colonel Banno for punishment – he would be in real trouble.

But in spite of such horrors there were still moments of lightness in Gloegoer One, at least in the early months. That July a rumour circulated around the camp that the Solomon Islands had been retaken by the Allies. The Japanese had seized the Solomons – a chain of islands lying far to the east of Sumatra – during the first half of 1942, in an effort to cut supply lines between Australia and New Zealand and the USA. The Allies had counter-attacked, with the landings at Guadalcanal and neighbouring islands, initiating a series of savage battles fought by land, sea and in the air.

The news that Allied counter-offensives had begun proved a massive morale booster for the Gloegoer One prisoners. They celebrated as only they could – by holding a special race in the

British barrack block. The hut was around 100 yards long, and makeshift 'hurdles' had been put up using empty kerosene tins. Judy was tasked to race up and down the length of the block, leaping the hurdles at each end, ears flapping crazily and her tail streaming out behind her, as the prisoners roared and cheered. As everyone agreed, Judy of Sussex was quite the character at Gloegoer One, and an incredible boost to their collective morale.

They would defend her with their lives, as Judy would on pain of death theirs.

Chapter Thirteen

For Judy the main struggle was to keep out of the guard's clutches, while still getting her paws on enough food. In this she was to be aided by a fellow prisoner, one of the first brought into her family of friends from outside of the gunboat crews. Private Cousens, of the 18th Infantry Division, was one of the many British foot soldiers captured after the fall of Singapore. Cousens had fought alongside Indian and Australian forces in Malaya, in an effort to halt the advancing Japanese, most notably in the Battle of Muar.

But after the mass surrender at Singapore, Cousens had ended up as a Japanese POW. Even once he'd been sent to Gloegoer One, Cousens remained a happy-spirited young man, with a cheeky grin and a ready wisecrack for his fellow prisoners. Cousens had a special skill that proved both a blessing and a curse in the camp: he was an accomplished maker and repairer of shoes. On learning this Colonel Banno had set him up as the official Gloegoer One cobbler – but not for the prisoners, of course.

After months of fighting, fleeing, trekking the jungle and now labouring as POWs, few prisoners had any proper footwear. Instead, they'd fashioned crude wooden sandals, which were fastened to the foot by a length of rag or a scrap of wire flex, or whatever else could be found. Real leather boots were the luxury of the victors, which meant for now the Japanese. The upside for Cousens was that it got him out of the more strenuous work parties. The downside was that he was forced to have regular contact with the Japanese, which was always a hit and miss affair.

Cousens was forever having to visit the Japanese officers' quarters, to measure up one or another who fancied a new pair of knee-high jackboots. Cousens would take with him a large hessian sack stuffed with half-finished boots for 'try-ons', strips of leather, knives, hammers and nails, and all the rest of his shoe-making equipment. The visits were invariably fraught with danger. Close contact with the officers was best avoided, in particular Colonel Banno, but worse still his second-in-command, Lieutenant Matsuoka.

An exceptionally ugly man, Lieutenant Matsuoka was better known to all as 'Piggyeyes'. He was feared and hated by his own men, as well as the prisoners. The next senior in rank was the so-called camp 'doctor', a man whose giant, two-handled sword was so large it seemed almost taller than he was. The Japanese guards knew their doctor to be so incompetent and careless that they would quietly consult the British or Dutch medics if ever they were ill.

Below the doctor came the camp interpreter, who on the face of it appeared rather like Colonel Banno – a kindly, almost distinguished-looking old man. But looks can be deceptive. Many thought the interpreter to be just that – a harmless, friendly sort – until the day he was spotted smashing a Dutchman's head against a concrete block wall, and for no other reason than that the prisoner was tied up in the punishment block, and hence made an easy target.

The most junior officer was Takahashi, and he was the exception that proved the rule. Takahashi was either quietly pro-British, or he'd realized that Imperial Japan was unlikely to win this war and was cleverly hedging his bets. He was super-smart, an arch-disciplinarian, and one whom many Allied soldiers would have considered to be a good officer. He was scrupulously fair to all prisoners, regardless of rank or nationality.

On one occasion, Takahashi came to the British hut late one night and passed a brown paper bag to the hut honcho – its leader. 'Keep well hidden,' he had whispered, before leaving. The bag contained a photograph of Winston Churchill, beneath which was the caption 'The man of the hour.' At other times he'd notice a prisoner turn his face skywards as an aircraft flew overhead, scrutinizing it for Allied markings. When invariably it turned out to be Japanese, he'd shake his head, and remark, 'Never mind. Better luck next time.'

More was the pity when Takahashi was transferred to Changi, an infamous POW camp in Thailand. With Takahashi gone, Cousens was left having to deal with the old guard, who were unrelentingly unpredictable, and capable of fits of savage violence, seemingly without provocation. Yet Cousens proved himself willing to risk all in the cause of keeping Judy alive, and in doing so he exemplified a simple truth about her existence here in Gloegoer. In this awful place, Judy had gone from being a ship's mascot to being the mascot of an entire community of prisoners of war. She had become the talisman of the Gloegoer One camp.

In her dogged survival, and her unfailing humour and her sense of occasion, Judy embodied the spirit of the one thousand-odd prisoners who inhabited this place. They had come to see her as a symbol of their resistance, and her renown had spread far and wide. As she had become Gloegoer's mascot, so in a sense the thousand prisoners had become her wider family. But Cousens, through his cobbling and his brave generosity, would enter into the first tier of her companions.

Cousens had got into the habit of sitting in the shade of an overhanging roof, where he could work on his shoes and boots in the open air. The Japanese provided him with the leather to do so, and like everything that was in very short supply, its use was carefully monitored. But as he cut the leather to craft a new pair of boots, he would hack off a piece especially for Judy, who was very often to be found lying at his side. It was tough and only just bordering on the palatable, but it was after all animal skin, and it never proved too unpalatable for a half-starved dog.

Over the days and weeks Cousens the Cobbler grew to care about Judy deeply, and especially her welfare. He knew full well that she couldn't survive on the odd scrap of tough leather. As with the rest of the prisoners, the weight was slowly dropping off her. Her flanks showed sharp and bony through her coat, which was losing the last of its shine. What they all needed – man and dog alike – was food in bulk, and the only way to get that would be to steal it off those who had it – the Japanese.

Being a part of Judy's core of diehard companions, it was only natural that Cousens would recruit Les Searle to be his partner in crime in his harebrained yet audacious scheme. Cousens waited until he had a large and heavy sack of boots to deliver to the camp officers, whereupon he enlisted Les Searle as his fellow sack-carrier. When he explained his intentions, Les baulked at what Cousens was planning. The irrepressible cobbler intended to use the boot-delivery as an excuse to steal a bulk consignment of rice from right under the noses of the Japanese officers.

The two men crossed the camp compound, heavy sack held between them, with Les Searle feeling like a fly walking into a very hungry and venomous spider's web. Having delivered the boots to the officers' quarters, they now had an empty sack into which they managed to manhandle their intended loot – a sack stuffed full of rice, and set aside for the officers' consumption. With the booty hoisted between them, they hurried back to the British hut, fearing every moment to be discovered. As luck would have it the theft went without a hitch. It was the aftermath that neither man had anticipated, or prepared for.

The next day a pair of Japanese guards entered the British hut and announced a surprise inspection. No one doubted they were searching for a large sack of rice that had mysteriously gone missing. Les Searle and Cobbler Cousens had hidden the purloined rice rolled up in a blanket and stuffed beneath one of the sleeping platforms. But one thrust from a guard's bayonet would soon uncover the theft.

As the guards moved systematically down the length of the hut, both men felt the fear rising in their guts. You could cut the atmosphere with a knife as bit by bit the guards neared the hiding place.

Ever since meeting her, Les Searle reckoned that Judy could sense just about every human emotion there was. Fear, happiness, sorrow, loss, dread – somehow she was able to pick up on them all. Right then, she must have sensed the utter terror that seemed to have gripped the hut, or at least held two of her closest companions – the rice thieves – in its thrall. She could feel that the air was replete with mortal danger – for the guards would happily decapitate a prisoner with a savage swipe of a shovel, or bayonet them to death for a far lesser misdemeanour than this.

Just as the nearest guard seemed poised to reach beneath the sleeping platform and thrust his bayonet into the forbidden bundle, so Judy came tearing into the hut with something gripped between her jaws. Upon spying her, the guard closest to the hidden rice sack froze. An expression approaching fear spread across his features, as Judy charged down the length of the hut, her ears flying, her eyes glowing red and crazed, and her jaws wide with the macabre object that she had grasped between them.

In her mouth was a gleaming human skull.

She tore past the guards, leaping any obstacle in her path, reached the far end, and in a rerun of the recent hut hurdling races, she turned and started back on her second lightning-fast lap. The guards began to scream crazily at the dog and to yell at each other in alarm. As every prisoner knew, the Japanese guards coupled their predilection for savagery with a seemingly unreasoning fear of anything to do with death. Skeletons, bones, graves, skulls – all of it had them utterly spooked.

As Judy raced past them for a second time, skull gripped tightly in her mouth, their cries rose to ones of sheer panic. Cobbler Cousens and Les Searle were expecting at any moment to hear a shot, as one or another of the guards levelled their rifle and fired upon the camp's beloved mascot. Judy must have sensed it too. With a final mad dash between the two guards, she turned and sprinted from the hut, skull still grasped firmly in her yawning jaws.

No one had a clue where Judy had got the skull. Presumably, she must have dug it up from the camp graveyard. But of one thing Les Searle and Cobbler Cousens were certain: she'd done what she had in the full knowledge of the grave danger two of her closest family were in, and of the impact her actions would have upon their would-be aggressors.

Few in the hut who were aware of the rice theft doubted that Judy knew what she was up to. Hers had been a mission of trickery and deception. She'd sought to trick the guards into believing she was some kind of a hellhound – a devil dog possessed by the spirits of the dead. In that she had succeeded spectacularly.

The guards were utterly spooked. Ashen-faced and gabbling away to each other, their voices unusually high-pitched and squeaky with fright, they turned after Judy and hurried out of the hut. With that the impromptu inspection was over, the purloined sack of rice lying miraculously undiscovered.

As December 1942 approached and with it the dire prospect of their first Christmas as POWs, the men were to receive a morale boost as fantastic as it was unexpected. In the officers' hut they had managed to cobble together a clandestine radio. Its very existence was a closely guarded secret. Only a handful of officers were 'in' on it, and for very good reasons. Were the radio to be discovered, the men of Gloegoer One would lose a very fragile link with the outside world, quite apart from the terrible consequences facing those who had been operating it.

News was disseminated from the radio in dribs and drabs, and only as the operators saw fit, so as not to raise the suspicions of the camp guards. More often than not it was released long after the event had taken place, when the officers perceived a real need to boost camp morale. Perhaps that was why in the run-up to that first Christmas in captivity the news of the heroic raid on St Nazaire was made known.

Earlier that year British Commandos had launched one of the first – and among the most daring and successful – cross-Channel raids on occupied France. An ancient British destroyer, HMS *Campbeltown*, was packed full of explosives and rammed into the vitally important dry-dock at the French port of St Nazaire. The charge was hidden inside a sarcophagus of concrete and steel secreted in her bows, and it was fitted with delayed action fuses. By the time it exploded the dry-dock was destroyed, and the Commandos had got ashore to sabotage the dock machinery.

Five Victoria Crosses would be awarded for the raid, in which 169 were killed and 215 were captured, mostly Commandos who had fought until they were surrounded and all out of ammunition. When news of this stunning operation – which became known as *The Greatest Raid of All* – was circulated around Gloegoer, the men jumped to the conclusion that the long-awaited liberation of Europe had finally begun. Finally, the English lion had found her roar, and those who had for so long felt utterly defeated – including one doggedly defiant English Pointer – began to hope and to believe once more.

As they headed out of Gloegoer's gates on their work parties, Les Searle and others began to take up the words of a poem written in Judy's honour. It had become like a sacred chant, embodying the spirit of those who found hope, where there was precious little to find, embodied in the mascot of Gloegoer One. They would sing it as they marched, to bolster flagging spirits.

They would stagger to their work place
Though they really ought to die,
And would mutter in their beards,
If that bitch can, so can I . . .

In light of the St Nazaire raid, the POWs started to examine the possibility of escape with newfound vigour. It had been discussed endlessly during the long months of captivity, but it had always been viewed as nearly impossible. Getting out of camp would be easy enough, but then what? A white man couldn't exactly blend in with the local population. Plus it wasn't as if this was a German POW camp in Europe, where the escapee could head for the nearest border with a neutral or friendly country.

The only escape route lay hundreds of miles across the India Ocean. An escapee would need to lay his hands on an ocean-going vessel, and to get one he would need serious money, which few if any had any more. But most of all he'd need the help of the locals, and they were fully in the thrall of the Japanese. Moreover, Colonel Banno, the Camp Commandant had warned that anyone caught trying to escape would be tortured and then shot, as would all the men in his hut who had 'helped him' make his getaway.

In spite of this, every soldier knew that it was his duty as an Allied prisoner of war to try to make a bid for freedom – regardless of how impossible it might seem – and news of the St Nazaire raid had quickened that sense of duty. But it was now that the Japanese chose to strike a blow that would dash utterly their newfound spirit of resistance.

Only the Japanese could have dreamt up such an idea – a contract that every single Allied POW had to sign, binding him under 'law' never to try to escape. This was simply a case of the conquerors lording it over the vanquished, and it felt like it too. But to sign such an agreement ran against every tenet of international law, and all in the camp were agreed – they could not and would not sign.

It was late in 1942 when Colonel Banno had the prisoners stand parade, so he could storm about in front of them, raging and issuing dire threats. Not a man stepped forward to sign. Colonel Banno ordered that the guard numbers be doubled. A vicious-looking machine gun was set up, covering the entire parade ground – but still the prisoners stood firm in their decision not to sign away a precious liberty. Of course, with Judy not being on the official camp roster her paw print wasn't required, but she sure as hell wasn't volunteering it, either!

Finally, on Colonel Banno's orders the British prisoners were herded into the Dutch barracks, together with the Dutch POWs, whereupon the doors were locked on the overcrowded hut. Moments later the wooden shutters were slammed closed, after which the hammering began. The Japanese guards were nailing the shutters tight. To those inside it felt like being sealed inside a gigantic coffin.

The rest of that day and night was spent in increasing torment, as the air became fouler and the heat grew to intolerable levels. No food was provided, and there wasn't even enough space to lie down and sleep. The siege continued all through the burning heat of the following day. In the rancid, sauna-like conditions of the hut's interior men were going down with malaria and dysentery. Nothing could be done to help them. Some urged the hut leaders to give in. Others were equally determined to hold out.

A second day and night passed in such hellish conditions. It was clear that the Camp Commandant wasn't going to buckle, yet nor were the prisoners. But how far would the Japanese go?

Was Colonel Banno really prepared to let every prisoner – dog included – die?

Chapter Fourteen

Two things combined to break the impasse in that accursed hut. The first was an ultimatum given to Sergeant Major Dobson, the man in charge of the British contingent of non-officers: either he and his men would sign, or they would be starved to death and even denied water. The second was the advice of the British and Dutch doctors who urged that sense prevail. Much more of this and there would be an epidemic of dysentery and deadly typhoid, with horrific consequences.

It was late that afternoon when a message was finally sent to Colonel Banno, accepting capitulation. A small table was set up on the parade ground. One by one the prisoners stumbled out to sign. The officers held out for a while longer, before they too were forced to capitulate. But a signature obtained under threat of death had no standing in law, as all the prisoners were told. For those who had resisted for so long, a victory of sorts had been won.

As for Judy, she went delirious with delight when finally she was released from the barrack-prison, and could tear around the camp, relishing the taste of relative freedom once again. Spirits rose still further that late November, when some extraordinary news reached the camp: a vessel had docked in Balawan harbour carrying Red Cross parcels for the prisoners. Every man was dreaming about what impossible luxuries that mercy ship might hold.

The air was electric with anticipation as a work party was sent out to unload the unexpected bounty. The first trucks arrived around dusk, and it was as if Christmas had come early. There were tins of bully beef and condensed milk; cases of canned fruit; sacks of sugar, beans and cocoa; boxes of chocolate and cigarettes; plus there was the old faithful from the Indragiri River trek – *Marmite!*

For half-starved prisoners this was booty beyond their wildest dreams. The consignment had been put together by the British Red Cross and shipped out from East Africa, and was intended for British POWs only. Some who remembered how the Dutch had done so little to help their fellow prisoners back in Padang wanted nothing to go to the Dutch hut. But that wasn't the spirit that prevailed. Many of the Dutchmen had the added burden of knowing that their wives and children were incarcerated in the nearby 'family camp' in Medan, and most Gloegoer One inmates – regardless of their nationality – pitied them for it.

The food was distributed to all, with a good deal being set aside to send to the family camp. Each man at Gloegoer One got a dozen tins of bully beef, several tins of condensed milk, fruit and other delicacies. Soon, the interior of the huts looked more like your average corner shop than the prison cells they were. With Christmas just a few weeks away, men deliberated on what to do with such plenty. Some would be eaten in a celebratory feast right away. Some would be saved for Christmas festivities. And a proportion would be kept in reserve for emergencies and barter.

With the unexpected provisions now on hand Les Searle, Jock Devani, Punch Puncheon and Cobbler Cousens were able to prepare a feast fit for a queen – for Judy. But the unexpected bounty was also the cause of a rare spot of trouble between some of Judy's gang. Unsurprisingly for men who had suffered such interminable hunger, the hoarding of the food stocks became something of an obsession.

One evening the workers arrived back at camp after a long day's toil, only for Jock Devani to become convinced that someone had stolen one of his tins of bully beef. He eyed Les Searle's neat stack angrily. In an accusing tone he announced that he was going to count them all. He stretched out his hand to do so, but equally forcefully Les Searle pushed it away. In the struggle that followed Jock's false teeth were knocked to the ground, and Les accidentally trod on them. There was a sharp crack as the denture snapped in two.

The argument over food was instantly forgotten. Jock bent to retrieve his precious teeth, cursing Les for having trodden on them. He made a beeline for the Australian hut, where it was reckoned they could fix just about anything. Jock returned a while later, grinning broadly and with the denture back in place. It had been patched up using a length of sticky tape.

In the spirit of reconciliation Jock brewed up some coffee from his Red Cross supplies, and the two men drank to their mutual good health. Trouble was, for Jock the toast ended in a strangled gasp. He went puce in the face, grasped his throat and choked as if he was going to die. Under the influence of hot coffee the sticky tape had lost its stickiness and got stuck halfway down Jock's throat when he swallowed.

Once his throat was finally free of sticky tape, Jock's spirits were revived in part due to the wheeling and dealing he was able to embark upon, courtesy of the Red Cross. He now had goods with which to barter. In theory, bartering was punishable by a savage beating or even death – depending on the mood of the guards. But the British block had developed a covert means by which it might flourish in relative safety. The hut still had its shower room and toilets, which flushed via narrow chutes leading to the outside. It was through these that the barter-in-secret was effected.

The system required absolute trust between prisoner and local, for more often than not the two parties to a deal never got to set eyes on each other. But amazingly, promises were kept and deals completed without anyone ever cheating. The main danger in these transactions remained the guards, and so a strict watch had to be maintained. It was organized on two levels. The first set of eyes and ears were Judy's, for she could always be relied upon to issue a warning bark if ever a guard were in-bound towards the hut.

The second watcher was a human lookout. Whenever Judy yelped in alarm, the lookout would call out a coded warning – *red lamp*. With the Red Cross parcels having enabled a resurgence in barter, so the camp guards must have grown accustomed to their every arrival being greeted by a loud cry of 'Red lamp!' One of the friendlier among them even took to calling out proudly 'Red lamp' whenever he was approaching, so as to pre-announce his own arrival.

With 25 December 1942 all but upon them, the men of Gloegoer One were facing their first Christmas in captivity. Those who'd cried out 'See you in Blighty for Christmas' when leaving Padang had been sorely mistaken. Fevered preparations got underway for the festivities – and the feast, made possible largely thanks to the Red Cross. Grudgingly, Colonel Banno agreed to recognize such a 'heathen festival' by allowing a day off for the work parties, and from somewhere he even secured a barrel of captured port for the coming occasion.

Christmas morning was spent singing carols, the British, Dutch and Aussies joining one another in belting out each other's favourite hymns. Courtesy of the Red Cross, the cooks had managed to cobble together a fantastic feast, as opposed to the usual slop of rice. Steak, new potatoes, kidney beans and brown gravy were served to all. And in spite of her not being on the Gloegoer One official camp register, Judy of Sussex was invited to sit down with the rest and enjoy her plateful.

Following the feast came the pantomime, a take-off of Snow White and the Seven Dwarfs, which was a skit on prison life. The Japanese officers and guards formed part of the audience, and they joined in the uproarious laughter – though thankfully they didn't seem to understand that the joke was largely on them. During the raucous and bawdy panto songs, Judy was seen to lift her fine head and howl along an accompaniment, just as any camp mascot should do – and just as she had done in the Strong Toppers Club, back in the heady days of gunboat diplomacy on the Yangtze.

But when all was said and done, the Christmas merry-making at Gloegoer One was forced. Refusing to be cowed, the prisoners were making the best of a bad job. The sense of awfulness, the separation from family and loved ones, the homesickness – none of that could be banished by one good meal and a jolly sing-song. All in Gloegoer longed for 1942 to end – ushering in a New Year that they hoped would bring a turnaround in the fortunes of the war, and see the Allies victorious; a New Year that would see their dream of liberation from the prison camps become reality.

In truth, 1943 would be the year in which the chill wind of death would be felt, even among Judy's gang of fellows. The Japanese decided to launch the New Year with a massive new labour project, one that would become known as the White Man's Mountain. Little would better demonstrate Imperial Japan's bloated sense of destiny – her belief that this one small nation alone could conquer China, India, South-east Asia and the USA – than the temple mount that the Gloegoer prisoners were ordered to build.

The work began with the clearing of an overgrown tobacco plantation, after which the labourers were given the Herculean task of piling up a man-made mountain. It took fifty men weeks of sweat-soaked toil, using billhooks and parangs – locally made hoes and machetes – to hack away the vegetation. With the blistering sun beating down, dark swarms of mosquitoes, giant stinging ants and other savage insects took full advantage of bare, unprotected bodies to bite, sting and feast to their heart's content.

But among the dangers there were also opportunities abounding in the thick bush: notably, the sudden appearance of a Sumatran water monitor – a 'giant lizard'. As big as a croco-dile, they looked to those who had never laid eyes on one like a mythical Chinese dragon. And while Judy had never seen one either, it didn't stop her from barking furiously, spooking one that was in hiding, and sending it tearing across the cleared ground in search of safety.

For their size and ungainly appearance, these giant lizards can move incredibly swiftly – but not as fast as Gloegoer One's dog could. With Judy snapping at the tail of the spitting and hissing creature, a giant lizard hunt could be strung out for a good hour or more, in large part to avoid the grinding monotony of the work. In spite of their gnarly, prehistoric appearance, the monitor lizards made for fine eating, the flesh tasting like chicken, but with a faint hint of fish.

Once the vegetation had been scoured away it was burned, after which the soil had to be sifted by hand for any tiny scrap of root, seed or vegetation. The work went on relentlessly, the guards driving the prisoners like slaves, until the area resembled a badly ploughed field. Next came the gruelling job of levelling the earth, after which the only way was up. Building the temple mount proved the most exhausting task both physically and mentally that the prisoners had yet been given. Tons of earth had to be shifted onto the growing 'mountain', and the only way to move it was using a pair of wicker baskets slung on either end of a pole.

Staggering under the weight, the pole balanced across emaciated, bony shoulders, the work became an agony of endurance, as the guards aimed blows from rifle butt or boot at any who faltered. They insisted the baskets were always filled to the brim, disregarding the fact that the thin scarecrows before them could barely lift their load off the ground, let alone stagger to the far side to dump the contents on the cursed hill. The higher it rose the more the hillside became a slurry of mud, up which the prisoners had somehow to haul their burden.

By the time the White Man's Mountain was nearing completion, conditions in Gloegoer were worsening daily. Even as the wooden temple itself was erected atop the hill – ornately carved dragons writhing above the doors to a 'house' in which the souls of the ancestors could dwell – the brutal working conditions and the lack of sustenance were claiming their first victims.

As the temple mountain had risen from the earth, so the food ration at Gloegoer – chiefly the rice slop – had shrunk in size almost as if the two were inversely linked. And even that pathetic amount of sustenance wasn't guaranteed to all. Those who formed the work parties got their daily share. Those who were too weak and were confined to 'light duties' were placed on half-rations. And those too ill to work at all received practically nothing to eat – meaning that men already sick were further weakened by starvation.

It reached the stage where the daily slop of rice simply *had* to be supplemented by extra food, or the prisoners – especially those forced to labour so mercilessly on the White Man's Mountain – would die. But at the same time the Japanese currency – on seizing Sumatra the Japanese had replaced the Dutch-issued coinage with an occupation tender, the Sumatran or Nippon Dollar – had plummeted in value.

The prisoners were paid a few cents a day for their labour, a pittance that might buy them a few eggs or vegetables at best. But as Imperial Japan's fortunes in the war began gradually to worsen, her legal tender became increasingly worthless. By the time of the temple mount's near-completion, two weeks' wages were needed to purchase a single egg. It was the cruellest of blows, coming on top of a constellation of circumstances that seemed designed to sicken and to kill.

Weakened by hunger, Private Cousens was struck down by disease. The ever-cheerful cobbler – he who had fed Judy surreptitiously from the scraps of leather reserved for the Japanese officers' boots – was carted off to the 'hospital hut'. There, with an ever-faithful four-legged companion more often than not at his side, Cousens sickened further and died.

On more than one occasion the soldier-cobbler had risked his life for the Glocgoer One mascot, and they had grown close. After his shock disappearance, Judy would be found lying under the overhanging roof where he used to work, still and silent and with her head resting on her outstretched paws. There was a deep sadness in her eyes, as yet another of her special protectors had been taken from her at just the time when she was most in need.

Perhaps it was this resounding sense of loss that would send Judy in search of a new companion, or perhaps it was the cumulative effect of being repeatedly parted from so many of those who had grown to love her. For whatever reason, it was now that Judy opted to seek out and choose her 'master'.

Shipwrecked in the Berhala Straits just hours prior to the *Dragonfly* and the *Grasshopper*'s sinking, Leading Aircraftman Frank George Williams had found his way to Gloegoer One via a similar route to that of Judy and her fellows. From the tropical island where he'd found himself marooned, Williams had travelled by tongkang, launch, truck, RAF warplane and other means in an effort to escape the encircling Japanese, but had nonetheless ended up in Gloegoer, via a short stay in Padang.

Williams was a tall, softly spoken individual blessed with a ready wit and a boyish appearance that belied his apparent wisdom and maturity. One of six siblings, he'd lost his father when he was nine years of age and life after that had been hard. He'd had to save up for two years to buy his first bicycle, perseverance becoming something of a Williams family trait. Aged sixteen, he'd joined the merchant navy, which was a tough and challenging career, but one that offered the considerable benefit of travel to the four corners of the world.

Hailing from Portsmouth, in Hampshire, he'd only just turned twenty when war broke out. He had enlisted in the Royal Air Force, service number 751930, joining the RIMU – the RAF's Radio Installation Maintenance Unit. He was duly posted to Singapore, joining the ground crew that supported those gallant RAF airmen flying sorties against the Japanese. Outnumbered and outgunned by the far superior Japanese warplanes, the RAF crews had battled to the very last, but with the fall of Singapore many had been taken captive, Frank Williams among them.

With his kindly face beneath dark, wavy hair, Frank Williams wasn't the toughest or roughest of the POWs in Gloegoer One, and he certainly wasn't the most outspoken. But he was a lover of animals almost without equal, with a correspondingly big-hearted loyalty to boot. Perhaps it was for this reason that Judy was to discover her 'master' in Frank Williams – although 'life-companion' would be a far better description for the extraordinary relationship that they would forge.

Frank was squatting in his hut, gazing into the tin containing his meagre rice ration, when he felt a pair of eyes upon him. He glanced up to find that a striking-looking dog was staring at him intently. The two eyed each other for a long moment before Judy began to advance. She seemed slow and uncertain in her movements, as if unsure of the reaction she might receive from a stranger – especially at 'feeding time'. But still there was the faintest suggestion of a wag in her slender tail, and just the hint of the love that was to be forged between them in her intelligent, sombre eyes.

Frank could see how thin she was and how hungry she had to be, but even so she remained a strikingly beautiful English Pointer. He eyed the gooey mess in his tin once more. It looked and smelled as revolting as ever, but every prisoner faced the same unpalatable choice at mealtimes: eat, or die; eat, or die. Everyone received the same ration, so it was his alone to consume – and most felt they had only themselves to look out for whenever the slop was doled out.

He hesitated for just a moment, before tipping a dollop into the palm of his hand. He held it out to Judy. Her eyes flicked to the proffered food, but still she wouldn't move. She let out a low, plaintive whine, but stayed where she was, eyes flicking from rice-slop to Frank and back again. It was obvious she needed some sort of reassurance, some sign from Frank that his was an entirely friendly, selfless gesture, and that he was not trying to trick her somehow.

Over the year or more that she'd spent in the camps, Judy had learned to be suspicious and guarded until someone proved themselves worthy. Frank understood. Placing the tin of precious food on the ground he reached forward and fondled her behind the ears.

'It's okay. It's okay,' he murmured, softly. 'Make yourself at home.'

Only then did Judy seem to relax. She took the food that he'd offered, lapped it up, then settled contentedly at his feet. Frank was by no means the first to share his ration with her, but he was one of the first 'strangers' to do so – someone who lay well outside of Judy's normal fellowship. Neither quite knew it yet, but each had found in the other a companion for life.

From the very first Frank Williams seemed to have a near-magical way with Judy. In short order she appeared to learn many a whispered instruction from the young RAF man, almost as if she understood his every word. He even had a command that he'd give when he wanted her to go and lift some of the fresh fruit that the Japanese guards would lay on the graves of their dead, their cemetery lying just outside the camp boundary.

The Japanese practise two forms of religion, which run side by side: one is Shinto, an ancient animistic or nature-based worship; the other the more modern form of faith, Buddhism. The wooden spirit house built on the newly completed White Man's Mountain would be a Shinto or Buddhist shrine – they would often be placed side by side. But for prisoners dying of starvation, fresh fruit was far better in their bellies than being left to rot above the bodies of the dead, or so Frank and his fellows reasoned.

As the food situation worsened, such risky forays by Judy became ever more vital to keeping both man and dog alive. But each time she ventured forth she risked being nabbed by the camp guards, whose own rations were often not a great deal better than those given to the prisoners. Very soon now, Judy would find that one of her daring expeditions outside the wire would put her life in mortal danger.

But it would do so in the most unexpected of ways.

Chapter Fifteen

For those of Judy's companions who had always believed that sex was the prime human motivator, Gloegoer One had soon taught them otherwise. Les Searle, Jock Devani, Punch Puncheon – and now Frank Williams – had found that food had long become the foremost inspiration for both waking dreams and sleeping nightmares.

Not for months had any of the prisoners talked about women or told the usual soldiers' smutty stories. Talk about the fairer sex had given way to endless discussion about food. Sometimes it was the wonderful meals they used to eat at home. At other times, it was the wonderful meals they would eat when they got home. Even the scant news cobbled together from the secret radio eventually got boiled down to food: when might they get out of there and get to a place where they might enjoy all the wonderful meals they had planned.

Judy's fellows had presumed that sex was very much off her menu as well. How wrong they were. Not long after finding Frank Williams, Judy returned from one of her nightly forays with more than a little extra food: *she was pregnant*. At first no one could quite believe it. How could it have happened? Every dog in the area seemed to have been shot and eaten long ago.

The men joked among themselves that maybe she would give birth to a litter of tiger cubs or maybe even goats!

But beneath the humour there was real jeopardy. The larger Judy became, the more sustenance she needed – for she had a hungry litter of young ones now growing inside her. For Frank and his fellow Judy-protectors, the daily struggle to find enough to eat for themselves was challenge enough: now they had Judy and her unborn offspring to fend for as well. Their greatest worry was this: the fatter the expectant mother became, the more she appeared like a feast fit for a Japanese or a Korean guard, not to mention a local Sumatran family.

Judy's protectors banned her from leaving the camp, unless she was in the company of a work party so she could be better protected. Every now and again a precious tin of food from a dwindling Red Cross hoard was volunteered for her. Daily she grew plumper, until the puppies were about due. And perversely, it was in their impending birth that Frank Williams saw an opportunity finally to secure for the Gloegoer One mascot the protection that she was due.

Under the care of Dr Kirkwood, Gloegoer One's British Medical Officer and himself a POW, plus a team of Dutch POW medical staff, Judy gave birth to nine puppies. It was four fewer than she'd managed aboard the *Gnat*, and these certainly weren't pedigree English Pointers. But under the circumstances, she had done incredibly well. As she licked them clean and nuzzled them onto her teats, four were clearly too weak to suckle and survive. They were passed to one of the men for proper disposal, leaving her with five healthy pups.

So, amid the misery of Gloegoer One Judy became the proud mother of those five mischievous balls of blind fluff and hunger. Even if it was half the number of pups she had managed aboard the *Gnat*, in its own way it was even more of a miracle. On a diet of bully beef and condensed milk – courtesy of the Red Cross food parcels – Judy's puppies grew fat, healthy and strong. Five balls of boundless energy started to totter around the British hut, causing amusement, havoc and chaos in equal measure wherever they ventured.

Once they were as chubby and irresistible as ever they were going to be, Frank put his plan into action. Judy never had been able to hide the loathing she felt for the Korean and Japanese camp guards. Indeed, only recently she'd gone for one of them whom she'd sensed was threatening one of her pups. But for some unknown reason she just about tolerated Colonel Banno. In fact, over time the Gloegoer One mascot and the Gloegoer One Camp Commandant had developed a kind of playful antagonism, which Frank hoped betrayed an unexpected softness on the Colonel's part – that he was secretly a dog-lover.

The Colonel loved nothing more than to draw his sword and pretend to threaten Judy with it, seemingly with the aim of making her growl and snarl, at which he'd burst into laughter. He seemed to find it great 'sport'. Frank also knew that the Colonel had a special friend in Gloegoer – a young and beautiful local lady. He'd also noticed how Colonel Banno's ladyfriend always made a real fuss over Judy. Whenever she was about she'd sing out 'Judy – come!' – which were about the only words that she knew in English.

One evening when he was sure that Colonel Banno was drinking alone, Frank took 'Kish', one of the most irresistible of the pups, and made his way to the Colonel's quarters. Any prisoner approaching the Japanese officers' part of camp did so with utter trepidation. A story had done the rounds recently of how sickeningly and inhumanely Colonel Banno and his fellow officers had treated one of their own soldiers.

A while back the Colonel had ordered tea for himself and his officers. A soft-footed orderly had entered, tea tray perched in one hand, and he had succeeded in bowing so low that his head almost touched the carpet, all without spilling the tea. Unbelievably, the man had a white lint mask over his nose and mouth to prevent him breathing any of his lowly germs over his superiors. The orderly had finished serving tea when he turned to leave and happened to stumble over a polished boot of one of the officers.

Before he even had the chance to utter an apology, the boot had slammed into his groin area. The orderly collapsed in silent, writhing agony. The rest of the officers grinned and nodded their satisfaction, as the assaulting officer got to his feet and proceeded to kick the orderly unconscious. Colonel Banno smiled his approval once the job was done, and promptly rang for another orderly, whose job it was to drag the bloodied and unconscious figure away from their esteemed presence.

That was that kind of environment that Frank Williams, a mere prisoner, was voluntarily heading into now. He didn't underestimate the dangers. More often than not, a prisoner who had the effrontery to approach the Camp Commandant's quarters without being summoned faced a long stretch in the solitary cell, or even summary execution.

Fortunately for Frank, Kish proved to be an instant success with the quick-tempered, irascible Colonel. Frank placed the tiny puppy on the desk before him, and the Colonel seemed to find the scene of her wandering her wobbly way towards him almost as funny as he did her mother snarling at his swordplay. But what really seemed to do it for him was when Kish stopped, flicked out a tiny pink tongue and had a few licks of the Colonel's sword-hand.

Trying to keep the tremor out of his voice – he knew just how much he was walking on eggshells here – Frank explained to the Colonel that Kish was a gift for his esteemed lady-friend. The Colonel nodded and chortled his enthusiasm. This was a very fine idea indeed; very fine. Seizing his chance, Frank asked whether perhaps the pup's mother might be rewarded by being made an official Japanese prisoner of war? She was after all a Royal Navy mascot and a serving member of His Majesty's Armed Forces, so it was perhaps the least she deserved.

The Colonel appeared to weigh the suggestion for a long moment. His face darkened. Much that he regretted having to refuse, he could see no way in which he could explain a sudden new addition to the camp roster to his superiors. It was then that Frank truly risked all. He had a suggestion to make, he ventured. If the suffix 'A' were added to his own prisoner number – Hachi-ju-ichi; Eight-one – then Judy could become 'Prisoner 81A'. That way, everyone would be happy. Kish's mother would be happy; the Colonel would be happy; and most importantly, his lady-friend, Kish's new owner, would be happy.

Left: Judy on duty. On the deck of HMS *Grasshopper*, one of the British gunboats that cruised the mighty Yangtze River in the pre-War years. Judy's in suitably attentive pose as she listens to a sailor's instructions. *Imperial War Museum*

Below: The Insect Class gunboat HMS *Gnat* on patrol on the Yangtze – Judy's first home afloat. When she was acquired from the Shanghai Kennels and adopted by the ship's crew as their official mascot, little did they realize how often this truly remarkable dog would save their lives. *Imperial War Museum*

A remarkably lifelike wooden figurehead of 'Judy of Sussex', as the ship's crew named her, carved by one of her extended family – Petty Officer Clark of the Yangtze Gunboats Association. *Imperial War Museum*

One of the 'large China gunboats', HMS *Grasshopper* was Judy's home for many a month, hunting for river pirates and dodging increasingly aggressive air attacks, as the Japanese military invaded China in a prelude to World War Two. *Imperial War Museum*

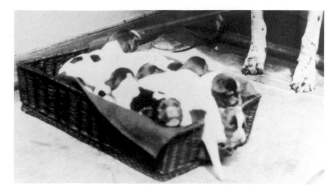

Above: Judy had her first litter of puppies aboard HMS *Grasshopper*, courtesy of Paul, the mascot of the French gunboat *The Francis Garnier*. *Below:* a sailor takes four of them for a stroll on deck. *Imperial War Museum*

Below: British and Allied forces surrender to the Japanese in the fall of Britain's 'island fortress', Singapore. 80,000 troops were taken prisoner. Packed with civilian refugees, the Yangtze gunboats tried to escape Singapore with all hands, Judy included, but they set sail into the teeth of the mighty Japanese invasion fleet. *Popperfoto/ Getty Image*

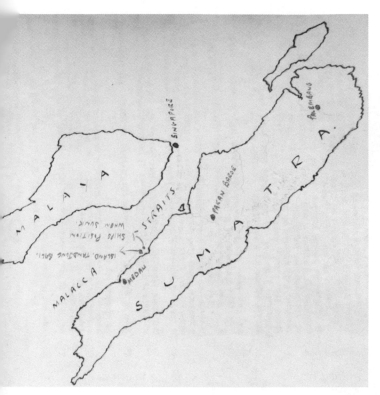

A sketch map drawn by an escapee showing where the fleet of little ships fleeing Singapore ran into the Japanese destroyers and battleships, plus her squadrons of warplanes. Judy and many of the *Grasshopper's* crew were washed up on a deserted island, from where the long flight to captivity began. *Photo courtesy S. Fowler*

MY HEALTH IS EXCELLENT.
I AM CONSTANTLY THINKING OF YOU. IT WILL
BE WONDERFUL WHEN WE MEET AGAIN.
THE JAPANESE TREAT US VERY WELL, SO DONT
WORRY ABOUT ME, AND NEVER FEEL UNEASY.
RECEIVED YOUR SIXTH LETTER RECENTLY, ALSO
LETTERGRAM. HOPE YOU HAVE PLEASANT
CHRISTMAS AND HAPPY NEW YEAR.
            LOVE TO ALL
                LES.

Postcard from hell. Les Parsons was an Australian prisoner of war held by the Japanese, one of many hundreds who shared the fate of Judy, the mascot of the hell railway prison camps. Although the POWs were starved, beaten and worked to death, the rare postcard home was strictly censored. *Photo courtesy Les Parsons*

Above: For Judy and her fellow prisoners the first few months of captivity at the hands of the Japanese were unpleasant, but far from the nightmare that would follow. Transferred to Sumatra's dreaded hell railway, Judy's morale-boosting presence helped save many who otherwise would have perished, and she would earn the reputation of being 'a dog in a million'. *AWM 019382*

Left: By the time the Pakan Baroe hell railway camps were liberated, POWs were dying from starvation and disease in their droves. Any living thing – snakes, rats, maggots even – was captured, cooked and eaten. But no one other than the brutal Japanese and Korean guards ever tried to seize and eat Judy! *AWM P00444.193*

"JUDY"

This is a sketch made by POW Stanley Russell, who amazingly managed to keep a secret diary of his time in the camps. He used to bury it in the camp graveyard, banking on the Japanese fear of the dead keeping it safely hidden. *Illustration taken from the collection of Museon The Hague*

HER FAVOURITE QUARRY

A second sketch from Stanley Russell's diary, entitled 'Her Favourite Quarry.' It shows Judy hunting for rats between the rickety bamboo huts in which the POWs lived and died. Judy would share whatever she'd caught with her gang of fellow prisoners and protectors. *Illustration taken from the collection of Museon The Hague*

Below: After the Japanese POW camps were liberated, Judy travelled to the UK with her then master, RAF ground crewman Frank Williams (on the far right of this photo). She was duly awarded the PDSA Dickin Medal – known as the Animal VC – for her life-saving acts aboard the gunboats and in the POW camps. *Topical Press Agency/Hulton Archive/ Getty Images*

Above: Judy, right of photo, in suitably regal pose, at the ceremony to receive her Medal. This is the photo that first inspired the author to research and then write her story. *TopFoto.co.uk*

Left: Judy's grave, in Tanzania, East Africa, where she went to live with Frank Williams after the war years. The first lines of the inscription read: 'In memory of Judy DM Canine VC. Breed English Pointer. Born Shanghai February 1936. Died February 1950. Wounded 14th February 1942 . . .' followed by a list of the theatres in which she served. *Imperial War Museum*

Frank Williams giving Judy a good groom. The devotion between man and dog is clear to see. Judy had numerous companions during the war years, and was cherished by so many – but immediately upon their meeting in a Japanese POW camp Frank Williams became the one that Judy loved the most, and vice versa. *Fred Morley/Fox Photos/ Hulton Archive/Getty Images*

The Colonel rolled the puppy backwards and forwards a few times, his hand buried in her pudgy tummy. He was clearly enjoying the play. He reached across his desk with the other hand for his official writing pad. There and then he began to scrawl out an order making it so. Judy was being given the Japanese prisoner of war number 81A-Medan, just as Frank had requested.

But as Colonel Banno scrawled out the precious missive, so Frank felt his heart sink to his boots. Beneath Kish's bottom a puddle had started to spread across the Colonel's polished desk. Frank had to hope and pray it didn't reach the writing pad before he was done scribbling. Barely had Colonel Banno handed him the precious slip of paper and dismissed him, than Frank practically ran from the room.

As no insanely angry voice yelled expletives after him in Japanese, Frank figured he must have got away from the officers' quarters before the puddle was discovered. By the following morning Judy was sporting a new metal tag on her collar, one fashioned by her protection committee using the flattened piece of a tin can. On it was etched in fine lettering: 'POW 81A-Medan'.

The news of Judy's 'promotion' in status spread far and wide, just as would word of the exploits of the four remaining pups. With Kish gone, Rojok, Sheikje, Blackie and Punch proved bundles of maverick-spirited foolishness, and they got them-selves into all sorts of trouble. They were too much for their mother to keep a watchful eye over. Fortunately, claims were about to be made on them. The women in the family camp – Gloegoer Two – had heard about the puppies. They sent word with a local fruit-seller, which consisted of a scribbled message hidden in her basket.

'Please, can we have one of your puppies?'

None could refuse such a request, especially as the men of Gloegoer One dreaded to think what life must be like for the Dutch women and children in their camp. Les Searle argued that Sheikje was the most beautiful of the four pups, which made her the most fitting to send. When the fruit-lady again visited, a space was made at the bottom of her basket. Sheikje was put to sleep by a tiny dose of chloroform administered by Dr Kirkwood, wrapped in a cloth and covered over with some bananas before being whisked out of the camp in the basket balanced upon the woman's head. Risking all kinds of reprisals from the camp guards the fruit-seller smuggled Sheikje out of Gloegoer One and into the family camp. And once she'd woken from her chemical-induced sleep and settled into her new home, Sheikje did no end of good to raise the morale of the women and child prisoners.

As the three remaining pups grew bigger and stronger, feeding them and controlling them became ever more of a challenge. The next to go was Rokok. He was passed through a hole in the camp fence, to be given to a Swedish Red Cross Official who was based in Medan, as a long overdue thank you for the food parcels.

But a horrific fate awaited one of the remaining pups – Blackie. Perhaps the most curious and nosey – a trait inherited no doubt from his mother – one dark night Blackie ventured out of the hut on some whim or fancy. Sadly, he ran into a drunken Korean guard, who proceeded to beat the puppy to death. The Koreans in particular were like spoiled children, and they could fly into a savage rage for no apparent reason. They were even worse whenever they had been drinking.

Poor Blackie had found himself in the wrong place at the wrong time.

There was no doubt about it – in recent months the disposition of the guards had been worsening. Many put it down to the fact that things weren't going all Imperial Japan's way in the war. For months now the guards had been boasting about the Japanese Army's invasion of India. A huge map of India had been displayed in a prominent window, with arrows indicating the line of the Japanese march. But for several weeks now that line had remained static at a hill station called Kohima, on the Imphal to Kohima road, on India's eastern border.

The Battle for Kohima would become known as the 'Stalingrad of the East'. From 3 to 16 April 1944 the Japanese attempted to storm the Kohima ridge, which dominated the road via which the British and Indian troops at Imphal were supplied. The tiny force at Kohima held out against all odds, and by mid-April the siege was broken. British and Indian troops then counter-attacked, forcing the Japanese to abandon the positions they had captured, driving them off the road and away from Imphal completely.

Imphal had been marked on the map at Gloegoer One with a prominent Japanese flag, as had the next several objectives in line all the way to Delhi itself, the Indian capital. But after weeks during which the flags had remained firmly fixed, the map was quietly taken down. It was never to reappear.

The prisoners at Gloegoer couldn't know it yet, but Imphal marked a decisive defeat for the Japanese. From there on General Bill Slim's magnificent 14th Army – the so-called 'forgotten army', a polyglot force of dozens of nationalities speaking numerous different languages, but united in their fight against the Japanese – would drive the Japanese Imperial Army back into Burma and beyond.

But with the turning of their fortunes in the war, the spirit of those guarding the Sumatran POW camps would turn darker still.

It was the second week of June 1944 when Colonel Banno left Gloegoer, to be replaced as Camp Commandant by one Captain Nissi. The moment of the Captain's arrival was a dark day for all. At the crack of dawn on his first morning as Commandant, Captain Nissi ordered all prisoners to appear on parade. And when he said 'all' he meant *all* – no matter how sick or injured anyone might be.

Those who were unable to stand were supported by their fellows. Those who couldn't walk were carried. Even the stretcher cases had to be formed up in one rank of the sick, the lame and those close to death's door. Captain Nissi stood in the centre of the parade ground, lord of all that he surveyed. His cane slapped against his long leather jackboots as he gazed over the pathetic stream of humanity that had stumbled and crawled and been carried forth from the huts.

But as he ran his gimlet eye down the emaciated figures, his cane stopped slapping quite suddenly. He had spotted Frank Williams, with a distinctive four-legged figure at his side. Captain Nissi had gone quite rigid. His eyes bulged in disbelief at spying the English Pointer, sitting to attention as if she was one of his prisoners. A dog? *A dog!* What was a dog doing on his parade?

Captain Nissi moved towards man and dog at a slow, predatory pace, his face dark as thunder. His sword-hand crept towards the hilt of his weapon. Frank Williams watched the Captain's approach with a quaking heart. At his side was a thin and worn Judy who was still recovering her strength after raising her brood. Her body was trembling slightly at the new Commandant's approach and her lip had curled into its barely audible snarl.

Captain Nissi came to a halt.

The atmosphere was fraught with tension.

Not a man spoke – neither prisoner nor guard.

Frank knew this was balanced on a knife-edge now. If the Captain were allowed to bark out an instruction for something unspeakable to be done to Judy, then the guards would be duty-bound to execute it. He had to strike the first blow, and before the Captain started yelling orders.

With a shaking hand he delved into the pocket of his ragged shorts. He pulled out the piece of paper that Colonel Banno had penned for him – Judy's 'official' POW permit. Gesturing with one hand at his dog, he held out the 'permit' in the other, Colonel Banno's swirl of a signature prominently displayed.

The Captain stared at that dog-eared scrap of paper for a long second, before snatching it away.

As he read it, incredulously, his cronies gathered around, nattering away and gesticulating at both the note and the dog. Finally, there were a series of head-scratchings and blank-faced stares between the Captain and his fellow officers. However implausible it might seem, this note about the dog seemed to come from Colonel Banno himself, a superior-ranking officer to Captain Nissi. The Colonel appeared to have conferred upon Judy official POW status, and in the rank-obsessed Japanese Army no one ever went against the decision of a superior officer.

For now at least Judy was no longer a legitimate target of Captain Nissi's ire. Instead, he turned his attention to the men. Everyone but the wakeful dead was sent out on forced-labour parties. The guards had clearly been given orders to up the work rate, or face the consequences. Captain Nissi seemed determined to drive the men to exhaustion and death in record time, and the prisoners were soon dropping like flies.

Day two was even worse, and if this were kept up the hospital hut would soon be filled to overflowing. But on day three came a reprieve of sorts. Mustered again at dawn on the parade ground, the men listened to Captain Nissi as he barked out a new order.

'All prisoners are to be shipped forthwith to Singapore.'

The news came as a total surprise, but it was greeted with barely disguised elation among the men. *Singapore*. It was a bustling metropolis compared to Sumatra – this jungle island where the prisoners had laboured for so long in forgotten isolation. *Singapore*. It was sure to offer news of the outside world, and perhaps a sense of how the war was going in Europe. *Singapore*. Surely there might be better treatment there – *and more food* – and perhaps even letters from home.

If nothing else, the urge to leave Gloegoer was so strong and surely anywhere had to be better than this. Les Searle used a rag to wipe the perspiration from one of the stretcher cases laid next to him on the parade ground.

'Cheer up, mate,' he whispered, 'you'll soon be out of this.'

That evening the huts were a scene of frantic activity, as men packed and repacked their meagre belongings in preparation for departure. Each hut received a visit from the guards, warning all to be ready for the off at first light the following morning.

For Frank Williams, there was to be a different kind of a visit. Captain Nissi himself came to have words with Judy's chief protector. The Commandant delivered a curt directive. *He wished to make himself clear: the dog would not be going to Singapore. As Judy was Gloegoer One's mascot, so at Gloegoer One she would have to stay.*

Once Captain Nissi was gone Frank took a few quiet moments to try to digest the news. But he felt truly shaken. He sat in one corner of the hut with Judy clasped between his knees and he tried to think up a plan – a plan to thwart the cruel Camp Commandant and keep Judy with her fellows, her natural family. He knew he could rely on Les Searle, Jock Devani and the others to help him, but the main risk in all of this would have to be his own.

He eyed Judy for a moment. He couldn't expect any of the others to sacrifice their life for her – and certainly, disobeying Captain Nissi's order would be life-threatening in the extreme. The Japanese – and especially ones like the new Camp Commandant – were incapable of dealing with 'loss of face'. If the plan now forming in Frank's mind was successful, when Judy was discovered gone everyone would know that the Captain's order had been disobeyed, and by a lowly POW. The loss of face that entailed was incalculable, as would be the punishment that would inevitably follow.

But Frank was absolutely determined: where he was going his bitch was going too. No matter who might be issuing the orders, they would not be parted. Man and dog hardly slept that night. They were up for many an hour as Frank went about teaching Judy a new trick – a variation on the fetch-the-fresh-fruit-from-the-Japanese-grave game.

The prisoners were going to be shipped to Singapore aboard an old freighter. Frank spent those few quiet hours before dawn – when the hut was filled with the groans and snuffles of hungry and exhausted men lost in the uncertain release of troubled sleep – teaching Judy to run to a hessian sack that he was holding, at his signal. When she seemed to have grasped that much, he taught her to jump in and out of the sack at a quiet click of his fingers.

Regardless of their breed, dogs respond best to training where the reward offered is play or praise. Frank had little else to offer Judy but play and praise in abundance.

As the first rays of dawn broke across the roofs of the Gloegoer One huts, Judy seemed to have mastered her new trick perfectly. She didn't quite grasp what it was for yet, but she trusted her teacher implicitly.

Little did she know it, but her life was hanging by a slender thread.

All they could do was to wait and hope.

Chapter Sixteen

At dawn the prisoners were ordered to muster for their final parade. But one, prisoner 81A-Medan, was left tied to a post in the British hut. Thanks to his days serving in the merchant navy, Frank knew just about every seaman's knot there is to tie. He'd used a slipknot to fasten Judy, one that would come loose under moderate pressure. Knot tied, he'd ordered her to 'stay' and left to join those lining up in the dim light outside.

After less than a week of Captain Nissi's brutal rule there were now two rows of stretcher cases. God only knows how the prisoners would have fared had they been forced to endure his murderous rule for any longer. Les Searle, Jock Devani and the other old faithfuls were 'in' on Frank's Judy-rescue plan, and each had their part to play. They waited tensely as the guards counted and recounted the POW numbers, and checked and rechecked their bags of pitiful possessions.

It was crucial to Frank's plan that he was seen to be carrying a bulging sack, although in truth he possessed little of anything that was worth taking with him. He'd stuffed his sack with an old blanket, so that it appeared bulging fat and full to those who might scrutinize it. At last the guards seemed satisfied with their inspections, and they reported to Captain Nissi that all were present and correct.

The Captain gave the order to move out.

For the last time – at least for these prisoners – the camp gates were swung open. The first to move off were those interred from the hospital hut, borne on hastily improvised stretchers. As the stretcher-carriers passed through the gates of Gloegoer One bearing their living skeletons, it was as if the tombs of the dead had opened. These were once men, but through a combination of brutal forced labour, tropical disease and starvation they had been reduced to wraiths.

Those who were still 'fit' – though that term in Gloegoer One had a very different meaning from the norm – watched this ghostly procession of the barely living in stunned silence. While busy on the work gangs, few had had the energy, the want or the need to venture into the hospital hut. Under Captain Nissi's orders that hut had been forced to disgorge its secrets. Many a man felt himself biting his lip or driving his nails into his hands, as he struggled to master the hatred he felt for those who had done this, and to resist the urge to strike back. Anyone who did so would end up either dead, or in the hands of the dreaded Kempei-tai, which was a fate worse than death.

The Kempei-tai were the Japanese equivalent of the Gestapo, Nazi Germany's secret police. Among this procession of the walking dead were those who had had cause to fall into their clutches. Mostly they were Dutch officers who'd been interrogated and tortured in unspeakable ways as the Kempei-tai had sought intelligence on the territory that they had overrun. They had returned to Gloegoer broken men: it wasn't so much their bodies that were finished, as their minds. They stumbled along like zombies, lost in a world to which their tortured psyches had, in desperation, retreated.

Frank lingered at the rear of the line of those deemed 'fit', waiting his turn to move. As the column began to snake ahead he joined the very end, so he would be last out. The moment he was through the gates he gave a faint whistle, the call that Judy would recognize as the signal for her to come. But as he followed the last in line towards the nearby railway siding – they were catching a train from the camp to the docks, the first leg of the coming journey – there was no sign of his beloved Judy anywhere.

Frank was worried sick that he'd tied the knot too tightly. But what could he do? He could hardly turn back for her. He was bound to be spotted, the questions would begin, and Judy would quickly be discovered. So he did the only thing he could do, moving along the line of men queuing to board the train, his eyes searching everywhere for any sign of his dog.

It was then that he saw it – a dark and moist nose and a pair of shining eyes, half-hidden in the shadows beneath a railway truck. He went down on one knee and a screen of bodies formed around him – Les Searle and Jock Devani herding others in closer, to hide what was about to happen. Once he was completely surrounded, Frank whipped the blanket out, clicked his fingers and Judy darted out from her place of hiding and leapt inside the empty sack.

With the blanket packed down on top to better hide her, Frank hoisted the heavy sack on his shoulders and climbed aboard a waiting railway carriage. With Judy thus hidden, the journey to the dockside proved a bittersweet affair. Much that the future was uncertain, the British and Australian prisoners were mostly relieved to be getting out of Gloegoer One. But for the Dutch prisoners there were distant and anxious farewells to be said as they streamed past the family camp and desperate rags and handkerchiefs were waved out of the carriage windows.

On reaching the harbour the carriages juddered and squealed as the brakes were applied. Now came the real test of Frank's plan. He released Judy from the sack, and she darted from the open door to her hiding place beneath the wagons, and almost before the train had come to a stop.

Again the men were formed up in ranks, as the Japanese did the second head-count and baggage inspection of the day – just to ensure no one had made a break for it during the train journey, or was carrying any hidden contraband. The prisoners eyed the ship that lay before them with some concern. The ship's name – the SS *Van Waerwyjck* – had been painted over with a Japanese one, the *Harukiku Maru*, and the tall, grey-painted hull was streaked with rust and dirt.

The SS *Van Waerwyjck* was a Dutch vessel captured and pressed into military service by the Japanese. Built in 1910 as a passenger steamer, the Royal Dutch Navy had commandeered her at the outbreak of the war, then scuttled her at the entrance to Tanjung Priok harbour, in Java, the island lying to the south of Sumatra, in an effort to prevent a Japanese invasion by sea. But once the Japanese had been victorious across the region they had refloated the ship, repaired her and pressed her into service as a transport vessel. She was the biggest ship that any of the prisoners had ever seen in the port of Balawan.

The head-count seemed to go on for ever, as did the inspection of the prisoners' possessions. Once his sack had been searched and the coast seemed clear Frank gave another whistle. Word ran down the line of waiting men whispered from mouth to mouth that Judy was coming. Having made as much progress as she could crawling beneath the train, she popped out and weaved her way between the ranks of prisoners, making directly for Frank's position.

Not a man among them so much as glanced down as she passed by. Seizing his moment Frank bent again and whisked her into the sack, and moments later he had her hoisted onto his shoulders. So far, so good. The waiting men began to shuffle their way up the gangways leading onto the *Van Waerwyjck*'s main deck. The prisoners were divided into two parties – officers and wounded for the front hold, all others for the rear.

There were some seven hundred prisoners gathered on the quayside, and it was taking an age to get them loaded, especially the wounded. The midday sun beat down mercilessly from a cloudless Sumatran sky. Sweat poured off the men standing unmoving in their ranks. Frank felt his limbs weakening with exhaustion, but he was determined not to buckle under the heavy weight slung across his shoulder.

He sensed the tall Australian beside him lean across and place something on his head. It was a wide-brimmed Aussie bush hat.

'If I fall down, someone'll pick me up,' he muttered, cheerfully. 'But if you fall down, mate, you've had it – you and your dog.'

Quite suddenly, Captain Nissi materialized right before Frank. For a second or so he scrutinized the wide-brimmed hat perched atop the prisoner's head. Frank could see the Captain's mind working away feverishly behind brutish eyes. Captain Nissi had seen Judy tied to a post, back in the hut in Medan. He'd seen Frank's sack inspected, once back at the camp and once here. Presumably, the dog had been left behind, as ordered.

'Ino wa arimasen deshita?' – The dog's not come? – he demanded menacingly.

'Ino wa arimasen deshita . . .' Frank confirmed unhappily.

He did his best to look utterly crestfallen at the loss of his faithful friend, eyes cast at the ground, but at the same time the heavy sack was biting deeper into his bony shoulder. If Judy so much as breathed right now the Captain would be bound to notice.

'Ino wa arimasen deshita!' Captain Nissi affirmed, a triumphant smile spreading across his features.

With a curt nod he moved on.

His knees shaking, Frank made it to the top of the gangplank, the contents of his precious sack still undiscovered. Rough hands grabbed him and shoved him towards a series of steep iron ladders leading down into the forward hold. No lifejackets were issued to any of the prisoners. They remained locked in the wooden cupboards on the upper deck, adjacent to the ship's lifeboats.

With the sack slung over his shoulder, Frank was all but thrown down the steps, joining the mass of bodies in the darkness below. At the bottom of the stairway he found that the ship's hold had been converted into a 'prison ship'. Rough wooden platforms ran along either side of the interior, dividing it into two floors. Those first down the ladder had been herded into the all-but-total darkness of the lower level.

Conditions were abominable. With only four feet of head-room, those on the lower level couldn't stand, and they were packed so tight there was no room to lie down. Instead, they squatted, row upon row upon row. Frank found himself a place on the upper floor. It was little better, except that there were portholes, which at least held out the promise that when the ship began to move there might be a little air.

Frank settled down with Les Searle, Jock Devani and the others, his back to a steel bulkhead. The heat was already intense. The entry hatch to the hold appeared like a small square of daylight above them, a shaft of sunlight streaming through it and piercing the thick darkness. But, shortly, even the hatch was slammed shut, sealing the men inside a giant metal oven. In no time the prisoners were sitting in pools of their own sweat.

With the hatch locked shut Frank felt he could finally risk releasing Judy. She poked her head out of the sack, tongue lolling and panting heavily, as she gazed around at her new surroundings. An instant later Frank had her out and she was lapping thirstily at the water that he'd brought with him from the camp. That done, they settled down to endure as best they could the sea voyage to Singapore.

It was mid-afternoon when the SS *Van Waerwijck* slipped her moorings and steamed out of harbour. Once she hit the open sea she formed up in a convoy with two oil tankers, another cargo ship and a pair of Japanese Navy corvettes, for protection. She steamed onwards, keeping close to the Sumatran coastline, the rhythmic slap of the waves beneath the hull lulling many into an exhausted sleep. But it was fitful and uneasy. With limbs entwined there was little room to lie down, and less still to move about.

Les Searle found himself desperate to stretch his legs. He was curled up tight against the bulkhead, with another prisoner lying in his path. As for Judy, in spite of the terribly cramped conditions she seemed happy enough. She was with Frank and her wider family – her fellow conspirators – and for now at least she had escaped whatever fate had awaited her at Captain Nissi's hands.

With dusk the ship came to a halt and dropped anchor. The engines were shut down, but still the oppressive heat in the cramped hold lasted long into the night. With dawn the *Van Waerwijck* was quickly underway again. It was 26 June 1944, a day that would be burned for ever in the minds of those aboard that ill-fated ship.

After repeated complaints to the Japanese guards, some respite from the terrible conditions below deck was granted. In small batches, prisoners were allowed up into the fresh air twenty minutes at a time. But of course, prisoner 81A-Medan was going nowhere. Judy-the-stowaway would have to remain ensconced in the darkest recesses of the hold, or she risked getting discovered.

A constant stream of buckets of hot water was lowered, so the men could brew tea. But the quicker they drank the quicker the sweat seemed to pour from their bodies. By midday the fierce heat was reaching its zenith. From stem to stern a deathly quiet gripped the vessel. The prisoners suffered in numbed silence – the oven-like conditions seeming to roast their very brains. It was only the malaria and dysentery patients who kept disturbing the mute stillness, the eerie moans and cries of their fevered delirium echoing back and forth.

Tucked away in her corner, Judy sat so still and so statuesque that it was almost as if she knew that she was a stowaway, and what the costs of discovery might be. Once again, just her presence among the prisoners proved a massive morale booster. The very fact that she was still there showed how they had had one over on the Japanese. She was a symbol of their stoic resistance and their survival – survival that in her case had been achieved against all the odds.

Across the hold from Judy sat a young British Army Sergeant called Peter Hartley. Hartley had distinguished himself during the battle for Singapore by being one of those who had refused to surrender when the order was given to do so by his commanding officer. Instead, he had stolen a boat from Singapore harbour, and via the Indragiri River he had embarked upon a journey to Padang that was almost a carbon copy of that undertaken by the gunboat crews – both man and dog.

He'd reached the besieged city at the same moment as Judy and her fellows, so missing the final ships sailing to safety, and he had likewise ended up in Gloegoer One. There a strange series of events had unfolded. Being a particularly religious man – he was a strong Christian even before the outbreak of the war – Hartley had been recruited by the camp's British padre to assist in his services and especially to help officiate at burials. But before the padre had been able to instruct Hartley very much, he had himself sickened and died.

Hartley – not properly trained and certainly not ordained – had become by default the 'padre' of the British at Gloegoer One, and in that he had done a sterling job. Ensconced in the hold of the SS *Van Waerwijck*, he gazed at the large liver-and-white dog across the way from him, marvelling at the incredible life she had led. All in Gloegoer had heard of their mascot's string of wild adventures – on the gunboats, in Singapore, and during her long flight to the POW camps – and it strengthened their determination to have her remain one of their number.

Now here she was again – smuggled aboard, and miraculously still with them. Hartley thanked God that she had not been discovered. Having her there on that hellish ship was oddly comforting. Hartley watched the Gloegoer One mascot lay her fine head between her forepaws, as if to rest. Gradually, he felt his own eyes closing, the stultifying heat and the motion of the vessel lulling him to sleep.

Neither man nor dog would rest for long.

In the seas off eastern Sumatra 26 June was a calm and sunny day. The *Van Waerwijck* steamed onwards toward Singapore, her Captain and crew remaining blissfully unaware that a British submarine had spotted her.

The first sign that Commander Robert Alexander, the Captain of HMS *Truculent*, had detected of the small convoy was a plume of smoke on the distant horizon. Minutes later he'd spotted an aircraft circling overhead, forming some kind of an escort. He'd closed to within 3,500 yards – a range from where he could study the vessels properly.

As he hunched over his periscope, gazing intently at the enemy ships, the British Commander realized he'd stumbled upon a small Japanese convoy. Having scanned the cluster of vessels from end to end, one – a twin-masted steamer with a single funnel churning out a dark plume of smoke – clearly presented the largest and most juicy target. Unaware that she was carrying hundreds of British and Allied POWs, Commander Alexander unleashed four torpedoes, then dived, settling upon the bottom at 58 feet depth.

On board the *Van Waerwijck* Les Searle had just been called onto the open deck. It was a chance to grab a little fresh air. The sense of relief after the punishing conditions below was unbelievable – even though he'd been summoned to help with a decidedly unpleasant task, that of cleaning the ship's latrines. Midway through the work some sixth sense made him glance out to sea. He froze. Just below the surface were the unmistakable tracks of white turbulence formed by torpedoes. Four of them, and bearing down on them fast!

Les felt overcome with shock and disbelief, yet still he managed to yell out a warning. 'Torpedoes! Torpedoes off the port side!'

His cry came too late for the ship to take any kind of evasive action. Moments later the first torpedo struck the SS *Van Waerwijck*, throwing up a geyser of white water high into the air. It tore into the ship's hull just to the rear of the forward hold, and adjacent to the coalbunker. Those who were on deck knew instantly what had happened, and several threw themselves into the sea. But those packed into the rear hold had heard only a deafening thud reverberating through the vessel, and they couldn't know what calamity had befallen the ship.

As Les raced across deck to warn them, the second torpedo was ahead of him. The blunt-nosed projectile tore into the rear hold, where several hundred prisoners and one dog were packed like sardines. The explosion proved so violent it buckled the deck, blasting several Japanese guards high into the air. Seawater began pouring into the ruptured hull.

The *Van Waerwijck* let out a tortured groan and started listing badly to port. In the forward hold the bulkhead that had separated the prisoners from the engine room collapsed. Blasted coal dust turned the air black as night, as ghostly, soot-covered figures fought each other for a place on the ladder and the chance to climb to safety. On the deck above a Chaplain was crying out 'Hail Marys' and 'Our Fathers' at the top of his voice as he wrestled open the cupboards holding the lifejackets and handed them around to those fighting to get clear of the sinking ship.

Drums, chests and falling planks of wood crashed about the badly listing deck, trapping those who were struggling to be free. The ship was sinking stern-first, and the water was already claiming its first victims. In the rear hold it was utter chaos. Figures clambered over each other to get access to the stairwell. As the ship heeled over still further the wooden platforms disintegrated into heavy planking, massive splinters crashing down on top of bodies and trapping many. The huge covers for the hatches had been blown inwards by the force of the explosion, crushing those below.

As the ship heeled over still further, the packing cases that constituted the deck cargo broke free and crashed into the hold. Seawater swirled and gurgled, as bodies fought to make their escape. Les Searle peered in through the open hatch, searching amid the mass of twisted metal, wood and seawater for Jock Devani, Frank, Judy and the others. He leant into the darkness and hauled figures upwards, as he joined those trying to drag as many as possible out of that giant steel coffin.

But Jock, Frank and Judy were nowhere to be seen.

When the first torpedo struck, Peter Hartley, Gloegoer's makeshift padre, had woken with a start. He'd got to his feet, a sense of panic sweeping through the hold, only to be blasted down again by torpedo number two. Moments later sounds began to filter into his numbed brain: rushing water, splintering wood; the agonized screams of those who were trapped. The harsh wail of the ship's siren rent the gloom, while the floor beneath him rocked and shook as if an earthquake was tearing through the ship.

High above him he saw a square of daylight – the hatch – with figures clustered desperately around it. The ladder was besieged. There was no way he could make it out via that route. Instead, he began to climb up the jagged mountain of packing cases that had tumbled into the hold. If he could make the high point, he might just be able to attempt a leap for the open hatch.

For an instant he glanced across at where Judy had been sleeping, her head resting on her paws. The most amazing sight met his eyes. Frank Williams had hoisted Judy up and was trying to post her out through a porthole. When the torpedoes had struck, Judy had been nestled comfortably between his knees. He'd known that there was no way he could carry her through the mass of men who had began to fight for the one escape route – the ladder leading out of the hold. Instead, he'd turned to the nearest porthole, wrenched it fully open, and lifted Judy towards it.

Trusting to the last, she'd allowed him to ease her head and forelegs through the opening, even as the ship had begun her final death throes. She'd turned her head towards the stricken vessel, eyes searching for Frank, as if she'd expected him to be following after her.

Instead, he'd uttered a few encouraging words. 'Out you go, old girl! Swim for it!'

With that he'd given a final push on her hindquarters, and Judy of Sussex had tumbled into the sea.

Chapter Seventeen

It was four minutes past two in the afternoon when the SS *Van Waerwijck* gave up the ghost and was claimed by the waves. It had taken just twelve short minutes for her to go down. But not all of the ship had disappeared. The stern was stuck in the mud, and the bow section remained likewise just proud of the waters. She'd broken in two, but she hadn't been lost from the survivors' view completely: there were hundreds in the water all around her, fighting for their lives.

Meanwhile, her nemesis HMS *Truculent* was doing her best to make her escape as the Japanese corvettes came hunting. A pattern of six depth charges was dropped, massive eruptions showing where they'd exploded deep beneath the waves. This first salvo hit wide of the mark, so the corvettes swung around to release a second, this falling much closer to the British submarine. A third attacking run sent more depth charges churning up the waters around their target, the shock waves pounding out a deathly rhythm against the British submarine's hull.

But by now Commander Alexander had got his vessel underway, and he managed to creep away silently and make good the *Truculent*'s escape. The British submarine left behind her a sea that was littered with debris and flotsam, plus hundreds of men struggling for their lives.

The *Van Waerwijck* had been sunk in the Malacca Straits some 500 kilometres north of Singapore. The shore was several miles distant, and there were few who were able to swim for it. Instead, figures clutched onto just about anything that might provide some form of buoyancy – broken wooden beams, life rafts, scattered life vests. Amid the thick, oily scum that covered the water, crates of live chickens bobbed about, their worried clucking adding a surreal touch to the ghostly scene.

A flight of Japanese bombers with fighter escorts appeared overhead, searching for the British submarine, but to no avail. HMS *Truculent* had slipped into deeper waters just as stealthily as she had appeared. With the threat gone, the Japanese tanker ships steamed back into view, having moved closer to the shore in an effort to hide. Lifeboats were lowered, but the crew had strict orders to prioritize the rescue of their fellow Japanese and Koreans. The British, Dutch and Australian prisoners would have to wait their turn.

Among the first POWs finally to be plucked from the sea would be Frank Williams. He'd been in the water for a good two hours, clinging to a lump of wreckage. For all of that time he'd kept his eyes peeled for a familiar figure, one that he was so desperate to spot – a liver-and-white English Pointer doggy-paddling through the oily swell.

When Frank was finally able to clamber up one of the nets thrown over the tanker's sides he was exhausted from the time he'd spent in the water, his eyes showing as white circles in his otherwise oil-blackened features. With a last despairing glance over the ship's rail, he allowed himself to be led aft to the galley.

As he did so, he consoled himself with the thought that he had done all he could to save Judy.

It was in the lap of the gods whether she lived or died, though he very much doubted whether the Japanese would make much of an effort to save a dog, especially one that was a forbidden stowaway. His biggest worry was that she might have gone back aboard the stricken ship to search for him, and had failed to get out before the vessel went down. After all, she'd got herself trapped aboard the *Grasshopper*, and only the spirited action of Petty Officer White had saved her.

Along with the rest of the rescued prisoners, Frank was given a ball of sticky rice to stuff into his mouth with his oil-smeared hands, plus a mug of tea. As more and more soot-blackened figures joined them, the deck became horribly crowded. There was only the open steel above the oil tanks for the survivors to squat on, and the afternoon sun was heating it up like a furnace. Soon, it was impossible to so much as step on the deck without burning the soles of the feet. All the men could do was squat under the burning sun, and suffer in a shocked and a stunned silence, as the search for more lives to save went on and on.

Unbeknown to those rescued prisoners, the greatest ever four-legged lifesaver was hard at work out there on the water. Les Searle had managed to escape from the stricken *Van Waerwijck*, whereupon he'd set out to swim for the nearest Japanese tanker. As he was stroking his way through the wreckage-strewn seas he came across the most incredible sight of all. A finely shaped, dark head was arrowing through the water, powerful forepaws thrashing at the surface. There was a figure at Judy's side and he had one arm thrown across her shoulders, as she pulled him towards safety.

Les could barely believe it. Why didn't the poor bitch shake him off, he wondered? Surely, under the dead weight of a fully grown man she'd drown?

But Judy made it to the nearest rescue boat – a local tongkang that had arrived on the scene – after which her shipwreck victim was hauled aboard. Yet still she wasn't done. With cheers of encouragement ringing in her ears she turned around and set off to find others. She helped bring in a good half-a-dozen survivors before she became too exhausted to drag any more to safety – at which point she resorted to pushing lengths of driftwood towards those who were the most in need.

Eventually, she allowed herself to be hauled aboard the tong-kang. Bedraggled and smeared in oil, Judy was more dead than alive. She was totally exhausted, her ribs showed sharp and angular through her emaciated, sodden flanks, and her eyes were red-rimmed and smarting – but she was still very much the heroine of the hour.

Sadly, there was little opportunity to treat her as the champion lifesaver that she was. Instead, she had to be hustled under a length of canvas that had been used to cover the bodies of some of her most hated human oppressors – a pair of Korean guards who had drowned during the ship's sinking. Judy would have to keep those corpses company for the remainder of the voyage to Singapore – otherwise the guards might discover her presence, and remembering Captain Nissi's orders, unleash savage retribution.

One of the last men to be plucked out of the sea was a Captain Gordon of the Royal Artillery. He'd managed to swim to a native fishing trap set off shore, and cling to that for several hours. From there he was picked up by one of the Japanese corvettes. Having thanked the ship's Captain for rescuing him and many others, Captain Gordon asked the Japanese Commander if he would be willing to make one last search of all the wreckage. He agreed, and by four-thirty that afternoon all the survivors had been plucked from the sea.

The convoy formed up and got underway once more, steaming south for Singapore. But with sundown the decks that had been boiling hot during the day were transformed into a freezing cold, icy bed for the night. Without any blankets and with many lacking clothes even – they'd lost them during the shipwreck – survivors huddled as close together as they could, trying to share some body warmth. As a chill wind whipped across the exposed deck, the curses and shivers of the survivors mingled with the hollow, despairing cries of the wounded.

Among those who had escaped the *Van Waerwijck* sinking were Les Searle, Jock Devani, Frank Williams and Judy of Sussex, plus Gloegoer One's makeshift padre, Peter Hartley – but they were spread across various vessels. Ahead of them lay a journey during which they would be frozen at night, baked under the burning sun by day, and forced to bury at sea many of their comrades – the worst wounded, who would not survive.

By the time the battered convoy sailed into Singapore, most were too numb with shock and exhaustion to register anything other than a dumb recognition that they had arrived.

Over two years had passed since Frank Williams had served with his RAF unit here in Singapore, or since Les Searle, Jock Devani and Judy had striven valiantly aboard the gunboats to escape the encircling Japanese, or since Peter Hartley had refused the order to surrender and made his desperate escape bid. The vessels that were carrying them chugged by the sunken forms of the wrecks that still littered the harbour, before passing the sleek grey forms of a pair of German U-boats, emblazoned with huge red-and-white swastikas.

The first ships pulled alongside an empty wharf. The reality of what had happened started to sink in for the shipwreck survivors, crouched like naked scarecrows on the decks. Naked and smeared with oil they might be, but somehow five hundred of the *Van Waerwijck*'s contingent of seven hundred POWs had survived. Dirty, bloodied and bare they might be, but few felt ashamed now they were back in 'civilization'.

Instead, they gave thanks for being alive.

But for one prisoner, 81A-Medan, the most life-threatening moment of this nightmare journey was still to come. The tong-kang carrying Judy pulled into dock, where there was a convoy of waiting Japanese Army trucks. A distinctive figure stood among the grey vehicles, looming head and shoulders above his fellow officers – Colonel Banno. After the horrors of Captain Nissi's rule, some of the prisoners – Les Searle and Peter 'the padre' Hartley among them – almost felt glad to lay eyes on Gloegoer One's former Commandant once more.

At first the Colonel greeted their arrival with a smile. But it soon gave way to a look of horror, as he surveyed the human skeletons clustered along the deck, and the awfulness of what must have happened hit home. As changeable as ever, the sight seemed to move him to a rare show of pity. He turned to his guards and began issuing orders, gesticulating wildly with his hands at the figures on the vessel.

The tongkang scraped its way along the concrete dockside and came to a halt. The gangplank went down and volunteers were called forth to carry the wounded, including those Korean guards who had jumped from the ship in the first seconds after she was hit, only to be caught by the shockwaves of the second torpedo and suffering horrific internal injuries as a result. Then there were the prisoners from the rear hold, who had been injured in the explosion caused by the second torpedo. A few Japanese guards had jumped into the sea with a supposed ready-made life raft gripped between their legs – a length of wooden planking from the ship, perhaps – only for its impact to cause serious injuries.

With the wounded unloaded, the order was given for the able-bodied men to disembark. As Les Searle coaxed Judy out of hiding he had no sack in which to hide her, nor any means to click his fingers and get her to dart inside. He had no choice but to lead her down the gangplank in full view. Together with padre Peter Hartley he and Judy half-stumbled the short distance, for they were in a terrible way. Hartley's legs and arms were cut to shreds from all the splintered wood that he'd had to fight his way through, and neither Les Searle nor Judy were in very much better condition.

But as soon as the three survivors made the quayside the Gloegoer One guards noticed Judy. The atmosphere surrounding the disembarkation changed completely. Two of the guards stormed forwards, mouths spouting invective and arms jerking maniacally at the dog, at Les Searle and then at the sea. The meaning was clear: they were threatening to throw Judy into the harbour, and very possibly her human companions with her. Les Searle doubted whether he could survive another immersion, and, as for Judy, even she was looking half-beaten.

As the guards went to snatch up the errant dog a powerful cry rang out. Hands froze in mid-action. It was the voice of Colonel Banno. Having seen what was happening, the Colonel had barked out some form of counter-order. The guards jerked stiffly to attention, then bowed before the Colonel, before stepping away from the dog.

Colonel Banno strode forward. The guards bobbed their heads in cringing subservience as he tore into them. Then, rather than drawing his sword to bait Judy, he bent down to pat her oil-stained ears, clearly signalling that she had won her reprieve. In the eyes of many of the prisoners, in that one moment Colonel Banno had atoned for many of the past cruelties that he'd visited upon them at Gloegoer One.

The POWs were formed up in ragged ranks. Many were completely naked, their only covering being a thick layer of greasy soot and oil. More trucks pulled up at the quayside. Head-count completed, the men – plus one dog who'd won an eleventh-hour reprieve – were ordered to board the waiting vehicles. But beside one of the newly arrived trucks stood another familiar figure, and this one was far less welcome.

It was the dreaded Captain Nissi, fresh onto the scene. As Les Searle went to hoist Judy into the rear of one of the trucks, the

Captain let out a strangled scream of rage. A torrent of abuse shot forth from his lips. A pair of soldiers stepped forward, rifles at the ready.

In her appearance Judy was very different from her heyday on the Yangtze gunboats. She was painfully thin; her white coat was stained black with oil from repeated forays into the sea; her teeth were yellow beneath snarling lips, and her red eyes burned with hatred for those about to seize her. Yet just at the moment when they were about to strike, an older, more commanding voice rang out. It was Colonel Banno once more, and this time he was countermanding Captain Nissi's orders: *prisoner 81A-Medan was not to be harmed.*

Much as he hated having to do so, Captain Nissi was forced to give way. Before there could be any further attempts to do her harm, Les Searle bundled Judy into the truck and vaulted after her. Shortly they were off jolting along the harbour road, every man lost in a dark corner of the vehicle and entombed in his own thoughts. Not even the fact that they'd succeeded in frustrating Captain Nissi's murderous intentions could lift the men's sagging spirits.

The convoy roared through the streets of what had once been Britain's island fortress, but which was now transformed into a stronghold of the hated enemy. Just a short drive across the city the trucks pulled to a halt. The prisoners were ordered out. They had been brought to a new camp – or at least it was 'new' to them, but a more dilapidated and dispiriting place they'd yet to imagine.

The huts were made of rough-hewn wooden frames, sup-posedly topped off with *atap* – rough thatch harvested from the jungle. But with many the roofing had blown away or rotted through completely. This accursed place was called the 'River Valley Road Camp', presumably because there was a garbage-choked drain running through the centre of it.

The first survivors from the SS *Van Waerwijck* marched into the camp, passing through a group of huts that were already occupied by Allied POWs. They were forbidden from stopping or talking to anyone. They were herded across the stream-cum-sewer, through a barbed-wire gate guarded by sentries, and into what appeared to be the most godforsaken corner of the entire godforsaken place.

This end of the camp was strewn with garbage and filth. On the far side was a rank of bare huts, each equipped with wooden sleeping platforms. For now, this was home.

These men had lost everything when the SS *Van Waerwijck* went down. What few possessions they'd taken with them from Gloegoer One had gone to the bottom of the Malacca Straits. Reduced to numbed, naked 'animals', suffering from shock and exposure, their hair matted and oily and with faces covered in filthy stubble, most were almost as crazed as they looked – for right now the survivors of the *Van Waerwijck* sinking were close to being an army of the insane and the damned.

Rubbish tips were ransacked for empty tins to use as mugs, or bits of sacking from which to improvise clothing. A meal was served. It was rice and dried, salted fish. The men were forced to eat with their hands, using leaves cut from the trees as their 'plates'. Harsh, unsweetened black tea was sipped from rusty, dirt-encrusted tins. But the ration drove some even closer to the brink, for it wasn't enough even to begin to satiate their gnawing hunger. There had been little to eat after the sinking of their ship, for the tongkang's crew hadn't expected to need to cater for dozens of Allied POWs.

And now this – *starvation rations*.

When Les Searle retired to his hut to rest his aching limbs, his shrunken stomach grumbling painfully, he expected Judy to come with him. But oddly, she refused. Instead she went from hut to hut, checking each in turn. That done, she proceeded to quarter the entire length and breadth of the camp. By now Les had an inkling what she might be up to: she had to be searching for their missing friend – for Frank Williams. But he could think of little to say or do to comfort her.

It was as much as he had been able to manage to save Judy from Captain Nissi's ire – with Colonel Banno's help. He had no idea if Frank Williams had survived the shipwreck or not. They'd all heard the story of Frank posting Judy through the porthole, but after that – who knew? Yet Judy was not to be deterred from her quest. Once she was certain that Frank wasn't anywhere in the camp, she settled down at the gate, her head resting on her forepaws, and her sombre eyes fixed in the direction in that she hoped her 'master' would miraculously reappear.

For two days she kept her lonely vigil. Judy's was a watch that would not be broken. Too often in life she'd been parted from her greatest protectors – Petty Officer Jefferey and Tankey Cooper of the *Gnat*, Petty Officer George White of the *Grasshopper*, plus Private Cousens the Gloegoer One shoe-maker, to name but a few. Losing Frank Williams was something that Judy simply refused to accept, as if by force of will alone she might bring him to her alive.

And so she waited patiently for a reunion that she felt certain was coming.

Some forty-eight hours after the first arrivals had reached the River Valley Road Camp, Frank Williams made it there too. Weakened by exposure, physically and mentally exhausted from the shipwreck, he was doubly traumatized by what he believed to be the loss of his beloved dog. Bit by bit, he seemed to be losing his will to live.

He clambered down from the truck, every movement causing him agony, and stumbled into the dreadful camp. He was blind to much of what was around him and lost in a dark world of his own. So cut off was he from his surroundings that when he felt the first blow to his shoulders as he staggered through the barbed-wire gate, he shrugged it off as just another exhausted prisoner stumbling into him.

The second blow had the power to send him sprawling face down in the dirt, so weakened was his physical condition. He lay there feeling little but dull incomprehension, as someone or something scrabbled anxiously at his head and shoulders, as if desperate to attract his attention.

And then he heard it. At first he couldn't – *wouldn't* – believe his ears. A low, insistent whine had reached him, cutting through the hunger, the trauma and the crushing exhaustion that had so befuddled his mind. As if to confirm his impossible hopes, he felt something cold and wet nuzzling into his face – and now the whining was right in his ear.

His hearing wasn't playing tricks on him! *It was her! It was Judy!* Somehow the dog he thought had perished in the seas around the stricken *Van Waerwijck* – the dog he'd posted through the ship's porthole in an effort to save her – had come back from the dead!

Sensing that he recognized her at last, Judy flung herself upon Frank's prostrate form in a wild frenzy of delight. Managing to roll over, he clasped his arms around her and gazed into her suffering, but ever-hopeful eyes. He felt the thick crust of oil and soot that matted her fur. He felt how dreadfully bony were her ribs and her haunches. He sensed too how desperate she'd been to find him.

They embraced for a while, miraculously reunited, and with nothing needing to be said between them. It was one of the sweetest of moments. Frank felt as if his heart would break with sheer unadulterated joy. As for Judy, her long wait had been rewarded. And in this one moment Frank seemed to have found the will to live again. He clambered to his feet, and summoning up his newly found reserves of strength, he scooped up his dog in his arms.

'Come on, old girl,' he told her, with tears in his eyes, 'and stop acting so daft.'

Together, man and dog moved into their new quarters.

That first night Judy lay stretched out at Frank's feet. In spite of her recent ordeal, she remained ever watchful over the one that she loved the most. At any movement from across the slumbering camp she'd open one eye, sniff the air and flick her ears forwards, checking for the barest hint of any danger. Judy was determined not to lose her best friend ever again.

Only when she was certain that nothing wicked was approaching did she close her eyes and drift into an aching, exhausted sleep.

The next few days were spent in rest and recuperation – not that the camp provided much of the means for either. It – and Singapore in general – offered none of the 'luxuries' that these desperate men had so longed for. There would be no mail from home; little news of the fortunes of the wider war; their rations were worse than they had been at Gloegoer One; and the camp itself was a shabby, leaking, windswept ruin of a place, when compared to their solidly built barracks on Sumatra.

The daily ration of rice and dried fish lacked the essential green vegetables or fruit needed to stave off beriberi, a debilitating disease caused by acute vitamin deficiencies. Already, every green and edible leaf had been stripped from the trees around camp. Occasionally, a dollop of dried seaweed accompanied the daily ration, but it looked and tasted like salty old rope. The Dutch and British doctors were forecasting dire consequences should the rations not be improved, both in quality and quantity.

But nothing changed.

The Japanese issued 'new' clothes to replace those lost in the shipwreck – yet these were mostly patched and repatched Japanese Army uniforms, ones that looked as if they had been removed from the bodies of the dead. A few battered British Army boots were handed out, but there were nowhere near enough to go around. For the first time since being taken prisoner a blanket was issued to each man. They were sorely needed, for the huts leaked like sieves. Time was spent trying to sleep and recover, or manufacturing crude spoons and plates from old tins, plus makeshift 'toothbrushes' from tree branches.

On the first Sunday after their arrival Peter Hartley – Gloegoer One's make-do padre – cobbled together a makeshift service. He had no Bible, having lost everything when the *Van Waerwijck* sank. He managed to beg and borrow some scraps of paper and a pencil, and he scribbled down as much as he could remember of four hymns, filling in forgotten lines with the help of other prisoners. The service was held in one of the skeletal huts. The singing would have raised the roof had it not been so rotten, as those who had survived the worst mourned friends gone but not forgotten, and offered thanks for their own deliverance.

But in truth, that deliverance was a mirage. Their stay here would last only four weeks – the time that the Japanese reckoned the POWs needed to recover from their ordeal. This was but a transit camp, and in the last week of July 1944 the announcement was made that the Gloegoer One POWs were moving on. In Gloegoer – and now here in River Valley Road Camp – these men had thought themselves in a place very close to the Underworld. But where man and dog were headed next would take them into the very jaws of hell itself.

They were returning to Sumatra, to work as slave-labour on the hell railroad.

Chapter Eighteen

It was in the late 1800s that the Dutch had first considered driving a railroad through Sumatra's seemingly impenetrable central highlands. The terrain was impossible. It consisted of rugged peaks wreathed in mist and cloud, their perilous slopes cloaked in a carpet of dense jungle, one criss-crossed with fast-flowing rivers and deep gorges, and undercut by a labyrinthine network of caves and tunnels. But the prize was also potentially stupendous: *black gold*. The Sumatran mountains harboured some of the richest coal reserves on earth.

The route that the Dutch railway engineers had first explored was only a little different from that taken by Judy and her fellows in the spring of 1942, as they travelled up the Indragiri River, trying to escape from the encircling Japanese. Much of it followed a knife-cut gorge where the Kwantan River – a tributary of the Indragiri – carved its way between jagged-toothed ridges. The sides of the gorge were near-vertical slabs of rock, and where massive boulders had tumbled into the river its flow was rendered into a series of tortured rapids white with foam.

At places the river appeared almost to disappear entirely into the earth, only to gush forth again like a giant geyser further downstream. At one stage a dark, bat-infested cave led off from the river valley some four kilometres into the stony heart of the mountains. At first it seemingly offered the Dutch engineers the promise of a route to push the railway through the worst of the terrain, only for all further progress to be blocked by a massive underground lake.

W. Ijzerman, the Dutch engineer leading the perilous expedition, never had a chance to see the fruits of his labours realized. He was standing in shallow water in the Kwantan with his measuring instrument in hand, when all of a sudden the sand beneath his feet gave way and he was sucked into a swirling, subterranean abyss. His body was never found.

Subsequent surveys confirmed that the route Ijzerman had pioneered – from the riverside town of Pakan Baroe south-west to Moera, via the Kwantan gorge – did offer the possibility of driving a railway through this daunting terrain. But still the Dutch government baulked at the prospect: it would prove staggeringly expensive, there was no guarantee of success, and the railway would have to penetrate an area largely uninhabited by man, but rife with wild animals and diseases like malaria and typhoid. Such an undertaking would very likely prove costly in human lives, and so the project was abandoned before it ever really got up a head of steam.

For the Japanese in 1944, however, there were to be no such limitations, blessed as they were with thousands of Allied POWs making up a free – and wholly dispensable – labour force. As the fortunes of the war began to turn inexorably against Imperial Japan, she was in ever more desperate need of natural resources. In particular, the Japanese motherland was bereft of reserves of raw energy, and many of the older ships feeding her war machine were coal-fired.

The untapped coalfields of the central Sumatran highlands were capable of producing 500,000 tonnes of the finest black gold a year. So it was that the Japanese, in extremis, resurrected the long-abandoned colonial Dutch railway project. Their aim was to open up a rail and river route into the Sumatran highlands, so the rich coal reserves could be dug out of the ground and shipped east to fuel their ships, first in Singapore and then to all corners of the Japanese conquests.

By far the largest contingent of forced – slave – labour earmarked for the railroad were locals, the so-called 'romushas'. *Romusha* is the Japanese word for 'labourer', and tens of thousands were forced to work on the railway at the end of the barrel of a gun. But on Friday 19 May 1944 the first contingent of Allied POWs arrived in Pakan Baroe, to join the romushas driving the iron rails into the jungle. Frank Williams, Les Searle, Jock Devani, Judy of Sussex and their fellows from the SS *Van Waerwijck* shipwreck were only a few weeks behind them.

The SS *Van Waerwijck* survivors re-entered Sumatra on 27 July 1944, following a route that all but mirrored many of the prisoners' first forays into this harsh but beautiful land. The main difference was this: now their journey's end would be the remote settlement of Pakan Baroe, surrounded on all sides by a seemingly endless expanse of swampy, malaria-infested jungle – as opposed to potential escape via an Allied ship from the port city of Padang, on the coast.

Upon arrival at Pakan Baroe, the *Van Waerwijck* survivors were met by the Japanese Camp Commandant, Lieutenant Miura, who informed them of their fate. To that point they'd been led to believe they were being sent to work on a 'fruit plantation'. Lieutenant Miura rapidly dispelled all such misapprehensions. The prisoners were to have the 'honour' of building a railway line for the Emperor of Japan. When finished, they would all receive a medal from the Emperor for their efforts.

From the muttered comments of those gathered to hear the Lieutenant speak, it was clear where they felt the Emperor could stick his medal. Luckily, neither Lieutenant Miura nor his fellow officers understood enough English to catch the under-the-breath remarks. The Japanese – and Koreans – in charge of the railway construction were experienced in such work, most coming direct from the infamous Thai–Burma railroad. They'd grown accustomed to seeing thousands of Allied POWs worked to their graves.

Peter Hartley had made it to Pakan Baroe, and before leaving River Valley Road Camp the Japanese guards had procured for him an English Bible. It was darkly fortuitous – for now more than ever before the make-do padre would need it, as he was called upon to officiate over the burial of the dead in their droves.

The *Van Waerwijck* survivors were placed temporarily in Camp 2, about five kilometres along the route of the proposed railroad. Camp 2 was supposedly the hospital camp, but it would soon become known as the 'Death Camp'. There they fell under the leadership of Wing Commander Patrick Slaney Davis, himself only recently arrived in Sumatra from the prison camps of neighbouring Java.

The Japanese had appointed Wing Commander Davis as the Allied Commander responsible for all POWs labouring on the railway. Tall, emaciated and with dark rings around his sunken eyes, he would forge for himself a somewhat conflicted reputation. While some of the POWs saw him as 'distant and aloof', he would earn unsurpassed renown for his fearlessness in the face of Japanese brutality, and for his courageous and wily negotiations to manipulate and compel the enemy on behalf of his human charges.

But the task facing this twenty-eight-year-old RAF officer was a near-impossible one. Wing Commander Davis would have thousands of Allied POWs under his purview, spread across a 220-kilometre stretch of railway traversing horrendous terrain which was served by as many as seventeen separate camps along its length. Out in the far jungle, where the word of the sadistic and brutal guards would be law, there was precious little the Wing Commander could do to protect his POWs.

After resting up in Camp 2 for just long enough to prove they were – in the eyes of the camp guards – 'fit', the shipwreck survivors were sent down the line into the jungle. Their destination was Camp 4, at Teratakboeloeh, some twenty-five kilometres along the route of the still barely nascent railway.

The Japanese had fitted an old diesel truck with steel railway wheels for shuttling prisoners to and from the camps. As the truck chugged its way along a perilously thin knife-cut slashed through the jungle, towing two railcars in its wake, the atmosphere among the prisoners was at its darkest. Like many of his fellows, Les Searle sensed that their fortunes had reached their very nadir.

All had heard stories of the terrible privations and degradations of the Thai–Burma railroad. There was every reason to fear that this would be as bad, and possibly worse. Les Searle was sure that ahead of them, to paraphrase Churchill, lay only 'blood, sweat and tears', but here they would be shed not to defend Britain from Nazi domination, but to further the war effort of the hated Japanese. To be used as slave-labour of the most expendable kind, and all to fuel the enemy war machine – what fate could be less enticing?

As the converted truck motored down the line, Judy and her fellows felt utterly forgotten – lost men in a lost world. Most had accepted that their chances of survival were at best slim. Perhaps the most awful thing of all was that to the outside world they were already 'dead'. They'd received not a postcard or letter from Britain, and the few official cards that the Japanese had handed out for them to write home had been burned on the camp fire. As they were sucked into this wilderness without end, a place utterly lost in time, the sense of being dead to the world was all-consuming.

Yet in the midst of this truck-load of the damned sat an emblematic figure – the erect and apparently undaunted figure of Judy. Dogs have long been bred to embody particular traits, one of the most important of which is to be 'man's best friend'. Their faithful companionship is a quality that we value in them possibly above all others. Over the millennia they have become extraordinarily well attuned to human emotions. In that cursed rail-truck rumbling through the wet, rotting heat and the suffocating riot of vegetation, Judy's companions could sense that she knew how they were feeling.

Her gaze fell upon them and it was full of a gentle warmth and empathy. One look from her long-suffering but caring eyes spoke volumes. It spoke of compassion and understanding. More than that, there was something in her panting, open-mouthed smile that was utterly maternal and reassuring. It was if she was saying, *I know how you're feeling; but trust me – we're going to be fine.* Judy's very presence among them, plus her indomitable spirit, gave these men the strength to face whatever lay ahead with shoulders just a little more squared.

Of course, Judy would be sharing the same fate as all, and indeed her chances of survival were arguably less than those of her fellow human prisoners. In the eyes of the railway guards she was a much-loathed but entirely edible dog. And as unspeakable brutality was unleashed upon her fellow companions she would feel compelled more than ever to protect them, which in turn would incur the guards' savagery and ire as never before.

That first night in Camp 4 provided a searing indication of things to come. Les Searle, Frank Williams, Jock Devani, Peter Hartley: each was allotted a slice of hard wooden shelf eighteen inches wide as his new 'home'. POW 81A-Medan got nothing, but she was happy enough to curl up at Frank's feet, content in the knowledge that she was still – miraculously – with the one she loved the most, plus their fellows. By the crude light of a home-made lantern – a scrap of rag floating in a tin of coconut oil – the appalling state of the hut in which they were billeted was clear to see.

Wall and roof were made of nothing more substantial than palm leaves bound to rough bamboo poles. Under the sleeping platforms tropical weeds reached out their hungry fingers, and the interior of the hut was thick with the voracious insect life that infested the jungle. A swarm of biting, blood-sucking flying things circled around the light, unidentified critters peeling off to left and right to attack one or other of the hut's human occupants. And from the jungle on every side the rhythmic *preep-preep-preep* of the insect chorus rang out deafeningly. Who could ever manage to sleep through all of this?

The air in the hut was thick with the stench of damp, water-logged wood and of rotting vegetation, to which was soon added the stink of unwashed sweat and of sleepless fear. Bullfrogs took up a chorus of damp, throaty croaks, calling to each other across the darkened jungle. Howls and shrieks of unknown beasts sent eerie echoes rebounding back and forth through the trees, like crazed laughter. At times they sounded spitting-distance close. It was mind-bending.

A warm bath; the feel of a clean towel; the caress of a loved one; the comfort of a home-cooked meal – all the norms of life seemed so impossibly distant.

On that first night the men felt as if they had only been asleep for a matter of seconds, when the harsh call of a bugle tore through the fetid hut. It was pitch-dark still, but no doubt this was their wake-up call. Life began at seven o'clock on the railway – but that was seven o'clock *Tokyo time*. Here in Sumatra it was four-thirty in the morning; the depths of the night. No matter: in the minds of their Japanese taskmasters everything from Imperial Japan was superior, and that included even time itself.

Responding to the blare of the bugle, figures stumbled about in the dark trying to find the hut doorway and get out on parade. There was a brutish simplicity to life here that reflected how low these men had fallen: there was no need to change into day clothes, for there were none; no need to pull on shoes, for most had none; no need to scrape a blade across angular features, for their thick, matted beards would have defeated all but the sharpest of cutthroat razors, and few had any shaving kit, less still the facilities with which to wash or to shave.

Under the ghostly light of the moon the prisoners lined up for parade, plus the obligatory head-count. Before them in the shadowy half-light lay the smoking silhouettes of oil drums with fires burning beneath them, signifying that breakfast was served. The first light of dawn was filtering into camp by the time each man received his one ladleful of grey-brown slop in battered tin or bowl. This was the entirety of breakfast – so-called 'ongle-ongle', a sludge of tapioca flour boiled in water, which set like tadpole jelly as it cooled.

Tapioca is made from the pounded root of the cassava plant, a kind of tropical potato. Devoid of sugar or salt, ongle-ongle was entirely tasteless and completely lacking in vitamins or sustenance, other than a small dose of carbohydrates. Yet this was the ration upon which these men were supposed to embark upon a full day's – invariably more than a full day's – hard labour on the railway.

The work gangs were divided by task. One group of men were sent deep into the jungle in front of the railhead, to build successive camps for the main body of labourers to follow. A second, larger body of men was tasked to raise the embankment for the railway itself – digging out sand or mud by hand, and carrying it in woven baskets to the rail route. This was some of the toughest work of all, and it was mostly given to the romushas – the local slave-labourers, most of whom hailed from the neighbouring island of Java – the living dead of the railroad.

Further gangs cut wood from the forest for the railway construction, or loaded sleepers and iron rails onto the rail-truck for movement forwards, or planted those sleepers on the raised embankment, or laid the rails on top of those, with a final gang bringing up the rear to hammer the rails in and fix them to the sleepers.

At Camp 4 the SS *Van Waerwijck* survivors were allotted their tasks as the Japanese Corporal in charge saw fit. Les Searle was one of the lucky ones: he joined a party of thirty-odd men being sent forward of the railhead to build a new jungle camp. Frank Williams – and Judy with him – got the grim task of unloading the iron rails from the rail-truck, carrying them up the line, and laying them on the sleepers.

From the very first the casual brutality and the apparent cheapness of life here was shocking. For Les Searle's party work was announced with the screamed command of 'Kura! Kura! Kura!' Few knew exactly how that word translated into English, but all understood its meaning: 'Oi!' Here on the hell railway it meant – *get to the storehouse now and grab your tools, or else!*

For the new camp the Japanese engineers had chosen a site near a stream, so it would be close to water. The first task was to clear the area of vegetation, after which piles of bamboo had to be cut and split battering-ram fashion, by lashing an axe-head to a tree and running the bamboo into it. This bamboo was as thick as a man's forearm, and it grew to sixty or more feet in height.

Lashed together with jungle vines, the bamboo lengths formed the frame upon which all huts were constructed, after which they were thatched with vegetation cut from the jungle. All of this required orders to be both issued by the guards and understood by the prisoners, and in a language that one side barely understood. Invariably, the prisoner who failed to catch on faced an outpouring of savagery.

Les Searle was sickened to witness one such prisoner get beaten to death with a shovel simply because he didn't understand Japanese. It was such a senseless way to die. Certainly, there had been beatings before now and terrible abuses – like the punishment cell back at Gloegoer One. But the casual and sadistic violence here would come to be a daily occurrence, one seemingly designed to snuff out the prisoners' lives as quickly as possible. It constituted an inhuman and murderous cruelty that many would never get inured to.

Being a Sergeant, Peter Hartley the makeshift padre was appointed the 'honcho' – head – of one of the labour gangs. The honcho had less work to do himself, but he was directly responsible to the guards for ensuring that those under him did whatever was required and exactly as instructed. As such the role was to be avoided at all costs, for the wrath of the guards more often fell upon the honcho's shoulders when anything was misunderstood or went wrong.

One morning Hartley saw a Japanese guard set about one of his men for no apparent reason. The guard swung a heavy shovel edge on, aimed at the man's head. It was a blow designed to maim terribly, if not to kill. The guard missed by a hair's breadth, but he recovered his balance and went for a second swing. Acting on instinct, Hartley reached out and grabbed the guard's arm, so preventing the shovel from hitting home. After that he had no memory of how he got back to the camp – only that he woke later heavily bandaged and scarred for life himself from a shovel's blade.

But conditions were the very worst for those tasked to labour at the railhead itself. At least Les Searle and his gang were able to work mostly in the shade of the deep jungle, but out on the open railway prisoners were exposed to the merciless sun. Just south of Camp 4 the projected route would cross the equator. Once the early morning mist had burned off the jungle, the temperature here was unbearable, especially for semi-naked men forced to work without a break for every hour of available daylight.

Frank Williams made up one in an eight-man rail-portage gang. First, the men had to line up in descending order of body height, so as to keep the crushing weight of the iron rail evenly distributed across their bony shoulders. On command, the rail was hoisted into the air. Moving with 300 kilograms of iron slung between two lines of starving, emaciated, semi-naked men, most of whom possessed no shoes, would be a perilous activity at the best of times. Doing so along a slimy, steaming, uneven rail embankment in the burning heat of the day was sheer murder.

The two lines of men had to march in sync, in an effort to prevent the load from becoming unbalanced, falling and crushing someone's feet. But newcomers to the rail-gangs – like Frank and his fellows – had yet to learn the tricks of the trade. Under the relentless sun the iron rails heated up to searing temperatures, and unless a pad of protective cloth was placed on the shoulder the bare metal would burn and scorch itself into bare skin. And always the work had to be done at the double – any 'slacking' being punished by kicks or blows from rifle butts.

A guard waited at the delivery end, where the rails were to be set into place on the sleepers in line with the ones behind. On a shouted word of command the dead weight would be lifted off shoulders and held in position, before being carefully lowered. The sleepers weren't anchored to the ground yet, and if they hadn't been laid true they could flip up with the weight of the rail, so injuring the nearest prisoners.

Each time a rail was successfully positioned, a stick was handed out to that gang's honcho. When the team had accumulated a dozen such sticks they were permitted to go for a cup of 'tea' – swamp water, boiled in an old oil drum at the side of the railhead and with a bare sprinkling of black tea leaves. No dawdling during the tea breaks was allowed, for a guard was always on hand to kick the team back to work.

At the approach of midday the sun hung directly overhead, huge and blindingly bright. It had become the rail-layers' single greatest enemy. The earthen embankment shimmered in the heat haze. It threw back the glare, dazzling unshielded eyes. The air itself seemed to be on fire, each breath dragged into heaving lungs in a painful inrush of burning. The merciless heat of the sun sucked moisture from unprotected skin and burned into bare heads and shoulders.

The midday meal offered a few precious minutes of relief. But all it consisted of was a single cup of boiled rice, levelled with a stick by the server, plus a watery soup made of cassava leaves. No sooner had the lunchtime ration been wolfed down than the work began again, and minds began to wander to the evening, when ravenous bodies might again be able to rest and to eat. As they lifted the heavy rails Frank and his fellows found themselves calling out time to the men opposite.

'Left, right, left, right, left, right . . .' they cried, as they marched under the crushing load.

If their movements were not completely synchronized, one bony shoulder would be going up as the rail came whipping down, with agonizing consequences.

As for Judy, she would be harrying back and forth just ahead of them, snuffling for anything of interest in the jungle to either side of the tracks. Every now and again she'd turn to check on the rail-carrying party, and to make sure the guards weren't causing any trouble. In spite of the bad company they were forced to keep, Judy loved being out in the jungle. There were all sorts of weird and wonderful creatures to sniff out, and in parts the thick vegetation was full of a dog's most favourite thing in the world – fresh bones.

Perhaps the hardest work of all was already done by the time the POWs reached the railhead – that of clearing the route and heaping up the embankment. In places this had involved moving massive quantities of earth to harden up the terrain where it was low-lying and boggy. In other places an army of human excavators had had to cut through steep ridges and hill-sides using only hand tools. That army consisted of tens of thousands of romushas, and already they were dying at the staggering rate of *one hundred or more per day*.

Unlike the Allied POWs, there were few if any camps constructed for the romushas. The POWs might be painfully underfed, but the romushas received zero rations from the Japanese. *Nothing.* And each night after a day's torturous slave-labour they were left to fend for themselves in the jungle. They were literally used as disposable beasts of burden – for excavation, clearance and transport – and they were discarded once they were too sick or too weak to move.

The bush was littered with the remains of the dead and the dying. Their corpses attracted scavengers: rats, giant iguana and tigers. Their skeletons lay everywhere, stripped of what little flesh had remained on their bodies at their hour of dying. For Judy, bones discarded in the jungle were always a temptation – especially as she received zero food rations herself.

But the main issue for Judy was: how she could shield her loved ones from suffering a similar fate to that of the romushas?

Chapter Nineteen

The rations doled out at the end of the first day's hard labour reinforced the dominant theme – starvation. The only difference was that the single cup of rice was heaped up, and the watery soup had some lumps of tapioca root and okra floating around in it. Just as the sustenance provided by the midday meal had been burned up in a few minutes lugging iron rails, so the evening's repast left every organ in the body crying out for more, and every prisoner dreading the long hours of the night that would be racked with hunger pains.

For Judy there was no ration, of course. Yet still Frank and his fellows were unwilling to see her starve. The emotional link between Frank and Judy had become so palpable that many of his fellows feared that if she sickened and died, so would he. Likewise, if Frank were the first to perish they were afraid that Judy would lose her will to live. It was as if man and dog shared a common life thread. So it was that a small portion of rice was set aside by those with the biggest hearts, so that a dog might also live.

Those in Judy's party – sailors, airmen and foot soldiers alike – had long learned a vital lesson, that the outer reflected the inner in any prisoner of war. Those POWs who had let their appearance go had very likely given up on the unequal struggle, and were heading for the 'hospital hut', from where few ever returned. It was vital to try to maintain a modicum of cleanliness and self-respect. But here in the ragged camps along the dark and serpentine railway, the chances of keeping body and mind together were slim indeed.

Camp 4's 'washing facilities' consisted of a slow and muddy river that wound through the forest. The only time allowed for washing was in the evening, and in order to reach the river the prisoners had to flit through the darkened forest, cross a swampy area balanced on a series of half-submerged tree-trunks, and clamber down to the slippery water's edge. It was one hell of an undertaking for men who had been worked half to death already, and had only bile and hunger in their bellies.

Such were the grim realities of their first days in the camps that fed the insatiable maw of the railway. With the Sumatran monsoons just around the corner, the SS *Van Waerwijck* survivors would learn soon enough that there was only one alternative to the muddy river-as-bathroom. It was to wait for a tropical downpour, when the heavens would open and the rain would sheet down, and to dash out into the curtains of pounding water for a makeshift 'shower'.

Perhaps inevitably, during those first nights in Camp 4 minds drifted to memories of the comparative 'plenty' of before: of scavenging in the Dutchmen's dustbins at Padang; of the magical arrival of the Red Cross parcels of Gloegoer One; of the miraculous delivery of the Bible at River Valley Road Camp. At Gloegoer, Frank Williams and his fellows had even felt able to set aside a little of their daily sugar ration – coarse, brown native sugar; but sugar nevertheless – to sabotage the Japanese war effort.

Whenever a guard's back had been turned they'd managed to slip a few spoonfuls of sugar into the drums of aviation fuel they were tasked to unload, plus the barrels of petrol. Popular folklore has it that sugar provides the perfect sweet revenge – that it can ruin a combustion engine. Sucked along the fuel lines it gets heated into a sludge that glues up the engine's innards. But the real killer is supposedly when the motor cools and the sucrose-slush cools with it, turning rock solid, thus fouling up the engine's arteries for good.

While those risking it at Gloegoer would have faced a spell in the punishment cell if caught, they were unlikely to have been beaten to death with a shovel on the spot. And whereas the idea of sacrificing a little sucrose to get back at the enemy was entirely feasible at Gloegoer, here on the railway sugar itself was soon to become an impossible dream.

After a long night of sleep tortured by hunger, the next day at Camp 4 began as had the previous – the only variation being what kind of overseer would be assigned to the work parties, for the infamy of the guards went before them. In Camp 4, as in most, the Koreans were by far the most sadistic and vicious. Korea forms part of the Asian continent abutting the islands of Japan, and in 1910 Korea – which was at that time still one country – had been annexed by Imperial Japan.

Most Koreans grew to despise the Japanese occupiers, and those who were recruited into the Japanese military were invariably the dregs of society: they had little to lose by throwing their lot in with the conquerors. Given a uniform, a gun and the power of life and death over their charges, there was little mercy to be expected from them. By contrast, some of the Japanese showed a grudging respect for the Allied POWs, who were at least fellow warriors and thus men of 'honour'.

In Camp 2 – the 'hospital' camp or death camp – Korean guards stubbed out their cigarettes on the faces of the sick and dying. Pencils and other sharp objects were rammed into patients' ears to perforate their eardrums. Every camp had its roster of monsters, whose nicknames betrayed the kind of savagery they excelled in: The Wrestler (a giant of a Korean who challenged the skeletal POWs to wrestling bouts); The Pig (a thickset monster and a brainless savage of a bully); The Basher (a name requiring no further explanation).

But perhaps the worst for those at Camp 4 was a dark-bearded Korean known as the 'Black Corporal', or more commonly as the 'Black Bastard'. At the railhead the work teams often ran out of sleepers, without which all work would grind to a halt. Some of the *Van Waerwijck* survivors were sent into the jungle, with orders to fell trees and to craft makeshift sleepers. Among their number was Engine Room Artificer (ERA) Leonard Williams, every inch a gunboat man and the most senior surviving rank from the *Dragonfly*'s original crew. Unfortunately, their overseer was to be the dreaded Black Corporal.

ERA Williams was a longstanding fan of Judy of Sussex. He'd been with her on the gunboats, been marooned with her on Shipwreck Island, drank the water she'd miraculously unearthed there, and shared her adventures ever since. He'd often refer to her as the prisoners' 'marvellous lifesaver', and 'a dog in a million' – and he meant every word. But there was only one Judy, and she wasn't able to be with everybody who might need her at all times.

Leonard Williams and a Lance Corporal Smith were in the process of chopping down a particularly large forest giant. The locals normally left such trees untouched, due to the menaces they harboured. Some had hairy undersides to their leaves, and as the tree shook under the assault of an axe the hairs would rain down, causing horribly red and itchy rashes. Other had been colonized by fire ants – a particularly aggressive and painful adversary.

The tree being the ants' home, they protect it ferociously. Within seconds they swarm all over the arms, legs and head of any axe-man, until his entire body feels as if it is on fire. The most hated of all the Korean guards had even fashioned his own torture using fire ants. His nickname was Porky, and he liked to tie a prisoner to a post, naked, and with their feet barely touching the ground. He'd then collect some fire ants, and place them in the man's mouth, nose and genitals, after which he'd leave the victim to fry in the sun and twist in the ants' venom.

In time, Porky would threaten to become Judy and her fellows' chief oppressor, as they were moved further down the railway. But for now the Black Corporal was the foremost worry. You had to be very careful when felling the giant trees that made up the deep jungle, and even more so when doing so under his baleful gaze.

For a moment Lance Corporal Smith must have let his mind wander from the task in hand, for he'd started to natter away to the prisoner at his side. The simple effrontery of *talking* was enough to raise the Black Corporal's murderous ire. As Smith swung his axe, the Korean guard smashed his rifle butt down onto the prisoner's unsuspecting head. Smith was thrown off balance by the powerful blow, and instead of hitting the tree as he had intended, he drove the axe deep into his own foot.

To the Black Corporal, Smith was just another of an endless series of victims to be thrown aside when their usefulness expired. A badly wounded British POW was useless for the task in hand, that of building the Emperor's railroad. The Black Corporal ordered the injured man – who was bleeding profusely – to be dumped by the railhead. The rail-truck that brought the men to work would carry him back to camp. Williams and his team did just that, and while in transit they managed to improvise a tourniquet for Smith's leg, to stop him bleeding to death.

It was seven o'clock that evening when they were finally done with their work, and the poor victim was still lying by the rail tracks. They managed to get him back to camp, but by that time Corporal Smith was at death's door. His life could only be saved by amputating the injured leg – a process that the British camp doctor had to perform with practically no surgical instruments, medicines, nor even any painkillers – and all because Smith had had the temerity to talk while working on the Black Corporal's labour gang.

This time, Judy hadn't been there to shield a fellow prisoner from the savagery of one of the guards, but the time was fast approaching when she would – and then battle would be joined.

As remarkable as it may seem, hardly any of the *Van Waerwijck* survivors had yet lost the will to fight, or their spirit of resistance. Their earlier shock and anguish at being brought to the hell of the Sumatra railway was starting to wear off. In its place there bubbled up the typical bulldog spirit and grim humour of British soldiers everywhere, and the burning desire to find a way to hit back at their oppressors in however small a way possible.

The men of the devil's own railway began to joke among themselves. They would form the Pakan Baroe rail workers' union, or the 'PBRWU' for short. All were welcome to the PBRWU regardless of nationality and of species: four-legged comrades were as appreciated as two-legged ones. They would demand higher wages, shorter working hours, better conditions and statutory holidays. They would have a canteen, a social club with bar, plus an annual conference with a few short speeches and the best beer and sandwiches money could buy.

Such humour served to raise morale, and with it the idea of sabotaging the railroad even as they built it began to crystallize in the minds of those most inclined to the spirit of resistance. Frank Williams, Leonard Williams, Jock Devani, Peter Hartley – all knew that by deliberately damaging the Japanese Emperor's railroad they were putting their lives in great danger, but they faced death on a daily basis anyway, so what of it. And in her own inimitable fashion Judy of Sussex was going to play a vital part in such a perilous enterprise.

The method of sabotage that Judy's gang hit upon was ingenious, yet simple. When not laying the iron rails they very often formed up the gang that fixed them to the sleepers. Normally, this was done using long bolts that fastened the iron to the wood below. However, because the Japanese were in an impossible hurry they opted to use massive metal spikes instead. The spikes were hammered through lugs in the rail and driven deep into the wood, using heavy sledgehammers.

Spike-driving under a burning sun proved backbreaking work, but it also offered a delicious opportunity for sabotage. The spikes were like large, blunt-ended chisels. If the 'chisel' edge was driven into the wood in line with the grain a weakness could be formed. Under the weight of a passing locomotive the wood might well split, breaking the sleeper in two. In the best-case scenario it might even cause a derailment.

Of course, this was something of a double-edged sword, for the workers rode the rail-truck to and from the railhead, so they would very likely be such sabotage's first victims. But so be it. Risks aside, a little sabotage was better than no sabotage at all.

Alternatively, when working as a sleeper-laying gang, Frank Williams and his team could choose to place the wooden cross-beams on a soft or uneven patch of ground, in the hope that those sleepers would be forced sideways by the weight of a speeding train, thus buckling the track.

Somehow, Judy always seemed to sense when such skulduggery was afoot. All her thoughts of hunting in the forest would be instantly forgotten. Instead, she'd take up the post of chief sentry, positioning herself between the saboteurs and the most likely direction of a guard's approach. From a distance she'd appear to be fast asleep, resting her belly on a sun-warmed sleeper and her head cradled on outstretched forepaws.

Yet long before a guard might be visible she'd have inched open one watchful eye. Moments later she'd be up on her haunches, ears pricked forward and nose hoovering up the scent as she detected The Wrestler, King Kong or the Black Corporal's approach. Just as soon as she was certain one of them was coming she'd let out her signature growl – the one that she only ever used to warn of the approach of a hated guard. And never had Judy of Sussex been known to cry wolf. If she growled you could be certain a Japanese or Korean was in-bound. Time and again it proved a lifesaver.

Yet it was nature itself that would prove to be the greatest collaborator in helping the saboteurs derail the devil's railway. As September 1944 blew around so the monsoon rains began to sweep down from the dark mountains, massive cloudbanks piling up into the heavens over raging tropical storms. The lightning flashed and the thunder roared, and with it the largest of the animals began to move, heading for the drier ground of the highlands.

The jungle was teeming with life. Judy had often sniffed out the spoor of what had to be a big cat around the railhead. At one time a group of prisoners had even been saved from a vicious beating by a huge pile of elephant droppings. They'd begged their guard's permission to go into the forest to answer the call of nature. In truth, they were desperate for a smoke. Just occasionally, a little tobacco found its way into the camps and Peter Hartley had found his Bible in correspondingly high demand, for the wafer-thin pages made excellent rolling paper!

There was a serious side to this craving for a smoke: for a while at least it dulled the pangs of hunger. The smoking party must have dawdled too long, for the guard came looking for them. Catching the scent of tobacco smoke, he'd demanded to see the evidence that they had indeed needed to defecate. It was then that one of the prisoners had spotted a pile of fresh elephant droppings. He'd pointed it out: *there – wasn't that proof enough?* The guard stared at it incredulously. 'Many-man *benjo*,' the prisoner explained – *many-man crap*. The guard scratched his head in amazement, before ordering the prisoners back to work.

As the rains came in ever more ferocious downpours, herds of elephants were on the march seeking drier ground. They soon ran into this strange linear formation that unexpectedly barred their path. They instinctively shied away. But there was no way around it and no way under it, and so the bull elephant leading the herd clambered up and over, with his charges following. In the process, sleepers weakened by sabotage-spikes were pounded into matchwood, and badly laid rails were left twisted and misaligned.

Other animals that had previously kept away were driven closer to the camps. One evening the Japanese guards yelled out a warning that a 'tiger' had got into their livestock and taken some of the 'Japanese pigs' (they kept livestock in an effort to supplement their own meagre rations). In spite of the prisoners' exhaustion, there were howls of laughter from the huts, and cries of 'Which guards have the tigers got, then?'

Yet in spite of such rare moments of levity the monsoons brought added suffering. The rain that fell like a waterfall from a dark sky was surprisingly icy. A sustained belt of storms drove down the temperature, rendering the nights chilly and damp. For healthy, well-fed adults equipped with proper sleeping gear this would have posed little problem. For starving, emaciated prisoner-slaves, who were lucky if they had the one blanket to sleep under, it could be a killer.

More than ever food became paramount. All conversations dealt with it; all dreams featured it; all schemes concerned how to get one's hands on it. Finding enough calories to drive out the cold and stave off death had become all-consuming. Anything even remotely edible would be caught and eaten, and the absolute master in all of this was an English Pointer called Judy of Sussex.

Not for her the pointing out of prey any more – or at least, not normally. Every day they were at the railhead, and every day she would be off in the jungle hopping, dancing and darting forward to snatch her prey. Often it was a snake. The Sumatran jungle abounded with them and many were highly venomous. She'd dance a duel with the serpent until it was exhausted and disoriented and then she'd dart forward to strike. She'd snatch it by the tail, shake the body violently like a whip until the neck snapped, then carry it proudly to lay at Frank's feet.

Judy proved such an accomplished hunter that even the guards learned to appreciate her talents. They did so because they might profit from it. Most prey she was happy to take on herself, but just occasionally she'd come across something that was too hot even for her to handle. There were wild pigs, deer, bears and tigers in the jungle. Whenever she encountered something of that size she'd start to bark ferociously. The guards soon learned what that signified. They'd come running with guns at the ready, in the hope of bagging some fresh meat. Of course, they'd keep the best for themselves, leaving the offal, the hide and the bones for the prisoners.

Each evening at Camp 4 dozens of 'hobo stoves' – small cans rigged up to cook in – would be balanced over wood fires. The prisoners would cluster around whatever brew was cooking, fanning the flames like witches at a cauldron. Snake proved to taste a lot like chicken and it made for delicious soup. But the jungle harboured a plethora of other exotic prey – giant cane rats, giant lizards, monkeys even – and nothing escaped a ravenous dog's attentions, or that of her half-starved human companions.

The prisoners themselves learned to scavenge during the midday work breaks. Fungi, roots, berries, fruit – anything that was remotely edible was harvested. From the Dutch – who had inhabited this wild country for generations – they learned about what was poisonous and what was best avoided. But it was from the romushas that they learned most about what was edible and could be eaten in an effort to supplement their starvation diet, and so up the chances of survival.

It was not long after the Black Corporal's murderous actions on the tree-felling gang that Leonard Williams found himself working at the railhead again, along with Judy and her fellows. He'd noticed that the dog that they all cherished hadn't been herself of late, and he'd surmised that she must have been bitten by a snake. He and his fellow prisoners were ordered to work alongside a group of romushas, clearing vegetation.

Leonard Williams watched them closely, hoping perhaps that they knew of a native cure for a dog suffering from a snake-bite. In the process he noticed how the romushas had these odd, bright green tips to their fingers. Via sign language, he managed to ask them why. By way of explanation one of the romushas took the British sailor to a certain shrub and ran his forefinger and thumb down the stem. The leaves peeled away, and he caught them in the bottom half of his hand.

The romusha mimed cooking and eating the leaves. There was iron in them, he explained. Iron was one of the many vitamins lacking in the prisoners' diet. Leonard quickly spread the word. The leaves didn't taste very pleasant, but even so from then on his fingers and those of his fellows would often be stained a bright green.

While plucking the odd leaf or mushroom was tolerated by the guards, barter with the locals was not. Shipwreck victims who had lost practically everything would at first sight seem to have little left to trade. But many still possessed a precious ring – perhaps an engagement ring, a much-cherished wedding ring, or even one handed down from parents – and gold has a value everywhere. The trouble was that any contact with the locals was strictly against the rules and would attract savage retribution if found out.

Again, in bartering along the railway Judy was to play a key role. She'd lope along beside the rail-laying gang, alert to anything of interest. Frank Williams had learned to read her body language quite perfectly, and one particular form of behaviour signalled that an opportunity for barter was at hand. Judy would stop and sniff at a bush, then stick her head and shoulders right into it, her rear end stock still apart from her long white tail swishing gently to and fro. This indicated that there was a local hiding in there, awaiting the opportunity to trade.

Jock Devani proved to be the arch bargain hunter, but once again the incredible thing was how such trade was conducted under the very noses of the guards, with both sides sticking to the terms of the deal. One day a prisoner offered up a battered gold ring. It was worn and broken, but it was still a band of gold. Over repeated passes by the bush that Judy had directed him to, a whispered deal was struck.

In exchange for the ring, the prisoner received what to him was a king's ransom in tobacco and coffee, plus a clutch of eggs and bananas to boot. Tobacco and coffee were highly valued because they were the unofficial tender of the camps. They could be traded with others for whatever they might have on offer – hopefully edible and nourishing food.

Barter and scavenging were vital to staving off starvation and death. Sabotage was vital to staving off the death of the spirit, after which the body would surely die. But all such activities were punishable by death in the eyes of the worst of the guards.

Skeletons labouring under a merciless sun – this had become the life of the *Van Waerwijck* shipwreck survivors. The weeks became months and the inhuman conditions took an increasing toll. As the prisoners weakened, normal bodily functions began to fail.

Yet illness was no excuse for avoiding the never-ending toil on the hell railroad.

Chapter Twenty

One sick prisoner, Tom 'Geordie' Scott, found himself on the rail-laying gang under the watchful eye of Judy, plus Frank and their fellows. But they were cursed with the very worst of guards as their overseer – the Black Corporal. In his emaciated, weakened condition Tom Scott was caught short for a pee. He was forced to do it right where he was standing, on the rail embankment. Unfortunately, the Black Corporal caught him in the act and flew into a terrible rage.

The prisoner has desecrated the Emperor's railroad, the Black Corporal howled. *For that he deserves to die!*

The enraged guard took his rifle in the one hand and brandishing a thick bamboo pole in the other he charged towards the guilty figure, murder in his eyes. Tom Scott stood there petrified, believing that his last hour on earth had come. His knees were shaking and he felt utterly unable to move. But the Black Corporal charged right past him and pounced instead on the gang's honcho, whose 'responsibility' it was to stop his prisoners from urinating on the esteemed Emperor's railroad.

The Black Corporal set about the honcho – a Sergeant in the RAF – with wild yells of rage, repeated blows from his bamboo pole slamming into head and shoulders. He was screaming invective, as he evoked the name of the Imperial Japanese

Armed Forces, plus His Imperial Majesty Emperor Hirohito himself, both of whom had been irrevocably insulted by such an act of wanton desecration.

Once he was sweaty and breathless from his exertions, the Black Corporal demanded that the honcho in turn beat the offending prisoner. British POW was forced to face up to British POW, as an enraged Korean guard continued to crack the honcho over the head, while demanding that he in turn punch the living daylights out of his fellow prisoner. The honcho made a few half-hearted swipes at Tom Scott, but this only served to enrage the Black Corporal still further, who redoubled his blows with the bamboo stave. In the Black Corporal's eyes the honcho was supposed to deliver his beating with the greatest possible enthusiasm, for he had the 'honour' of punishing the offender.

If something wasn't done soon to save him, the honcho was in danger of buckling under the blows, and everyone knew what happened to prisoners who went down. If you couldn't stand and take it, a guard like the Black Corporal would very likely proceed to kick you in the head until you lost all consciousness.

Tom Scott stepped closer to the bloodied, swaying victim. 'Hit me, Sarge!' he yelled. 'For Christ's sake, hit me!'

At last the RAF Sergeant began to respond as the Black Corporal intended, landing powerful blows on his fellow prisoner with clenched fists. Now it was Tom Scott who went staggering backwards under the onslaught. It was clear that someone was going to end up very badly injured or even dead, unless . . .

To one side of all of this a figure was watching. Judy was growing increasingly agitated. Her lips had curled into their signature snarl, and her eyes glowed red at the horrors she was being forced to witness, and her fellow prisoners forced to endure. All of a sudden she whirled around and darted off into the bush. Moments later there was that unmistakable bark – *aroof-roof-roof-roof-roof* – the one she reserved for when she came up against a large animal and needed a guard with a gun to help her bring it down.

Somehow, the fierce yelping seemed to cut through the Black Corporal's blind rage. The blood-smeared bamboo pole froze in mid-air. The Black Corporal glanced off into the bush, his brain trying to process the new information that was reaching him, and to make a choice between competing priorities: *to uphold the Emperor's honour by beating the prisoner to death, or to shoot the animal for meat?*

His sense of hunger clearly won over his sense of duty to the Emperor, for he dashed off into the bush in the direction of the barking, rifle at the ready. The two victims of the beating needed no further urging. Covered in blood and badly bruised as they were, they stumbled off towards the railhead, aiming to get as far away from the Black Corporal's savagery as humanly possible.

Of course, there was no large animal in the bush. There never had been. Judy had witnessed the savage beating, realized a diversion was needed to save the victims, and decided to provide it. She'd taken a major risk in doing so. A guard like the Black Corporal might opt to shoot her, once he realized that she'd put one over on him. But it was in her nature to come to the aid of the little guy, and here on the hell railway the under-dogs were very much her fellow prisoners of war.

This time at least Judy managed to dart through the jungle unseen. She gave the Black Corporal the slip and was soon back with her work gang. But here on the trans-Sumatran railroad it felt as if she was very much living on borrowed time. She had cheated death in so many ways and for so long, and eventually everybody's luck runs out. It always does some day.

Judy had first defied death as a tiny puppy when she'd snuck under the Shanghai kennel wire; she'd done so next as an adolescent dog tumbling from the deck of the *Gnat* into the Yangtze. She'd done so again in Hankow harbour, at the wrong end of a Japanese sentry's rifle; when trapped in the *Grasshopper*'s flooded mess-deck; when gnashed by a croco-dile's hungry jaws on the Indragiri River; when smuggled out of Gloegoer One in a sack, under pain of death; when posted out of the porthole of a sinking SS *Van Waerwijck*; and upon arrival in Singapore harbour, when she was spotted by Captain Nissi's murderous eye.

By anyone's reckoning she was eight lives down by now, and it was anyone's guess as to how much longer she could keep cheating death along this railroad steeped in blood.

As if to remind the SS *Van Waerwijck* survivors of all that they had endured, another group of shipwreck victims were about to join them. If anything their story was even darker and more replete with tragedy. In mid-September 1944 the Japanese cargo ship the *Junyo Maru* had set sail from neighbouring Java with around 2,300 Allied POWs crammed into its hold, plus some 4,200 romushas. All told there were some 6,500 slave-labourers packed into that rusting relic of a hell ship; more than nine times the number that had boarded the *Van Waerwijck*.

On 18 September 1944 the *Junyo Maru* was torpedoed by the British submarine HMS *Tradewind* off the coast of Sumatra. The ship, hit by two torpedoes, sank stern first in a matter of minutes. Some 5,600 POWs and romushas perished, making this the single greatest maritime disaster in terms of confirmed loss of life to this day.

On 22 September just over 400 of the *Junyo Maru* survivors turned up at Camp 4 to join their fellow shipwreck victims as slave-labour on the hell railroad. They stumbled into camp like a legion of the damned. Among their number was one Rouse Voisey, a young British soldier captured at Singapore. Rouse had already served as a POW-slave under the Japanese on the island of Haruku, in the Moluccas – the so-called 'Spice Islands' – hacking a runway out of the bare, dust-enshrouded, sandpaper-like coral terrain.

He had survived the *Junyo Maru* sinking by hanging onto a raft cobbled together from a glass-fronted cabinet that had floated free of the ship, with some planks lashed to its sides. He'd looped his arms around a length of rope and tied himself to the raft, as the only way to keep afloat. After forty-eight hours at sea the rope had rubbed him raw under the armpits, and he was hallucinating. He swore that he could see a vision of an earthly paradise calling him – bright lights ashore, with music and laughter and dancing. He was finally saved by a Japanese ship, on which he was brought to Pakan Baroe and the railway.

On seeing the terrible state of Rouse and the hundreds of other shipwreck victims at Camp 4, the 'established' POWs volunteered to take the heavier workload out on the railhead. The *Junyo Maru* survivors were given lighter duties around camp – fetching water, cutting wood for the fires and digging latrines. It gave Rouse plenty of time to get accustomed to his new surroundings, which in some ways resembled the jungle-clad island of Horuku that he'd come from. The one thing that amazed him about Camp 4, however, was that they had a dog.

Rouse, like Frank Williams, was an incurable devotee of animals, and even the recent hell that he'd suffered hadn't managed to kill his greatest love of all. But to see such a striking, comparatively healthy-looking and so clearly *edible* dog still alive here in this hellish camp – well, it defied all comprehension. How on earth her protectors had kept her from someone's cooking pot Rouse didn't know. It was such a daily struggle for survival that *anything* on four legs was being eaten, and that made Judy a walking miracle.

Back on Haruku, to his eternal regret, Rouse himself had eaten a cat. The gnawing hunger had driven all normal considerations out of a man's mind. Here on the hell railway prisoners were being forced to eat anything that came to hand. In Camp 4 every living thing had its price, no matter how small and seemingly inedible. A mouse was worth one guilder (the local Dutch currency), a rat two-and-a-half guilders, and in an extreme perversion of the natural order of things even flies had their price.

In the topsy-turvy, nightmare world of the prison camps, the Japanese had decreed that those too sick to work had to catch two hundred flies per day to receive their *half-ration* of food. The Japanese reasoned that sick men needed less sustenance, for they were doing no work – hence the reduced calories. Flies spread many of the diseases that were rife in the camps and so the sick were tasked with making themselves useful, and catching their allotted quota – or no food.

A sick man who needed proper rest had to buy his peace, by paying another to catch his allotment of flies. Some prisoners had even managed to cobble together ingenious fly-traps, so as to have excess bugs to sell. Others made a little money on the side by carving whatever a fellow prisoner might need – wooden-soled sandals being the most common item. Several of the *Junyo Maru* survivors had lost their dentures during the sinking. A certain prisoner became an expert at carving custom-made dentures out of lumps of hardwood cut from the forest.

Shortly after the *Junyo Maru* survivors joined the railway gangs, Les Searle was taken off the forward camp construction and rejoined his old colleagues. He was shocked by the scenes of horror that he found at the railhead. Dreadful skeletal figures heaved, toiled, sweated and groaned until the day was done, or they dropped where they worked. Those injured on the construction, or rendered too sick to continue, were sent to the dreaded Camp 2 – the so-called Death Camp.

In the terrible conditions and with such extreme levels of malnutrition, the slightest injury or cut failed to heal. Practically every prisoner had developed ghastly tropical ulcers, some as big as saucers. They ate flesh right through to the bone. Malaria, dysentery, beriberi and heat exhaustion were rife. But at Camp 2 there were few if any medical supplies, and in spite of Wing Commander Davis repeatedly pointing out to the Japanese how desperately they were needed, nothing was ever done.

In fact, the Japanese commanders appeared perfectly content for the injured and sick prisoners to die. This led many to suspect that the Sumatran railway was as much an extermination project as it was a construction one. By October 1944 POWs were dying at a rate of ten or more a day. On average, each kilometre of the cursed track claimed another twenty Allied lives, and those of some four hundred romushas.

Yet incredibly, some four months into their time on the railroad the spirit of the Allied POWs had yet to be broken. As Les Searle observed, 'We grimly joked and we encouraged each other. Somehow we hung on to the slender thread of life.' And as luck would have it a much-needed morale boost was about to fall into the laps of those slaving in that living hell.

As there had been at Gloegoer One, here on the hell railway there was a secret prisoners' radio. News was disseminated along the line as 'rumour', in an effort to disguise its timeliness and accuracy. The radio was thought to be operated by one of the officers, who had a hollow leg in which he kept it hidden. It was an aluminium prosthetic and supposedly each night after use the radio was dismantled, and the parts carefully wrapped up and hidden inside his leg!

It was towards the end of October 1944 when the rumour mill began churning big time, courtesy of the secret radio. Camp 4 had in it one of the few American POWs on the Sumatran railway, a Captain George Duffy. Like Frank Williams,

Duffy had served as a merchant seaman, until his vessel, *The American Leader*, was sunk by a German warship. Taken as a POW by the Germans, Captain Duffy had in turn been passed to the Japanese, which was how he had managed to end up in Camp 4. For Duffy and the handful of other Americans their nationality was about to become both a blessing and a curse here in the Sumatran jungle.

One night in the last week of October 1944 the Japanese guards held a drunken party. The *sake* – Japanese rice wine – was flowing, and wild celebrations and what sounded like victory songs echoed across the camp. In the morning the guards were boasting about a decisive Japanese naval victory. The battle of Leyte Gulf, the largest naval battle of the Second World War, had just taken place in the waters off the Philippines. According to the guards His Imperial Majesty's Navy had sunk a string of American warships, including one light aircraft carrier, two escort carriers, two destroyers and one destroyer escort.

The prisoners' clandestine radio soon gave the lie to the guards' claims. In truth, Leyte Gulf had constituted a crushing defeat for the Japanese. While the losses boasted about on the Allies' side were true, those suffered by the Japanese Navy were far worse. One fleet aircraft carrier, three light carriers, three battleships, ten cruisers and eleven destroyers were sunk, with the loss of 12,500 lives. Twenty-eight Japanese ships had gone down, as opposed to six Allied vessels.

As tight as it doubtless was, the Japanese propaganda machine couldn't keep such losses secret from her troops, not even those living in a world lost in time. The Japanese and

Korean guards couldn't fail to notice the changed atmosphere around the camps. The supposedly invincible Japanese war machine had suffered a major defeat at Leyte Gulf, and thanks to their clandestine radio the prisoner-slaves knew all about it.

It was around now that those at Camp 4 were moved to Camp 5, at Loeboeksakat, twenty-three kilometres further along the railway. The move was to keep pace with the onward progress of the railhead. Frank Williams, Les Searle, Padre Peter Hartley, plus Judy joined the relocation, as did the American Captain George Duffy. In Camp 5 were gathered together around one thousand POWs, the majority being Dutch, British and Australians, plus a handful of Americans – those who had achieved the seemingly impossible and crushed the Japanese forces at Leyte Gulf.

Over time George Duffy had taught himself to speak Dutch from the prisoners in the camps. As a result, he was often mistaken for a Dutchman. At Camp 5 he was appointed honcho for a group of mainly Australians, who were tasked with loading gravel into small, open-topped wagons along a spur track leading into the jungle. When the wagons were full the rail-truck would pull them up to the railhead to be emptied.

Duffy had allocated a place beneath a certain tree for those who became too ill to work. By mid-morning there were six skeletal figures lying in the shade, and he noticed a Japanese guard approaching them. He hurried over, explaining that the men were far too sick to work. This irritated the guard. He demanded if Duffy was an Australian. Duffy pretended that he didn't understand the question.

'English-ka?' the guard asked – *Are you English?*

Again Duffy shrugged his shoulders, acting as if he didn't understand.

'*Blanda-ka?*' the guard demanded – Blanda being the Malay word for Dutch.

When Duffy tried to claim that he still didn't understand, the guard went to unsling his rifle, a sure sign that the American was about to be clouted. Seizing the moment, Duffy leaned forward and stabbed the guard in the chest with his finger, before pointing at himself.

'America! America!' Duffy announced. '*American!*'

The guard's eyes practically popped out of his head. He clearly had no idea that the dreaded American enemy was anywhere near his railway. He waved Duffy back to his task, but word soon came down the line that the guard was working himself up into a towering fury. When the break came for midday meal the guard struck. On some imagined provocation he grabbed his rifle by the muzzle and swung it like a baseball bat into Duffy's torso, hitting him with all the force he could muster, just below the ribs. The blow was powerful enough to fell the American. Knowing he was in danger of being kicked unconscious, Duffy scrambled to his feet. He was knocked down two further times before the guard finally decided he had had enough.

After eating their lunchtime ration, some of his fellow prisoners tried to persuade Duffy not to go back on the work gang, for he was still in considerable pain and the guard clearly had it in for the American. But Duffy refused to back down, and oddly it was the Japanese guard who failed to return to work – so boosting the confidence of the American that, in defeat, the Japanese could be faced down.

A resurgent spirit of defiance swept through those Brits, Aussies and especially the handful of Americans resident in Camp 5. As the monsoon rains strengthened, and even as the floodwaters rose throughout the forest, so the prisoner-slaves were buoyed by further news of US victories emanating from the railway's secret radio.

Camp 3 was flooded out completely and had to be relocated. At Camp 5 work gangs were sent out to shore up the rail embankment near a swollen stream. All of a sudden a pair of forest buffalo appeared on the far bank of the watercourse. The nearest guard, a Korean, raised his rifle excitedly and fired. All his shots missed. Standing next to him was an American POW. Unable to bear the thought of so much potential food going to waste, he wrested the weapon off the unsuspecting Korean guard, dropped to one knee and fired two shots in quick succession, felling both animals.

The American thrust the rifle back at the startled guard, after which he proceeded to take charge of the meat-retrieval operation. He called for a rope, slung it around his skeletal frame, and waded into the fast-flowing water. Perhaps the Korean had heard of the Americans' military prowess, and was starting to worry about whether he'd chosen the right side in this war, but for whatever reason he let the American continue with his mission until both carcasses had been loaded aboard a rail wagon. That evening, in an unprecedented show of even-handedness, the buffalo meat was divided between guards and prisoners alike at Camp 5.

But such shows of solidarity were rare indeed, and they were destined to become rarer still as Imperial Japan's fortunes in the war worsened. Much as it might defy belief, as defeat stared them in the face the Japanese would drive their prisoner-slaves ever more remorselessly, forcing them to work ever longer hours on ever decreasing food rations – or die in the process.

Christmas Day 1944 was fast approaching, and for the SS *Van Waerwijck* survivors it would prove their darkest in nearly three years of captivity.

Chapter Twenty-one

Six months had passed since the SS *Van Waerwijck* survivors had first laid eyes on Pakan Baroe, the starting point for a railway whose progress would be measured in the futile sacrifice of so many lives. Repairs to the bridge damaged in the monsoon had been completed and a huge quantity of new sleepers and rails were being shipped down the line. It seemed as if the railway's taskmasters had redoubled their efforts to finish the line, come what may.

Such was their urgency to drive the iron rails onwards that Christmas was almost cancelled. But sensing a revolt among the POWs the Japanese Commander declared a rare 'holiday' for 25 December 1944. Each camp had two cookhouses, one for the guards and one for the POWs. The prisoners' kitchen was staffed up by those assigned to 'light duties' – more often than not the recovering sick or the walking wounded. On Christmas Eve 1944 rumours abounded that the cooks at Camp 5 had something special in store for the morrow.

Not for the first time all thoughts turned to food.

For weeks now the cooks had hoarded supplies, and sure enough that Christmas morning breakfast proved to be an impossible feast: five *ongol* balls per man, plus – joy of joys – coffee. *Ongol* balls were nothing more than the standard tapioca flour, but fried into 'doughnut holes' and flavoured with cinnamon and precious sugar. Lunch was more impossible still: *Ikan Daging, Nasi Goreng* and more coffee. *Nasi Goreng* is stir-fried rice, and *Ikan Daging* is a dish made of tiny dried and salted fish.

But it was dinner that proved the real miracle: from somewhere the cooks had rustled up brown bean stew, *Sambal Katjang* – hot peppered beans, plus *Trassie Balls* – pongy, but decidedly tasty golf-ball-sized nodules of fish-paste, and . . . more coffee. But while the feast was as fantastic as it was unforeseen, the increasingly jumpy and resentful Japanese guards still found a way to pour cold water on the festive spirit.

Christmas itself wasn't cancelled, but they decreed that *singing* was. There were to be no carols.

There would be no repeat for Judy of her yowling serenades at the Strong Toppers Club on the Hankow Bund, or even of her performance at the Gloegoer One Christmas pantomime, when she had howled out a wild accompaniment to the merry-making. As for Padre Peter Hartley, while he insisted on holding a Christmas service, by now he was so sick that he had been consigned to Camp 2, the hospital-cum-death camp, and it proved a sorry and joyless affair.

In Camp 5 the healthy joined the sick and immobile, cramming themselves into the hospital hut, where a service of sorts had been cobbled together. It was one in which carols would be played by musical instruments, in an effort to get around the singing ban. Wretched skeletal forms packed together on the rough-hewn sleeping platforms, spluttering lanterns throwing eerie shadows across the flimsy leaf-walls.

When the musicians struck up the tune for 'Silent Night, Holy Night' the hollow-eyed walking dead could no longer hold themselves back. The hut was filled with a soft, gentle humming to accompany the notes that the prisoners knew so well . . . but that was all. Not a voice could be raised in full song.

In spite of the day's feasting it turned many a man's stomach, and brought tears to many an eye. It beggared belief that in the upside-down crazed world of the hell railway the Japanese had even banned singing.

Four days later the entire population of Camp 5 was on the move again. This time they were heading for Camp 7, at Lipatkain, some fifty kilometres further along the railroad. Lipatkain actually translates as a rather poetic name for such a hellish location. It means 'fold in a sarong' – sarong being the traditional multicoloured wrap-around skirt worn by the natives of the region.

It was the kind of garment most of the shipwreck survivors would have given their eyeteeth for right now. Very few had any clothing left, apart from the single dirty grey loincloth that the Japanese issued to all prisoners.

Camp 7 proved similar to those that had gone before, only it was more remote, and the huts were even less substantial. There was a new accompaniment of guards, each of whom came with a peculiarly apt nickname: King Kong, Slap Happy, Howling Monkey, and so on. Among their number was Porky, the guard who specialized in using fire ants to torture his victims. Porky was the very worst – a stocky, fat beast of a man with near-invisible eyes, his buck teeth sticking out below a thick and fleshy upper lip. He radiated an evil cruelty, from his pockmarked wedge of a head to his flapping ears.

But as luck would have it, Porky was about to get his come-uppance, and before he could visit too much of his malice on the new arrivals at Camp 7. He was sent forward to Camp 9, the railway storage depot, to collect a new consignment of rails. In the midst of the loading a heavy storm blew up. Fork lightning stabbed out of the heavens. Fearing that the iron rails might attract a strike, all moved into the fringes of the jungle, to shelter.

Suddenly, there was an unearthly scream followed by a volley of rifle fire. Porky had been relieving himself in the jungle, only to be set upon by a tiger. He was badly mauled before his fellow guards managed to drive it off. He was evacuated down the line, to Pakan Baroe and the Japanese medical facilities based there, which in contrast to the POWs' hospital camp were lacking in very little. But Porky was too far gone by the time he got there, and he died from his injuries.

Upon hearing of his passing there were few at Camp 7 who shed a tear. In fact, Porky's death would inspire some remark-able mimicry. There were one or two prisoners who managed to perfect an utterly convincing tiger's snarl. Upon a dark, moon-less night they'd start their roaring, which would send the guards into paroxysms of worry. With the Japanese and Koreans refusing to leave their huts, the prisoners would sneak into the livestock pens and steal a chicken or a goat. All signs of the purloined animal would have utterly disappeared come morning. If any questions were asked, the livestock theft was blamed on the tiger that had supposedly visited during the night.

On 10 January 1945 the first direct signs of the turning fortunes of the war appeared in the skies above Sumatra. The sleek, silvery form of an American B29 Superfortress – a massive, long-range bomber that was super-advanced for its time – was spotted over Pakan Baroe, returning from a bombing run over the nearby port of Padang. Finally, this island lost in time was back on the radar of the Americans – the long-hoped-for liberators.

Few of the guards were able to ignore the fact that the American enemy was able to operate such a sophisticated warplane over the territory of the railway, and seemingly with impunity. Consequently, they started carrying tin hats and gas masks wherever they went . . . and the prisoner work parties started to catch hell.

The men would be woken by the seven o'clock bugle call, often not to return to camp until past ten o'clock at night. They'd be out on the work gangs for fourteen hours, being driven relentlessly by their merciless taskmasters. Yet the more the Japanese and Korean guards upped the pressure, the more ingenious became the methods the prisoners adopted to sabotage the thing they hated most – the railway that was killing so many of their fellows.

With Judy standing fierce guard, Frank Williams, Les Searle, Jock Devani and crew set about packing an earthen embankment that they were tasked to build with rotten wood, which they patched over with a thin layer of mud and sand.

From a distance it looked firm enough, but when a fire-snorting Hanomag locomotive tried to pass over it the embankment should crumble, sag and disintegrate into a mini-landslide.

In recent weeks Judy's gang had also learned how break off the heads of the iron spikes used to secure the rails to the sleepers. Hammering in just the head alone gave the impression that a spike was in place, whereas in truth there was nothing substantial holding the rail in place at all. This was a surefire way of causing havoc with the rail alignment, but being caught with a supply of de-headed spikes, or just the heads themselves, would be a one-way ticket to the grave.

More news of Allied victories percolated down the eighty-odd kilometres of the railroad to Camp 7. This time the secret radio, which was located at Pakan Baroe's Camp 1, was reporting British and Commonwealth forces in action, as Bill Slim's fabulous 14th Army drove the Japanese out of Burma. The guards were faced with news of defeat on several fronts, and at the hands of almost all of those nationalities that made up the prisoners in their charge.

Unsurprisingly, tensions were reaching fever pitch.

There were signs that the Japanese were moving vital materiel out of the area: tanks and field artillery, plus trucks loaded with military equipment, were driven east, on the first stage of the long journey to Singapore. It looked as if the Japanese might be preparing for a major defence of what had once been Britain's 'island fortress'. It was a delicious prospect for the POWs, so many of whom had been driven out of that island stronghold as a lost and vanquished army, a defeat for which they had for too long hung their heads in shame.

By February 1945 some 120 kilometres of the railway had been completed, but there remained 100 kilometres or more to go, and this final stretch would have to cut through the most difficult terrain of all – the Barisan Mountains. The death rate began to accelerate terribly. During March, forty-one POWs died at Camp 7 alone. The following month proved even worse. In the first seven days of April, twenty-five of the Camp 7 prisoners passed away. At such a rate all the POWs in Camp 7 would be dead inside ten months, and the death rate just kept rising.

The Allies might have been winning the war, but the worry of all in the camps was whether victory would come soon enough for any of them. There weren't enough able-bodied men to keep pace with the need for grave-diggers, pall-bearers or burial parties. Those on light duties gathering firewood to fuel the kitchens were redirected to carry bodies to the cemetery or to dig the graves themselves.

Yet somehow Judy and her core of fellow prisoners endured. Having clawed himself back from the dead – miraculously he had escaped Camp 2, the Death Camp, and returned to the railhead – Padre Peter Hartley found himself called upon to officiate at burials. During the nightmare weeks at Camp 2 the self-taught padre had come close to losing his faith even in God. Twice he'd been consigned to the Death House, the hut reserved for those who were destined for the other side.

The lack of medicines, painkillers, sterilizers or any proper surgical instruments at the Death Camp was so acute that the doctors had taught themselves to use fly maggots to treat tropical ulcers. They'd pack a wound with them, bind it with a rag, and let the grubs eat out the dead and infected flesh until the ulcer was rendered clean. With no malaria drugs, they'd also taught themselves to make a form of quinine using the bark of the Cinchona tree that grew abundantly in the surrounding jungle.

Ground up and formed into a paste, the foul-tasting and nauseating DIY medicine could be mixed with the morning ration of ongle-ongle to make it vaguely palatable. The nasty skin infection scabies was rife, and lice and fleas were everywhere. The DIY cure for scabies was to use raw sulphur dissolved in old motor oil. The oil was drained from the sumps of some disused Japanese Army trucks, and the dark, gluey 'ointment' had to be smeared over the body from head to toe, and left on for forty-eight hours.

Tropical ulcers, scabies, malaria, beriberi – Padre Peter Hartley had had just about every disease going. Yet still he had done the seemingly impossible and twice beat the Death House – and in large part thanks to Padre Patrick Rorke, a Roman Catholic priest who, oblivious to the risks of infection, had spent hours squatting on a homemade wooden stool, comforting the sick and dying, regardless of whether they were believers or not. That Catholic padre had helped restore Peter Hartley's faith, and given him the strength to perform his funeral duties, as the graveyards along the railroad swelled to overflowing.

Whenever a man died he was taken to the 'preparation area', where his body was washed and wrapped in a straw mat. If he possessed four good and able friends, they could request a formal burial service for that evening. If the dead man possessed too few able-bodied buddies, his body was laid outside the morgue. The wood-cutting party would pick it up after their lunch break – along with any other corpses, and invariably there were several – and carry it to the cemetery, whereupon the grave-diggers would bury it without ceremony. Such was the casual nature of death here on the bestial railway.

Losing life had become so commonplace that those who survived had become inured to the loss. But the Grim Reaper was also stalking the ranks of the enemy, as the Allies closed the noose around the Axis powers. Mid-April brought a rash of rumours flying along the railway. Via the secret radio there were reports of landings by Allied forces on Kyushu and Honshu, two of the main islands of Japan, plus news of the death of the American President, Franklin Delano Roosevelt (FDR), due to a stroke.

Roosevelt had indeed died, but in fact there had been no Allied landings on those Japanese islands. Even so, such rumours, which couldn't fail to reach the ears of the railroad's overseers, only served to up the ante still further. Unbelievably, on 23 April 1945 the Japanese ordered the POWs' daily rations be cut to 200 grams of tapioca flour and 270 grams of rice for workers, and less for those who were too ill to labour.

Four days later the death toll in Camp 7 was seventy-nine individuals for the month, and April wasn't even done yet. The prisoners were struggling to bury the dead fast enough as the sick and the incapacitated were starved into their graves.

In desperation, one of the camp doctors had an inspired idea. He figured they could secure a free and protein-rich source of food. He'd watched the camp chickens growing fat foraging around the latrines, and he realized they were eating maggots. In due course he and his fellows started to haul maggots out of the latrine by the bucket-load. They were washed, cooked and fed to those who were on death's door. For many this revolting but protein-rich diet would prove an absolute lifesaver.

But in the tense and febrile atmosphere of the railway there was little that could be done to defend against the guards' growing predations. Staring defeat in the face, their tolerance was at near-zero, while their aggression levels were soaring. At the same time – and perhaps sensing that the end was near at hand – Judy of Sussex was becoming ever more defensive of her flock.

Judy never had been able to hide her hatred of the guards, but now she seemed determined to do everything in her power to bring the worst of the savagery to an end – at least on her patch. Whereas once she had been content to dodge a kick levelled at her flank from a guard's jackboot, now she stood her ground. She'd crouch low, barely feet away from her adversary, muscles tensed and ready to spring, her jaws a row of yellowing fangs, and a deep snarl issuing forth from her throat. With blatant daring she'd face down the murderous bully. But Judy was up against those for whom a POW's life meant little, and even less so when the prisoner happened to be a dog. And with guards armed with rifles it was an unequal contest which, if continued, could only end badly for the dog that had for so long refused to die. Judy's fellows could sense that their railway hell had to end sometime soon now, and none could face losing their miracle dog at the eleventh hour.

Over the months that they'd been together Frank Williams had developed an unspoken, almost telepathic means of communication with Judy. He was always able to reach her. She seemed permanently on the prowl now, almost deliberately seeking confrontation with the guards, but at one word or a gentle touch from Frank her fierce red eyes would soften, and a potentially deadly altercation would be brought to an end.

Sensing the way the wind was blowing – that Judy was on a collision course with one or other of the guards – Frank developed a new 'trick' in an effort to protect her. It was a variation on the jump-into-the-sack routine that he had employed when smuggling her out of Gloegoer One and onto the SS *Van Waerwijck*. At the soft click of his fingers Judy would disappear into the thick jungle at the rail-side. There she would remain, utterly silent and obscured from view, until the coast was clear, whereupon a gentle whistle from the one she loved the most would bring her back to his side.

But the day inevitably came when Judy went a step too far. Frank Williams, Judy and her gang were out at the railhead, the prisoner-slaves as usual being driven to the brink of collapse by their guards. Perhaps there was nothing specific that had triggered it: in the dark spring of 1945 the railway's overseers needed little provocation to unleash their worst. For whatever reason one of the guards set upon a prisoner, screaming obscenities and slamming him around the head with the thick bamboo pole that he carried.

The prisoner's head whipped backward with the first blow. More followed. The horrific scene had become all too familiar, as a figure who was barely skin and bone staggered under the onslaught, and fought to remain upright. He flinched under an extra-powerful swipe and looked sure to lose his footing, when into his place sprang a four-legged champion. Snarling and barking with undisguised ferocity, her hackles raised and her eyes blazing, Judy stopped the guard in his tracks.

Hitherto all-powerful and utterly unprepared for any kind of resistance, for a moment the guard's brute confidence wavered. Then one hand lowered the bamboo pole, as the fingers of the other curled around his long-barrelled Arisaka rifle. Many a time Judy had witnessed the effects of these oddly shaped thunder-sticks. She's seen them fell any number of beasts that were far larger and more powerful than she was. She'd come to appreciate both the thunder-stick's range and its deadly effect.

Judy knew instinctively that it was time to make her getaway. In any case her work here was done: she'd turned the guard's aggression away from the prisoner onto her own gaunt and fleshless shoulders. In a flash she whipped herself around and fled, racing for the cover of the thick bush at the bottom of the embankment. But even as her thin white tail disappeared into the dense undergrowth, the guard levelled his rifle and took careful aim.

The long, bolt-action rifle barked once, the muzzle spitting fire. A bullet tore after the fleeting figure of the dog. It had all happened at such speed that Frank Williams and his fellows had been powerless to intercede. They were horrified at the prospect that the bullet might find its mark. Thankfully, there was no canine cry or yelp of pain from the undergrowth, and it looked as if Judy had yet again escaped unscathed.

Either that, or the bullet had killed Judy stone dead, silencing her for ever.

Chapter Twenty-two

It was a long time before Frank felt able to risk a faint, low whistle to call her back to his side. Several hours had passed and their work party had moved a good way along the embankment. When finally Judy came to him, Frank noticed that she was limping. He was shocked to discover an angry and bloodied furrow running across her shoulder. The 6.5mm bullet had missed Judy's head by a bare few inches, her heart by just a few more.

In the dark and malevolent world that was the hell railroad there was no reward fit for a dog as brave or as spirited as Judy, apart from Frank Williams's boundless affection and love. Yet Judy went ahead anyway and found one for herself. A while later there was a bout of sustained and excited barking from within the forest. Frank went to investigate, fearing that Judy might have come up against some animal too large for her to handle, or maybe even that same vicious guard.

Instead, he discovered his dog with an utterly goofy expression on her features, as she tried to drag the world's biggest bone into a hole that she had been digging. She paused for a moment to give him that look of hers – *guess what I've found?* – before going back to her task. It was so large it could only be an elephant bone, Frank reasoned.

It was certainly a reward big enough for a dog of Judy's enduring spirit, if only she could manage to get her jaws around it and give it a good gnaw.

On 29 April 1945 the guards marked the birthday of the Mikado, the Emperor of Imperial Japan, with a drunken feast. The POWs of Camp 7 – Judy of Sussex included – marked it with a grim milestone, the deaths of ten of their number on that day alone. To celebrate the 'auspicious' occasion, the Japanese deemed it worthy to give a gift of a pig to the camp inmates, but just as quickly they decided to take it back again, leaving only the head and guts for several hundred prisoners to share between them.

Bitter resentment and hatred seethed back and forth between the guards and the POWs. Across the camps the means of sabotage became ever more desperate and full of bile. Prisoners who were able to get access to the kitchen spat infected mucus into the drums of porridge being prepared for the guards. Faeces from the dysentery patients were even slipped into the guards' food.

One prisoner learned that the hairs from a certain type of bamboo bush were toxic, and would cause internal injuries if ingested. He slipped some into the coffee being prepared for a newly arrived team of Korean guards. Those who drank the poisoned brew became critically ill. Within days they were seen stumbling around camp with wet rags tied around their horribly inflamed throats. A week after they had drunk the evil brew they were removed and replaced en masse, for nothing could be allowed to impede the construction of the railway.

But by early May 1945 progress on the railway had slowed to a painful crawl. During the first two months of construction twenty kilometres had been built. Now, a few dozen yards were being completed a day. Weakened though they were, it wasn't the labour force that was failing: the prisoner-slaves were being driven even harder than ever. POWs and romushas alike were forced to work round-the-clock shifts, the railroad lit by smoky, spluttering rubber torches that drove away the darkness, so allowing the torture to continue even during the night hours.

It was the rugged terrain that was the problem. Teams of romushas were sent ahead to cut a route through the most impossible ground of all – the cavernous gorge lying ahead of Camp 11 at Moedikoelo, which was the 200-kilometre mark of the railroad. There the Kwantan River had cut deep through the heart of the Barisan Mountains. This was the very area that had claimed the life of W. Ijzerman, the Dutch engineer who had first surveyed this route, over fifty years before.

In May and June 1945 it would claim countless more lives.

For the surviving POWs emotions seesawed between ecstasy one moment and utter misery the next. Stunning news of Allied victories would raise the collective hope that surely this had to end soon, only for there to be no change in the camps or at the railhead. The lethal, soul-destroying and utterly futile work continued, day after night after day, seemingly without end. It was all so entirely pointless – for what could be the point of continuing with the railroad, when the Japanese were so clearly losing the war?

In the second week of May the seemingly indestructible Jock Devani was able to deliver the most incredible news yet. He returned to Judy's crew's hut after a hard day's labour, complete with a quantity of fresh fruit and vegetables hidden on his person. As he handed the unexpected goodies around the old faithfuls – Les Searle, Frank Williams and Judy among them – he revealed to man and dog that a special celebration was in order.

Somehow, Jock seemed always to be the first to hear of any news, and today he'd hit the jackpot. The war in Europe was over, he announced. Germany had surrendered, and all across Europe the Allies were victorious.

'And as a very special treat,' he added, 'I've brought you the fruit, to celebrate!'

He had liberated the fruit and vegetables from a Japanese grave, he explained. One of the camp guards had died recently, and in keeping with Japanese tradition and beliefs his fellows had piled his burial place high with fresh bananas, mangoes, cassava and the like.

'It would all have been gone by the morning any road,' Jock remarked, with a grin, 'and who is there more deserving than us lot?'

At first the prisoners refused to believe Jock's news. But of course, it was true: 8 May 1945 marked Victory in Europe – VE Day, although it had taken a while longer for the news to filter in through the POWs' clandestine radio, and to make its way down the accursed railway line to Camp 7.

With Nazi Germany having capitulated the rations deteriorated still further. There was less food handed out, and what there was seemed of an ever poorer quality. General Saito, the supreme Japanese Commander in South-east Asia, had issued orders to reduce the food rations of all Allied POWs. They were to be fed only enough to keep them functioning as prisoner-slaves. They were to be deliberately deprived of any levels of sustenance that might 'encourage' them to launch a prisoner uprising.

Just days prior to VE Day, the prisoners in Camp 7 had been forced to sign a similar declaration to that which they had already 'agreed' to at Gloegoer One – a second non-escape contract. It stated that under no circumstances would they attempt any kind of breakout. In short the Japanese position was characterized by paranoia and not a little schizophrenia: the prisoners needed to be worked like slaves to finish the railway, but starved to death to keep them docile, and incapable of rising up against their 'masters'.

By mid-June the overall camp leader on the Sumatran railroad, Wing Commander Slaney Davis, was complaining on a daily basis to his opposite number, Japanese Lieutenant Doi, in the most strident terms possible. He confronted the man with statistics, proving how the death rate among the POWs was spiralling out of control. Lieutenant Doi's response was that the Allied prisoners were deliberately trying to sabotage the railway, and the Japanese war effort, by dying.

Increasing numbers of terribly ill prisoners were arriving at Camp 2, but due to the Japanese quota system, wherein each camp had to deliver up a set roster of 'fit' workers, the newly arrived sick had to be replaced by a similar number of 're-covering' patients, who were sent back down to the railhead. Of course, there were few if any remotely healthy individuals left at Camp 2, and so the barely living were forced to rejoin the work gangs.

Then, in mid-June, Wing Commander Davis was presented with an ultimatum by his opposite number, which was as unexpected as it was perplexing. Lieutenant Doi declared an irrevocable finish-by date for the railway. No matter what, it had to be completed by 15 August 1945. Accordingly, every prisoner who was capable of getting to his feet was required to get out and work – no exceptions. In spite of the Wing Commander's spirited protests a roll call was held, and any skeletal, ghostly figure even vaguely capable of standing was marched off to the railhead.

In every prisoner's mind was now being nurtured the spark of hope that the end really was in sight, if only they could just hold on. But the flip side was the fear – rarely vocalized, but felt by all in the darkest corner of their hearts – that in truth the Japanese would allow none to survive; that none would be allowed to emerge from this hellish reality and reveal to the outside world all that had happened here. The fear was not without justification.

Work parties were formed to carry out an alternative 'light duty' task. Their orders were to dig air-raid shelters for the camps. The trouble was, they looked nothing like any such defences any Allied soldier had ever seen before. Air-raid shelters have to be dug narrow and deep, with high earthen walls, and to be roofed over by massive beams and thick layers of earth, to provide adequate protection from blast. What the work gangs were being made to dig along the railway were long, shallow troughs, with no roofs whatsoever.

It didn't take a genius to guess what in truth their intended use might be: they had all the right dimensions for mass-graves.

299

Most were situated near the parade grounds, where the men stood for their early morning and evening roll calls. It wasn't too hard to imagine prisoners being called out one morning, only to be machine-gunned where they stood, and their corpses rolled into the open pits.

Unbeknown to the POWs, orders had in fact been circulated to that very effect. The Japanese high command had decreed that should the Allies set foot on Imperial Japanese soil and threaten the Emperor, then all Allied POWs were to be executed. In other words, if a decisive ground assault was launched against Japanese territory by American and Allied troops, POWs across Japanese-held territory were to be slaughtered.

In these days that were rife with uncertainty, fear and desperation, Judy proved a rock around which many a prisoner could moor their restive spirits. Frank and Judy never seemed to spend a moment apart. Wherever he went she followed, and vice versa. Frank was down to around half his weight by now – as were Les Searle, Jock Devani, Pastor Peter Hartley and their other long-standing companions – but together Frank and Judy were somehow still able to remain strong.

Under the growing pressure there were those in Camp 7 who did crack. One was a young prisoner only ever known to all as 'Catcher'. Les Searle witnessed what happened when Catcher snapped. He was accused by a Korean guard of forgetting to salute and bow properly before him. Screaming abuse, the guard proceeded to beat the young British soldier about the head.

When Catcher flipped, he did so in spectacular fashion: the shocked guard fell back under a hail of blows from Catcher's bony fists, which were going like a windmill. Other guards came running to their fellow's aid. Catcher was quickly overpowered and carted away. The following morning his fate was clear for all to see: he had been placed in a tiny bamboo cage, which was positioned in full view at the edge of the parade ground.

Catcher would be locked in there come rain or shine for days on end. He would be starved, beaten and eaten alive by insects and vermin day and night. It was a fate that would drive many a lesser man to madness and beyond.

On 27 July 1945 a full year had passed since the *Van Waerwijck* survivors had arrived at the hell railway. Many had spent over a thousand days in captivity by now, and still their suffering wasn't at an end. As impossible as it might seem the iron rails snaking through the Kwantan gorge had all but reached the far side, though few liked to contemplate how many human lives – both Allied POWs and romushas – that dark valley had swallowed.

Batches of prisoners had even been shipped to the far end of the railway, to Moeara, so they could start the building from that end. The plan now was for the two ends of the line to meet somewhere in the middle. But practically everywhere were signs that the Allies were closing in. Seemingly a day didn't go by when a US B29 Superfortress wasn't spotted high over the camps. Many speculated that some at least were reconnaissance flights, helping plan a campaign to liberate all of South-east Asia, including Sumatra.

But no one could know for sure.

Chapter Twenty-three

Then came stunning news. In the second week of August 1945 a bizarre rumour flew up and down the railway. It would become an impossible to believe yet apparently genuine fact. An inconceivably powerful weapon had been dropped on the Japanese city of Hiroshima. Prisoners and guards alike spoke about it in hushed, disbelieving tones: this one American super-weapon had apparently flattened an entire city.

It was of course the atomic bomb codenamed Little Boy. Little Boy had been dropped by a US Air Force B29 Silverplate long-range bomber – one specially adapted to carry a nuclear weapon – on 6 August 1945. Three days after the bombing of Hiroshima a second atomic bomb, codenamed Fat Man, was dropped over Nagasaki. Together, the two bombs would end up killing as many as a quarter of a million people, but the alternative to using them – an invasion of Japan that would without doubt lead to many millions of casualties – had been equally unthinkable.

After the dropping of the atomic bombs the Japanese guards seemed lost in a blind frenzy. Work gangs were sent out having had only four hours' rest. Some spent days away from camp slaving on the railhead. American merchant seaman Captain George Duffy was one of those sent to the far end of the line, to

Camp 12. Rations were so non-existent there that he and fellow POWs resorted to eating rubber tree nuts, which are full of deadly cyanide. They had to be laboriously prepared – sliced, soaked, washed and dried – to render them edible. Prisoners who got the treatment wrong died a horrific death of cyanide poisoning.

With Judy's party at Camp 7, odd and unprecedented things seemed to be afoot. With no apparent explanation or ceremony Catcher, the young prisoner who'd turned on his abusive guard, was released from the bamboo cage. Barely able to stand, let alone walk, the mumbling, half-crazed figure was helped to the hospital hut. With food, proper medical treatment and rest Catcher's body might recover; it was his mind that no one could be certain about.

Then, from out of the blue it was announced that all prisoners were to have their heads and eyebrows shaved, to help rid the camp of lice. Rarely had the guards demonstrated the barest modicum of concern for the health of their human charges. Speculation was rife that the Japanese overseers were beginning to accept the inevitable: that the war was lost, that the camps eventually would be liberated, and that they in turn might be held accountable for the unspeakable horrors that had transpired here.

But for Frank, Judy and their cohorts, the lice-eradication programme was to have much darker consequences. The guards announced that Judy, the heroine of the trans-Sumatran railroad, was likewise lice-ridden, and she was to be handed over to them so she could be shot. Frank, Les, Jock and her many faithful fellows suspected that this was no lice-eradication measure. The guards were more or less starving alongside the prisoners. In their extreme hunger they had their eyes fixed on the hell railroad survivor extraordinaire – its mascot dog – for the pot.

It was now that Frank and Judy's disappearing act truly came into its own. Overnight, she became a ghost dog. At a flick of Frank's fingers she'd dart into the bush, and stay there for as long as her master deemed necessary – basically, until there wasn't a starving or a baleful-looking guard in sight, at which point Frank would whistle her out again. In this way man and dog managed to avoid the worst of the guards' famished predations, until the day upon which the impossible came to pass: the completion of the railway.

The final few days had been a madhouse. Torrential rains falling for hours on end had turned the last few hundred metres into a treacherous mudbath. Prisoners were whipped until they dropped. Sleep was snatched here and there at the railhead, and meals eaten three in one go, as the prisoner-slaves laboured around the clock. But on 14 August 1945 the two work gangs – one building from the Pakan Baroe end, the other from Moeara – finally met.

The next day, 15 August, dawned bright and sunny over the Sumatran jungle. The men in most of the camps were given a rare day off, apart from a handful that were required for a special duty at the juncture of the two ways. The atmosphere everywhere was utterly surreal. After the murderous pace of the past few days, and the widespread cursing and beatings – not to mention the deaths – the guards seemed abnormally chatty, even friendly.

The vast majority of the prisoners wondered what on earth this might mean. A few were tasked to attend a ceremony at the very point of the joining of the rails.

The prisoners were ordered to set up wooden tables and chairs, adjacent to the spot where the final rail lay waiting. Bottles of *sake* and biscuits were arranged on the table. The prisoners were told to make their way into the bush, and remain silent and out of sight. The ceremony began at close to midday. The sun was high and it was sweltering as a Japanese officer delivered a short speech. When he was done the last rail was lifted into place, and the officer produced a golden spike – one modelled along the lines of the iron ones used to anchor the entire railroad.

The golden spike was loosely tapped into place, whereupon a Japanese General was handed the ceremonial hammer and invited to hit it home. That done, there was a reverential silence for several seconds, after which the assembled party took up the formal cry of *banzai*: '*Banzai Nippon! Banzai Nippon! Banzai Nippon!*'

Banzai translates as meaning 'ten thousand years' and it was both a traditional battle cry and a call of respect to the Emperor.

The Japanese officers' words echoed across to the prisoners crouched in the bush, but they seemed to lack a certain conviction. It was little wonder. At 00.00 hours that very morning Imperial Japan had surrendered to the Allies. On the day of completion of the trans-Sumatran railway – one laid in suffering, degradation and blood – the war was already over. As they nibbled on their biscuits and sipped their *sake*, the Japanese officers were aware of this, yet still they had proceeded with the railroad's formal opening ceremony.

Of course, none of the POWs crouched in the bush could know that the war was over, and the Japanese officers weren't about to tell them. All along the railway the guards were keeping very quiet. At their camp, Judy and her fellows knew that all was not as it had been and that change was afoot – but what exactly the nature of that change might be few could tell.

That evening the camp commanders up and down the line made a similar kind of announcement: the railway was finished, the prisoners could rest, and rations would be increased once the Japanese had the supplies to make it happen. And no one was permitted to leave the camps.

Days passed in this weird, otherworldly kind of limbo. There were signs everywhere that the war had to be over, and the rumour mill was working overtime. In several places the Japanese were seen to light huge bonfires, as they sought to burn all the camp documents. British prisoner and *Junyo Maru* survivor Rouse Voisey spotted them doing so in his camp. Were they destroying incriminating evidence? he wondered. It certainly looked that way.

The daily rice ration – the Japanese still had ample supplies of rice, it seemed – was increased to 2,600 grams a day, ten times the starvation ration of the last few weeks. It was too much food for most, whose stomachs were shrunken and shrivelled. Padre Peter Hartley could barely believe it when a consignment of Japanese Red Cross parcels arrived, along with the massively increased food rations. There was little of use in the parcels, but surely it had to signify that the war was over and that the prisoners were finally free?

*

Fittingly, in Judy's camp it would be the miracle survivor dog who finally barked the good news, confirming that liberation had come for those who had survived over a year on the railway.

On the morning of 4 September 1945 the prisoners awoke to another day in limbo, only to hear a very strange sound indeed: it was a loud, insistent and somehow clearly joyous round of barking. Judy had spent the last few days living as a ghost dog, only risking the occasional appearance whenever Frank whistled for her. But this morning, she was barking her head off unreservedly.

Judy had long learned to keep her counsel in the POW camps. Barking had only ever served to attract unwanted attention from those who might seek to do her harm. But this morning, as the sun rose above the surrounding jungle, she was truly letting rip. Frank hurried out to quieten her down, but he quickly realized that all was somehow different about the camp. No matter where he looked there didn't seem to be a Japanese or a Korean guard in sight.

It was then that he understood just what it was that Judy was so joyously barking over. She approached Frank accompanied by two heavily armed figures. They were dressed in the smart uniform of British Royal Marines. Judy cavorted around them, knowing instinctively that the good guys were here at last.

Four parachutists commanded by a Major Gideon Jacobs had been dropped from a Liberator long-range bomber near the location of their former prison camp, Gloegoer One. From there they had made their way to Pakan Baroe, and up the length of the railway. Incredibly, the Allies had had not the slightest idea that the trans-Sumatran railroad had been under construction until Major Jacobs had parachuted in to discover it.

As skeletal prisoners tumbled out of their huts to greet the newly arrived troops of liberation – some with wild cries of joy, others with cheers and laughter, but many with a quiet and uncomprehending lethargy – makeshift Dutch and British flags were raised above the camp over which only the Japanese rising sun had ever flown.

But even now news of the longed-for liberation proved too much for some. Even now some would prove too debilitated by their long ordeal to survive. Tragically, some who had fought so doggedly to make it through would perish during these final days, as the camps of the trans-Sumatran railroad were dismantled. Yet for Frank Williams, Les Searle, Jock Devani, Peter Hartley, Rouse Voisey and George Duffy – as for so many other Allied prisoners – this day marked the deliverance for which they had so long dreamed. And for Judy of Sussex, the much-loved dog of the hell railroad, this was the start of her long journey home.

Perhaps it was inevitable, but along the way there would be one last hurdle, one final attempt to separate man from dog. When it finally came time for Judy and her fellows to set sail for England, they would be ordered to depart via Singapore on the troopship *Antenor*. For the first time in Judy's life – she was approaching ten years old by now – she was about to board a ship that wasn't under threat of river piracy, or bombing or torpedoing by the enemy. But that was only if she was going to make it aboard.

When Frank received his embarkation papers, a footnote read: 'The following regulations will be strictly enforced: no dogs, birds or pets of any kind to be taken aboard.'

Frank gave Judy a fond look, where she was curled up at his feet. 'No dogs allowed, old girl,' he murmured, softly. 'Only ex-POWs: and that, of course, means you.'

There was no way that Frank was willing to even contemplate abiding by the order, and neither were Judy's fellow ex-prisoners. This time, no sack was required to hide her from a murderous Captain Nissi, but still the operation to smuggle Judy aboard the *Antenor* was organized with the precision, flair and efficiency without which these resourceful and brave men might never have saved her from a long string of dangers.

Frank waited until the gangway leading onto the ship was largely clear. Leaving Judy hidden between some rows of kitbags, he went aboard, trying to act as casually as he could. Les Searle and the others followed, but they paused at the top of the gangplank and fell into apparently easy conversation with the staff supervising the boarding.

Once all were seemingly engrossed in the chat, Frank gave a faint whistle in the direction of the dockside. In a flash a streak of liver-and-white had sped up the gangplank and Frank and his fellows were able to welcome Judy aboard.

Finally, the dog that had so many times snuck under the wire was homeward bound.

Epilogue

During their long voyage to Great Britain Judy was helped by several trusted fellow POWs and others, most notably one of the ship's crew working in the galley. An irrepressible dog-lover, he provided her with all her meals prepared by his own loving hands. But man and dog's trials were far from over.

Upon docking at Liverpool, Judy had to endure six months' separation from Frank and fellow POWs, in keeping with Britain's strict quarantine laws. Unsurprisingly, Judy was bewildered and upset to be separated from her fellows at the Liverpool docks, where she was taken to the nearby Hackbridge Quarantine Kennels. But the subsequent reunion with Frank was made all the sweeter in that by then, Judy the POW dog had become something of a national sensation.

Reunited, man and dog were feted by the British media and military alike. Judy emerged from the Hackbridge Kennels to a joyous reception from the waiting public. As flashbulbs popped the now-very-famous POW dog that had survived the hell railway warmed to the cheering crowds. Judy even enjoyed the distinction of being 'interviewed' on a special Victory Day BBC radio programme, in which her barks were broadcast to grateful listeners all across the nation. No one seemed to complain that they couldn't understand what this hero dog had to say.

Judy visited London and was enrolled in the Returned Prisoners of War Association as its sole canine member. She was presented at Wembley stadium as one of four war dogs – the 'Stars of Blitz and Battlefront' – and featured on the BBC. She was made an official mascot of the RAF, and given a flying jacket embroidered with the RAF's crest to wear. Frank Williams won the White Cross of Saint Giles, the highest honour awarded to humans by the animal charity the PDSA, and Judy won the PDSA's Dickin Medal, more commonly known as the 'Animal VC'.

The press ran headlines typified by the following: *Gunboat Judy saves lives – wins medal and life pension*. Judy was even given a generous grant from the venerable animal charity the Tailwaggers Club, so she could 'enjoy life in peace for the rest of her days'. Proudly sporting her Dickin Medal – inscribed with the motto 'We also serve' – Judy and Frank toured schools, children's hospitals and other venues, as the great British public feted a truly deserving four-legged heroine of the war.

Judy's uniquely apposite Dickin Medal inscription reads:

For magnificent courage and endurance in Japanese prison camps which helped to maintain morale among her fellow prisoners, and also for saving many lives through her intelligence and watchfulness.

Saving lives through her intelligence and watchfulness indeed. Judy DM had saved the lives of her fellows – both soldiers and civilians – on so many occasions during her long journey from the Yangtze River patrols to the hell railway, and back again.

*

The ill-fated railway that had been forced through the Sumatran jungles at such a terrible cost in human life was completed the day Japan surrendered to the Allies. What had driven the Japanese overseers to force it to completion in the face of their inevitable defeat remains a mystery. All the research that I have carried out seems to offer no explanation for this pointless and grossly inhumane imperative, other than that it was pursued in an effort to prevent losing face – something which was seen as being of the utmost importance in the Japanese culture of the time. If the last few weeks of frenetic and murderous construction were pursued in that name, the waste of thousands of Allied and Indonesian lives is all the more reprehensible.

The railway, completed or not, was never going to serve the Japanese war effort, for even as they pushed the prisoner-slaves to exhaustion and death, it was crumbling all around them. There are detractors of the use of the atomic bombs at Hiroshima and Nagasaki. They need to remember this: without their use, the unspeakable suffering of the Allied POWs and the local forced-labourers held by the Japanese would have lasted far longer than it did, at a cost of countless more lives. Indeed, as documents have subsequently shown, the Japanese camp overseers had orders to execute all the POWs should the Allies set foot on Japanese soil and 'threaten the Emperor'.

In many of the trans-Sumatran railroad camps prisoners had been forced to dig what were clearly planned to be their own mass graves. This could have been for no other reason than preparation for their mass execution, should the feared Allied invasion of the Japanese motherland have ensued. The use of the atomic bombs ensured that such an invasion wasn't necessary. The bombs dropped on Hiroshima and Nagasaki forced the Japanese to the negotiating table and to sue for peace – a peace that would grant those POWs strong enough to survive the first few weeks of liberation their right to go home.

As to the railway itself, its impotence and futility was demonstrated most starkly in the months immediately following the end of the war. It was never put to use. After the departure of the vanquished Japanese no locomotives ever ran on that ill-fated railway. Not a year after the Japanese surrender many of the bridges along its route had been washed away in the monsoons, and the iron rails were already being ripped up and sold for scrap.

In 1951 Indonesia's national railway authority did carry out an inspection of the Pakan Baroe to Moeara railway, or at least what remained of it. The recommendation of that study was that only the section from Pakan Baroe to Logan – the first 100 kilometres – was worth saving, a length that would give access to the Sapoe and Karoe coal mines that the Japanese had been so eager to exploit for their war effort.

That recommendation was never acted upon, and today most Indonesians have no recollection of the railway ever having existed. They have no idea how the rusting hulks of locomotives lying in the jungle or in village clearings – those that their children use as makeshift climbing frames – ever came to be there. Nearly all traces of the railway that was hacked and hewn from jungle, cliff-face, rock and mud with the loss of so many lives have vanished.

The railway has been reclaimed by the jungle, along with so many of the bones of those who perished while trying to build it. One fact often ignored by those relating its history is the appalling death rate suffered by the romushas, the local slave-labourers who were forced to work on the railroad alongside the Allied POWs. It is over 80 per cent, bringing it very close to that of the German concentration camps.

Absolutely accurate numbers will never be known, but the Pakan Baroe to Moeara railroad claimed the lives of some 700 British, Dutch, American, Australian and other Allied POWs, and over *eighty thousand* Indonesians. That doesn't include some eighteen hundred Allied POWs who drowned when their transport ships the SS *Van Waerwijck* and the *Junyo Maru* were torpedoed and sunk off the Sumatran coast. All of that untold suffering by so many prisoner-slaves had been for naught.

Petty Officer White – the seaman who had rescued Judy from the trap of the *Grasshopper*'s flooded mess-deck, after the ship had been run aground – did complete his epic escape. It took him and his fellows several weeks by small boat to India, but by a process of dead-reckoning and navigating by the stars they did make it to friendly landfall, and just a few dozen kilometres from the coastal city of Madras. By then of course the main body of survivors from the *Grasshopper* had been taken captive by the Japanese, Judy included.

After the war Judy and Frank spent two happy years in his native Portsmouth. He'd often take her to his local, the

Stamshaw Hotel, and regale fellow drinkers with tales of her adventures. But he remained reluctant ever to speak about his own experiences as a POW. The one thing he did discuss was how Judy contributed to saving his own and so many other lives in the camps.

'The greatest way . . . was giving me a reason to live. All I had to do was look at her and into those weary, bloodshot eyes and I would ask myself: What would happen to her if I died? I had to keep going. Even if it meant waiting for a miracle.'

By 1948 Frank Williams had grown restless living in Britain and he sought wider horizons. He accepted the offer of a job with the Overseas Food Corporation, in Tanzania, East Africa, running a large groundnut (or 'peanuts' as we more commonly call them) plantation. Judy, of course, was going with him – and so the man and dog who had survived so much in foreign climes were once again headed overseas.

Unsurprisingly for a dog so well-travelled, Judy thrilled to their new adventure. She had her third and final litter of pups in Tanzania, and she grew adept at chasing after the exotic East African wildlife, all except for the baboons. They'd form a troop and dance and cavort around her, daring the distinguished-looking liver-and-white English Pointer to single out one of them to chase. More often than not she found it so beguiling that she'd try to dash after them all, and the entire troop would spring away, chattering and laughing.

But there were bigger and wilder things out there in the bush than playful baboons. One evening Abdul, Frank's houseboy, left a tin bath full of water outside their house on the plantation, intending to empty it the following morning. In the depths of the night Frank and Judy were woken by the sound of loud slurping coming from outside their window. Judy rushed to investigate, only to find an enormous, muddy-brown animal sucking up the last of the bath water. The elephant took precious little notice of Judy's spirited barking and continued to drain the last of the suds.

Only when Frank joined his dog shooing the massive beast away did the elephant finally decide to leave, its thirst well and truly slaked. But Judy remained incensed. She grabbed the tin bath – now noticeably lighter – and started to drag it into the house. Frank tried to object that there was nothing much left in the bath to save, but Judy was having none of it. Once the tin trough was safely inside, she returned to bark at the receding bulk of the elephant, which was fading into the silvery shadows of the moonlit African plain. Elephant gone, she curled up in the doorway and settled down to sleep, keeping one eye on her master's precious bathtub.

Frank's plantation work took him by air all across Tanzania and wider East Africa. He always tried to take Judy, his faithful companion, with him. On one such flight he was surprised to see her happily squeeze herself into the onboard kennel, a process more normally met by fierce barking and resistance. Frank wondered why she had gone in so easily this time. He was mystified.

Upon touchdown he got his answer. The top of Judy's cage had an opening large enough for her to poke her head through. Above her had been packed a cargo of freshly killed game. Judy had had a veritable in-flight feast, and much of the meat had been wolfed down.

It seemed that the ultimate survivor dog had never forgotten the lesson she had learned in the Japanese POW camps: if there was food to be had she was best to grab it, and hang the consequences.

In February 1950 – with Judy fourteen years old – Frank took her on a work trip in their jeep. There had been heavy rains and he didn't want to stray too far from their place of abode on the plantation, near the town of Nachingwea. After the short drive Frank and his workers proceeded to make a camp in the bush, as Judy did what she always did when they were out in the field – darting off to scout for any danger.

At first Frank wasn't particularly worried. But when three hours had passed and still Judy was nowhere to be seen, he got together a search party. His workers joined Frank in whistling and calling out her name, but still Judy wouldn't come. With dusk approaching, Frank was getting seriously worried. Then one of his local foremen, Abdullah, discovered some tracks in the bush, which were clearly those of the missing dog.

Abdullah used his native tracking skills to follow her, with Frank at his shoulder. Frank became all the more alarmed when they noticed a leopard's tracks apparently shadowing those of his dog. They tracked her for miles along a narrow path that led to an isolated village, but when they got there no one had seen any sign of the dog. Her tracks appeared to peter out. Judy, it seemed, had disappeared.

Frank posted a reward for 500 shillings – a considerable amount of money in what was then pre-independence Tanzania – for his dog's safe return, and sent messages out to all the surrounding villages. Three days passed and there was still no news. Frank was getting desperate when, on the afternoon of the fourth day, a local ran into the camp and announced to Abdullah that Judy had been found. On hearing the news, Frank and Abdullah jumped aboard their jeep, with the local acting as guide to take them to the missing dog.

A village elder received them and took them to a hut. He opened the door and there was Judy. But so exhausted was she from her ordeal that she could barely stand. Seeing Frank, she struggled to her feet, wagged her tail weakly and promptly collapsed again. Wrapped in blankets, Judy was driven back to their homestead. There they treated her by removing the hundreds of cattle ticks that had attached themselves to her during her long sojourn in the bush, bathing her wounds and dousing them with disinfectant.

Judy ate the food Frank gave her, seemed much comforted and fell into a deep sleep. Over the ensuing days she gained strength and Frank hoped the worst was past. But on the night of 16 February – some days after her disappearance – Judy began to cry and whine. Frank sat with her during the hours of darkness, but whenever she was awake Judy cried and was clearly in pain. Come sunrise she was unable to stand and in obvious discomfort.

Frank carried her through the streets of Nachingwea to the hospital, his dog still crying as she lay in his arms. Doctor Jenkins, the English surgeon at the hospital, found she had a mammary tumour and operated immediately. At first the operation seemed to be a success, but a few hours later the dog who had survived so much succumbed to a raging tetanus infection.

She was still trying to fight but she was in obvious pain, and it was clear to the surgeon that she was fading fast.

'Let me end it, Frank,' he suggested.

Wordlessly Frank nodded his acquiescence, and on 17 February 1950 at 5.00 p.m. Tanzanian time Judy was put to sleep.

Judy's body was wrapped in the Royal Air Force jacket that she'd been given when she was made an official mascot of the RAF, and laid in a simple wooden coffin. She was buried in a grave not far from the home she had shared with Frank in Nachingwea. Using pieces of white stone collected in the bush, Frank and his workers fashioned a polished sarcophagus over the grave, topped off with a plaque that reads:

In memory of Judy DM Canine VC
Breed English Pointer
Born Shanghai February 1936, died February 1950.
Wounded 14 February 1942.
Bombed and sunk HMS Grasshopper
Lingga Archipelago 14 February 1942.
Torpedoed SS Van Waerwijck
Malacca Straits 26 June 1943.
Japanese Prisoner of War March 1942–August 1945.
China Ceylon Java England Egypt Burma
Singapore Malaya Sumatra E Africa.
They Also Served.

A Short Bibliography

Ambushed Under the Southern Cross – the Making of an American Merchant Marine Officer and His Ensuing Saga of Courage and Survival, Capt. George W. Duffy. An American merchant navy Captain's memoir of his ship being sunk by a German raider and the Japanese POW camps spread over Java, Singapore and Sumatra that he survived.

Beyond the Bamboo Screen – Scottish Prisoners of War Under the Japanese, Tom McGowran, OBE. A compilation of articles and stories from the Scottish Far East Prisoner of War Association.

Escape to Captivity, Peter Hartley. The story of a young Sergeant in the British Army who refuses to surrender at Singapore, and ends up being captured by the Japanese and imprisoned on Sumatra.

Marines Don't Hold Their Horses, Ian Skidmore. The story of Colonel Alan Warren, CBE, DSC, who having helped many escape the Japanese via Sumatra ended up as a prisoner of war himself.

Prisoner in Nippon, Ray S. Stubbs. Tells the story of the author's retreat from Singapore and capture by the Japanese and the years he spent as a prisoner of war.

Prisoners in Java – Accounts by Allied Prisoners of War in the Far East (1942–1945) Captured in Java. As the title suggests, the book contains collected articles written by former POWs, compiled by the Java Far East Prisoner of War Club.

Prisoners of War – Australians Under Nippon, Hank Nelson. Stories of the Australian servicemen and women held in Japanese prisoner of war camps.

Spice Island Slaves, Leslie J. Audus. Presents a history of the Japanese prisoner of war camps in Eastern Indonesia during the war years.

Survivors of the Sword – Prisoners of the Japanese 1942–45, Brian MacArthur. Compelling stories from survivors from across the Japanese prisoner of war and slave-labour camps. An excellent read.

The Animal Victoria Cross – the Dickin Medal, Peter Hawthorne. Compilation of short stories covering the Dickin Medal winners throughout its history.

The Animals' VC – For Gallantry or Devotion, David Long. Compilation of short stories covering the Dickin Medal winners throughout its history.

The Conjurer on the Kwai: Captivity, Slavery and Survival as a Far East POW, Peter Fyans. Superb first-hand account of a British POW who used his skills as a magician and conjurer to stay alive in the Japanese labour camps, and to save countless other Allied lives.

The Defining Years of the Dutch East Indies, 1942–1949, edited by Jan A. Krancher. Contains survivors' accounts of the Japanese invasion of what was then the Dutch East Indies and the incarceration of the European, American and local POWs and their forced labour on the death railway.

The Judy Story, E. Varley. A short but engaging book written with the assistance of some of the Yangtze gunboat crews, telling of Judy's life and adventures.

The Jungle Journal – Prisoner of the Japanese in Java 1942–45, Frank and Ronald Williams. The story of a young Royal Artillery officer who was held as a Japanese prisoner of war in the Dutch East Indies, as told through his diaries.

The Sumatra Railroad: Final Destination Pakan Baroe, 1943–45, Henk Hovinga. One of the very few books telling the story of the other death railway – the one pushed through the Sumatra jungles by the POWs. Encyclopaedic. Definitive.

Unsung Heroes of the Royal Air Force, Les and Pam Stubbs. A useful and informative record of the RAF airmen held as Japanese prisoners of war.

Yangtze River Gunboats 1900–49, Angust Konstam. Short but excellent book about the Yangtze gunboats, including fine photos and illustrations.

Appendix: Original Documentation

I have decided to include in this book a sample of official documents obtained from The National Archives, The Admiralty, the Imperial War Museum and other sources capturing the flavour and essence of some of the key moments in the extraordinary story of Judy and her fellows. What is especially striking is the underplayed, deadpan way in which those present at such events – which were extreme, even for a conflict as all-consuming as the Second World War – relate them. They give a real sense of the nature of Judy's comrades during the war, and from reading these and more it seems clear why she was so devoted to her fellow sailors, airmen and soldiers, and especially when they became fellow prisoners of war. Each document is accompanied by a note outlining the genesis and purpose of the report.

Document One

Author's note – this is a report on the sinking of the Grasshopper, *the vessel on which Judy was shipwrecked as they attempted to evacuate Singapore.*

Narrative 7.
Note – There are probably officers, survivors, P.O.W. in Sumatra & Siam.

> Prisoner of War Camp,
> Mile School,
> PALEMBANG.

P.N. Sherd, 9/9/45

4th April, 1942.

STATEMENT BY Mr. H. BARDEN, Eastern Bank, SINGAPORE – Ship 'GRASSHOPPER' (800 tons approx.)

We left Singapore 1730 hours on 13th February, 1942, but with Dragonfly: returned about midnight when we sailed again about 1000 hours on 14th February, one aircraft dropped one bomb that missed us. About 1230 hours two waves each about

25 aircraft bombed us. We were hit and the engine room began to flood. The ship was then beached near a small island in the Rhio Archipelago. Stores were offloaded and magazines destroyed. All personnel including 60–80 civilians were taken ashore. The skipper (Hoffman) arranged for us to go to Daboe where we arrived on the 18th or 19th February. Owing to the effect of blast on my back from bombing I went into hospital where Captain Kirkwood, I.M.S., had just arrived. On 23rd of February the Dutch from Djambi took about 40 of us to the hospital there. Another launch containing fit survivors from Daboe followed us, but went through to Padang. They were mostly serving personnel.

On 1st March we tried to go to Padang but the ferry launch had been destroyed by the Dutch as we retuned.

The Japanese arrived in Djambi on 6th March. We stayed in Hospital until 27th March, and after 2 days in the military barracks Djambi we were taken to Palrumbang where I arrived 31st March as prisoner.

In the party which went to Padang were Commander Alexander R.N., and Lieutenant Commander Reid.

Mr. H.M. James (Planter) died in Hospital at Djambi.

We left in Djambi Hospital a Mrs. Parr with a badly injured arm, Dalrymple (R.A.F.) wounded by schrapnel in the leg, Marine Faint (wounded), Miss Hartley, an elderly lady with slight schrapnel wounds in the leg, two Chinese nurses from the General Hospital, Singapore, and two Eurasian nurses. I regret I do not know what happened to the many people who were left in Daboe.

Document Two

Author's note – this is a report on the sinking of the Dragonfly, *sister ship to the* Grasshopper, *which was shipwrecked as they attempted to evacuate Singapore.*

Statement by Capt. R.L. Lyle (now Major) on loss of H.M.S. 'Dragonfly' including statement on possibility of survivors landing in other places and a list of names of those known to have embarked, seen killed etc.

I have divided this report into three:
(1) Circumstances under which H.M.S. Gunboat 'Dragonfly' was lost
(2) General itinerary of survivors from the place of loss to Colombo
(3) List of names of those seen killed etc.

e. Loss of M.M.S. Gunboat 'Dragonfly'

   At about 0200 hrs on the 14 Feb 1942 H.M.S. 'Dragonfly' in company with H.M.S. Gunboat 'Grasshopper' removed detailed evacuation parties of the various Brigades and Divisions which then remained on Singapore Island. At this period both ships were very badly shelled but appeared to sustain little damage and no casualties.

After steaming at probably maximum speed the remainder of the night, at 0930 the same morning (i.e. 14 Feb) a Japanese Flying Boat was sighted which was very obviously on reconnaissance. At this time H.M.S. 'Dragonfly' was leading and H.M.S. Grasshopper was following about a mile astern.

The Flying Boat flew over the 'Dragonfly' and dropped two bombs of small calibre. Both however were near misses and no damage was done. The ships guns went into action. The Flying Boat paid no attention to H.M.S. 'Grasshopper'. As this plane was so obviously a reconnaissance aircraft, the Commander of our Gunboat decided to get under the lee of one of the small islands in the vicinity, in an endeavor to evade any aircraft which might be sent after us. To put this into effect our course was changed slightly. The Commander of H.M.S. 'Dragonfly' was to the best of my knowledge by name of Commander Sprott. The Commander of the 'Grasshopper' being Commander Hoffman. However, before reaching cover of the islands, large numbers of Japanese Bombers were seen to be approaching from a northerly direction and I was informed by the first Officer Lieutenant P.P. Shellard R.N.V.R. that he had counted some 123. On sighting of aircraft the alarm was sounded and all non-naval personnel were ordered below. I myself was put into the corridor between the Officers' quarters forrard along with a number of other Army officers, and spare gun crews of the ship's forward guns.

By some means or other the Commander of the ship had been able to supply all personnel with life belts. There had not been a great deal of time to check up on the exact numbers on board the ship or get their names and Regiments, particularly as in getting to the ship on Singapore Island our parties had been very badly shelled and cut up, and many of the other ranks had lost their Officers in charge. It was however estimated that the Naval crew amounted to 73 and that the total number of persons on board was about 225 i.e. 152 Army personnel of various Regiments that were made chiefly of men from 2nd Battalion The East Surrey Regiment, The 1st Battalion Manchester Regiment, my party of Headquarters, 6/15 Indian Inf Brigade, a few R.A.F. and a few miscellaneous people such as Intelligence Corps. The majority of the other ranks were quartered in, what I believe, was the ratings Mess Deck, aft.

From below we soon heard the aircraft circling overhead which carried on for some minutes, and from my position, which was sitting on the floor forrard, the next thing I knew was a colossal explosion and a complete ceasing of all avoiding action by the ship and the immediate stoppage of the engines, which had appeared to be going full out.

It was obvious to us that something very serious had happened and we therefore filed up the companion-way on to the deck.

On looking round I was able to see that the very worst had happened and that the entire ship, aft of the smoke stack, was just a mass of twisted metal, and the stern of the ship had completely disappeared. It is my belief that the depth charges which were in position for use had exploded, causing the chaos. On going closer to the gap it appeared that it would have been impossible for any man to be alive who had been in the after Mess Deck. However, we managed to get one or two very badly wounded men out through a bomb hole. It was not possible to do very much as the ship was by this time a good deal more than half submerged.

One leading seaman by the name of Brennan (I have reported this to the Navy C/O H.M.S. Sultan Colombo) by great presence of mind managed to get the one sound Whaler into the water. We also got clear two small khali floats. We managed to get the wounded that were lying about the deck into the one boat and a certain number of other able-bodied personnel got into it as well, before it became obvious that we would have to push her away or she would sink with the Gunboat. I along with a number of others remained on deck until Commander Sprott gave the 'abandon ship', when we jumped overboard and swam away from her. At this time Commander Sprott was still on the bridge.

It was now a little after half past ten in the morning. I got some 100 yards away from the ship and turned round just in time to see her take take the final plunge. As she was going under I saw two Naval Officers jump out of the bridge onto the ship's side, slip down her bottom and into the sea. All that remained of her to be seen after this was a short piece of her bows, and she remained in this position for some hours. The actual period which she took to sink from the time of the bomb hitting her I estimate as being a maximum of 5 minutes.

The next thing I saw was the Whaler on the far side of the wreck from me with a number of people hanging onto her life ropes. One empty khali float and the other with a number of men on it.

All this time large numbers of aircraft were circling round in squadrons and I was able to vouch for well over 60 planes. They had by this time seen our fate and had turned their attention to H.M.S. 'Grasshopper'. They were doing the same to her as they had done to us. Pattern bombing by squadrons. For a time she appeared to bear a charmed life and never seemed to be hit. Literally hundreds of bombs must have been dropped near her. She was at this time perhaps up to half a mile away from us circling round in avoiding action. It is possible that some of those bombs severely shook some of those people swimming in the water so as to render them unconscious. We eventually saw the 'Grasshopper' circle as if in avoiding action and make for an island which we could see in the far distance. I estimated that she had been hit, which turned out to be correct, and she was endeavoring to beach herself which she eventually did success-fully before her after-magazine blew up.

I was given to understand later that H.M.S. 'Grasshopper' only sustained some 8 or 9 fatal casualties.

To turn back to the plight of the survivors of the 'Dragonfly' the Whaler was now collecting those that she could find in the water and she was getting very full.

The empty float had been occupied by large numbers and was seen to be making away in a direction that I presumed to be Sumatra where a very vague outline of coast could be seen.

The other float was making off to the nearest island which I have mentioned before.

There were still a number in the water who were some distance away from the Whaler. I found myself, after endeav-oring to collect people into a bunch as I considered that way we should have a better chance of rescue or getting ashore by swimming, the only officer, I took charge of those that I had collected, a number of about 6 and shouted to others to join us. There were a few whoever who swam off on their own in the direction of the nearest island. I only saw one of them again. I should mention here that all the personnel I had been able to collect were Naval ratings.

By shouting and making signs at the Whaler, which was too far away to recognise persons, we were led to understand that she was too full to take more than the men that were in her immediate vicinity. I and my party therefore decided to endeavor to swim ashore which we set out to do.

By this time the aircraft, their mission fulfilled, had flown away, but some half an hour later we saw a squadron approaching us at a very low level coming from a direction which I presumed to be East. Before long it was obvious what they were going to do and that was to machine gun the life boat. They came down to what I believe is termed, naught feet, and machine-gunned the life boat in tiers of 2 & 3 at a time, the whole time keeping formation. They repeated this twice on the life boat and having dealt with them passed on and machine-gunned myself and party in the same manner. It was very obvious, even from the distance that we were away from the life boat, that they had sustained very heavy casualties. We were more fortunate in that no one was hurt.

Having, as already said, repeated this twice they flew off in the same direction from where they had come. We saw no more of them.

We saw the Whaler re-arrange itself and start off for the nearest island for which we were also making.

At about half passed six that evening the Whaler which had been waiting behind picking up people, caught up my swimming party and some of us were able to assist the few able-bodied men in the boat to get the last half mile to the shore, which we reached about 7 o'clock that evening.

We took a count and if I remember correctly there were 27 men composed of 22 in the boat and the 5 who had swum with me, about 8 of those in the boat were in a very serious condition. Unfortunately we found the island to which we had got possessed no food or water and nothing very much could be done for the wounded, numbering considerably more than half of those remaining. I do not know the name of the island.

The following morning a Sub-Lieut, whose name I believe was Clarke, a New Zealander, arrived walking along the beach with 8 others. They had been on the second float and had got ashore a little further up to coast. This made the total count of 36. Others may possibly have got ashore by swimming to other islands in the vicinity, but in my own opinion, I am afraid that they must have been very few, as the majority of the ships' total complement, particularly those of the Army, must have been killed outright in the first explosion or were killed during the machine-gunning of the life boat.

The names of personnel that I can remember are give in part III under the heading of having landed or having died in the particular action.

(Sgd.)

<u>General itinerary of survivors from place of loss to Colombo.</u>

ċ.   Referring to the last sentence of War Office Cable which says 'state where he landed and possibility of survivors landing elsewhere', I shall give a short itinerary as it is just possible that other of the ships company did land elsewhere.

As I have said in part (a) of this report the name of the island on which I landed is unknown to be but from having talked to the naval crew of H.M.S. 'Dragonfly' I gather that is was estimated to be approximately 100 miles south of Singapore in the vicinity of the Sinkep Group of islands about 10 miles from one by the name of Pongpong. I do not know whether this is the correct spelling but to pin-point it, it may be of interest to sat that Pongpong was where S.S. 'Kuala' foundered with a large number of nursing sisters on board.

As can be seen from the map there are many hundreds of small islands in this area many of which were visited by various officers in an endeavor to collect more survivors of the large number of ships which sank in that area on our about the 14th Feb. 1942. I believe the number to be sunk within a radius of some 40 miles numbered 9 of various sizes, one other of which I believe, was the 'St. Briac', which I gather was a tug and was towing barges of explosives.

Having remained on this small island for 48 hours and having endeavored to make the Whaler more or less seaworthy we eventually were able to contact the crew of the H.M.S. 'Grasshopper' by means of a native in a small sampan. We were told to go to another small island where they would endeavor to get a few medical supplies to us.The name of this island to which we eventually got was called I believe Pisec (spelling doubtful). Unfortunately we were not met here by anyone and it is believed that there must have been a number of places of similar name and we had arrived at the wrong one. Between the time of landing and arriving at this island we had lost a number of the wounded, they having died. See part (c) of the report.

We had been on the second island for about 24 hours when a number of large sampans arrived which were sent by a Dutch Controller of another island some 40 or 50 miles away, he having heard of the various disasters. The town from which they had come was a small Dutch settlement by name of Dabok. We took over the sampans, as by this time the Whaler was completely unserviceable, due to its many bullet holes, and we decided to try and find the personnel of H.M.S. 'Grasshopper' which after a night's travel we were able to reach. They were on still another island some 10 or 15 miles away from where we had been, the name of which I do now know, as the village in which we stayed was completely devoid of all local inhabitants who had, it was presumed, gone into the jungle for safety.

It may here be interesting to note that a few of the locals which we had met previously had informed us that the Japanese had been round these islands previously dressed as fisherman, warning all the natives that they would suffer very considerably if they gave help to any British personnel.

Shortly after joining up with the personnel of H.M.S. 'Grasshopper' a motor launch arrived to take us off to Dabok which had also been arranged by the Controller of that particular island. It took us three nights to clear all personnel from this one island. However, all that were there arrived safely at our destination (Dabok). Here many of us were put into the local hospital inclusive of myself. While I was in hospital a Committee was formed consisting of the Controller, Commander Hoffman and one or two others and it was decided that all able-bodied personnel including a large number of civilians which were on this island should be sent off in large country boats to Sumatra, which we were informed was about 80 miles away. While I was still in hospital large numbers of personnel left Dabok for Sumatra in this manner.

It is interesting to note that of H.M.S. 'Dragonfly's' ships company, apart from those which were in hospital with me, I never saw any again. I can only surmise that either they landed on a different part of the Sumatran coast to that which I did or they must have got across the country a good deal quicker than myself and caught a previous boat out of Padang. I have, however, only seen one Naval Officer of our party since I arrived in Colombo, and he being very sick was sent off a good deal earlier than most of the others. The Navy are in possession of all his particulars although I forget his name.

Some days after arriving in hospital I was sent off in a motor launch along with a party of walking wounded to Sumatra. We made for the mouth of the Indragiri River and eventually landed at Tembhilahan. It is my opinion that those who had left before us in country boats probably landed at Jambi, which of course was considerably further south, and it is therefore possible that in view of the fact by this time, the Japanese had landed at Palembang, and were making their way north, that many of them were cut off and unable to make the west coast of Sumatra.

From Tembhilahan we went by river to Rengat and from there on to Ayermulek staying a day or two at each place. From there was were able to get a lorry which conveyed us to Sawerleunto and eventually down to Padang. Some of the wounded party which I came over with were not sufficiently fit to complete the whole journey, and a number of them were left in the various hospitals on route. I eventually left Padang in the early morning of the 3rd of March 42 which I believe was after S.S. 'Rosenbloom' left the same Port and has been reported lost with all hands. I understood that some 300 persons embarked on this ship although there was no definite method of checking the numbers. I am, however, very much afraid that personnel who left Dabok three or four days before I did may have been unfortunate enough to have embarked on this ship.

I left Padang in the K.L.M. SS 'De Weert' and on the day we left, Padang was completely clear of personnel with the exception of a Colonel Warren, Royal Marines, who was in charge of the evacuation from that Port. A wire, however, had been received that same day from the East side of Sumatra, I do not know whether it was Jambi or the Indragiri landing place, but it said that there were some 700 persons still to come through. However, as it would have taken anything up to a week for them to arrive, the 'De Weert' could not possibly wait for them.

Documents Three & Four

Author's note – two reports on the sinking of the SS Van Waerwyjck *– renamed the Werweck by the Japanese –* the vessel on which Judy was shipwrecked for a second time.

Tranby Lodge,
Hessle,
E. Yorke.
25th May, 1946.

To: The Under Secretary of State,
       The War Office,
       Edge Lane.
       Liverpool. 7.

From: Captain J.G.Gordon,
       Royal Artillery.

Sir,

In answer to your letter of the 24th May. reference M/954 I will do my best to answer the seven questions, but would point out that I have issued a full report on this disaster to the Judge Advocate General's Office and have made several trips in connection with this and other War crimes to London. However, I will repeat for your benefit.

The Japanese vessel on which I was sailing was making a trip from Medan to Singapore, not Palembang as stated by you.

<u>Answers to your questions.</u>

(4)   S.S.Van Warweak.

(5)   1400 hours, July 26th 1914.

(6)   Two hundred and seven. (Not quite certain).

(7)   Sixty-seven including three who died immediately on arrival at Singapore as the result of wounds.

(8)

    a.   Sixty miles south of Medan on Sumatra side of Malacca Straits, seven or eight miles from shore.

    b.   Three enemy ships in the vicinity which picked up survivors. One Tanker which took the bulk, and two Corvettes.

    ci.   Completely out of sight within five minutes, actually under water in three.

(6)   All British were rescued by being picked up by an enemy vessel (to the best of my knowledge and belief).

(7)   I regret that this is quite impossible owing to all my records being removed from me on more than one occasion by the Japanese during later imprisonment. However, practically all the information was computed and filed with the records at the base camp at Pakan Baroe, Sumatra, the C.O. of which being Wing Commander P.S. David, R.A.F., the Senior Medical Officer of the S.M.O. Officer being Lieut. Col. E.M. Hennessy, R.A.M.C. The latter in

the final stages of Japanese surrender was responsible until his transfer to Singapore for all records of lost personnel. If these records were not complete and you care to ask me for the particulars of any individual, and I am able to remember, I shall be only to pleased to help.

In conclusion I would add that I personally reached a Fishing trap just off the shore by swimming, and was then picked up by one of the small Corvettes. On getting on board, I went up to the Japanese Captain of the ship to thank him for rescuing my party, and asked as best I could if he would go round the wreckage to see if anybody else was left alive on the spot, the main bulk of survivors having already left the scene of the sinking in the other two vessels. To my astonishment he agreed. We then proceeded to go round all the remaining wreckage and rafts, stopping sometimes to examine bodies thereon, and I am therefore able to state that at approximately 1630 hours on the same afternoon there was nobody left alive at the scene of the sinking.

When I later was transferred back to Sumatra I discovered that four allied P.O.W.'s all of whom were Dutch had been picked up by a fishing vessel and taken to the shore of Sumatra. After careful investigation I could find no other trace of any other allied P.O.W.'s who had been rescued in this way or who had reached the shore. It is there to be concluded, unless picked up by the Japanese, which was extremely unlikely with an unfriendly local population, and the knowledge that the Japanese brought all Allied P.O.Ws in Northern Sumatra to the base camp at Pakan Baroe; that there were no other survivors other than those contained on the list held at Headquarters Pakan Baroe and at Changi, Singapore, the Changi list being taken to Changi camp by Major P.E. Campbell, Indian Army, approximately a fortnight after the sinking.

J.G.Gordon,
Captain Royal Artillery.
28–5–46.

To: Officer Commanding, Command Medical Store, Harefield, Middlesex.
From: 7259601 W.O.11. Eckersall, K.P.J., R.A.M.C. Det. 12 Company R.A.M.C., Command Medical Store, Harefield, Middlesex.
Date: 28th May 1946.

Sir,

In reply to War Office Letter No. MA/OR/954 dated 24th Mar 1946, asking for information on the subject of loss of British personnel, who while P.O.W. in the Far East, were lost by the sinking of an enemy vessel by Allied action on the 26th June 1944, the following particulars are submitted:

The route was Medan to Singapore and not as quoted in the above mentioned War Office letter.

(9)   The name of the vessel I am not quite sure of, it was some-thing like 'Kwewegem', which prior to capture by the enemy, was a cargo cum passenger vessel of the K.P.M. Line. The vessel carried the enemies' serial No. P.1406, this number is to the best of my knowledge correct

however, no doubt the Allied submarine commander recorded this prior to sinking the vessel.

(10) Time of sinking – 1347 hours (Tokyo time) on Monday 26th June 1944.

(11) Approximately 300 Allied personnel of British, Americans, Australian, and mixed European Nationality, also approx. 450 Dutch personnel.

(12) A total of 62 Allied personnel (other than Dutch) were found to be missing when a check was made at River Valley Road Camo, on the 28th June. A further three died as a result of the action in the P.O.W. Camp Hospital at Changi Gaol, Singapore. Their names are as follows:

Sgt. Fowler, R.A.   )
Sgm. Conley. R.C. of Signals.   ) – This gives a total of 65.
P.O. Christopher, R. Navy.   )

The full total missing was approximately 200, including Dutch.

Of the 65 missing I am certain, as after the fall of Japan in August 1945 I complied a list of all casualties (excluding Dutch) known in the Pakan Baroe Area P.O.W. Camps, from 1st July 1944 to August 1944. This list including full details of personnel (Excluding Dutch) lost in the sinking of the vessel in question. The details were as follows:

Nationality – Number – Rank – Name – Initials – Officer or Other Rank as applicable to the various arms of the service.

Copies of the list quoted above were taken from the Pakan Baroe Allied H.Q. Camp Office by Lieut. Colonel E.M. Hennessey, R.A.M.C. (Regular Army) and handed over to the

British Representative at R.A.P.W.I. Headquarters at the Goodwood Park Hotel, Scott's Road, Singapore, in early September 1945.

Further copies of these lists were handed over by me, together with lists of deaths in the Pakan Baroe area and in Medan area, and sick lists categorised for evacuation, to a Captain Carey, R.A.M.C. (Airborne) of the occupying forces, to whom Lt. Col. Hennessey handed over prior to leaving for Singapore in early September, after release.

Note: Dutch records were maintained by their own clerical personnel.

All other Allied statistics were compiled by British P.'s O.W.

5a.   Time of leaving Medan – 4pm Tokyo time, on Sunday 25th June 1944, steaming at approximately 6 knots. Vessel anchored at dark and proceeded at dawn. (8pm to 5.30am approx). Note: Owing to clocks being advanced to Tokyo time after April 1st 1942, by Japanese Order, it was light until nearly 8.30pm.

Convoy of three of four vessels, other vessels were tankers, and escorted by three small corvettes, carrying depth charges and small A.A. guns. Two Jap Bombing planes also acted as escort during steaming time.

The ship was sunk by Allied Submarine off Tandjong Bali, a small island about 7 Kilometers off shore, at 1347 hours 26th June 1944, by two torpedoes fired into the Port side from possibly a distance of 6 miles away.

The convoy hugged the coastline all the way from Medan up to the time of sinking, steaming about 4 to 5 Kilometers off shore.

There had been sinkings of other vessels in the same area as wrecks could be seen partially above the water level.

This particular ship after sinking had still approximately 12 feet of its masts showing above the water level.

5b.   There were no friendly ships in the vicinity. Enemy ships in the convoy refused to pick up the P.O.W. survivors until Japanese Merchant Navy crew and native crew survivors, also Japanese Military Guards, were picked up.

All P.O.W. survivors were finally recovered from the water by approximately 1645 hours 26th June 1944, either by ships in convoy or small escort corvettes.

This excludes two or three Dutch, one of whom was a doctor, by name A.L. Yurgens, Captain 1st Class, Dutch N.E.I. Forces, who reached shore by swimming and gave themselves up to native police at the nearest village, and were finally returned to a P.O.W. Camp in the Pakan Baroe area at a later date, approximately August 1944.

5c.   The vessel was not longer than seven minutes in sinking after being struck.

6a.   Two or three are stated in 5b.

6b.   Approximately 550 were picked up by the enemy merchant vessels and corvettes.

f.   I have previously stated in answer to question No. 4 where complete particulars of personnel lost, or died as result of the action (other than Dutch) may be obtained.

For your information I have added the following details:

The final destination as a result of this move was Pakan Baroe, Central Sumatra. The reason we were conveyed by sea from Medan to Singapore was, the enemy did not at that time possess adequate road transport to convoy from Medan to Pakan Baroe by road, a 4 day journey.

The solution being, transfer P's.O.W. from Medan to Singapore in a large vessel, transfer at Singapore to small flat bottomed river craft in order to return to Sumatra and navigate the long narrow rivers which have their source in mountain ranges on the west coast of Sumatra, in order to arrive at Pakan Baroe by the sea and river route.

I trust that the information given herein will shed some light on this most unfortunate incident.

I have the honour to be,
Sir,
Your obedient servant,
K.P.J. Eckersall
7259601 W.O.11. R.A.M.C.

Document Five

Author's note – a report on forced labour parties working in the Sumatran jungle as POWs of the Japanese, one that captures the stark horror of the camps and the unbreakable spirit of resistance of the Allied internees.

<u>Report of a POW work party in the Gaje Country, S Atjeh, Sumatra</u>

1. On March 3rd 1944 a POW work party of 300 Dutch, 200 British left Glegeer POW Camp, Medan, Sumatra. The Allied senior officer was Capt. Van der Lande. The British senior officer was Lieutenant L. R. T. Henman, the British Medical Officer was Captain P.M. Kirkwood. The whole party was commanded by Lieutenant S. Miura of the Japanese Army.

2. On arrival at Keta Tjane at the end of a day's lorry ride Lieutenant Miura informed us that we must on the following day commence a march of 135 kilometres (approx 85 miles) to Blangkedteren, S. Atjeh. After protest by the senior Allied officers, including medical officers, one more days grace was allowed before the march was commenced. All belongings that could not be carried had to be left at Keta Tjane.

3. This march was made in four stages with one whole days rest on the way. Food supplies consisted of rice, soya beans and meat. Owing to bad organization on the part of the Japanese the proper quantities were not always available at the stopping places. Many of the British particularly had no water bottles and in spite of warnings men drank from streams on the road and thus laid themselves open to attacks of dysentery. The men had not marched for two years or more and on the way suffered very severely from blisters. Nevertheless very few British fell out. The RN party of 45 (under Second Lieutenant H. Hedley, Mysore Regiment) completed the march in fours, with only one casualty in the last stage.

4. After about one month the British contingent (consisting of four parties – RN, Army, RAF and AIF) were finally billeted at a camp at 28 kilometre Blangkedteren Takengong Road. This road was being constructed by the Japanese with POW and native labour. The camp was at a height of approximately 3000 feet and consisted of bivouac attap huts built by POWs themselves immediately after arrival. Lieutenant Hedley, the RN party and some of the Army men had to spend two nights amongst native coolies in hovels made of bracken, in the midst of a sea of mud and excreta (human and otherwise) before being allowed to move into the camp at 28 kilometres. This they built as best they could with a small quantity of attap and wood cut in the jungle.

5. The men were driven out to work as soon as possible and no fit men were allowed to stay in camp other than a bare minimum for cooking and wood chopping. Work consisted of labour on a

mountain road, tree felling, bridge building, stone carrying, earth removal with Java hoes and bucket, and metalling of the road surface. Average days work about nine hours in all weathers, and while carrying stones men sometimes had to walk 30 kilometres a day.

6. Sick men were continually persecuted and many men were forced to go out working when they were in no way fitted to do so. A certain percentage of men were required. If these were not forthcoming the sick were paraded (irrespective of what diseases they had) and the Japanese would choose those who in their opinion were fit for duty. Attached correspondence between Captain Kirkwood IMS and Lieutenant Miura gives an idea of the situation. Officers who protested were merely beaten up by the guards in front of the remaining POWs.

7. Food at this period consisted of 300 grams of rice and 200 grams of soya bean per day, salt fish was also provided, approximately 2 bullocks per week (amongst 500 men) and a small quantity of vegetables (see report by Second Lieutenant J. Hedley, Mysore Regiment). Many men could not eat the soya beans as they caused diarrhea (see report by Captain Kirkwood, IMS). Naturally, the diet was totally inadequate for the work being done.

8. Particularly at first there were many cases of dysentery. Those were treated in a so-called hospital at Blangkedjeeren where a Dutch Army doctor named Duringa did splendid work with practically no equipment. As soon as these patients were pronounced temporarily fit they had to walk back to the

camp from which they came (23–28 km.) and bring with them a bullock which was the meat ration for the camp concerned. Delay in sending men to Blangkedjeeren Hospital was in my opinion the cause of the death of Pte. Lahay, AIF, one of the three British casualties in Atjeh.

The two letters were attached to the original of this report submitted to MI5 War Office.

(13) As a consequence many men sold their clothes and with the proceeds bought extra rice, fruit and native sugar. To do this they had to break out of camp at night. When some of them were caught the whole camp was punished by being made to stand to attention in the evening, after the day's work for approximately 2 hours per day. The guards said that they would make arrangements for fruit to be bought legitimately but, having done so once, they would then forget their promise in true Japanese style and so no more official purchases would be allowed.

    g.   The spirit of the men during this period was very high, particularly after news was heard of the invasion of Europe, and this was as well, because without it there would have been far worse casualties on the march down into the plains which began on October 6th.

    cii.   On October 5th at 18.00 hours I was informed by Miura that on the following day we were to commence a march of approximately 85 miles which had to be completed in as short time as possible (actually the march took 81 hours including all stops for food and sleep and rest).

(8)   Many of the men had no boots, many more were suffering from diarrhea or amoebic dysentery, the roads were steep and shockingly surfaced and Korean guards (until they themselves got left behind) used sticks and riffle butts on any stragglers. Capt. Kirkwood was himself suffering from amoebic dysentery but nevertheless gave every possible assistance to the sick.

13. The worst part of the journey was a night march between the hours of 20.00 hours and 04.00 hours. During this period I was marching with the Navy party and the singing by them and the Army and R.A.F. of songs such as 'The Eagle they fly high in Mobile', 'Lily of Laguna', and 'The beer is on the table' helped a good deal.

14. A Korean guard named Matsuoka was especially vicious during the march. On one occasion when P/O. Sparks, W. No D/JX 125134 with blistered and festered feet as being helped along by Capt. Kirkwood and P/O. Northcott, C.J. No. D/JX 137479 his guard used his rifle butt on all three of them, because they were not walking fast enough.

15. We finally arrived at Kota Tjane with 6% of our strength having fallen out against 25% of the Jap and Korean guards. The streets were festooned with bananas – but Lieut. Miura had given orders to his Sergeant that on no account were the P.O.W's to be given or allowed to purchase any fruit at all.

16. This man Miura provides a most interesting study. He spoke English (and Malay) extremely well and had apparently been in some large business firm in Japan, where he said he

had many foreign friends. He was always anxious to try to convince me that he was trying to do everything in his power for the P.O.W's. Had his actual behavior, particularly towards the sick, borne out his fine words I should have been more impressed with his good intentions. 'Sick men,' he said to me on more than one occasion, 'are of no use to the Japanese Army. It is better for them to die'. The hospital too he said, should be made to resemble a prison as near as possible. 'You yourself,' he added, 'complain far too much. It is not gentlemanly'.

17. He had no control over his Korean guards who did more or less as they pleased. He did indeed at my request forbid them to take action into their own hands by inflicting physical punishment themselves, but when, as soon happened, they began to disobey this order, he seemed quite unable or unwilling to see that it was enforced. 'Do not punish your men,' he told m   e when I asked for some powers of punishment (with regard to sanitary matters), 'Always be kind. I never punish my guards'. Quite true.

18. Under the circumstances the discipline of the men was very good and for this credit must go to the officers under me (especially Lieut. Hedley and Lieut. D.S. Matthews, G.S.) and equally to the N.C.O's of the various parties (R.N., Army, R.A.F. and A.I.F.) These N.C.O's had not only to work and live with the other men, but, on return to the camp each evening, had to distribute food, collect money for canteen purchases (when

allowed), detail working parties and settle all minor disputes without having any disciplinary powers at all.

R.N. Party	P/O	Northcott, C.J.R.	D/JX 137479.
	P/O	Bosward, F.	D/JX 140525.
	P/O	Sparks, W.	D/JX 125134.

Army Party	Sergt.	Maverty, R.A.S.C. (18th Div.)	
	Sergt. Powell, T.F. R.A.		1454735.
	(head cook)		

| R.A.F. | Sergt. | Appleton, J.G. R.A.F. 522620 |

| A.I.F. | Cpl. | Mackay, L. | 2/29 Btn. A.I.F. |

I would also especially like to recommend Lieut. Hedley for the excellent work he did as ration officer on the march down from Blangkedjeren to Kota Tjane and at other times.

19. Capt. Kirkwood, I.M.S. succeeded under the circumstances in preserving the men's health, or what was left of it, to an astonishing degree (though for most of the time he was sick himself with amoebic dysentery). In all during the eight months period only three men died.

Pte.	Hopson.	A.I.F.
Pte.	Lahay.	A.I.F.
L.A.C.	Willis.	R.A.F.

Although the hard times which the men underwent was probably the original cause of the many casualties which we suffered afterwards in the Pakan Baree area. (See report by Capt. Kirkwood, I.M.S. and Capt. J.G. Gordon, R.A.)

20. The whole Atjeh party (Dutch and British) were drafted to Pakan Baree after approximately three weeks rest in a camp (Sungei Songkel) near Medan. On the way we (500 men) were kept at Fort de Kock (Nr. Padang) for four days in two rooms which in normal times formed the police courts of the town in question. During these four days we were given very little to eat, the only sanitary arrangements consisted of a trench dug in the yard, and it was only possible to have a bath by standing in the bin. There was just sufficient room for each man to lie down on the floor. The sick lay in the middle of one room in a space which we cleared for them.

21. At Petai Camp (Pakan Baree area) Lieut. Miura put cost and difficulties in the way with regard to the digging of latrines. He would not allow sufficient time for the work and forbade me to use the timber (for our big latrine) from the jungle nearby. However by disobeying orders we managed to get the latrine completed, upon which he sent for me and congratulated me on its efficiency. A few days previously he had complained that the British, though they always obeyed him, did so 'with a sulky face'. The next day (Nov. 23rd) he went to Pakan Baree and bought back Capt. Gordon, R.A. as Senior British Officer.

22. This officer, who had worked untiringly on the troops behalf in Medan, took over the duties of Senior British Officer from me. He was faced with the last (and most difficult) period which we went through as P.O.W.'s, and in my opinion carried out his duty until I left him in Legas in August 1945, in a most admirable manner. He has details, which I handed over to him,

of the personnel of the Atjah Party and all casualties which we suffered then and in the Pakan Baree area.

23. Finally I would like to say how much the British Contingent in Atjah appreciated the great organizing ability and general efficiency of Capt. J.J.A. Van der Lande and his S.M.O. Capt. Linggen (Royal N.E.I. Army) in particulary in connection with medical matters the work done by Sergt. Major Bougels (R.N.E.I. Army) is worthy of the highest praise.

(SGD) L.R.T. HERMAN

Lieutenant, R.N.V.R.

Index

SMOKY
THE
BRAVE

ALSO BY DAMIEN LEWIS

SMOKY
THE
BRAVE

The World's Smallest Dog
The World's Biggest Heart

DAMIEN LEWIS

Quercus

First published in Great Britain in 2018 by Quercus.

Quercus Editions Ltd
Carmelite House
50 Victoria Embankment
London EC4Y 0DZ

An Hachette UK company

A CIP catalogue record for this book is available
from the British Library

HB ISBN 978 1 78648 307 2
TPB ISBN 978 1 78648 308 9
Ebook ISBN 978 1 78648 309 6

10 9 8 7 6 5 4 3 2 1

Text designed and typeset by CC Book Production
Printed and bound in Great Britain by Clays Ltd, Elcograf S.p.A.

For the fallen of the 26th

Captain Sheldon P. Hallett
1st Lt. Donald W. Christians
1st Lt. William McDaniels
T/Sgt. Harry R. Rogers
1st Lt. Clair J. Bardsley
1st Lt. Lee G. Smith
2nd Lt. James H. Morrison
1st Lt. Karl M. Booth Jr
1st Lt. Madison E. Gillespey
2nd Lt. Clarence E. Cook
F/O James L. Wilson
F/O Henry R. Willis
1st Lt. Samuel Dunaway

They shall grow not old, as we who are left grow old:
Age shall not weary them, nor the years condemn.
At the going down of the sun and in the morning,
We will remember them.

Laurence Binyon

Photo Joe

Now, Photo Joe is an altitude fiend.
He flies way up high where he can't be seen.
He flies at thirty thousand in his P-three-eight,
Getting drunk on oxygen at a rapid rate.

He tells all the bombers of every hot spot.
He flies over places where the fighters will not.
The bombers have top-cover and the fighters have a gun,
But all Photo Joe can ever do is run.

There's a little more to this sad, sad story:
The bombers do the work and the fighters get the glory.
And here's another thing that you ought to know –
There aren't any medals for a Photo Joe!

Anon

AUTHOR'S NOTE & SOURCES

The time served by Allied servicemen and women during the Second World War was often traumatic. Memories tend to differ and apparently none more so than those concerning operations flown deep behind enemy lines. The written accounts that do exist of such missions tend to vary in their detail and timing, and locations and chronologies can prove contradictory. That being said, I have done my best to provide a proper sense of place, timescale and narrative to the story as depicted in these pages.

Where various accounts of a mission appear to be somewhat confused, the methodology I have used to determine when and how events took place is the 'most likely' scenario. If two or more testimonies or sources point to a particular time or place or sequence of events, I have opted to use that version as most likely. Where necessary I have very occasionally re-created small sections of dialogue to aid the story's flow.

The above notwithstanding, any mistakes herein are entirely of my own making, and I would be happy to correct them in future editions. Likewise, while I have endeavoured to locate the copyright holders of the photos, sketches and other images and material used in this book, this has not always been straightforward or easy. Again, I would be happy to correct any errors in future editions.

Of particular use during the writing of this book were the 5th Air Force, 26th Photo Reconnaissance Squadron's own accounts of the war years. These include the Flight Reports, Intelligence Reports and other official squadron records held at Maxwell Air Force Base, in Alabama, USA. The 26th being a photo reconnaissance squadron, the photo archive held at Maxwell AFB also proved particularly useful. So too did the 26th Photo Reconnaissance Squadron's own war diary, entitled simply 'Squadron History – Twenty-Sixth Photographic Squadron (L)'. Likewise, the squadron's more informal photographic and written legend of the war years, entitled '26th Photo', and published by 26th Photo Reconnaissance Squadron, proved hugely insightful.

ACKNOWLEDGEMENTS

In researching this book I was able to speak to and receive assistance from a number of individuals, who were especially generous with their time. My special thanks and gratitude are extended to all, and my apologies to those that I have inadvertently forgotten to mention.

In no particular order I wish to thank the following, who assisted in many ways: research, proofreading, recollections and subject matter expertise. Author Taylor Dowling was kind enough to alert me to the existence of his superlative account of the British reconnaissance pilots of the Second World War, when we shared a platform at an Imperial War Museum Duxford event, and to discuss same.

Sim Smiley, for your expertise and inspiration, gleaned from the various archives in the USA. Simon Fowler, for your expertise and inspiration, gleaned from the various archives in the UK. Paul and Anne Sherratt, for your perceptive comments and guidance.

The staff at several archives and museums also deserve special mention, including those at the British National Archives, in Kew, London; and those at the Maxwell Air Force Base archives, Alabama, USA. I would like to make particular mention of

Tammy Horton, archivist at Maxwell AFB, for your diligent help and assistance.

I'd like to thank in particular nonagenarian Rouse Voisey, a survivor of the the Second World War years in the southwest Pacific theatre, who was captured by the Japanese and survived many months of hellish forced labour, not to mention journeys on the so-called 'hell ships', shipwrecks and the Sumatra 'hell railway'. Thank you, again, Rouse, for sharing with me your extraordinary memories and recollections of your time serving in this theatre of war, over seventy years ago.

My gratitude also to my literary agent, Gordon Wise, and film and TV agent, Luke Speed, both of Curtis Brown, for helping bring this project to fruition, and to all at my publishers Quercus, including, but not limited to, Jon Butler, Charlotte Fry, Ben Brock and Hannah Robinson. My editor, Richard Milner, deserves very special mention, as does Josh Ireland: your unstinting enthusiasm for this story is, I hope, rewarded in these pages.

I am also indebted to those authors who have previously written about some of the topics dealt with in this book and whose work has helped inform my writing. These include, in alphabetical order of author: *Smoky the War Dog*, Nigel Allsopp (New Holland Publishers, 2013); *Dogs of Courage*, Clare Campbell (Little, Brown, 2015); *Spies in the Sky*, Taylor Downing (Little, Brown, 2011); *Beyond the Call of Duty*, Isabel George (HarperCollins, 2010); *The Eight Ballers: Eyes of the Fifth Air Force*, John Stanaway and Bob Rocker (Schiffer Military History, 1999); and finally *Yorkie Doodle Dandy*, William A. Wynne (Smoky War Dog LLC, 1996).

Enormous gratitude is also due to Fiona MacDonald and all at the charity Glenart and their Bravehound initiative, which helps match service dogs to deserving ex-servicemen, those who have either been wounded in combat or suffered from the modern-day trauma-related disabilities (akin to those I have described in this book as assailing some of the Second World War veterans). Thank you for those events that you organized to support the publication of this book: I'm honoured to be able to raise the profile of the fantastic and hugely valuable work that you do.

And thanks are due as always to the ever-patient Eva and to the wonderful David, Damien Jr and Sianna, for not resenting Dad spending too much of his time locked away . . . again . . . writing . . . again.

CHAPTER ONE

The image painted on the side of the aircraft's fuselage was eye-catching. It showed Donald Duck riding on a speeding cloud, one eye squinting down a camera lens as he snapped off a photo of the earth far below, his webbed feet thrust before him, dashing pilot's scarf and leather flight helmet flapping in the slipstream.

It was the patch of the 26th Photo Reconnaissance Squadron, part of the aptly named Hawkeye Group: their task was to dash across hostile territory at altitude, grabbing daring images of enemy positions – images that would prove key to winning the war.

The pilot flying the powerful but graceful P-38 Lightning – nicknamed the fork-tailed devil, *der Gabelschwanz-Teufel*, by the enemy, due to its distinctive twin tail planes – was one of the best. First Lieutenant Lee G. Smith, a hugely popular figure in the squadron, was blessed with dark good looks, his square-jawed features set below a steady, self-possessed gaze, offset by a thin, somewhat wry and lopsided smile.

Right now, Smith's jaw was locked tight as he wrestled with the Lightning's controls and the demands of flying such a mission.

It wasn't his aircraft's capabilities which worried First

Lieutenant Smith. Known as a hugely robust and forgiving airframe – the 'sweetest-flying plane in the sky' to many – the twin-engine Lightning could take any amount of mistreatment and abuse. It was the photo recce pilot's age-old adversaries – the weather, plus any marauding enemy aircraft that might be menacing the skies.

Smith banked tightly, turning his head as he did so, scanning the cloud-enshrouded earth as he tried to identify the distant target that he intended to capture on celluloid. At the same time he kept flicking his eyes to either side and behind, as he checked anxiously for hostile warplanes.

The standard combat model of the P-38 Lightning (the 'P' stood for pursuit) packed a devastating punch: one 20mm cannon and four Browning machine guns were positioned in the aircraft's bulbous nosecone, primed to unleash a torrent of heavy-calibre bullets at any adversaries. No wonder it had produced so many combat aces.

But Smith's aircraft – the F4 reconnaissance version – was a very different kind of machine. A bulky K 22 camera – as large as any man's torso and operated by a clunky lever bolted to the pilot's control column – was positioned where the weapons normally sat. In place of the gun button Smith had only a hot switch to enable him to fire off nothing more deadly than . . . photographs. And whereas normally the pilot was ensconced within a sarcophagus of protective armour, on the photo recce version of the Lightning that was all stripped away to save weight.

Less weight meant more speed, which was the key to surviving such solo dashes through enemy airspace, or so the photo recce fliers reasoned.

The eerie, alien suck and blow of the oxygen mask echoed in Smith's ears, accentuating the loneliness and isolation of flying such a mission. He was alone on the roof of the world up here – tearing along at pushing 435 miles per hour and 20,000 feet of altitude. Without the oxygen, he'd last barely minutes before losing consciousness.

At such height, the air outside the Lightning was at minus 12 degrees; far colder with the wind-chill factor. So frigid was it that the K22 camera crammed into the nosecone had its own bespoke heating system, to prevent the lenses from fogging up or the mechanism from freezing solid.

Smith was blessed with few such comforts. He was hunched in the unheated cockpit, his clawed hands aching from the glacial conditions and the hours spent gripping the flight controls, his thick sheepskin flying jacket buttoned tight.

The heavens stretched above him, a deep, icy blue. Towards the eastern horizon, the sun peeped a fiery eye above thick clouds, gilding their billowing tops a fierce orange. Smith had taken off early in an effort to catch his target in the fine morning light – the best time to secure the kind of images he was after.

But the cumulus stretched from 3,000 to 14,000 feet, where towering updrafts of moist tropical air punched high into the atmosphere, and Smith found himself having to steer a path around heavy rainstorms. Above the cloud cover the visibility was pretty good at around ten miles, but within the dark and torrential cloudbursts it was close to zero.

It was 12 March 1944, and all that month the squadron had been dogged by bad weather here in the southwest Pacific theatre. Repeatedly, pilots' Final Mission Reports had concluded with the dreaded words: 'Unsuccessful due to weather'. It was a phrase that did little to reflect the drama and heartache of being dogged by such treacherous conditions. Even worse was being forced to file the report: 'Did not take off due to weather'.

At least Smith had got airborne. But in spite of his best efforts, he feared today's flight was destined to earn that hateful epitaph: *Unsuccessful due to weather.*

He pressed on, eyes searching for a break in the cloud and determined to bring back something – anything – that might be of use to the Allied commanders presently plotting death and destruction to the enemy. At the same time he tried to ensure that his hunger to bring back some positive results didn't blind him to the dangers inherent in his task.

He had to avoid creating a 'contrail' – a double line of cloud formed when the water vapour from the Lightning's twin-engine exhausts condensed in the freezing blue and froze. Such a trail thrown across the heavens would appear like a giant arrow, leading the eyes of any watchers to the tiny, isolated speck of an aircraft.

Repeatedly, Smith scanned cloud cover, temperature and altitude, running a series of complex computations through his head. At the same time he kept his eyes peeled, checking if the enemy might have left any telltale signs of their own. Spotting their contrails would give him a few precious seconds warning, allowing him to push to full throttle and dive to shake off any pursuers.

The cockpit was freezing cold. Agonisingly so. Smith ran his aching eyes across the controls, checking for any that might have frozen solid, so giving him a potentially catastrophic mis-reading. Crystals of frozen moisture could even form around

4

the Lightning's sharply raked canopy, frosting up the windows and obscuring his vision.

Momentarily, his gaze flicked downwards, to the map folded into the knee pouch of his flight suit. He'd been airborne for two hours, and it required pinpoint navigation to bring his Lightning directly over today's target – the Cape Gloucester headland, set to the far west of New Britain Island, one of the key enemy positions hereabouts.

Menaced by the 6,000-foot volcano of Mount Talawe, and clad in thick jungle and treacherous swamps, any pilot forced to eject over such terrain stood little chance of survival. Below lay a clutch of enemy airbases and ports, ones that Allied commanders hoped to secure as part of Operation Cartwheel, a series of island-hopping missions designed to isolate and neutralize Japanese strongpoints across the Pacific.

But planning such a complex series of amphibious and airborne assaults called for the kind of detailed intelligence that air recce photos supplied, which is why Smith had been sent out to brave the weather this morning.

Smith's camera pointed vertically downwards and was set to fire off a series of photographs at regular intervals, which would allow him to cover a continuous strip of terrain. Each shot would overlap with its predecessor, forming one uninterrupted image. Each large, 7 x 8.5-inch strip of celluloid would capture a patch of ground roughly one square mile. Such was the quality of the camera equipment that it could capture enough detail to identify individual vehicles moving across the terrain. But only if a weather window opened, and there was little sign of that happening right now.

Eventually, Smith was forced to turn for home – which presently consisted of the airbase at Nadzab, situated on the coast of New Guinea, which lay off the northern coast of Australia. Nadzab Airbase was never the easiest place to land: it had been hacked out of the deep jungle flanking the Markham River valley and was menaced by rugged mountains on either side.

Seven months earlier Allied forces had seized the area in a series of airborne assaults. In response, the Japanese – hungering for revenge following one of their first setbacks in the war – had launched a series of ferocious counter-attacks. Waves of Japanese warplanes flew repeated bombing missions, forcing the men of the 26th Photo Recce Squadron to pitch their tents directly beneath the jungle canopy, in an effort to hide from hostile eyes. Still they'd taken casualties, both men and machines getting blasted on the ground.

Yet there was little that the Photo Reconnaissance pilots could do to retaliate or to fight back. Their planes had been stripped of the guns that would have allowed them to do so – it was up to their comrades in the fighter squadrons. In the meantime, men like Smith had to carry on with the task at hand: speeding through enemy airspace to locate their target, capture it on film, and return as quickly as possible, so that their precious photos could be rushed into Allied commanders' hands.

As he set a course for home Smith checked his fuel gauges. After being airborne for several hours, dodging the weather and enemy aircraft alike, he might return only to find the airstrip cloaked in cloud. By then his aircraft might be sipping on fumes, and just at the moment when he was forced to delay landing. The Lightning used more than a gallon of fuel every minute, and

Smith needed to keep a constant watch on speed and bearing. There would be little scope for loitering above Nadzab, waiting for the cloud to clear.

It took a certain type of temperament to volunteer for such work. A certain kind of courage. Bomber and fighter pilots were accustomed to flying in formation, enjoying the company of fellow aircrew and a shield of friendly aircraft to ward off the enemy. By contrast, the recce pilot flew alone, unarmed and unescorted.

Serving in a photo recce squadron called for a rare combination of common sense, daring, self-reliance and initiative. Such pilots had to make a virtue out of the fact that their aircraft flew unarmed. If his P-38 carried guns, Smith would be tempted to turn and fight at the approach of an enemy warplane. As it was he had no option but to concentrate on avoiding combat, securing his photographs and speeding them back intact.

All too frequently recce pilots failed to return to base. They were flying solo missions across airspace where 'enemy fire and interception were probable and expected', as the mission briefings expressed it. More often than not those who failed to return were simply listed as Missing in Action (MIA). The chances were that no one would ever know what calamity had befallen them on their long and lonely flight.

If a pilot went down in the sea there was little likelihood of his body or any wreckage ever being found. If a plane came down on land, a report might filter in from local resistance fighters or villagers, and the wreckage might be identified from its tail number, but it was often difficult to determine whether the pilot had lost his life due to enemy action, mechanical failure or adverse weather.

Such dangers were all too real. A month earlier this had been brought home most powerfully, when the squadron's Commanding Officer (CO) had been lost in action. The 26th had been founded a year earlier, at Colorado Airbase, Colorado Springs, in western USA. First Lieutenant Sheldon P. Hallett had been appointed its founding officer, and he had been in command ever since.

Fresh-faced and youthful, yet with a direct intensity to his eyes, Hallett had nurtured a fierce pride in the 26th, one defined by rigour. His was the only photo recce squadron to have passed out of training in that autumn of 1943 with an 'Excellent' rating. On Sunday 31 October they had deployed from the US, sailing for a 'secret destination' on a luxury liner hastily converted into a troopship.

En route Hallett had spoken to his men of the eternal quest for excellence that he wanted the squadron to embody. From the moment they had arrived in theatre Hallett had led from the front, earning enormous respect from all who flew alongside him. But then, on 29 February 1944 had come shocking news: Hallett had been listed Missing in Action. In the blink of an eye the squadron had lost its Commanding Officer, and it would be some time before anything was learned of his fate.

Such unexpected losses could be shattering – especially within such a tight knit unit – but it was offset by the knowledge of the crucial role they were performing here. The squadron's war diary made proud mention of the 'highly important pictures of the enemy's activities and dispositions' that their pilots were bringing home. It was not an idle boast. The US Army Air Force's Official Service Journal concluded that photo reconnaissance furnished 'ninety percent of modern military intelligence. Armies do not move without it.'

So important was their work that President Roosevelt's son, Colonel Elliott Roosevelt, had been placed in charge of developing the craft of the photo recce squadrons, continuously pushing at the boundaries of what was known and possible. Such knowledge of the war-winning scope of their missions helped put steel in the pilots' souls.

As he set a course for home, Smith likewise had to draw on his own reserves of steel. He had to remain razor sharp and one hundred per cent focused. A moment's distraction could prove fatal. He was looking forward to landing back at base, in spite of the failure of his mission. After hours of intense concentration he was dogged by exhaustion, and he longed for the relief that came from simply making it back again in one piece.

He was just off Karkar Island, on the western fringes of the Bismarck Sea, when he spotted something. Far below the thick cumulus swirled for a moment and then cleared. In the break in the clouds a stretch of glistening ocean opened before him. Right in the midst of the water were the familiar forms of two ships, steaming resolutely onwards.

Smith studied the vessels. They were positioned five miles off the coast of Karkar Island and heading southeast – most likely making for Rabaul, on the eastern shores of New Britain, a base that the Japanese had captured from its Australian defenders in February 1942. Under Operation Cartwheel, Rabaul – one of the enemy's most significant strongholds – was to be isolated by air and by sea, its garrisons rendered impotent.

From such altitude the two ships appeared as little more

than pin pricks, but Smith doubted they were friendly. A year earlier a major sea battle had raged here, becoming known as the Battle of the Bismarck Sea. A fleet of Japanese warships and troop carriers had been steaming for Nadzab, to intercept Allied landings. The troopships and their destroyer escorts were caught by Allied warplanes. All eight transports were sunk and 3,664 Japanese soldiers and seamen had lost their lives.

But despite the losses they'd suffered, the armed forces of Imperial Japan remained resolutely committed to holding this region, and supply ships regularly braved the Bismarck Sea. To be certain of the two vessels' identities Smith needed to take a closer look. He put his Lightning into a shallow dive, dropping to 12,000 feet.

From that height he was almost certain of the identity of the ships below him. During training he'd memorized the photos and diagrams depicted in the Department of Naval Intelligence's 'Standard Classes of Japanese Merchant Ships'. The two vessels had all the appearance of the Type D freighter – a 2,300-tonne merchant ship codenamed *Sugar Charlie Love* in the manuals.

The freighters looked laden with war materiel, but you could never be too careful with such vessels, for the Japanese were in the habit of packing them with unexpected cargo, including Allied prisoners of war. Those fighting in the Pacific had heard of these 'hell ships': they transported British, American, Australian and other Allied POWs across the ocean, thousands crammed into bamboo cages stacked into hot and airless holds.

In the months following Pearl Harbor a vast swathe of terrain – from Burma in the north to New Guinea in the south – had been overrun by the Japanese. It seemed as if nothing could stop the Emperor Hirohito's forces: in spring 1942 the Japanese had launched a raid on Sydney harbour, using a fleet of *Ko-hyoteki* class mini-submarines. One Australian ship, HMAS *Kuttabul*, was sunk and the mini-subs had shelled shore positions.

The damage done wasn't great, but the message sent was heard loud and clear by the Australian people: their nation was under threat of invasion. As Japanese forces scored one triumph after another, hundreds of thousands of Allied troops had been taken prisoner. Those Allied POWs were used as slave labour. Working in nightmarish conditions, they were forced to clear the jungle and build airstrips and railways across territory seized by the Japanese.

The two vessels that Smith had discovered might be packed with such long-suffering Allied POWs. He dropped lower, setting his cameras running. Most such Japanese freighters boasted gun emplacements set in the stern and prow, but at his current altitude he was well out of range. As the camera whirred, he felt a kick of adrenalin. In spite of the terrible weather, he'd found something of possible interest and captured it on film.

Just as soon as he touched down at Nadzab, the ground crew would rush into action. They'd slip the precious roll of film out of the camera, jump into a jeep and dash across to the photolab that lay beneath the dark fringe of jungle. Within an hour at most the negatives would have been developed and dried, and the specialist photo-interpreters would be poring over whatever Smith had found here.

Painstaking research had enabled a calculation to be made of a ship's speed, based upon specific measurements of the wake revealed in such photographs. That combined with the vessels' bearing would give a good indication as to both where the ships were heading and their present position. It was then just a matter of whether attack aircraft could be scrambled in time to reach the two vessels while they were still within range.

But first, Smith had to fly like the wind to get his precious images home.

As his Lightning approached the hills that lay to the east of Nadzab Airbase, little did Smith suspect what lay far beneath him, secreted in the jungle shadows. Likewise, the warplane would be invisible to the stray soul hiding under the thick forest canopy. But her ears would be drawn to the distant roar of the twin engines, even as she crouched, fearfully, in the deserted foxhole in which she'd taken refuge.

Abandoned long ago, she appeared like a shapeless mass of tangled, dirty hair. After days lost in the jungle this starving, emaciated animal was barely recognizable. But she was still breathing and still fighting for her survival, and even in such a state a dog's hearing remains many times more powerful than that of any human.

Perhaps she raised her head a little further and pricked up her ears. If she did, she would doubtless have associated the roar of the P-38's twin aero-engines with what she longed for most in the world right then – human company, for she was accustomed to the sights, smells and sounds of an airbase such as this. Wonderful companions because they are so affectionate, she was of a kind of dog that hungers for human companionship, and hates being cut off from its two-legged companions.

Left alone for even a short while, she was of a breed that suffers from separation anxiety. After days marooned in the hot and airless jungle, and with little conception of how she had come to be there, the dog's disquiet and distress was acute. She longed for a human voice; a human touch; someone to scoop her up in friendly arms and to cherish her once more.

As the P-38 thundered onwards one thing was for certain: this tiny ball of matted, dirt-encrusted hair could have little inkling how her fate, and that of the reconnaissance squadron with whom Smith flew were inextricably linked, for all of that lay sometime in the future.

Abandoned in the jungle and lost to her erstwhile human protectors, the future was one of fearful uncertainties.

CHAPTER TWO

The angular form of a Willys jeep pulled out from the motor pool at Nadzab Airbase and took to a dirt track that threaded through the jungle. At the wheel sat Edward 'Ed' Downey, one of the airbase's ground crew. With a rugged boxer's features and a shock of unruly red hair, Downey was forever to be found with a Lucky Strike cigarette glued to his bottom lip.

Where they'd felled and burned the jungle to expand the airstrip, thick kunai grass crowded in on the track, its spear-like heads rising as high as ten feet and blinding Downey to his surroundings. He was more accustomed to the rolling hills of his native Pennsylvania and its heavy winter snows, than to the thick and stifling jungle and the claustrophobic fields of kunai grass. It made for hellish terrain in which to fight.

The track snaked this way and that as Downey gunned the jeep through the toughest sections, which had worsened with the rains. There seemed to be no happy medium to the weather here. When the sun was out it was as hot as an oven. When the clouds built it was oppressively humid, like being trapped in a giant sauna. And when the rains came it was as if God Himself had turned on a giant tap over the airbase.

In places the track was completely flooded and Downey had

to slow to a crawl to ease the jeep through chocolate-coloured water as thick as custard. It sloshed about up to the level of his axles. In places it was deep enough to reach to his mudguards, the jeep's powerful 'Go Devil' engine straining to keep the vehicle in motion.

Such terrain took a heavy toll on the unit's vehicles, and Downey wasn't entirely surprised when the one that he was driving coughed and spluttered and came to a sloughing halt. Not for the first time since he had been deployed here, he clambered out of the driver's seat and went to open the vehicle's hood, trying to avoid the worst of the mud as he did so.

He lifted it, latched it, and leaned over the engine, feeling the heat rise from the straight-four. He reached for and jiggled a couple of wires, checking if those serving the vehicle's battery were still making good contact. Such damp and humid conditions weren't great for keeping any kind of machinery serviceable, or weapons for that matter.

As he fiddled with the engine, a P-38 roared across the sky and touched down on the airstrip. One of the squadron's recce flights, no doubt. Maybe First Lieutenant Smith, making it early back to base. Surrounded by the tall kunai grass, Downey couldn't see the runway, and his concentration was focused on the engine compartment of the jeep.

He was just about to give the engine a try when he heard a sound from over his shoulder. It was so utterly unexpected, but he could have sworn that he'd heard a dog whining. The sound transported him back to his native Pennsylvania and his childhood years. To Downey, it was a far from welcome noise and one that sparked distinctly unpleasant memories.

He didn't mind admitting that he was a die-hard dog-hater. He couldn't fathom his fellow soldiers' affection for the four-legged curs, nor how they were always going on about how they missed the pets they'd left back home. It didn't make the slightest bit of sense to him. He was about to ignore the sound – surely he'd imagined it? – when he heard it again: a plaintive whimper coming from just behind where he stood.

Later, when asked, Downey was never able to explain why he went to investigate. But for whatever reason – curiosity, perhaps – he turned and sloshed his way through the mud to the side of the track. He peered, cautiously, into the shadows that seemed to be the source of the noise. There was an abandoned foxhole by the roadside, and Downey had learned to love and loathe those shell-scrapes in equal measure.

During the rains they were invariably thick with clinging, stinking mud. During the drier periods, they became home to a variety of crawling, stinging, slithering life, much of which was lethal. At the very least vicious red fire ants were bound to have set up camp, and he'd learned to his cost what sharing a foxhole with those critters entailed.

But the foxholes could also be real lifesavers. When the enemy warplanes attacked, you had two basic choices: remain where you were and dice with death, or dive into a foxhole and take your chances with whatever jungle life had made a home there.

As he peered into the gloom Downey spied movement. A pair of dark eyes, glinting in the dull light, gazed up at him, imploringly. They seemed disproportionately large for the sodden floor-mop of hair they seemed to inhabit. He heard the noise again – a dog's pitiful whine. If it hadn't been for that, Downey would have doubted whether this sad, benighted creature really was a dog at all.

Even as he stared at the animal, trying to fathom what in God's name the breed might be, Downey saw it try to clamber out of the pit, its tiny paws scrabbling desperately at the earth. It jumped at him, tiny head bobbing upwards once, twice, three times. Downey couldn't help but admire the creature's sheer tenacity and will to survive. Perhaps it was that which spoke to him and prompted him to act as he did.

Almost against his will he reached out a hand, scooped up the tiny dog, turned back to the jeep and tossed it unceremoniously onto the passenger's seat. That done, he went back to fiddling with the wires. It was most likely a dodgy connection, maybe to the spark plugs. He tinkered for a while longer, eventually persuading the engine to cough back into life, and with barely a glance at the dog he continued on his way.

One of the greatest ironies of Downey's discovery was that he shared a tent with a man who was arguably Nadzab's greatest dog-lover: Bill Wynne. Wynne and Downey had trained as aerial photographers back in the US, before deploying to theatre together. Downey fancied himself as something of an athlete and a swashbuckling adventurer. He had a wicked sense of humour and was cocky and sharp-tongued. He and the dashingly handsome Wynne were the best of friends.

Their only differences seemed to be over the hotly disputed topic of dogs. And knowing of Wynne's all-consuming passion for man's four-legged friend, Downey was loath to let his buddy set eyes on his newfound discovery. If he did, Downey felt sure that this irritating mop of a hairball would end up moving into the tent that he shared with Wynne.

He wasn't about to let that happen.

Upon returning to camp Downey parked up at the motor pool and yelled across to his friend who worked there, Sergeant Dare. 'Hey, Dare, I found this in a foxhole.' He thrust the diminutive animal into the sergeant's hands, then banged a fist onto the bonnet of his jeep. 'And this damn thing broke down.' Another vehicle for Dare to fix. Downey spent a few more minutes explaining how he'd found the animal, before concluding by saying: 'I don't know what it is, but I know I don't want it.'

With very little ceremony – he was glad to be shot of the shaggy canine enigma – Downey left the animal in Sergeant Dare's care. He headed for the tent he shared with his friend and dog-lover, Bill Wynne, determined not to breathe a word of his discovery.

It was a little over two years since the 7 December 1941 surprise Japanese attack on Pearl Harbor had catapulted America into the war. Ever since deploying to this far-flung corner of the globe – to avenge Japanese aggression, and in defence of Australia – those based at Nadzab had grown accustomed to the nightly air raids. Powerful blasts shook the very foundations of the camp. The 26th's end of the airbase was stocked with any amount of highly combustible and explosive materials – gasoline for the trucks and jeeps, aviation fuel for the P-38 Lightnings, plus photographic film, paper and chemicals. A lucky hit would result in a cataclysmic explosion.

Their accommodation tents had been given suitably ironic names: 'GI Manor' or 'Target For Tonight'. If any soldier managed to sleep through the nightly air-raid sirens and remain in his cot, he'd certainly be wrenched awake by the time the first bombs had fallen. He'd make a mad dash for the comparative safety of the coconut log and earthen-roofed air-raid shelters, as the flash of detonating munitions tore the dark night apart.

Daylight raids were rarer. Generally, the only aircraft to menace the skies during daytime were the enemy's 'Washing Machine Charlies' – most often a lone Mitsubishi G4M twin-engine bomber, the nearest Japanese equivalent to the P-38 photo recce aircraft (although slower and more vulnerable). Those flights were the enemy's attempts to do exactly what the 26th were charged to do here – to spy on their adversaries.

Among the war debris scattered around the airbase, the men had retrieved some prized souvenirs. Foremost were the white cotton flags emblazoned with the symbol of Imperial Japan – a blood-red rising sun. Then there were the aircraft recognition manuals that had been issued to the Japanese troops, illegible with their vertical columns of spidery writing. But the accompanying diagrams of Allied warplanes dropping sticks of bombs over Japanese positions left little to the imagination.

You never knew what you might find here, abandoned in a Japanese foxhole. But neither Ed Downey nor Sergeant Dare had ever expected this – a mysterious and diminutive dog, with what must once have been a long and luxuriant coat of hair that fell to her ankles, but which now was a mass of dirt-encrusted knots and tangles.

Left with his new charge, Sergeant Dare wondered what on earth he was to do with such a dog in a place like this. He had his hands full with his duties at the motor pool, and the harsh rigours of jungle warfare hardly made this a fit place for pets. There was a saying popular among Allied troops then serving in the region: 'Heaven is Java; hell is Burma; but no one returns alive from New Guinea.' It sure wasn't an ideal location to try to nurse some life back into a sickly little dog.

Of course, there was a very real chance that the mystery dog shared its origin with the Rising Sun flags and aircraft recognition manuals the men had found around the base. After all, the Japanese were known to afford dogs similar veneration as Western cultures tend to.

In Japanese tradition a number of animals were renowned as lucky charms. The *Maneki-neko* – the beckoning cat – was a symbol of success, prosperity and happiness. The *Komainu*, known as Foo Dogs in English, were the ubiquitous lion-like statues that flanked the doors of Japanese Shinto and Buddhist shrines. Foo Dogs – as with their living brethren – guarded such places against those who would do them harm, even when their human occupants were absent.

Traditionally, the size of the Foo Dog was irrelevant: even a miniature one could do the job well. Maybe this tiny bundle of canine mystery had served a similar purpose for the Japanese forces garrisoned at Nadzab? Maybe the good luck that she supposedly brought had finally run out the day the fearsome armada of USAAF C47 Skytrains had released their paratroopers over this jungle-clad valley?

On the morning of 5 September 1943 a fearsome aerial barrage had saturated the Nadzab area with bombs. Immediately after, US warplanes had strung a thick smokescreen across the valley, into which the C47s had dropped their paratroopers in human waves. The US and Australian airborne troops had routed the Japanese defenders, even as General Douglas MacArthur, supreme Allied commander in the region, had circled overhead in a B-17 Flying Fortress, keeping watch as 'his kids' went into action.

The assault had been declared a 'signal step on the road to Victory' by the Allies. Once captured, Nadzab Airbase, which lies on the northeastern coast of what was then called New Guinea – today's Papua New Guinea – was rapidly expanded, until eventually four all-weather airstrips were in use, making it the most important Allied airbase in the region.

The loss of Nadzab Airbase, and the neighbouring port of Lae, had constituted a game-changer. No longer would Japanese commanders concentrate on new offensives aimed at overrunning nearby Australia and cutting it off from America – something which they had come so very close to achieving. Instead, they would focus their efforts on holding their positions, and preventing the Allies from approaching any closer to the Japanese homeland. That was to be prevented at all costs.

The battle for Nadzab was a good seven months old by now, and if the mystery dog retrieved from the foxhole was some kind of Japanese lucky charm, how on earth had she stayed alive in the interim? Any way Sergeant Dare looked at it, the dog's very existence here just didn't seem to add up. Regardless, she had been handed into his care and for now at least the Nadzab motor pool would be the diminutive mutt's home.

Japanese Foo Dog or not, the immediate priority was ensuring her survival. Though seemingly overjoyed to be back among human companions, the tiny little dog was emaciated and terribly weakened. Dare fetched some water and leftover rations. The food at Nadzab was atrocious – real potatoes were an unheard-of treat in the mess, fresh meat a thing of their dreams – and some US Army rations were the best that he could manage.

Once the dog seemed passably fed and watered Dare figured the tiny animal needed a shave. She looked horribly hot, and her long coat seemed beyond saving. Holding her down, he proceeded to slice off the worst of the matted clumps, until all that remained were short tufts sticking out at odd angles. That done, he fashioned her a collar and lead of sorts, a section of old belt forming the former, and a strip of cord cut from a parachute's shroud-lines making the latter.

With the dog shaved, 'dressed', and secured to a nearby tyre, Dare settled back to his duties. His newfound canine companion looked somewhat alarmed by the turn of events, and especially at her unceremonious scalping, but at least she seemed visibly less distraught than when Downey had first dumped her in the motor pool. No doubt the mystery surrounding her surprise discovery would be answered in time.

Dare had his work cut out right now with tending to the 26th's vehicles. The entire squadron was slated to move north to Hollandia – present day Jayapura – the capital city of the northern half of New Guinea Island and the next objective of Operation Cartwheel. No one was kidding themselves that wresting Hollandia from Japanese hands was going to be easy, especially with the calibre of enemy forces that were based there.

Just months earlier Roosevelt, Churchill and China's leader, Generalissimo Chiang Kai Shek, had met to determine the aims and future conduct of the war in the Far East. The resulting

Cairo Declaration had pulled no punches. The Allied leaders had pledged to continue military operations until Japan's unconditional surrender was secured. Japan would 'be stripped of all the islands in the Pacific . . . all territories Japan has stolen from the Chinese,' and any other gains it had made.

The priority for the Allies was to cut off Japan from its chief source of oil supplies, which entailed driving ever northwards to take the Philippines. The archipelago of islands making up the Philippines lay between Imperial Japan and the oil fields to the east. If MacArthur could seize back that territory, he could block all oil supplies from reaching Japan. Deprived of fuel, the nation's warships, tanks and warplanes would grind to a halt, and the Allies would be free to march upon Tokyo.

Of course, Japanese commanders had realized the threat this posed, especially after an airborne attack of breathtaking audacity had demonstrated Japan's vulnerability. In what had become known as the Doolittle Raid, in April 1942 Lieutenant-Colonel James Doolittle had led a flight of sixteen B-25B Mitchell bombers, which had taken off from the carrier USS *Hornet*, deep in the western Pacific Ocean.

They'd reached Japan largely undetected and released their payloads over a selection of military targets spread across six major cities, including Tokyo itself. Intended as retaliation for Pearl Harbor, and as a dramatic stunt for the Allies to boost spirits at home, the raids proved wildly successful. Fifteen of the bombers flew on to China, where they were scheduled to land, and most of the aircrew returned to the USA in triumph.

While doing little lasting damage, the raid convinced the Japanese that their homeland was threatened and vulnerable. Land, naval and aerial reinforcements were rushed to the southwest Pacific region. Provoked into action, Admiral Isoroku Yamamoto had steamed with a powerful armada to attack the US-held airbase on Midway Island, in the Central Pacific. Yamamoto planned to seize Midway and extend the reach of Japanese air power into US territory. Instead, his forces had suffered a major defeat, losing four aircraft carriers – *Akagi*, *Kaga*, *Soryu* and *Hiryu*.

The Battle of Midway represented a serious blow to the Japanese, but the losses were covered up and the Japanese high command announced Midway as a stunning victory. Yet Yamamoto knew as well as anyone the import of such a major setback, and especially in light of the subsequent airborne and amphibious assaults typified by Operation Cartwheel. The Allied advances would have to be halted on the island of New Guinea, which meant that the stakes could not have been higher.

The man charged by Imperial Japan to hold the line among the rugged jungles of New Guinea was General Hatazo Adachi, a figure whose reputation went before him. Adachi came from humble roots. Born to an impoverished Samurai family, he'd worked his way into the ranks of the Japanese military the hard way. When Japan had invaded China, in July 1937, Adachi – then a colonel – had led from the front, spearheading the fierce and brutal fighting around the Chinese port city of Shanghai.

Injured in a mortar barrage, he became known as a soldier's soldier, sharing front-line combat and the miserable conditions suffered by his troops. After being promoted to major general he played a leading role in the hellish policies pursued by the Japanese Army in northern China – the 'Three Alls': 'kill all, burn all, loot all'. Adachi oversaw a scorched-earth policy known as the *Sanko Sakusen* – the annihilation campaign – which had been signed off by Japanese Emperor Hirohito himself.

The *Sanko Sakusen* had involved the razing of Chinese villages, the targeting of 'enemies pretending to be local people', and of 'all males between the ages of fifteen and sixty'. Infused with the same sense of racial and military superiority that enabled Japanese soldiers to treat Allied POWs so mercilessly, the *Sanko Sakusen* policy had claimed more than 2.7 million Chinese lives.

More recently Adachi had cause to taste the Allies' mettle. Upon deploying from China to New Guinea, he'd been caught by US warplanes in the Battle of the Bismarck Sea. He'd seen Japanese ships sunk by Allied aircraft and witnessed thousands of Japanese servicemen losing their lives. Adachi knew what he was up against in New Guinea: he was determined to give no quarter and to fight to the last man.

Despite the savagery that he had orchestrated in China, there was another, more measured, cultured side to Adachi. He was a skilful composer of poetry, excelling at Japanese traditional short verse – *tanka*. Unusually for a Japanese officer of the day, he was exceptionally close to his men. He was accustomed to drinking quantities of sake – rice wine – with the rank and file, and encouraging them to speak freely about their concerns.

In short, Adachi was a formidable adversary. He considered it an enormous honour to have been given command over New Guinea, especially 'at a time when the issue of the day was to be settled'. He relished the challenge of being posted to the 'point of strategic importance in order to ensure that the tide of the war moved in our [Japan's] favour'.

Hollandia – the next clutch of Japanese positions on General MacArthur's shopping list – was to be the acid test. There, General Adachi was determined to make the Allied saying 'Heaven is Java; hell is Burma; but no one returns alive from New Guinea' into a grim and bloody reality.

If the mystery hound now tethered at the Nadzab motor pool was indeed a Foo Dog, the men of the 26th would need all the good luck and protection that she might bring.

Shortly, they would be sailing for Hollandia and whatever hell awaited there.

CHAPTER THREE

Before the squadron could move anywhere, Bill Wynne came to investigate sketchy reports of a dog residing at the motor pool. Wynne's tentmate, Ed Downey, hadn't breathed a word about her presence, but news had a way of getting out. Wynne had heard rumours about a four-legged fugitive that had arrived from out of the blue – a mystery dog that Sergeant Dare had apparently christened 'Smokums', after her smoky grey-blue colouring.

Wynne's first reaction on meeting 'Smokums' was surprise. The tall, dark-haired GI had never laid eyes on an animal as odd-looking as the one presently tied to the motor pool tyre. As her tiny tongue lolled out, panting in the heat, Smokums repeatedly tried to jump up at her newest visitor, desperate to demonstrate how happy she was that someone, anyone, was paying her a little attention.

She was so small it was almost unreal. When standing, she came to no higher than Wynne's boot tops. He squatted down for a better look, getting face-to-face with the dog. This close up her eyes were half-obscured by the shock of shorn hair: he could make out a set of fuzzy, grinning features, in a face exuding an impish sense of curiosity and canine mischief. Wynne's close scrutiny was rewarded with a generous lick from her tiny pink tongue. He was more than a little intrigued.

'Well, what kind of beast is this?' he announced, speaking more to himself than to Sergeant Dare.

All he could see of the motor pool sergeant was a pair of booted feet sticking out from beneath a nearby jeep. He repeated the question, Dare responding by extricating himself from the dark and oily engine compartment, his eyes blinking in the fierce sunlight.

The motor pool sergeant proceeded to relate the tale of how the dog had been found in the jungle, but that no one seemed to have a clue as to how she had got there, let alone what breed she might be. As Dare spoke, Wynne studied the dog some more. She was a compact little animal, that was for sure. Too compact: she was clearly half-starved. But regardless, she carried herself well, conveying an air almost of self-importance, with her head held high.

That head was petite, the nose short and finely-boned, the tip a glistening black button. The V-shaped ears were a rich tan colour and covered in short hair, as were her legs. But it was the eyes that struck him most powerfully. A deep amber-brown, they had a fierce sparkle in them that spoke of an innate loyalty and a quick-witted intelligence.

'So, what d'you think she is?' Sergeant Dare asked, once he'd finished relating his tale.

Wynne shrugged. 'Well, it's a dog . . . But it looks kind of weird thanks to the haircut. Some kind of dizzy little poodle,' he ventured.

He caressed her for a moment. Word was that Dare wanted rid

of the animal and was seeking a buyer. Her stubby tail wagged furiously, but still he could tell that the tiny dog was sickly. She weighed almost nothing, and the impression of scrawniness was hardly helped by the appalling haircut. Plus she seemed racked with anxiety, weaving this way and that and spinning incessantly on her tired legs.

A hopeless lover of dogs, Wynne did his best to comfort and calm her. Despite her tiny stature, the animal's big personality seemed to shine through. She had to be one feisty and courageous animal, to have survived all alone in the jungle for however long she had. Beneath the ragged shorn coat and sickly pallor, he could sense the dog's true nature – one replete with charm and a real love of fun.

'I'm not sure she's very healthy,' he remarked, as he fingered her uneven tufts of hair. 'Where exactly did you say you found her again?'

Dare repeated the story of her discovery, as told him by Downey.

'I'm not sure she'll live,' Wynne ventured. 'She seems so weak. But hey, I'll give you two pounds Australian for her.'

'Make it three and she's yours,' Dare countered.

Wynne considered this for a second. The price wasn't the issue. In American money it amounted to less than ten dollars. He was more worried about the risks involved in taking the dog. He sensed that they would bond incredibly quickly, but he was worried that she might die on him, and he would be bereft. It wouldn't be the first time that he'd lost a beloved canine companion, and the trauma had left him wary: once bitten, twice shy.

On the other hand she was a fellow creature caught up in the horrors of war, and that tugged at his heartstrings. Wynne marvelled at the series of events that had led to Downey's jeep breaking down at the exact spot where he could hear the dog's whining, not to mention a dog-hater such as him deciding to rescue her. He didn't doubt that Downey had saved her life, for she wouldn't have lasted many more days in the heat of the jungle with no water to hand.

A part of him felt that fate somehow had brought him together with this dog. Yet at the same time he had an instinctive feeling that nature might take its course with this tiny little life. He couldn't face carrying Smokums back to his tent, only to have to bury her in the jungle in a day or two's time.

Hailing from Cleveland, Ohio – a city on the shores of Lake Erie, which sits astride the US-Canadian border – Bill Wynne had known few moments when dogs hadn't graced the family home. Indeed, he'd come to view the families in the neighbourhood by the type of dog they kept. A quiet, happy dog signified a quiet, happy home, and vice versa.

His parents were of Irish and Welsh ancestry, but his father, Martin Wynne, had left before Bill had had the chance to get to know him at all. He hadn't seen or heard from him since. By the time he was six, Wynne's mother, Beatrice, was supervising a large staff at a factory making chicken incubators. She struggled to manage work and to find childcare for Bill and his younger brother, Jim, while striving to give them the care and attention they deserved.

Finally, she'd made the tough decision to send the boys to the Parmadale Children's Village of St Vincent de Paul, a Catholic orphanage, in Parma, a suburb of Cleveland. The orphanage was run by an overworked but immensely patient staff of Catholic nuns and it was an all-boys affair. That being the case, Bill's sister, Mary, was sent to live with a grandparent. Caring for boys aged six to sixteen, Parmadale boasted its own school, gymnasium, swimming pool, accommodation blocks and a convent. The boys rarely had cause to leave the grounds.

At first Wynne was horribly lonely, and it was fortunate that the orphanage came complete with a veritable menagerie of animals. To the consternation of Sisters Lucy and Hubert the boys kept bringing all sorts of creatures into their dorm, including snakes, turtles and raccoons. One day some of the older lads had returned from a nightly forage with a pair of owls carefully wrapped in their jumpers. The birds proceeded to hoot all night long, until Sister Hubert insisted an owl-release expedition was in order.

Bill Wynne had grown closest to Parmadale's dog, Rags, a big, shaggy-haired Airedale, which, with his fluffy face and kindly eyes resembled a giant teddy bear. Rags loved kids and he and Wynne ran wild through the grounds. But one day a big, sullen fourteen-year-old had decided to take out his anger and frustration on the defenceless dog. He threw acid at Rags, and the memory of the poor animal running in panic and agony was seared forever in Wynne's mind.

Playing in the orphanage baseball team had taught Wynne that apparent losers could become winners, if blessed with the right frame of mind. With spirit and hope and guts they'd won the local championship, even without any parents on the sidelines to cheer them on. But the discipline at Parmadale had been harsh and that, combined with the loneliness that plagued him over the two years he spent there, meant that Wynne returned home somewhat introverted and withdrawn. Again, it was dogs that brought him out of himself.

Queenie was a stray who followed him home one day. His mother decided to let her young son keep the dog. In time Queenie had six pups, which looked like a crazed Chow-Brindle Bullmastiff-Stafford Terrier-Bulldog cross. Unsurprisingly, they grew up to be bundles of pure grit and muscle. Wynne named his favourite Pal. Pal nurtured a love all of things human, but he turned out to be a true hellhound with any male dogs that crossed his path. Fed mostly on table scraps, his teeth got into poor condition, which at least meant that he didn't do too much damage when fighting his rivals.

Cleveland was a sprawling expanse of a city, with lots of wide-open spaces. It was a paradise for groups of energetic young boys. Wynne and his friends would take Pal to the sand field, a large area of derelict ground several blocks square, and pocked with 'Indian mounds' – low, angular hillocks which made for adventurous bike rides. Nearby was a patch of scrubby woodland thick with songbirds, and an adjacent swamp, thronging with water fowl. They were great places for Pal, Wynne and their gang to explore.

Pal was a fast learner and an eager pupil. Wynne taught the dog to jump up and snatch his woollen hat, without harming a hair of his head, and then to drop it the moment he cried out 'Stop!' During the heavy snows that often hit Ohio in winter, Pal learned to ride a sled downhill and then drag it back up again crammed full of eager boys.

Smart and fiercely loyal, Pal even managed to discover where Wynne attended school. Everyday he'd be there at 3.30, waiting to escort his young master the mile walk home. But one day Pal wasn't waiting in his usual spot any more. Wynne hurried back to the house, only to find that Pal wasn't there either. For months he waited for Pal to return, but the dog had simply disappeared.

Losing Pal broke the young Wynne's heart. He was sickened by the loss, which he never forgot. And now, as he crouched in the motor pool tent at Nadzab contemplating Smokums, he was assailed by similar worries; similar fears. Could he really take the risk of being hurt like that again? Could he really risk getting another dog, especially in a place such as the war-torn New Guinea jungle?

In war, everything seemed heightened: fear, adrenalin, brotherly love, sadness, hunger, thirst, loss, trauma, boredom and excitement. Wynne wasn't exactly eager to go through everything that he had suffered with Pal all over again.

Bidding farewell to Smokums, he wandered back to his tent lost in thought. He felt torn. He vowed to give it twenty-four hours. He'd go and visit the motor pool tent the following day, to see how the little dog was faring. Yet even if she had survived, he wondered how a unit like the 26th – one that thirsted for excellence – would take to one of their own adopting a mystery hound.

Ever since its formation a year earlier, the 26th had been pinned as a 'hot' squadron, one earmarked for overseas deployment and a leading front-line role. The men had prepared themselves by undergoing weeks of exercises under canvas, complete with daily hikes laden with weapons and rucksacks – all designed to simulate the kind of conditions they might encounter in the Pacific.

Wynne had trained as an airborne photography specialist, but the single-seater P-38 Lightnings had no call for such a role. At first, no one had been sure where best to utilize his skills: was he going to be most use in the camera repair workshops or the photo laboratory? As the lab was short of manpower he'd ended up there, processing the reams of precious images that the pilots brought back from their daring airborne sorties.

By its very nature photo recce work was top secret. Nothing – from the destinations of recce flights, to the images the pilots secured, to the intelligence the photos revealed – could be allowed to leak to the enemy. As a result, the squadron had to observe exacting standards of security. Just about every document emanating from the 26th – from Final Flight Reports to the monthly intelligence briefings – was stamped 'CONFIDENTIAL', 'CLASSIFIED' or 'OPS SECRET'.

Only the highest calibre officers could be entrusted with overseeing such levels of security. After First Lieutenant Hallett – recently listed as missing in action (MIA) – First Lieutenant Hartwell C. McCullough was one of the 26th's most senior officers. McCullough was a former photo reconnaissance instructor at Peterson Field, Colorado, then the centre of US photo recce excellence. Along with First Sergeant Joyce B. Howell, a squat, forty-something dark-haired Texan, McCullough constituted the heart and soul of this elite unit.

McCullough, who hailed from Louisiana in the American Deep South, was an absolute stickler for discipline. Among his many duties, McCullough was 'Custodian of Squadron Classified Documents' – the man charged with ensuring nothing of any import found its way into the enemy's hands.

McCullough ensured that rules and regulations, especially concerning security, were rigidly adhered to. Just that month he'd had to read the men the riot act, after wild rumours had swept through the ranks about the squadron's forthcoming move. Careless talk costs lives. It could also seriously dent morale.

Yet inevitably, there was also a real maverick streak to a unit like the 26th. The solitary seat-of-the-pants flying tended to attract single-minded, one-of-a-kind individuals, and the culture of daily risk-taking rubbed off on everyone, ground crew included.

Here at Nadzab, the men expressed their individualism in various idiosyncratic ways. Over the camp flew the iconic Texas colours – the Lone Star Flag – as opposed to the regular Stars and Stripes, reflecting the fact that sixteen of the squadron's two-hundred-plus personnel originated from Texas. In rare moments of downtime the Texans liked to gather beneath the flag to play poker and shoot the breeze. Hidden away in the jungle there was a still, for distilling moonshine – a fierce liquor the Texans like to quaff beneath their Lone Star Flag. Most prominent among the Texans was First Sergeant Joyce Howell, a self-confessed country-boy and a renowned practical joker who was in the habit of wandering about Nadzab wearing a pair of leather cowboy boots, as opposed to regulation army footwear.

But despite the squadron's decidedly maverick bent, Wynne could expect few special favours here at Nadzab, and who knew whether adopting a dog would pass muster? He ducked inside his tent – an inverted V of khaki green, sheltered beneath a forest giant laced with thick vines – and eyed Ed Downey, his so-called buddy and tentmate, accusingly.

'How come you didn't offer me the dog?' he demanded.

Downey turned an expressionless face on Wynne. 'I don't want a mutt in my tent,' he replied, flatly.

The whole thing was made even worse by the fact that Downey was well aware that Wynne hankered after a canine companion, for he was forever going on about it. Not only would Wynne have to risk the censure of the 26th's senior officers if he adopted the dog, he'd have to tackle his tent buddy, who clearly wasn't going to welcome a few pounds of cute and cuddly hairball into their communal living quarters.

First the dog had been abandoned in the jungle by persons unknown. Then she'd been discovered by a self-confessed dog-hater, and she hadn't exactly been welcomed with open arms in the motor pool, either. Right now she was for sale, but there weren't any buyers. Right now, it seemed as if Smokums wasn't particularly welcome anywhere. It struck Wynne that she was an orphan – and orphan from a foxhole – rather like he had once been, at least for a while.

Surely he was duty-bound to ride to her rescue?

CHAPTER 4

Before joining the military and training as an aerial photographer, Bill Wynne had done his utmost to use his canine experiences to help the US war effort. On his twentieth birthday he'd been given a dog by his sweetheart, Margie Roberts, who lived just ten doors down from his house on the same Cleveland street. It was 1942 and Wynne had answered the call to train the puppy, a Doberman-German Shepherd cross named Toby, as a war dog.

Bill and Toby signed up to the Cleveland All Breed Training School, part of a nationwide initiative established by the US military to boost the number of potential war dogs in circulation. The need was acute. At the time of Pearl Harbor the US had fewer than a hundred dogs serving in the Army, mostly sled dogs serving at snow-bound military bases in Alaska.

To begin with the US military had no plans for training any kind of expanded canine corps. Senior commanders had simply assumed that in the new high-tech form of warfare in this global conflict there would be little call for animals to serve. That thinking quickly changed. Dogs were wanted for wire-laying, message-carrying, mine-detection, sentry, first aid, scout, attack and trail duties, and demand for trained dogs far outstripped supply. Hence the War Dog Program was launched, informally known as the 'K9 Corps'.

A national publicity campaign solicited donations of semi-trained animals to join the Dogs for Defense initiative, run in conjunction with the American Kennel Club. Experience showed that German Shepherds, Dobermans, farm collies, Siberian Huskies, Malamutes and Eskimo dogs were the breeds most suited to such work.

Crosses of those breeds were equally acceptable, making Toby an ideal recruit. Wynne and his dog had started attending the Dogs for Defense obedience classes, which were held in a downtown Cleveland public square. Those open-air training sessions drew crowds of onlookers, attracting yet more owners and their dogs to volunteer for the War Dog Program.

Dogs for Defense received 18,000 donations, of which around half completed formal training with the military. Those disqualified were generally ruled out due to their small size, temperament, health, extreme excitability or for having a weak sense of smell. Wynne and Toby were halfway through the ten-week obedience classes when he had received his draft orders. Before Toby was able to graduate, his master had left to train for war.

In the spring of 1943 the US War Department decided that K9 units were needed for front-line duties, especially in the southwest Pacific theatre. Dogs could make a real difference in the close confines of the jungle, where visibility was often limited, but where scent and sound could still be detected over great distances.

Committing dogs to the jungle war presented a serious challenge. The K9 Corps didn't possess trainers with experience of such a tough and unforgiving environment, but they knew of those who did. At the British War Dog Training School they had been doing this far longer than anyone. Time was short and there seemed little point in trying to reinvent the wheel, so the US K9 Corps asked for help from Captain John B. Garle, one of the most experienced of the British trainers.

In February 1943 Captain Garle travelled to the US along with two fellow handlers and four veteran dogs, on what the American K9 Corps jokingly referred to as a 'lend-leash' basis. (Lend-lease was the system in which the US provided her allies with warships, warplanes, fuel and other vital war materiel, in return for leases granted on overseas bases owned by those Allied nations.)

Garle and his lend-leash team set to work at the War Dog Reception and Training Center, in Maryland, on the eastern coast of the USA. There they demonstrated how messenger dogs could be trained to carry urgent communiqués across the field of battle. Each dog had two handlers, to both of whom he or she demonstrated a fierce loyalty: one would give the dog a message to be carried, while the other would await its delivery. Such messenger dogs could cover great distances at high speed, presenting an elusive target to enemy snipers.

Garle and his team demonstrated how scout dogs could use their incredibly powerful senses of hearing and smell to identify hostile patrols at up to 1,000 yards away. Depending on the conditions – wind direction, vegetation cover, dampness of the ground – they could be used in amphibious landings to detect enemy positions on the shoreline, or on reconnaissance and combat patrols. But in all cases the dogs' effectiveness would depend upon how accustomed they were to gunfire and explosions.

Following the lend-leash training programme, the first American war dogs units had been dispatched to the Pacific, K9 teams going into action in New Guinea. Reports that filtered back from those units were highly positive. Both messenger and scout units gave 'consistently excellent performances'. Inevitably, such successes had made the dogs a target. A Marine Corps German Shepherd was shot by a Japanese sniper on Bougainville, an island off the east coast of New Guinea, and later would die of his wounds. There were dozens more such canine casualties.

In contrast to the US military, in the run-up to the war the Japanese had had a highly active K9 programme. The Japanese military had urged the public to donate their domestic pets, German Shepherds being the most sought after. As early as their 1937 invasion of China, some 10,000 highly trained dogs – mostly German Shepherds – served with the Imperial Japanese Army, as messengers, sentries, trackers and sled teams. The breed was praised as embodying the 'dauntless courage whose loyalty and bravery rank with the Imperial Soldier, and which would even make a fierce god weep'.

But that was the mighty German Shepherd; the diminutive dog tethered to a tyre at the Nadzab motor pool was an entirely different kind of beast. If Smokums had been a Japanese war dog, it stood to reason that a creature of her size could only have served as some kind of a mascot. As Bill Wynne wandered through Nadzab camp the morning after her surprise arrival, he didn't doubt that she was ready to serve a new master – that's if she'd survived the night just gone.

She had. Not only that, Sergeant Dare had decided that his need to be rid of the dog was ever more pressing. Indeed, he came seeking Wynne with a new proposition. There was a knock at the door of the photo trailer, Wynne's main place of work in the camp.

'Hey, Wynne, d'you want to buy the dog for two pounds?' Dare declared. He laughed, a little self-consciously. 'I need to get back in a poker game.' Dare had been losing and he wanted the money to help him reverse his recent ill-fortune.

Wynne eyed him, suspiciously. 'How is she looking today?'

Dare assured him that with a little half-decent food Smokums was making a remarkable recovery. Wynne was on duty, so he could hardly go and see for himself. He was a Private First Class (PFC) in rank and two Australian pounds was the equivalent of $6.44, a tenth of his monthly salary. But he was eager to claim the dog as his own, especially if she'd rallied as much as Dare claimed.

The deal was struck, and Wynne could hardly wait to fetch the odd little creature and lavish upon her the kind of care and attention he just knew she craved.

Just as soon as he had signed off duty Wynne hurried down to the motor pool. The reception he received from Smokums – Smoky now she was his – was everything that he'd been hoping for. She bounded about at the end of her lead, clearly overjoyed to see him again. Sure enough she seemed to have a new lease of life and was bubbling with energy and spirit. Wynne had to accept that Dare's assessment had been right: she had made a miraculous recovery.

He bent to inspect her for a second time, a little more

thoroughly now that the deal was done. He worked his thumb and forefinger around her back, just around her hips, and he could feel that she was bony still, but not as bad as the day before. Her eyes sparkled, her stubby little tail – docked at the first joint – flicked back and forth in a high-speed blur, and her ears pricked up excitedly. The look on her face seemed to be all about what adventures the two of them might have together.

Their very first adventure, which was hardly likely to be overly pleasant, lay right before them. Wynne whisked her up and made his way towards the tent that he shared with Downey. He soon realized that Smoky wanted a run around. He set her on the ground and she fizzed and buzzed around his feet. She was a real firework of energy, and Wynne made sure to scoop her up and tuck her securely under his arm again, as he ducked through the flap of his tent. There was nothing for it: he'd have to face down the dog-hater.

Downey was resting on his cot. He took one look at Smoky and his face darkened. 'I don't want that mutt in my tent,' he yelled.

Wynne stood his ground. 'She's staying,' he countered firmly, his voice calm but low.

There was a long beat of silence, a moment in which these two good friends might have come to blows. But finally, Downey seemed to back down. He gave a dismissive gesture, before adding, vehemently: 'Well, just keep the thing away from me.'

That was exactly what Wynne, the little dog's saviour, intended. He set Smoky down and she scampered over to his cot, making a beeline for the patch of drab olive material that served as a cover. It was spread out at the bottom end, and Smoky clearly had found her chosen spot. Under Wynne's careful gaze she circled a couple of times, before settling down for a nap. Smoky, at least, seemed very much at home.

Wynne let her rest, knowing this was very likely the first sleep in relative comfort and security that she'd had for some time. The crazed haircut made it look as if she'd been in some kind of savage fight, and he tried to imagine what her coat might look like when it grew back and was properly groomed. He could see why Sergeant Dare had chosen the name Smokums for her. Even shorn as it was, her hair had a gingery-brown tone with lighter, smoky tips at the ends.

Downey remained an issue, so this was hardly the perfect home for her, but it sure was a damn sight better than an abandoned foxhole in the jungle. What struck him most, now that he had her in his custody, was the responsibility that he'd just taken upon himself. Tiny she might be, but already he had a feeling that this was a little dog with a giant personality. He had no idea what breed she might be, but there was a fine elegance to her bearing that hinted at a real pedigree.

Smoky was something special, Wynne felt certain, and he was determined to discover her story. He wondered if she might be some kind of Japanese breed. There was an interpreter on camp who spoke fluent Japanese, and he decided to take Smoky to see him just as soon as she'd settled. If she responded to commands issued in Japanese – sit, stay, come – then that might go some way to solving the enigma that she embodied.

But for now, it was all about more prosaic issues. The first was food. Wynne and the rest of the 26th were fed on GI – Government Issue – rations, served in the squadron's mess tent and eaten at ranks of rough hewn wooden benches and tables. The food consisted mostly of dehydrated potatoes, powdered egg, bully beef (canned corned meat), canned Australian mutton (which had a terrible taste and smell to it), spam, plus citric acid to drink (which occurs naturally in citric fruits like lemons and oranges, and was taken to prevent scurvy).

There was a joke among the men of the 26th regarding the chow: 'Throw it in the mess tin, then go outside and throw it one way or another.' Fresh meat was a rarity, but fortunately canned fruit was in abundance and highly popular, though it would be no meal for a dog. Wynne worried that the kind of food available at Nadzab might kill a little animal like Smoky, causing pancreatic or kidney failure in a matter of months.

But there was little else to hand.

When Smoky woke from her nap he tried her on some bully beef. He opened a can and emptied half of it into his mess tin. Famished from her sojourn in the foxhole it seemed to go down a treat. Wynne figured that the key to keeping her safe and secure in the camp was going to lie in training. Between his duties at the photo lab and diving into the nearest shelter during air raids, he reckoned he could find the time to act as her instructor. He suspected that she was sharp-minded and would prove a quick learner.

The sooner that he could get her to understand the rules and constraints of such a place, the better. If he could teach her tricks, like he'd done with Pal and his other dogs, so much the better. She could entertain the men of the squadron, which should endear her to their number. A popular dog was far less likely to be on the receiving end of any ill treatment, or to fall foul of military rules or regulations. Even someone like Downey would have to rein in his antipathy if Smoky somehow became indispensable to the 26th.

Wynne knew a good deal about training champs. On the Parmadale orphanage's baseball field he'd learned how no-hopers could be melded into winners. In his teens he'd gone to Cleveland's West Technical High School, which had 5,600 students on its books. It was at West Tech that he'd first studied photography, which in time had led him to his role in the 26th. He'd also indulged his love of football, making it onto the high school first team, which was no small achievement in a school of West Tech's size and standing.

Torn ligaments in his right knee had put a premature end to his footballing career, but he'd learned a great deal about top-notch teams and their training regimes. A great coach-player partnership relied upon a combination of natural ability, the will to win, and trust. Sporting greatness didn't come easily. You had to have the drive to be the best, no matter what. His football coaches had called that quality 'intestinal fortitude', or the 'willingness to pay the price'.

Likewise, in a canine pupil-trainer team, each would only ever be as good as the other. He and Smoky would have to strive to be the very best, for the odds were stacked against them. Wynne knew instinctively that training, and forging an unbeatable partnership, would be the key to their survival.

He'd settled upon shortening Smokum's name to 'Smoky', in part because it rolled more easily off the tongue. It was smooth and quick for calls and recalls. Once he was certain she was fully fed and rested, he grabbed Smoky's DIY collar and parachute cord lead and took her for her first training session. He began by teaching her the basics: 'Heel! Sit! Stand-stay!' At that last command she had to remain exactly where she was, as he walked away from her and then returned to her side.

He sensed from the get-go that this was a dog who'd been trained before. She took to the commands so easily. He made sure to encourage her with an abundance of praise and play, as he'd been taught to do during the Cleveland Dogs for Defense classes. You never used physical punishment or harsh words with a dog. If you did, your aggression would tend to be transferred to the animal. A dog apes its owner. You had to use positive reinforcement to get the very best out of your dog.

At the Cleveland All Breed Training School they'd advised using a choke collar, a silver chain threaded through itself that would close tight and choke the dog if ever he or she tried to pull away. (It's something that many experts now advise is neither humane nor conducive to getting the desired results.) Here in Nadzab Wynne had only the makeshift leather belt that was threaded around Smoky's delicate neck.

Smoky loved the training, but she loved the breaks too. She seemed to have a massive drive for action and play. She thrilled to being taken for a run around the camp or playing tug-of-war with one of Wynne's socks, making throaty little growls as she tried to wrestle it from his hands.

For a moment, as they play-fought in this way, Wynne felt like a little kid again, though he was in the middle of the jungle and the wail of the air-raid siren might start up at any moment, signalling the need to dive for the nearest shelter. This was the beauty of owning a dog, even at war.

The obedience lessons would establish limits for the dog, allowing Smoky to settle into the more relaxed and calm animal that she doubtless naturally was. She seemed exceptionally eager to please, which made her a pleasure to work with. Bonds were forming quickly between the dog and her new master, and ironically, bearing in mind Wynne's concern for Smoky and her diminutive size, she seemed to be growing keenly protective over him.

Wynne decided to try her on a few choice tricks. One of the simplest and most effective acts that Wynne knew of was the 'play dead'. He taught Smoky to 'drop dead', the signal being him holding out his finger and thumb like a pistol and miming taking a shot: *Bang!* Right on cue Smoky had to fall down. She had to lie on her back, legs in the air and paws curled over, unmoving. She'd stay like that no matter what Wynne might say or do.

Then he'd give her the call: 'Smoky, okay! Okay!'

At the sound of his voice she'd spring back to life, jumping onto all fours and taking a bow. It was a simple enough trick but a compelling one, and Wynne felt certain they'd have audiences gripped in the palms of their hands (paws). Smoky also had a big voice for such a small dog, and she seemed to have an innate love of 'singing', or rather howling along to her master as he played his favourite tunes on the harmonica.

When Wynne blew a few exploratory notes, Smoky threw her head back and responded with a long, drawn-out 'Owoooooo'. Soon she'd learned to throw her head back in conjunction with her master, howling for all she was worth as he whistled along. But Smoky's singing was not without risk: it attracted the wrath off her chief detractor.

'When a dog cries someone's gonna die,' he growled, menacingly.

The threat was made in all seriousness, and for now at least Wynne decided to exercise Smoky's choral talents only when she was well out of anyone's earshot.

Very quickly, Wynne – still just twenty years of age – realized that Smoky had much to teach him. As man and dog trained together, so they appeared to be maturing alongside each other. Wynne felt ever more certain that this tiny bundle of mystery had been cared for, schooled and nurtured by whoever her previous owners might have been. It was more than a little intriguing.

As they got to know each other better, Wynne felt his earlier concerns about owning a dog once more gradually seeping away. After months soldiering in the loneliness and isolation of the New Guinea jungle and beset on all sides by dangers as they were, life could be incredibly stressful, and Smoky was proving a tremendous morale-booster.

As had happened so many times in Wynne's life, at the point of greatest need a dog had come to his rescue.

CHAPTER 5

After several days training squeezed between lab shifts, Wynne decided that Smoky was ready for her great unveiling. More to the point, he reckoned she might have a role to play within the finely tuned outfit that was the 26th Photo Reconnaissance Squadron. The capturing, processing, analysis and dissemination of photo intelligence were conducted round the clock. The labs, the drying machines, the analysis desks and the communications centre were never less than busy and they never closed.

Whenever an aircraft landed from a successful mission the images it carried were required by senior commanders as a matter of urgency. Combat missions were in the final stages of planning. Targets were being confirmed and apportioned to fighter and bomber squadrons. Beaches were being scoped for amphibious landings, caves and thick jungle probed for hidden enemy positions.

Usually, the first sign that a recce flight was in-bound came via the radio: maybe a P-38 had been detected on the base's radar, or the pilot had called in with an ETA. Once the landing time was known, the ground crew would head for the flight line to ease the half-frozen flier out of his cockpit. Once that was done, he'd report the basics of what he'd filmed to the squadron's intelligence officer.

The photo magazines would be removed and rushed by jeep to the lab. There the team – including Wynne if it was his shift – would develop the negatives in the darkroom, immersing them in pools of chemicals. They would be dried and viewed on a special light table. Prints were made of the most promising images, which were washed and run through drying machines that looked like giant industrial hair-driers. The finished images were sorted again, before being rushed to whoever had requested them. Often, they were packed aboard a light aircraft to be flown direct to the relevant headquarters.

It was intense, relentless work. The men found it hard to stay focused amid such a whirlwind of activity, especially as it was interspersed with long periods of simply waiting for something to happen, of hoping against hope that the recce squadron's Lightnings would come back safely. All too often there was the dark stress and strain of a flight going missing; of pilots simply not returning at all.

A few days after making her his own, Wynne took Smoky with him for her first shift at the photo lab. The laboratory was so hot – with gallons of chemicals being mixed by hand in vats, prints being washed in the steaming sinks and the oven-like driers whirring away – that the men tended to work shirtless and bare-headed. It lent an informal edge to the lab's otherwise intense and frenetic atmosphere.

Generators thudded in the background, for the photo lab – the driers especially – consumed huge amounts of electricity. Indeed, with the amount of power available Sergeant Waggoner, one of the 26th's engineers, had decided to form his own 'Power & Light Company'. He'd got men shimmying up palm trees, stringing cables from trunk to trunk as makeshift telegraph poles, providing electric lighting to those facilities that kept turning and burning day and night.

Nowhere burned the midnight oil like the photo lab, and Smoky's appearance there proved an instant hit. Most had already heard about the mystery dog, but few had managed to get sight of her up close. Smoky did a meet and greet with each of the lab team, starting with the lab chief Master Sergeant Irving 'Irv' Green, and she loved being the centre of attention.

Man and dog proceeded to demonstrate their first trick. Wynne pointed his finger at Smoky, forming a pistol shape. 'Boom!' he cried. Bang on cue she fell 'dead'. She lay rock-still, no matter what Wynne might do to her. He poked and prodded her several times, all to no avail. Squatting, he picked her up by her hind legs and rolled her over from hand to hand. She remained limp and lifeless as a ragdoll.

Wynne placed her on the ground, gently. He prodded her a few more times, as if doing a final check for any signs of life. Nothing. Then he turned and walked away, disconsolately, as if giving up on the little tyke. He waited a few seconds, before calling out: 'Okay!' At the sound of his voice the little bundle of shapeless fur exploded into life, jumping onto all fours and charging after her master.

The lab crew went wild.

Irv Green seemed more taken than anyone with his newest crew member. He had sandy hair cut longish and semi-quiffed at the front, and a quiet, pensive air. The demands of the photo lab could be all-consuming, the pressures debilitating. Methodical, calm, a little introspective – Green was the ideal kind of individual to run the place.

It was Green who came up with the concept of how Smoky might best serve on his team. Much of the work was endlessly repetitive, but the stakes were incredibly high. One wrong move, one moment of lapsed concentration, could ruin an entire roll of film and its irreplaceable images. The consequences of that were unthinkable. Smoky was the answer to livening things up a little, and to helping the lab crews stay focused.

In the shadows of the darkroom – it was lit only by dim, red-filtered bulbs, to protect the negatives – Wynne and Green got the tiny dog to squat in a tray of freshly developed film, ready to be passed through the 'light-trap', a hatchway sealed by thick curtains leading to the outside. Once all was ready, the tray was posted across complete with a tufty-haired, sparkly-eyed dog – for make no mistake, Smoky was loving this new adventure.

The crew outside, who were responsible for washing the freshly developed film, plucked her off the tray as she blinked in the bright sunlight. They caressed and cooed over the dog, the banter flying back and forth as they passed her around. Shortly, the tray was posted back, with Smoky taking pride of place once more. Irv Green declared himself delighted with the procedure. Smoky had found her niche in the laboratory: she was on Tray Duty. This was to become a regular procedure, one that helped the lab teams pass the interminable hours.

Shifts were long, hot and testing: twelve hours at a time. Mostly, the men of the 26th worked seven-day weeks, with no breaks. Nights, menaced as they were by air raids, were fraught with danger. Occasionally, there was a movie in the mess tent, whenever a new release managed to make it out to the wilds of New Guinea. Other than that, the pastimes for the GIs were writing letters to loved ones, listening to the radio or playing endless card games.

Isolated so far from home, it was an eternal struggle to keep morale high, one in which Wynne hoped Smoky could play a significant role. Though the Allies had started to turn the tide of the war in the Pacific, it didn't necessarily feel like that to the men on the ground, operating deep in the jungle facing a fanatical enemy, assailed by air raids and starved of news. Realizing this, the Japanese had started their own wily form of propaganda, which was beamed into Nadzab every day.

The squadron's typed Monthly Intelligence Summaries – stamped CONFIDENTIAL – listed the main issues affecting the unit, under such headings as 'RUMORS', 'PROPAGANDA ACTIVITY' and 'MORALE'. Alarmingly, that March 1944 – the month of Smoky's discovery – the morale of the 26th was listed as 'unusually low'. Much of the disquiet was due to the squadron's rumour mill, which seemed to have gone into overdrive, and one of the key reasons for this was Radio Tokyo.

In November 1941 Japan's national broadcaster – NHK, their equivalent to the BBC – had been nationalized by the Imperial Japanese Army. In fact, all news, whether newspaper or radio, was now to be regarded as an official pronouncement of the Imperial Army General Headquarters, in Tokyo. The 'Tokyo Rose' programmes had become the foremost weapon in the Japanese propaganda arsenal.

Those broadcasts were made by fluent English speakers, all of whom were female and whose identities remained a tantalizing mystery. They consisted of a clever blend of music, comedy and entertainment, interspersed with 'news flashes' that accentuated the privations and the losses suffered by the Allies. They aimed to demoralize Allied troops, who were already facing tough and testing conditions.

Marooned amid the mountainous jungles of Nadzab, those Tokyo Rose broadcasts became compelling listening to the men of the 26th. With carefully crafted disinformation slipped into genuine news stories, such propaganda proved remarkably effective, especially as the newscasters were fluent and soft-voiced young women, who the lonely soldiers couldn't help but imagine as pretty and alluring.

That March an extraordinary rumour swept through the squadron: President Roosevelt's wife, Eleanor, was demanding that all soldiers returning from the southwest Pacific theatre be sent to an island lying off the coast of the mainland USA, where they would be subjected to as much as eighteen months' quarantine. If true, it would mean a year or more of miserable isolation.

Troops would be screened for malaria, lice and other diseases endemic to the Pacific area. New Guinea was plagued by such ills, so much so that the skin of GIs took on an unhealthy yellow pallor, due to all the anti-malarial drugs they had to take, first and foremost the notorious Atabrine. So significant was the threat from malaria, that at the entrance to New Guinea's main field hospital was a sign that read: 'These men DIDN'T take their ATABRINE'. On top of the sign were perched two empty-eyed human skulls.

Eleanor Roosevelt played a very prominent role in the political and social life of the nation, so the story appeared to have credibility. The Allies had declared their first priority in the war was to defeat Nazi Germany, with Japan coming second. Accordingly, troops in the Pacific tended to worry that they were the 'poor cousins' in the conflict. That fear was now being exacerbated by outrageous and unsettling rumours of long months of quarantine.

In short, the Radio Tokyo story was a masterpiece of propaganda. It had taken the soldiers' deepest fears – of exotic diseases, of isolation and of being forgotten by those at home – and apparently made them a chilling reality. There was no truth at all to the story, of course, but that didn't stop the men talking among themselves.

The squadron's spring '44 Intelligence Summaries stressed the efforts made to quash such morale-sapping loose talk. They concluded that the story was 'obviously a malicious rumour intended to damage the character of the First Lady; it was pointed out to the men as such.' But the novelty of the shows and the allure of the mystery female hosts ensured that Radio Tokyo continued to draw listeners.

An even wilder report began to do the rounds. 'Rumoured also was the belief that "Madame Tojo" of Radio Tokyo is Amelia Earhart,' the Intelligence Summaries noted. 'Rumour is not generally believed.' Whether or not the men believed it, the very idea that one of America's most famous and heroic figures might be pumping out enemy propaganda was hugely disheartening. It sowed the seeds of doubt – doubt that could become corrosive if left to fester.

In 1932 Amelia Earhart had become the first woman to fly across the Atlantic. Blessed with fresh-faced, tomboyish good looks, there was a swashbuckling side to her character that played well with the public on both sides of the Atlantic. Upon touching down at Culmore, in Northern Ireland, after her fourteen hour fifty-six minute trans-Atlantic journey, Earhart had been asked by a curious local if she had come far? 'From America,' was her teasing reply.

In 1937 she'd set out with a male pilot to circumnavigate the globe. They'd completed 22,000 miles of the trip, before going missing in the southwest Pacific. What made the Tokyo Rose rumour all the more credible, at least to the men of the squadron, was that Earhart and her fellow pilot, Fred Noonan, had taken off for their fateful last flight from Lae, the port adjacent to Nadzab itself.

In spite of extensive searches made along their flightpath, no sign was ever found of the missing aircraft. Earhart and her co-pilot had disappeared seemingly without trace. But now, according to the Tokyo Rose broadcasts, Earhart had resurfaced as a female propagandist for the Imperial Japanese Army. It was said she'd been captured by the Japanese when her plane crash-landed, and now was being forced to help spread their gospel of lies.

Because they were a photo reconnaissance squadron, the men of the 26th were allowed to undertake a 'limited amount' of personal photography. In his spring '44 intelligence reports the 26th's intelligence officer stressed how he had 'enforced a rigid censorship of all photos . . . the lab chief is responsible for a check on all negatives developed.' By doing so he hoped that the flow of damaging images that might be mailed home, or fall into enemy hands, would be 'considerably reduced'.

But the real challenge remained to limit the damage caused by the Japanese radio broadcasts, which were beaming daily into the soldiers' tents. Faced with such sophisticated propaganda, could the squadron's newest and smallest member help turn the tide of demoralizing disinformation? Could Smoky do something to help lift the men's spirits? As it happened, yes, she could.

Sport is one of the great morale-boosters. Trouble was, in New Guinea there weren't many football stadiums or baseball fields to hand. Finding enough flat, clear ground to build the Nadzab airstrips had been enough of a challenge. But all work and no play makes Jack a dull boy; a strip of land was bulldozed out of the jungle that fringed the Markham River so that an inter-squadron softball series could be started.

It made sense to play softball here, as opposed to regular baseball – its need for a smaller field and a larger ball was more suited to the terrain. Excitement mounted quickly ahead of the first game, one in which Smoky was about to demonstrate just what a huge spirit-lifter such a tiny dog could be. As the teams warmed up, tossing the ball into the outfield, runners dashed about 'shagging flies' – catching balls thrown wide.

By now Smoky, the dog who had appeared from out of the blue, was pretty much known to everyone around the camp, and she was in the thick of it, chasing every ball that came in her direction. As the softball was the best part of four inches in diameter, and Smoky barely stood that high off the ground, it was as if the tiny dog was chasing after a massive boulder, ears flapping and hair streaming as she dashed from pillar to post.

Warm-ups completed, the competition got underway. The 26th was playing a game against a team from the headquarters of the 5th Air Force Wing, their parent unit. A quick ball left the bat and skittered along the ground. Before anyone could stop her Smoky was after it like a bullet from a gun. The player on third base bent to scoop up the ball, just as a careering canine hairball overtook it.

Smoky leapt to seize the ball and was flipped head over heels by the fast-spinning projectile, landing in the startled baseman's glove. The ball itself powered onwards, smoking past between the guy's legs. He didn't know what had hit him, but at least he managed to refrain from hurling what he'd caught – *a dog* – to fourth base.

Predictably, the doggie stunt provoked a great deal of hilarity. All around the field figures were clutching their sides laughing. Smoky, meanwhile, had returned to the sidelines a little chastised, and noticeably shaken and stirred.

Days later the news bulletin printed by the 5th Air Force declared of the match: 'O'Hara went to second on an effort by Havel and Smoky, Lightning Dog Mascot.' In a sense they'd hit the nail on the head: the little dog *was* becoming an invaluable mascot to the 26th, those who flew the unarmed P-38 Lightnings into hostile skies.

Smoky's value lay in humour, in her ability to bring light amid the darkness of war. Under the stresses and strains of combat and in such an environment, Smoky constituted a rare slice of fun. And, crucially, she was a reminder of a distant and much longed-for place: home. She served as a symbol of the simple freedoms and pleasures of life that all here were fighting to preserve.

Indeed, the more the men of the 26th got to know her, the more it seemed that spreading fun and laughter and light was the very essence of Smoky's being. Tiny though she was, Smoky just seemed to be the gift that never stopped giving.

And she was about to reveal her powers in the most unexpected way.

CHAPTER 6

Yank Magazine was a US military weekly founded in June 1942, with a view to boosting the morale of soldiers, sailors and airmen deployed overseas. The idea for the publication was inspired by the *Stars and Stripes* newspaper, which served a similar purpose during the wars. Written by enlisted ranks, the debut June '42 issue of *Yank* had the US actress Jane Randolph, one of the GI's favourite chocolate-box pin-ups, gracing the cover.

A few weeks after Smoky had been discovered in the jungle, *Yank Magazine* launched a competition to find the best mascots in the southwest Pacific theatre of operations. When Bill Wynne heard of it he was determined that he and Smoky would give it their best shot. It was an inspired idea guaranteed to occupy the minds of the troops, and Wynne sensed a real opportunity for him and his tiny dog to make a splash.

Soldiers mostly had to make their own entertainment at Nadzab, especially if they didn't fancy another night in with Tokyo Rose. Some made carefully crafted models of their trusty P-38s, using empty shell cases to form the body of the aircraft and the engine housings. Occasionally, a group of three or four might pay a sightseeing visit to a native village, and some had resorted to making collections of the giant butterflies that flitted through the jungle.

Indeed, Smoky herself found the huge, low-flying iridescent insects irresistible. Many a time Wynne had caught her bounding after a Queen Alexandra's birdwing, a butterfly whose wingspan could grow to twenty-five centimetres – enough to dwarf the dog's girth. There was something captivating about the way she pranced and danced and snapped beneath the giant creature; she looked like a crazed paratrooper desperately trying to recover a wayward parachute. But Bill Wynne was all too conscious of the dangers associated with such seemingly harmless fun.

Like a diminutive Pied Piper, the butterfly would flit and flap its way deeper into the jungle in an effort to escape its pursuer, drawing Smoky inexorably after. And that risked one of two outcomes. In the first, Smoky might lose her way once more – and there was no guarantee that this time she would be found. In the second, she might stumble into the path of one of the many predators that slithered and crawled through the dank shadows.

The ghastly thought of losing his new friend made Wynne intensify Smoky's obedience training, which he hoped might also give them an edge in the forthcoming *Yank Magazine* pageant. He was under no illusions as to how stiff the competition would likely prove. Indeed, one of their sister squadrons had a long-standing mascot who had already achieved a high profile. 'Colonel Turbo' had earned widespread infamy at Nadzab due to his wild, bad-tempered and downright destructive ways.

Colonel Turbo was a Rhesus Macaque – a monkey native to Asia, but not to the New Guinea region. Standing some twenty inches tall, and with brownish-grey fur and pink, hairless features, the Rhesus tends to look red-faced and angry at the best of times. There was no worse-tempered macaque than Colonel Turbo, though his tantrums were mostly tolerated because he had a fairly good excuse for such behaviour.

A pilot had acquired Turbo from a zoo in the States. Subsequently, that aviator had been killed in a plane crash. Feeling sorry for Turbo, his parent squadron had adopted him as their mascot. When they deployed from the US, Turbo had been dosed with sleeping tablets to keep him quiet during the long sea voyage. He'd been stuffed into a soldier's duffle bag to be smuggled aboard ship, and subsequently he was hung out of a convenient porthole on the end of a leash as a way of hiding him during ship's inspections.

By the time they reached New Guinea, Turbo's ways were pretty much ingrained. He took either an instant like or dislike to whoever he met. You'd know if it was the latter when he sunk his teeth – all thirty-two of them – into your arm or leg. Whenever he was free he'd race from tent to tent causing chaos and mayhem, ripping open cigarette cartons, shredding letters and parcels from home and eating whatever goodies he could find.

One of Turbo's chief sponsors at Nadzab had warned Wynne that Smoky would never get the better of their notorious mascot. 'Colonel Turbo can handle anything,' he'd boasted. Colonel Turbo, he'd bragged, would grab a tiny little thing like Smoky and eat her alive.

The monkey was known to have a wily way with dogs. He'd square up to any that he encountered with his head held low to the dirt, hips set high and hands reached back between his hind legs. When the dog approached – all ground-snuffling curiosity – those hands would shoot forward in a flash, grab the dog's front legs, and wrestle it to the ground, whereupon Turbo's jaws would clamp shut on the poor animal's ears. In no time the dog would be howling in pain and would beat a rapid retreat.

Wynne wasn't overly keen on Smoky fronting up to Colonel Turbo, but he sensed a certain inevitability about the showdown. There was only so long that these two larger-than-life animal characters could avoid running into each other in a place like Nadzab. He also had a sense of how big Smoky's attitude was, regardless of her size. There is an old saying: *it's not the size of the dog in the fight; it's the size of the fight in the dog.* It was to be more than borne out in the course of Smoky's first encounter with the infamous macaque.

Turbo was kept tied to a post most of the time. If not, he would run riot. He seemed to have little desire to escape into the jungle. Once or twice some of his less-forgiving victims had driven him deep into the forest, evicting him from their jeep and speeding away. But their efforts to free Turbo had always misfired. A while later he'd be seen sidling back into camp, moving with the side-swagger and crooked hop so typical of the species.

Upon first spying the monkey Smoky had been all perked-up ears and doggy curiosity. Bold as brass, she'd trotted over to check out this strange-smelling beast. Turbo had treated her well-meaning approach as he had that of a dozen dogs before her: in a flash he'd grabbed her by the nose, squeezing tighter and tighter until she was yelping in pain. Finally, Smoky had broken free and backed away in shock and surprise. But not for long.

Even as Turbo was basking in his apparent victory, she'd leapt forward on the counter-attack. Turbo tried to recover and nab her again, but she was too nimble and too quick. In an instant she'd darted beneath his arms and lunged for his face, snapping at and skinning his pink, protruding nose. It was Turbo's turn to yelp with pain. He'd jumped up into a tree above, and sat there rubbing his face and checking his hand for any sign of blood.

By now a crowd of curious onlookers had gathered. Sensing an audience, Smoky turned her back on the monkey. Believing his adversary was unsighted and vulnerable, Turbo dropped softly to the ground and lunged for her nether regions. But in a flash Smoky had whipped around and charged at him, barking in a wild, high-pitched yelp. It sounded as if the macaque had hold of some tufts of her hair and was ripping it out by the roots.

Nonplussed and panicked, Turbo fled, but Smoky was too fast for him. As he tried to leap for the safety of his tree again, she was upon him, snapping at his heels. Each time Turbo made a jump for the nearest limb of the tree, she would do the same again, putting him off his stride. Unable to reach the branch, the macaque was reduced to leaping repeatedly into the air to try to avoid the little dog's wrath. By now, the gang of onlookers was roaring with laughter.

Finally, Smoky allowed him space to swing into his tree. It was the first time a dog had got the better of Colonel Turbo, and from then on the two animals struck up a relationship based upon a measure of mutual respect. Whenever she tired of chasing butterflies Smoky would seek out Turbo for a runaround. He never forgot how feisty she could be and he never tried to bully her again. But as mascots went Turbo was still a legend and Smoky would have to go some to beat him.

Historically speaking, Smoky should have had the edge. The US military had a long tradition of keeping dogs as mascots. During the First World War the Germans were reputed to have referred to US Marines as the *Teufelshunden* – Devil Dogs – due to the ferocity with which they fought. The Marine Corps embraced the name, and before long a recruiting poster appeared showing a British bulldog snapping at the heels of a Dachshund. The iconography had taken root, with the Marines adopting both the name and a live British bulldog as their mascot.

As it turned out there were to be some 400 entries to the *Yank Magazine* mascot competition, most of which were dogs. Clearly, Smoky needed to find a way to stand out from the crowd. Fortunately, the 26th had two very strong cards to play: the dog's undeniably photogenic looks, and the fact that they were a photographic squadron. With this in mind, Wynne decided some truly creative images were called for, in combination with a little theatre.

First off he grabbed a camera from the 26th photo lab, and his GI helmet, with its distinctive bowl-like profile, jungle-green covering and canvas strap. From the moment Smoky had become such a seminal part of his life, he'd realized that grooming her was going to be of paramount importance, if her crudely shorn hair was to recover and if she were to survive the privations of jungle living. Searching around for a suitable bath he'd alighted upon his helmet.

It doubled as his daily wash-and-shave basin, so he could see no reason why it shouldn't serve a similar purpose for his dog. He filled it with water, placed Smoky inside, and it was perfect: deep enough for her to sit in, with her beady eyes peering over the side, hair shooting out like fireworks in all directions. As she gazed at him in excited curiosity, Wynne had proceeded to give Smoky her first proper bath and rub down since she'd been rescued from the jungle.

After treating her to a proper post-bathe grooming, he'd noticed that her hair seemed to have a natural parting stretching from the nape of her neck all the way to her tail. She'd shaken herself dry, and her hair had fallen straight down both sides of her body, from the ridgeline of her backbone. If he brushed it back again, with one shake it flopped into place once more, tumbling down from that natural parting. Smoky was full of surprises and again Wynne had been struck by a burning curiosity to find out what kind of breed she might be.

He readied his camera in preparation for the mascot competition photo, placing his helmet on the ground and knowing that Smoky would jump right in, as if taking a bath. Sure enough she did, and the shot he took served to emphasize her small size, for the helmet lent the photo a perfect sense of scale. Surely, no one at *Yank Magazine* could fail to be captivated by the image, or to be curious as to what kind of dog she might be.

But still he wasn't satisfied. Suddenly he had a flash of inspiration as to the type of dramatic image they could shoot for. It would need the assistance of a good number of the squadron, yet if they could pull it off it would surely be the clincher.

Wynne sought out Corporals Murphy and Piette, who were saddled with one of the unit's most onerous jobs. They were the 26th's parachute packers – charged with keeping the squadron's 'chutes in fine fettle. Murphy and Piette had to ensure that the parachutes were properly stowed, so if a pilot did have cause to bale out the expanse of life-saving silk would open on cue, blossoming in the skies above. The trigger system for this involved a small pilot 'chute that deployed once the rip-cord was pulled, which in turn would drag out the main parachute.

Wynne figured one of those pilot 'chutes was just about the right size to carry his dog. With his kindly, open features and receding hairline, Corporal Thomas Murphy was one of the old hands of the squadron, having joined in March 1943. He was the kind of guy who would do anything for anyone. His fellow parachute packer, Corporal Marion Piette, with his slicked-back hair and pencil-thin moustache, was the more sober of the two. But both men were noted for treating their craft with the seriousness that it demanded.

Fortunately, they were also big fans of Wynne's dog. In the parachute store-tent they tended to work bare-chested, but with a US military khaki field cap – similar in style to a baseball cap – jammed on their heads. They were surrounded by the tools of their trade: parachute harnesses, rigging, and shelves stacked high with bulging parachute packs, each about the size of your average day-sack. Just as soon as Wynne had explained his cunning plan, a pilot 'chute was quietly passed his way.

Normally, the pilot 'chute was attached to the main 'chute by rigging lines. But for Wynne's present purposes he had to fashion a parachute harness in which a seven-inch-high dog could hang suspended from those lines. He found the best material from which to do so was a bog-standard money belt. By lashing a couple together, he managed to form a cradle in which to strap his dog, which in turn was attached to the 'chute's rigging.

It was time to try Smoky out in her new apparatus. By now

man and dog were several weeks into their partnership, and it was almost beginning to feel as if they'd never been apart. In war, bonds tend to form far quicker than in peacetime. Extreme situations engender extreme emotions, extreme attachments. Already, Wynne and Smoky trusted each other implicitly. He fastened her into the DIY harness, tightened the straps and swung her about this way and that, aping the movements the 'chute was likely to make in an effort to get her accustomed to what was coming. Luckily, she seemed perfectly happy in her new rig.

That done, he went about recruiting his para-drop team. He needed a volunteer to cut the branches from the side of one of the trees that grew adjacent to the softball field; it would be from there that Smoky would make her first jump. Next, he needed someone to hold one side of the GI blanket in which they would catch Smoky as she fell. Wynne decided he needed to be one of the catcher-crew, and John Barnard, one of his buddies in the squadron, offered to hold the blanket's other side.

Finally, he gave the key role of official stunt photographer to Staff Sergeant Howard J. Kalt, a man whose thinning hair, protruding ears and self-effacing smile gave him something of a schoolmasterly appearance. A superlative organizer, Kalt helped run the squadron's movie nights, and he was forever taking stick for it.

However good or bad the film might promise to be, the tent was always packed, for a Hollywood release was a rare treat. But it was a major triumph to get through an evening's projection without something breaking down. The long-suffering Kalt had got used to all the catcalls and the jibes. How hard could it be capturing a parachuting Smoky on film, after facing countless movie nights at Nadzab, complete with their boisterous and disruptive audiences?

The man whom Wynne entrusted to release Smoky from the tree was Don Esmond, a fellow native of Cleveland. Esmond climbed into the branches, and Smoky was passed up to him with her parachute attached. Leaning out as far as he could, Esmond checked the reception committee was ready down below. He waited until the hot tropical wind that gusted down the valley had died down a little, and upon Wynne's yell to release her, he let Smoky and 'chute go free.

The silk blossomed above Smoky and she proceeded to float towards earth, her four legs splayed wide as if ready for a proper bail out and landing, her head peering forward and searching for the point to make touchdown. She landed right in the centre of the blanket, Wynne and Barnard breaking her fall, and the team let out a triumphant cheer. Smoky seemed to love the attention. She got to her feet and wagged her stumpy tail, gutsily. As she gazed at her team with a moist and shiny muzzle, tongue lolling out and eyes shining happily, they could have sworn she understood exactly what they were here for.

She seemed keen for more. Her para-drop team repeated the jump four further times, just to ensure that Kalt had it captured properly on film and from all possible angles. But when they sent her up again, drop number six was to prove a jump too far. The wind gusted fiercely across the softball field, just as Esmond set Smoky into motion. The blast hit the side of the 'chute, blowing it out of shape and collapsing it in an instant.

Moments later Smoky was falling, the 'chute balling up like a bundle of wet washing behind her. Wynne and Barnard rushed to reposition the blanket, but they were too late. Smoky tore past. As Wynne watched aghast, she arched her back, her four legs reaching wide, and disappeared into the foot-high grass. She bounced on impact, yelping with pain as she turned a somersault in the air, her head bent at an odd angle.

Moments later she hit the ground again and lay still.

Wynne raced to Smoky's side, feeling sick to the death at what he might have done. He was consumed with fear for his blameless companion. The others gathered in a stunned silence as Wynne held Smoky down, checking her for injuries. She continued to yelp and whine. Finally, he took her head in one hand and body in the other, and pulled gently. Something seemed to snap back into place, and Smoky stopped the agonized whimpers. She convulsed several times and vomited up the canned sausages that she'd eaten for lunch.

Wynne felt furious at himself, cursing his own stupidity for risking the life of the animal that he loved. Sure, there would be no better way to raise the morale of his squadron than to win the *Yank Magazine* competition, but that didn't mean it had to require a life-threatening stunt such as this. If Smoky died, or was left disabled, who knew what effect it would have on the spirits of the 26th?

Shamefaced, the team wrapped Smoky in the blanket and carried her back to her tent. By the time they reached it, she seemed to have recovered her spirits a little. She was still uncharacteristically quiet and inactive, but at least the pained whining was over.

Wynne sat up all night, watching over his dog. He didn't

know quite what he would do if she took a turn for the worse. All he could imagine was that he'd take her to the Nadzab Quartermaster Corps – the unit that oversaw administration for all military supplies routed via the base. If he was lucky there might just be a veterinarian within their ranks, or at least someone with that kind of experience.

Fortunately, he had no need to throw himself on the mercy of the Quartermaster Corps. Come morning, Smoky seemed almost back to her old self.

Kalt suggested they take a photo of her in a far less life-threatening role – fifty-five standing astride a 55-gallon steel drum. They would be extra careful with her this time. Once that image was developed, Kalt cut it out and pasted it onto a picture of a cloud, with Smoky's ears and her hair flying in the breeze. It was Smoky's version of the 26th's Donald Duck patch: all that seemed to be missing was the flying helmet.

That became her official *Yank Magazine* entry photo. Beside it Wynne wrote that her key responsibility within the squadron was morale. Whenever the men of the 26th had had a particularly bad day, all anyone needed to see was Smoky chasing after a giant butterfly, captivated by its every move, and they would find the heaviness lift from their shoulders. In no time they would be smiling and laughing again.

The *Yank Magazine* entry was submitted, the plucky little dog having survived her para-jumps apparently none the worse for wear. But little did Wynne realize how Smoky's para-training would prepare her for the rigours of what was coming.

For soon, she would be called upon to take to the skies.

CHAPTER 7

Throughout March and April 1944, the high-flying P-38 Lightnings flitted through the skies above Hollandia in an effort to capture images of the Japanese forces based there. Hollandia was the site of the single greatest concentration of enemy warplanes south of the equator, as well as being a vital staging post in the region for men, materiel and supplies. General MacArthur was determined to wrest those bases from enemy hands, and to do so he needed up-to-date recce photos. But the weather continued to be abysmal, which made securing those crucial high-altitude images a huge challenge.

Finally, a brief weather window opened and the fliers of the 26th were able to get airborne. They were able to buzz Hollandia fast and at 20,000 feet, capturing the images that senior Allied commanders hungered for. The negatives were rushed through the Nadzab photo lab, with Smoky performing her Tray Duty with admirable poise. The pictures so secured revealed hundreds of enemy fighters and bombers parked in serried ranks upon Hollandia's three airstrips, making for incredibly juicy targets.

Of course, the Japanese defenders had detected those lone recce flights sizing up their positions. But their commanders – foremost, General Hatazo Adachi – made the fatal error of underestimating their adversary. Assuming that Hollandia lay beyond the reach of any Allied air-attack squadrons, they had presumed that no airborne assault was possible. It was a mistake that would cost them dear.

Under Operation Cartwheel – MacArthur's grand strategy in the region – key enemy bases were to be subjected to 'Air Blockade', which had the following objectives: to destroy the enemy's air force on the ground; to destroy his airstrips and air defences, so no reinforcements or supplies could be flown in; to destroy the enemy's living quarters; and to destroy all stores and related installations.

The other key element of Air Blockade was surprise. As the official US Air Force journal from the time declared: 'Surprise is to air attack what mustard is to a hot dog. You can do without it, but it makes a big difference.' Following an Air Blockade, General George Churchill Kenney, overall commander of Allied air forces in the region, aimed 'to land troops with rifles on their backs and to have the enemy so thoroughly demoralized that the rifles are kept there as long as possible'.

Two factors would prove essential when it came to securing the element of surprise at Hollandia. The first was capturing those high-level recce photos: they confirmed that the Japanese had done little to make their warplanes any more difficult to target, which had to mean that they believed no attack was coming. Hundreds of aircraft were lined up like ducks in a shooting gallery. Indeed, General Adachi kept adding to his squadrons – building up his air power, in keeping with his orders to hold the line in New Guinea and repulse any Allied assaults.

The second factor was a cunningly crafted deception. General

Adachi rightly presumed that no Allied commander would risk an attack by heavy bombers without fighters in escort. He wrongly presumed that no Allied fighters had the range to make the thousand-mile round trip from Nadzab to Hollandia and back again. A new 'long-legged' model of the P-38 had just been introduced to theatre. The P-38F possessed underwing racks for carrying 'drop-tanks' – external fuel tanks that could be jettisoned when empty – an innovation that vastly increased its range.

The P-38F was deliberately kept under wraps, never venturing more than 300 miles from Nadzab, which further lured the enemy into a false sense of security. The Japanese were led to believe that Hollandia was safe, because their adversaries had no fighters that could cover the kind of distances required to engage in combat and defend their bomber squadrons. It was to prove a catastrophic oversight.

On 30 March 1944 the massed ranks of Allied warplanes took to the skies. The air above Nadzab darkened with the forms of hundreds of Consolidated B24 Liberators, the valley echoing to the roar of the heavy bomber's turbo-supercharged Pratt and Whitney radial engines. The Liberators formed up with their 'long-legged' P-38F escorts, and set a course for Hollandia, some three hours flying time to the northwest. It was the first time the Lightnings would venture that far from base.

The air armada reached Hollandia to find that surprise was almost complete. Of the 150 fighter aircraft that General Adachi had on the ground, only forty managed to get airborne in an attempt to intercept the Allied warplanes. They were scrambled in a disorganized and piecemeal fashion and they faced a perilous climb to the B24's cruise altitude. Long before they reached it the P-38F Lightnings fell on them with a vengeance, and half the Japanese fighters were blasted from the skies.

The Liberators, meanwhile, unleashed their payloads. Each heavy bomber was packed with 5,000 pounds of incendiaries, which were highly effective against the aircraft lined up on the ground. The closely packed Japanese warplanes – mostly prized Mitsubishi G4M high-speed, long-range bombers – were caught in long strings of blasts. In short order the aerodromes at Hollandia were wreathed in thick and billowing clouds of smoke and flames.

The following day the airborne raiders returned, wreaking further devastation. By the end of those forty-eight hours of action, 219 enemy warplanes had been destroyed in the air and on the ground, for the loss of only a handful of P-38s. Follow-up airstrikes pounded Hollandia's air-defences with 1,000-pound demolitions bombs, and ripped apart the stores and barracks areas that serviced them. By the end of the second week of April, 352 enemy aircraft had been destroyed, while Allied losses remained meagre.

But the Allies were not to have things all their own way: soon they would learn that they too could be taken by surprise.

On Sunday 16 April 1944 the weather turned. That day, which would become known as 'Black Sunday', a towering tropical storm darkened the skies above Nadzab, blocking out all sunlight. Out of the two hundred Allied warplanes that had set out earlier to raid Hollandia, scores would fail to make it back again.

Some three-dozen aircraft – Liberators, plus Douglas A-20

Havocs and their Lightning escorts – returned from the raids over Hollandia running short of fuel, only to find Nadzab Airbase blanketed in thick cloud.

On the ground, Bill Wynne and Smoky could hear the airplanes desperately circling in the dark skies. Some aircrew chose to bail out before their aircraft ran out of juice completely. Others flew on until all their fuel was exhausted, waiting for a weather window that never opened. Dozens of warplanes went down among the jungle-clad mountains that towered to either side of the Markham River Valley.

Black Sunday had delivered one of the worst blows the US air force suffered during the war in the Pacific, with the weather proving to be a more fearsome enemy than the Japanese. But all things told, the Hollandia operation was still regarded as a runaway success. 'The enemy's air strength, which he had been building for weeks, was wiped out as thoroughly as a janitor clearing a blackboard with a wet rag,' the US Army Air Force trumpeted in their report on the raids.

On the coat tails of the blistering air offensive, ground forces set sail for Hollandia, executing a 500-mile advance and catching many enemy garrisons by almost total surprise. With General Adachi's air power practically wiped out, he'd had little means to scour the seas for any approaching Allied ships. Less than a hundred hours after the amphibious landings had gone in, and after a series of intense and fierce ground battles, all three airstrips at Hollandia lay in Allied hands.

In some of the Japanese barracks breakfasts lay uneaten on mess hall tables. General Adachi himself was said to have evacuated his quarters leaving a pair of trousers in a clothes press.

The general had been caught with his 'pants down', the Air Force wrote gleefully, and 'must have made an incongruous sight tearing through the jungle dressed as a general only from the waist up'.

Indeed, Adachi had slipped into the thick tree cover that lay inland of Hollandia, taking 200,000 of his troops with him. On paper his options were limited. At his back lay the impenetrable New Guinea jungle. To his front lay the open sea. As they'd intended, Allied forces now dominated the airspace, and he could expect little relief or reinforcement from that direction.

But Adachi was far from done. He planned to lead his men through seemingly impossible swamp and jungle, in an effort to launch a counter-attack from where General MacArthur would least expect it. Leaving some of his forces to harass the new Allied positions, Adachi set out on a forced march through utterly punishing terrain, leading, as always, from the front.

With Hollandia lost, his army was isolated thousands of miles from home and effectively cut off from the rest of the Imperial Japanese Army. But by his example, Adachi intended to hold his men together and to strike a decisive blow. Putting himself on the same short rations as his troops, and disdaining old war injuries, he set out to fight a do-or-die battle.

As for MacArthur, he was already eyeing the next objective on his Operation Cartwheel shopping list: Biak Island, lying some 350 miles beyond Hollandia. Heavily garrisoned by Japanese troops, MacArthur needed his eyes in the sky to get airborne over Biak Island, to bring him the crucial intelligence he required. That meant the 26th had to get their aircraft up to Hollandia, just as soon as the runways could be made serviceable. But as the squadron began its move north, its man-and-dog team were struck down by one of the many mystery ills that stalked the New Guinea jungle.

Growing up before the war, Bill Wynne had been a big fan of the hugely successful movie *Bring 'Em Back Alive*, featuring the American adventurer Frank Buck. Filmed in the Malaysian jungle, it showed dramatic scenes of a giant python fighting a crocodile, and of a 'street brawl' between a tiger and a black panther. But what Wynne remembered most, now that he had Smoky to care for, was the scene of a python swallowing a pig, and the bulge the animal made in the snake's stomach.

He was determined that Smoky wouldn't suffer a similar fate here in Nadzab, and at night he kept her firmly tethered to the foot of his bed. But during daytime she loved to chase the helmeted guineafowl that ran wild around their tented camp. About the size of a chicken, the guineafowl has a grey-blue plumage spangled with white, and bright aquamarine and red colouring to its head.

Congregating in flocks of twenty-odd birds, the guineafowl were quite happy to fend off the occasional inquisitive cat. But not Smoky. Whenever she disappeared, Wynne knew exactly where to look. He'd follow the excited yelps, only to find his dog thrashing her way through the dense jungle to the rear of their camp, with a flock of portly guineafowl trotting along in front on spindly legs, issuing harsh calls of alarm.

It was obvious why Smoky found it such fun chasing the birds, but the bush was full of dangers. The worst were actually the invisible threats – first and foremost of which was Scrub Typhus, a disease caused by an intracellular parasite, carried by the mites that infested the jungle's thick vegetation. The bite of the mites – commonly known as 'chiggers' – caused a characteristic black welt on a human's skin. But not on a dog. And dogs were known to carry the disease, transmitting it to humans.

Scrub Typhus plagued those who were sent to fight in the New Guinea jungle. In some areas it had caused more casualties than combat. Symptoms included high fever, headaches, aching muscles, liver failure and haemorrhaging. Left untreated, it normally proved fatal. The way to avoid catching the disease was to avoid close contact with the vegetation on which the chiggers lurked, which was why Wynne called Smoky back whenever she went chasing the guineafowl.

He'd grab a low bush and start to shake it, enticingly, shouting: 'Here they are! Here they are!' Curious, Smoky would weave a path back towards him. They'd play that game for a while, before Smoky would wag her tail and cock her head to one side, eyeing Wynne knowingly.

Her expression seemed to say: 'Come on! Let's go! I know where loads of them are!'

But each episode chasing Smoky in the bush exposed Wynne to hidden diseases like Scrub Typhus. One evening shortly before the Hollandia raids, he had to work late in the lab. He returned to his tent, only to find that Smoky had disappeared. He figured he could hear her yapping in the distance. He searched high and low, but could find no sign of her. Horrible visions of bulging snakes filled his head.

Finally, he spotted some locals wandering along a path. In pidgin English – an English-based dialect used by the New Guinea tribes – he explained to them that his dog had gone missing. Using hand gestures he indicated her size, and pointing at his own hair he gave an impression of what her coat looked like. The locals nodded and grinned and disappeared into the bush. A few minutes later one of them was back, bursting through a thick curtain of vines. In his arms he held a squirming dog.

'Yah!' Wynne yelled; *you've done it!*

Before handing Smoky back, the villager turned her over and inspected her underside. He smiled. 'Smoky – Mary dog!' In pidgin all females were referred to as 'Mary'. Wynne nodded in agreement. Smoky was indeed a Mary dog. He had her execute a couple of tricks and the locals were amazed that she seemed to understand every word that he was saying.

Word must have spread about this amazing little dog. A short while later Smoky went missing again. In desperation, Wynne headed down to the nearest village to ask if his dog had been seen there. The locals had the reputation of being cannibals, at least in the remoter parts of New Guinea, but Wynne was less worried about himself being eaten and far more concerned about the fate of his dog. She'd make a tasty snack for any famished villager.

His first efforts in pidgin didn't seem to cut it. There were blank, uncomprehending stares all around. He resorted to a form of charades, miming a dog barking, raising one paw and standing on her hind legs. Eventually, it dawned on the villagers what he was after. They beckoned for him to follow and threaded their way deeper into the bush. Wynne had no idea where this magical mystery tour was taking him, but he hoped to discover his dog alive and well at the end of it.

Finally, they came to a clearing. He heard a familiar sound – a dog's yapping. It made his heart leap. It was Smoky all right. He found her surrounded by village children and running through her repertoire of tricks. Smoky was clearly in her element. The kids were laughing, cheering and egging her on to do more. The more she captured their attention, the more she wanted to captivate them all.

Wynne watched for a while, feeling torn. On the one hand he was overjoyed to have found her, and just wanted her back in his arms. On the other he was reluctant to break the magic of the moment. Finally, Smoky spotted him and came running. She looked proud as punch at her solo performances. He scooped her up and there were smiles all around from the children.

Wynne carried Smoky back along the path that meandered through the bush, jungle giants towering high above their heads, their trunks thick with vines. Finding Smoky here had been a surreal moment and a magical one, but each exposure to the wilds carried its own risks. Back at camp Wynne treated his dog to an extra-long soak in his helmet bathtub. Once her coat was thoroughly shampooed, rinsed and dried, they settled down to some serious grooming. Smoky's hair was growing back again, and it was getting longer, silkier and very much like that of a human.

Just like human hair tends to, Smoky's would get into knots if not regularly brushed. Repeated sojourns in the bush risked her picking up all kinds of parasites and pests, which could thrive in her coat. Caring for his dog – taking the time to properly bathe and groom her – was one of the means by which Wynne tried to counter such threats. But who was taking care of him?

When the sickness came, it hit like a whirlwind. Overnight almost, Wynne developed a raging fever. The alarm was raised, he was loaded into a field ambulance and rushed across camp to the 233rd Station Hospital. This was a tented field facility, which constituted the first line of care for front-line troops evacuated from battle all over New Guinea.

Wynne's fever was raging at 105 degrees, the level at which you start becoming delirious and hallucinating. High fever is a symptom of malaria, but the blood tests came back negative. If it wasn't malaria, it was most likely dengue fever, the doctors decided – another mosquito-borne disease, but this one caused by a virus. The symptoms of dengue are largely similar to Scrub Typhus: high fever, headache, vomiting, muscle and joint pains, plus a telltale skin rash. Again, if not treated properly dengue could kill.

While Wynne battled fever in the hospital tent, the medics ran more tests. As for Smoky, this was the first time that she'd been separated from her saviour for any length of time. The way Wynne was feeling, he had no idea how long he might be hospitalized, or when he might see Smoky again. He'd left her in the care of Francis 'Frank' Petrilak, a fellow dog-lover. With his fresh-faced looks, eager gaze and glasses, Petrilak appeared far too young to have been sent to war. But Wynne knew how fond he was of man's four-legged friend. He felt confident that Petrilak would care for Smoky, no matter how long they might be parted.

During the first night Bill Wynne spent in hospital, a casualty from the fighting around Hollandia was brought into the tent. Squadron Sergeant James M. Craig had been in the thick of

In early March 1944 a tiny dog was discovered by Allied troops, abandoned in a jungle foxhole. A total mystery – was she a Japanese military mascot that had somehow got left behind? – she was named 'Smoky' by Corporal William 'Bill' Wynne, the soldier who adopted her, due to her distinctive colouring. Though he was unsure even of what breed she might be, Smoky would go on to forge one of the most extraordinary records of any dog that served with Allied forces.

Facing suicidal resistance from Japanese troops, and fighting across horrendous terrain, Allied troops – and their diminutive canine mascot – were stalked by venomous jungle critters and exotic killer diseases, but it was then that Smoky really came into her own. When Bill Wynne was struck down with suspected dengue fever, Smoky was allowed to sleep in the field hospital on his bed. Overnight she became an informal therapy dog, comforting those traumatised on the frontline of war, and bringing light into shattered lives.

After many months of taking it, the anti-malarial drug, Atabrine, turned troops' skin a signature yellow. This sign, at the entrance to one of the main field hospitals, left little doubt as to what fate awaited those who missed their pills.

Smoky became the prize-winning mascot of the 26th Photo Reconnaissance Squadron. Pilots flew their lone, unarmed aircraft fast and at high altitude deep behind enemy lines to capture crucial photographs on film. Their distinctive aircraft, the P38 Lightning, was nicknamed the Fork-tailed Devil by the enemy, due to its distinctive twin tailplanes. Soon, Smoky too would take to the skies on a series of daring sorties.

Moments of downtime were rare, both for the men and their diminutive canine mascot. Smoky was determined to get involved, more than once being mistaken for the ball in the rough and tumble.

Colonel Turbo was a Rhesus Macaque, and a mascot of a rival squadron. But Smoky got the better of him, both in their first and only fight, and when she beat him to first place in a mascot competition.

Allied forces swept through the Islands of the Southwest Pacific, often moving so swiftly that they bypassed Japanese garrisons. But in the spring and summer months of 1944, enemy forces were found to have fortified deep caves on Biak Island, drawing Allied troops into a series of brutal close-quarter battles. Many suffered terrible shell-shock or combat fatigue, which meant that Smoky's healing powers were in even greater need.

Advancing towards the Philippines in convoy, for the Lingayen Gulf
Landings, Bill Wynne found that Smoky's powers of forewarning would
save him in the most miraculous of ways. In desperation, the Japanese
military had resorted to using kamikazes – suicide pilots – in an effort to
sink the Allied fleets and slow their advance. Wearing ceremonial belts and
headscarves, the Kamikaze pilots took off on their one-way trips, blessed with
flowers … Waves of such aircraft swept into attack the landing craft on which
Bill Wynne and Smoky were riding, as ships were hit and sunk in terrifying
kamikaze strikes. After she saved his life, Bill Wynne would nickname Smoky
'The Angel from a Foxhole.'

British serviceman Rouse Voisey would be captured by the Japanese, and forced to work as slave labour clearing airstrips from the jungle and on the notorious Sumatran 'hell railroad'. Worse still, when loaded aboard the Japanese hellship *Junyo Maru*, Rouse found the ship hit by torpedoes. Packed into bamboo cages in the hold, few escaped before the *Junyo Maru* went down. Those who did suffered terrible vengeance at the hands of their captors, but amazingly Rouse lived to tell the tale. When Bill Wynne and Smoky took to the war-torn skies, part of their mission was to scour the seas for such shipwrecked Allied survivors.

Incredibly, Smoky survived the long months at war on the ground, at sea and in the air, becoming one of the most famous mascots and therapy dogs of the Second World War. Bill Wynne, an amateur magician, taught her a raft of tricks with which to entertain war-weary and homesick troops. After the war, they forged a show-business career together in the USA, with their wartime exploits taking centre stage.

battle for days, rescuing his buddies from a fearsome enemy mortar barrage. Eventually, he'd been evacuated, complaining of stabbing chest pains, but the doctors had concluded that Craig's problem was more mental than it was physical.

Craig wasn't alone in suffering in such a way. Hundreds of troops were arriving from the front plagued by 'combat fatigue'. Known as 'shell shock' in earlier conflicts, combat fatigue constitutes a severe loss of 'normal' human functions due to the trauma of war. It was characterized by the 'thousand-yard stare', an unfocused, weary, lifeless gaze. Sometimes called 'battle neurosis', it was often the precursor to what we today recognize as post-traumatic stress disorder (PTSD).

Back in civilian life the blond, tousle-headed Craig had been a real live wire. He had a thick New Jersey accent, a ready smile, and an easy-going manner and was a perfect potential roommate for Wynne. He'd been moved to Nadzab so the medics could keep a close eye on him. Like so many others in that hospital, at the first hint of a distant explosion he'd dive out of bed and scrabble for cover.

Panic, extreme anxiety and depression are common symptoms of combat fatigue. This was the first real exposure that Wynne had ever had to it. Craig was a war hero: he'd earned a high-valour medal for his efforts at Hollandia. But his nerves were shot to shreds. For Wynne, more accustomed to the loss of aircrew at a distance, this was a hugely sobering experience. Having contracted this mystery illness, all of a sudden he found himself face-to-face with the debilitating effects of front-line fighting.

Wynne was hugely fortunate to have ended up in this particular hospital. It was commanded by Colonel Charles William

Mayo, a surgeon in the United States Medical Corps who happened to hail from the family who had founded the famous Mayo Clinic. Colonel Mayo had served on the Mayo Clinic's board since 1933 and he remained a powerful advocate of the Mayo's core philosophies, of which the most important was that the needs of the patient had to take priority.

On his third day in the hospital Wynne had visitors. Frank Petrilak and Staff Sergeant Kalt – Smoky's photographer for the *Yank Magazine* competition – came to see him. As a bonus they'd brought Smoky with them. Upon explaining to the nursing staff how inseparable were patient and dog, Wynne was permitted to have his canine visitor, which was all in keeping with the Mayo's core values of putting the patient's needs first.

Upon spying Wynne, Smoky became a veritable tornado of excitement, whirling around and yelping happily. She was clearly as overjoyed to see him as he was her. Wynne tried to get her to settle upon his bed, as Petrilak and Kalt handed him a bundle of mail. In pride of place sat a large brown envelope stamped with the logo of *Yank Magazine*. Despite his sickness Wynne felt his pulse quicken.

He ripped open the parcel, eager for news of the mascot competition. He ran his eye over the first line of the enclosed letter. 'Dear PFC Wynne, I am enclosing herewith . . .' The letter announced the delivery of his first copy of *Yank Magazine*, which would be mailed to him weekly from now on, free of charge. It had to mean that they had been successful.

'Wow!' he declared. 'We must've won!'

He grabbed the magazine and flicked through its pages, stopping at the one entitled 'Smoky – FIRST PRIZE.' Next to the headline was the photo of his dog peering impishly from an upturned GI helmet.

'First prize!' Wynne cried triumphantly, as he flashed the others the fantastic news.

Yank Magazine had even posted Wynne a silver 'loving cup' – a two-handled drinking cup, for ceremonial occasions – to commemorate their win. It was engraved: 'SMOKY. First Prize Yank Mascot. Australia 1944'. When it arrived, that cup would stand as high as Smoky was tall.

Word of the news quickly spread, and shortly Smoky was being acclaimed as the hero of the 233rd Field Hospital. Wynne couldn't help but notice how just as soon as Smoky had made an appearance the eyes of the war-wounded were drawn towards his dog. Their vacant, thousand-yard stares seemed to soften slightly, regaining their spark and focus whenever she was within their sight.

Some of the nurses must have noticed as well. They approached Wynne with an unusual request: might they be allowed to seek permission from the Field Hospital's commander for Smoky to accompany them on their rounds? It seemed appropriate, especially as she was now the champion mascot of the southwest Pacific area.

'The wounded fellows are flooding in,' they told him, 'and they're sure to love her.'

Amid all the surprise and the high spirits Wynne was feeling markedly better, which he figured was just the kind of thing the *Yank Magazine* editors had hoped to achieve with their competition. He didn't doubt that having Smoky pay the wounded a visit would lift their spirits. He told the nurses that he could think of no better way for his dog to serve.

The nurses went to speak with Colonel Mayo and they were back a few minutes later. They'd won his absolute blessing. Not only that, but Wynne was to be allowed to have Smoky sleep on his bed for as long as he was in hospital.

As Smoky began to make the rounds, Wynne was amazed at the effect she seemed to have. There was a total change whenever she entered a ward. A soldier lying glassy-eyed would perk up at her appearance, as if he couldn't believe what he was seeing. The looks on their faces were of surprise mixed with sheer delight. Seeing a dog like her in a place such as this was so utterly unexpected. Seeing her standing duty at their bedside was even better. If such a tiny, gutsy dog could be happy in the midst of this war, so for sure could they.

Wynne was hospitalised for several days, for all of which time Smoky was allowed to sleep on his bed. She was collected at seven o'clock in the morning to accompany the medical teams on their rounds, and returned to his care each evening. Casualties were flooding in from the front lines and there was much work to be done. Best of all was when James Craig cradled Smoky, his cap pushed back on his unruly mop of blond hair, his eyes sparkling and his face grinning ear to ear. Petrilak managed to grab a photo of the smiling war hero posing with the champion mascot in his arms.

Whatever breed she might be, Smoky seemed particularly suited to this role. She was six pounds of pure tomboy attitude. Her confidence and sparky personality rubbed off on all those she visited, and her love of being the centre of attention meant that she was always game for more. She never seemed to tire of the ward rounds.

It was amazing to see how much care and attention such a small dog seemed to lavish on each and every one of the war-wounded. When Wynne looked at her, he saw a dog that just radiated love. For him, Smoky truly was the gift that never stopped giving.

Unbeknown to Wynne – or anyone else for that matter – Smoky was performing a role now widely recognized: that of therapy dog. Nowadays it has become widely understood that the very presence of a dog can transform the heavy, oppressive atmosphere of a hospital. Caring for an animal helps individual soldiers focus on the dog's needs, rather than their recent traumatic experiences. It draws them out of their shadowed past – where they were trapped within a cycle of reliving the trauma – to socialize and play with another living being.

But in the spring of 1944, the idea that a dog might perform such a valuable therapeutic function for those wounded and traumatized by war had rarely been entertained. Using a dog to bolster the spirits of the injured – both in body and mind – was unprecedented. It was one of the many firsts that Smoky and Bill Wynne were to achieve together.

But all too soon their hospital interlude was over. In a matter of days Wynne had recovered from his illness. He was discharged, and with that Smoky's ward duties came to an end. Their time at Nadzab was over and the 26th was shipping out to Hollandia. The heavy vehicles and equipment were to travel by sea, but mostly the men and machines of the squadron were to be airlifted there by C47 transport planes.

Man and dog were heading north, into terrain freshly seized from a die-hard adversary that was hiding out in the hinterland.

The move to Hollandia would take them closer to the enemy than they'd ever been before, that was for certain. Or rather, it was for Bill Wynne. For all anyone knew, Smoky, the champion mascot of the 26th, might have made her first home with the enemy, as some kind of a Japanese dog of war.

Perhaps the move to Hollandia would reveal it, one way or the other.

CHAPTER 8

As soon as Adachi's forces had been driven out, the 26th Photo Reconnaissance Squadron began to ferry their P-38s north to the newly seized airbases. In short order the ragged bomb craters were filled in, and a series of hasty repairs implemented to make the runways functional once again. It was now crucial to get the Lightnings of the 26th on the ground and operational.

The key to MacArthur's Cartwheel strategy was never to allow the enemy a moment to rest or regroup. Allied forces had to keep pushing north at speed. But such a frenetic pace of operations brought its own challenges, and no unit seemed to have been left unscathed.

It was May 1944 by now, and the strength of the 26th lay at thirty-five officers, with 235 other ranks. The squadron was equipped with nine warplanes – all P-38 F5s, the reconnaissance variant of the standard combat aircraft. In the last month alone they'd flown seventy recce missions, and, perhaps inevitably, they'd suffered losses due to the hectic demands that were being placed on them.

On 20 May a P-38 flown by First Lieutenant McDaniels had ploughed into the sea at Madang Harbour, around two hundred miles north of Nadzab. McDaniels had been piloting a P-38 'piggy-back' – a modified version of the aircraft that allowed a passenger to crouch in a compartment set just to his rear. Both he and his passenger, Troop Sergeant Harry R. Rogers, had been killed.

The P-38 piggy-back was a configuration that never caught on, and the flawed design concept was soon dropped. But the 26th were two men the poorer for it, and two good men at that. The loss of the curly-haired, buck-toothed Rogers was keenly felt by the men. Forever with a smile on his face no matter what might be afoot, Rogers would do anything for his fellow soldiers. He and McDaniels would be sorely missed.

After his spell in hospital, Bill Wynne found that he was slated to make his way to Hollandia with the squadron rearguard, travelling by ship. He was reluctant to subject Smoky to a long and potentially storm-tossed voyage, so he asked one of his pilot buddies, Lieutenant William Bishop, if he might fly Smoky to their new base, as a special favour.

With his jet-black hair and dark, intense good looks, Bishop was a popular pilot and known as one of the real daredevils of the squadron. As photo recce fliers went there were few better. He agreed to Wynne's request, but he pointed out they'd need someone on the ground to care for the dog once she got there. With the best will in the world a guy like him tasked with executing daily recce flights couldn't keep tabs on a dog. Wynne got one of the ground staff to agree to look after Smoky during his absence.

As Smoky boarded Bishop's aircraft, her para-jump crew wondered if they should remind her of the bail out drills they'd taught her, when leaping from the tree on the edge of the Nadzab softball field. But on balance the dangers of the coming flight seemed slight. After seizing Hollandia, the skies above New Guinea were largely free of enemy warplanes. The battle had moved on.

Indeed, it was to be those left on the ground who would face the biggest dangers, and from unexpected quarters. Shortly after Lieutenant Bishop had flown Smoky safely to Hollandia, Wynne and the rest of those travelling by ship moved to the nearby port of Lae. Barely had they got there when the heavens opened. The storm was like nothing any of them had ever seen. They set camp as best they could in the tempestuous conditions, the nearby Markham River swelling to a raging torrent.

That night the river burst her banks. Wynne and his fellows awoke to find the waters swirling around their cot-tops, their kit bags soaking wet and pairs of boots floating off downstream. The water just kept rising. By dawn it was as high as a man's thighs, and it had made quagmires out of the dirt roads. They had no option but to retreat to higher ground, carrying anything they could with them. The rows of heavy, sodden tents had to be collapsed and rescued from the rising waters, and re-erected on dry land.

They were forced to board the waiting vessel – a cargo ship called the *Joseph P. Bradley* – using small landing craft, which pitched and rolled terribly in the sea's wild waters. Each man had to take his chances and grab for the ship's ladder, weighed down as he was with his cot, rifle and barracks bag. No one could wait to get out of that flooded, blighted camp, but they would find little comfort or relief on the journey north.

Wynne was doubly glad that he'd got Smoky sent ahead by

air. Aboard the *Joseph P. Bradley* they had two choices of quarters: either they could roast below decks, or they could camp topside in crowded 'tents' improvised from tarpaulins. The nightly tropical downpours made short work of such shelters. Those on deck were soaked to the skin for the majority of the voyage. Anyone hoping they might find relief at the dinner table was to be sorely disappointed: the less said about the food on offer, the better.

They reached Hollandia a drenched and famished lot, to find operations in full swing, with reconnaissance flights roaring into the skies above a hot and dusty airstrip. Wynne's joy at being reunited with Smoky was tempered by some surprising news. During his absence she'd been left to run wild somewhat, and rumour had it that she'd found herself a boyfriend. Wynne tried to tell himself that it just couldn't be true. It was challenging enough looking after one dog in the midst of war, but what if Smoky had fallen pregnant? How would he cope with a litter of puppies on his hands?

He forced such worries from his mind. There were other, more pressing concerns to address. The squadron was based adjacent to the airstrip at Sentani, named after the nearby lake, which was ringed with thick jungle. Sentani lay on the edge of the city of Hollandia, but still it felt as if it were a million miles from civilization. A further move to Biak Island was on the cards, so little had been done to establish even the most basic of facilities.

They'd set up camp in an area of forest sandwiched between the lake and a nearby mountain. The kitchen store was a cave that the Japanese had tunnelled into the hillside, in an effort to shelter from Allied bombing. The cramped hospital tent doubled as the mess hall. There wasn't even a shower or any form of laundry facilities. The men were mostly camped along the riverbank. They had to wash both themselves and their uniforms in the stream, beating their khakis clean on boulders.

The water in the creek originated from a seven-thousand-foot peak, so at least it was cool and refreshing. But at night searchlights played a blinding light show across the skies above the Sentani strip, scouring the heavens for incoming warplanes. Around the airfield lay piles of wreckage – mostly bombed – and burned-out Mitsubishi G4Ms, bulldozed into twisted heaps. The cockpits of some of those aircraft were remarkably intact. The instruments looked strikingly – eerily – similar to those used in the squadron's own aircraft.

Located as it was in dense jungle, the camp at Sentani was besieged by crawling, stinging, swimming, biting, flying, venomous things. Swarms of mosquitoes flocked to the water's edge. The lake itself was home to huge sawfish – a ray boasting a long, narrow, bony nose extension that resembles a many-toothed sawblade – which grew up to three metres in length. The sawfish used their sawblades to slice up and impale their prey.

Any food left lying around camp was an invitation to an ant invasion. Table legs had to be inserted into tin cans filled with water, to keep the swarms of ants from crawling up them. The water had in turn to be sprinkled with engine oil, to prevent mosquitoes from hatching out their larvae. Huge venomous centipedes – *Ethmostigmus rubripes* – lurked in the shadows. Two men were hospitalized as a result of their agonizing bites. One had gone to put his shoe on, only to find one of the revolting critters hiding out in the toe.

Smoky reckoned she could take them on. After her victory over Colonel Turbo, the fearless dog presumed the six-inch-long insects would be a pushover. With its garish orange-yellow body and black bands, plus numerous wriggling legs sticking out the side, going after centipedes proved irresistible for Smoky. Having cornered one angry beast, she decided to do a back flip in an effort to confuse it. But she ended up with the swift-moving centipede beneath her, whereupon it whipped its head around and bit her on the thigh.

The modified claws that curve around its head allow *Ethmostigmus rubripes* to inject venom deep into its victims. That is how it hunts and kills its prey – normally small insects, snails and worms – but it also uses the venom to ward off larger would-be predators. Having been bitten, Smoky howled and wailed pitifully. The cries brought her protector, Wynne, running.

He gathered up his precious dog and tried his best to comfort her. He had no idea what the effect of the venom might be. Did the centipede pack enough punch to kill a six-pound pooch like her? Wynne just didn't know. First he'd been struck down by a mystery tropical disease. Now this. In the jungle, danger red in tooth and claw lurked on every side.

Not knowing what to expect, he waited anxiously for the outcome. Rest seemed to be the cure that Smoky craved. After a spell of nurturing care and relaxation she gradually recovered, although it looked as if the giant centipede's powerful poison was still going to leave its mark. Where Smoky had been bitten a patch of hair an inch or so across dropped out. The bare skin turned jet black. It was to be a permanent reminder to the little dog never to go chasing after venomous beasties again.

It was a huge relief to have Smoky well again, for the 26th was getting seriously busy, and the laboratory as much as any other part of the unit. Dozens of recce missions were flown over the Palau and Molucca islands, Biak itself, and even distant Ambon, which was a round flight of pushing 1,800 miles. That was right at the very limits of what the P-38s and their pilots were capable of, and everyone knew the risks of such ultra-long-distance solo sorties.

Four pilots – Captain John Brown, First Lieutenant Michael Koziupa, First Lieutenant Warner Buchanan and Second Lieutenant Ercel Powers – were awarded the Air Medal that June, for completing one-hundred hours of operational flying over enemy territory. The squadron also won its first ever high-valour medal, a Distinguished Flying Cross, which honours 'heroism or extraordinary achievement while participating in aerial flight.'

The citation for Captain Carl D. Lindberg's DFC read: 'for flying 1,450 miles to take the first aerial photographs of Manokwari, Dutch New Guinea [now Indonesia]. He also sighted several large enemy naval vessels including a battleship, three destroyers and two cruisers.'

It was an epic flight that would have taken a minimum of five-and-a-half hours. With a top speed in excess of 414 mph, there was nothing that the enemy flew that could rival the Lightning. The ubiquitous Japanese fighter, the Mitsubishi A6M Zero, was some eighty mph slower. Even the Zero's replacement, the Nakajima Ki-84 *Hayate* – Storm – would be hard-pressed to catch a Lightning, but only if the P-38 pilot stayed totally focused. If he failed to spot an enemy aircraft's approach, he could do little to outfly or outpace it.

Pinpoint navigation was crucial on such missions, especially in a theatre that consisted largely of open ocean. On the Manokwari sortie, over half the flight had been executed across the Bismarck and Celebes seas – long tracts of water devoid of any landmarks. Managing the flow of aviation fuel was also critical. Throttling back the P-38's twin engines on those long and lonely stretches when sky and sea alike were empty was vital to husbanding fuel supplies.

By punching these high-altitude speed runs deep into enemy airspace, the pilots were earning a hard-won reputation. The risks and the hardships were extreme, so recognizing the gallantry exhibited by these unarmed recce fliers was crucial. It wasn't simply a question of helping to boost the pilots' morale. The secrecy of their work meant that their missions – their very existence – were rarely spoken of outside their own limited circles, so awards like Lindberg's Distinguished Flying Cross helped attract more recruits to the recce squadrons' ranks.

In the European theatre a handful of very high-profile reconnaissance flights had made it into the limelight. Most notable was the mission flown by RAF Pilot Officer Michael Suckling in May 1941. The fearsome German battleship *Bismarck* was reported to be lying at anchor in the shelter of the Norwegian fjords. If the 40,000-tonne behemoth – Germany's largest battleship – managed to break out she could wreak havoc among the Atlantic convoys, which were Britain's lifeline. The RAF were tasked to find her.

On 21 May Suckling had flown his Spitfire over the Grimstadfjord, south of Bergen, Norway's second city. It was 1.15 p.m. when he'd spotted what was possibly the elusive warship, nestling in a crook in the fjord. The photos he fired off from high altitude became known as 'the picture that sank a battleship'. From Grimstadfjord the *Bismarck* was tracked into the Atlantic, and eventually crippled by a Swordfish torpedo bomber, before being sent to the bottom by British warships.

More recently, the incredible high-altitude detective work executed by the recce squadrons in finding the V1 flying bombs and V2 rockets had also hit the headlines. One leading British specialist, the female photo-analyst Constance Babington Smith, would win glowing accolades in the US media: 'Connie Saves New York' ran one somewhat overblown headline. Babington Smith had played a key role in spotting the V1 launchers, at a time when German scientists had been developing rockets and missiles designed to hit the US eastern seaboard.

But those were the exceptions. Mostly, the high-risk, relentless and absolutely vital work of the reconnaissance squadrons was carried out wholly in the shadows. And at the 26th's new Sentani airbase it was beginning to take a heavy toll.

In the second week of July 1944, the Commanding Officer of the 26th himself was grounded by the base's medical staff, who cited combat fatigue. Barely five months earlier, the squadron's founding commander, First Lieutenant Shelton Hallett, had been lost in action. (Hallett's fate was known by now. He'd been shot down by enemy warplanes while executing a photo recce mission at sea.) Now his replacement, Captain Walter R. Hardee, had been pulled off flying duty, due to the cumulative stress of executing similar kinds of missions.

Hardee had once given a long-to-be-remembered speech to the men of the squadron, explaining how he'd been the valedictorian – the top student – at his high school, the one who delivered the final graduation speech. He expected nothing but the very best from those under his command.

It was in this spirit that he'd pushed himself to the edge, and perhaps beyond it, in New Guinea, flying more missions than most. Hardee – with his serious expression, swept back forehead and intense gaze – was finished in theatre. Just days after his grounding he was relieved of his command and sent back to the USA.

On 17 July 1944, Captain Orville L. Counselman took over command in Hardee's place. The squadron's new leader was cut from similar cloth to his predecessor. An archetypal recce pilot, he was a man whose kindly eyes and gentle smile belied the core of steel that lay within. Counselman would lead the squadron from the front, flying more often and further than just about any other pilot. He would push the risk envelope exponentially, and in time he too would reap the whirlwind.

But for now, it was to be Bill Wynne whose recent sacrifices were to gain him a little respite. After his severe bout of tropical fever and the rough sea voyage that had followed, Wynne was offered two weeks' 'recuperative leave' by the squadron's doctor. The 26th was scheduled to move to Biak Island any day now, and all knew they would need to muster their collective strength if they were to survive the trials and tribulations that lay ahead.

Allied commanders had sorely underestimated the numbers and tenacity of the enemy troops garrisoning Biak. They'd expected to face no more than 4,000 defenders: in truth, there were over twice that number. The island was a jumbled mass of mountainous coral, honeycombed with caves. Making maximum advantage of the terrain, the Japanese commander had refrained from opposing the amphibious landings in late May '44. Instead, he'd secreted his forces deep within the cover of the jungle-clad caves, overlooking key Allied objectives – including Biak's main airfield.

The enemy positions had been stockpiled with many months of water, food and ammunition. Within days of the Allied landings the battle for Biak Island had descended into a savage and bloody war of attrition. Air power could do little to help clear those entrenched cave positions. It took men on the ground to do so, and it had proved terrible, bloody work. But MacArthur needed Biak badly. It was a crucial stepping stone toward his overall objective: the Philippines.

Wynne, however, was heading in the opposite direction – to Brisbane, the capital city of Queensland, the state that lies on Australia's north-eastern coast. Sunny, semi-tropical and relatively untouched by war, it was a whole world away from the hell of New Guinea. Still, the trip was not without its challenges. Reams of US military regulations forbade the taking of anything other than official war animals on military transports. But bearing in mind what he had been told about Smoky's amorous adventures at Sentani, Wynne was damned if he was going to leave her behind.

He managed to hitch a ride in a C47 with a crew who were heading south towards Brisbane. He'd taught Smoky to lie quietly and peacefully in his musette, an army-issue canvas haversack. Secreted away, she was rendered largely invisible to prying eyes. Fearful that she would be discovered by the authorities at some point en route, he'd taught her to keep still and silent just as soon as she'd scrambled inside.

Smoky might be a *Yank Magazine* champion mascot, but

that would cut little ice with the C47 crew, or, for that matter, the customs officers who would greet them upon arrival. Once he'd tucked her little body into the base of the bag and closed the flap over her head, tightening it gently with the straps, Smoky knew that she was not to move a muscle or to make the slightest sound.

By the time man and dog were ready to depart, the C47 – nicknamed the Gooney Bird by US forces, after a long-winged albatross known by the same name – was hopelessly overloaded. The aircrew had packed the hold with two radial engines still in their wooden crates, plus a dozen infantrymen in full combat gear.

It was pelting with rain by the time the pilot took to the airstrip. Straining to get airborne, the C47 seemed to be heading into a wall of water that blocked out all visibility. Even as the aircraft thundered down the runway the crew chief hurried aft and asked Wynne to move up to the cockpit, as the C47 was too rear-end heavy. Wynne grabbed his musette bag and its precious canine cargo and did as asked, the dozen-odd infantrymen crowding forward with him.

The sight that met his eyes as he entered the cockpit was hardly an encouraging one. Through the C47's rain-lashed split windscreen he could just make out the wall of ragged trees that edged the Sentani strip. It loomed out of the murk, looking frighteningly close. Wynne pulled Smoky's form tighter to him, as the Gooney Bird thundered ever nearer to that fringe of jungle. Right now, Australia seemed a whole world away.

It looked impossible that the C47 would even make it into the air, before smashing into that dark line of trees.

CHAPTER 9

With throttles pushed to the max and with her twin engines howling, the Gooney Bird seemed to shudder along her entire length as she heaved herself upwards through the torrential rain. Moments later, with her undercarriage kissing the treetops, she thundered over the highest of the forest giants, emerging on the far side miraculously unscathed.

The overloaded warplane was past the wall of thick jungle. The C47 skimmed across the roof of the forest, the storm-lashed waters of the Setani Lake opening out below her. For now at least, man and dog could sit back and enjoy the ride. Australia – and all its wartime wonders – were but hours away.

US troops serving in New Guinea had been given orientation briefings about Australia – the nearest nation where they could expect some R&R – and her people. America it was not. Everything in Australia was rationed, so they should expect the locals to be after all the freebies they could get. The tone of voice of an Aussie was something like a London 'cockney' accent, they'd been told. They were cautioned not to remark upon it.

American cigarettes were prized. 'You gotta smoke, Yank?' was to be an oft-heard 'cockney-toned' refrain. The GIs had learned all about the local brand, Craven A. 'After smoking one you'd still be Craven A cigarette,' the joke went. With beer in short supply, the bootleggers were doing a roaring trade, in what the Aussies referred to as their 'sly grog shops'. There were reports that the Aussie girls tended to warm to American servicemen, because the 'Yanks' had what they termed real 'get up and go'.

But the first surprise for Bill Wynne and his dog upon touching down in Australia was the climate. It might have been a balmy sixty degrees, but to a man and dog accustomed to the intense tropical heat of New Guinea, it felt positively frosty. Wynne was freezing, and he could only imagine what it was like for Smoky, still hidden away in his haversack. Despite her thick coat of hair, he feared that a small dog like her would be sensitive to the cold.

Once he'd managed to smuggle her through customs, Wynne and Smoky spent their first night in Australia huddled beneath a heap of US Army issue blankets. Man and dog shivered all through the dark hours. After eight months in New Guinea, Wynne craved fresh milk and fresh meat, but clearly their first priority had to be to find some way to keep themselves warm, for the military-issue blankets just didn't seem to cut it.

The following morning Wynne made his way to a local 'hobby shop', an emporium that specialized in hobbies, including all sorts of games. He managed to find a green woollen tablecloth made for a card table. Fringed with beads, it looked about the right size, shape and thickness from which to fashion the kind of DIY coat needed to keep a small, shivering dog toasty warm.

Having purchased the tablecloth, Wynne headed for the local Red Cross office. Scores of volunteers were busy at banks of sewing machines, stitching rank stripes and unit insignia onto new sets of uniform to be issued to those fresh out of the jungle, so they could look dapper during their leave. Producing his dog, Wynne explained just who Smoky was, and that she too had completed many months of war service in New Guinea.

Then he outlined the little dog's requirements. Unsurprisingly, there was no shortage of volunteers to get stitching for Smoky. The Red Cross ladies fitted the little dog by cutting the tablecloth so that it would cover her from neck to tail and almost to her ankles. Straps to the front and beneath fastened the blanket to her chest and underside, while the beads would lie around the fringes to weigh it down.

Wynne himself had recently been promoted to corporal, and he figured the 26th's champion mascot should at least carry the same rank. Warming to their task, the Red Cross volunteers sewed a corporal's stripes to the front left side of the blanket, the same place where a soldier would wear them. Behind the stripes they added the shield of the 5th Air Force – the 26th's parent unit – consisting of a star-spangled comet bursting through a golden '5'. A Good Conduct Ribbon – rewarding honourable and faithful service – plus one or two other badges completed the eye-catching spread.

Smoky now had her coat of many colours, which served both to parade her credentials and honours and to keep her warm. Wynne decided to billet himself with the American Red Cross in Brisbane, for they offered free accommodation and first-class food. After months in the New Guinea jungle this was heavenly. Barbara Wood Smith, an American Red Cross worker, seemed particularly taken with Smoky. She asked if they were willing to pay a visit to the city's hospitals, so the champion mascot might do the rounds of the wounded.

Wynne was in something of a quandary. Fearful of the rules and regulations, he'd had to smuggle Smoky into the country. After much deliberation he agreed that she could visit the hospital wards, but only if there was a publicity blackout. The fact that *Yank Mag*'s champion mascot was there would have to be kept under wraps. Wood Smith agreed, and so the deal was cut: Smoky would do her tour and everyone would keep schtum.

This time, there was to be another major difference from their time in the Nadzab hospital. As Wynne was healthy, he could accompany his dog, and that meant they could employ their full repertoire of tricks. After all their practice and training, Wynne decided they were more than ready to give the war-wounded a special treat.

They began at Brisbane's US 109th Fleet Naval Hospital. In the stifling heat of New Guinea, wounds tended to fester, injuries taking an age to heal. Here in Brisbane the long-suffering casualties of the war faced a far better chance of recovery. But long enforced stints in hospital weren't good for anyone's spirits, least of all sailors who had steamed halfway around the world to fight.

Man and dog did the rounds of the injured sailors, covering around eight wards that first day. In each they ran through their whole box of tricks. First, Smoky dashed through some obedience trials, just to show how strict and soldierly this champion mascot could be. Then it was on to the highlights – Smoky's playing dead had the wounded rolling with laughter. But if anything, her singing duet with Wynne was even more of a show-stopper. As man and dog threw their heads back and crooned, there were tears running down the cheeks of men who hadn't had a great deal to laugh about of late. Wynne and Smoky rounded it off with a new trick – the 'grapevine' – leaving the ward with him stepping quickly and her weaving a figure-of-eight around his feet as he went.

Upon seeing Smoky's sterling performance, one of the Red Cross workers decided to claim her as their own: she pinned an American Red Cross badge to Smoky's coat. Two days later, a lady from the Women's Auxiliary Corps (WAC) – the women's branch of the US Armed Services – noticed the Red Cross badge and figured that she would have to top that.

'If Smoky's a female in the US Army, then she has to be a WAC,' she declared. She removed her own lapel badge and fastened it to Smoky's coat.

While it wasn't exactly what man and dog had come to Australia for – Wynne was supposed to be here enjoying some recuperative leave – their hospital visits certainly went down a storm. Barbara Wood Smith asked if they might be willing to do a repeat performance at the 42nd General Army Hospital. There, Wynne regaled the wounded with tales of Smoky's adventures in New Guinea, relating the miraculous way in which she'd first been discovered, and how she'd gone on to win the *Yank Mag* contest against such stiff competition.

The wounded were enraptured. Starved of any form of entertainment or light relief, the tales had them gripped. Man and dog received a euphoric reception, with Smoky's antics invariably earning wild applause. So captivated were some of the injured soldiers that they took to accompanying the performers from ward to ward, carrying Smoky in their wheelchairs with her diminutive form perched on their laps.

That was what was really so special about such a visit: in the midst of all the trauma and pain of war, it was an incredible treat simply to be able to hold and to cherish a dog like Smoky. Just as had been the case in New Guinea, the hospitalized soldiers noticed how she somehow reminded them of their homes, and of what they were all fighting for. The wounded soldiers kept firing curious questions at Wynne, most commonly: what did he feed her on in the midst of the jungle?

'Regular mess hall chow,' he explained, proudly. Smoky got no more or less than he did: spam, bully beef and canned mutton, plus the occasional vitamin pill.

Their tour of the hospitals complete, Barbara Wood Smith wrote Smoky a personal letter of thanks. In it she addressed the little dog as 'a lady artiste without temperament'.

Being so busy and in such high demand, Wynne and Smoky's two weeks recuperation leave seemed to flash by. In short order it was time to head north once more, back to war. It was late spring 1944, and the Gooney Bird that man and dog boarded would fly them into the heart of the hell that was the battle for Biak Island.

Flights into Biak made their approach across Cenderawasih Bay – Bird of Paradise Bay, in the local language. From an aircraft's window the scene below might indeed look paradisiacal: the humped folds of verdant green stretched to the horizon, towering volcanic peaks plunging into stunning aquamarine waters. But as the flight carrying man and dog neared the Biak Island landing beaches, they revealed a very different story.

Biak Island sits just four degrees south of the equator, and blinding white coral sands fringe the brilliant ocean waters. But crammed into the dense jungle of an island just forty miles long and twenty square were several thousand Japanese troops, well dug-in and ready to die for their emperor. The terrain testified to the ferocity of the combat: the fighting during the landings had been so intense that the palm trees had been stripped bare of their fronds. Ranks of battered trunks stood sentinel over the beaches, their skeletal tops reaching forlornly into the hot skies.

The camp of the 26th lay just to the rear of the main landing beach, looking out over shredded stands of palms and with views beyond to the white breakers of Bird of Paradise Bay. But here, even the sea itself had become a battleground: every day, platoons of Marines would chug across the bay in their General Motors 'Ducks' – the distinctive DUKW amphibious truck-cum-landing-craft – to flush die-hard enemy forces out of the jungle.

With little tree cover remaining to shield the squadron's quarters, the camp lay on the open grassy hinterland to the rear of the beach. Huge shell craters pock marked the terrain. One of the largest had been adapted to form the squadron's shower facilities: a spring bubbled up from the depths of the crater, and a rough screen of sacking had been erected around it.

When the tide came in, it washed right over the floor of the shower, which was fortunate, for it briefly cleansed its terrible smell. For whatever reason, the spring-water reeked of rotten eggs. It was possible to get passably clean, but only if you could stomach the stench for long enough to do so.

Unfortunately, the squadron's camp lay directly under the

flight path used by Japanese warplanes. It was sandwiched between the beach and Biak's main airstrip, at Mokmer Airbase, and the open bay provided the line of attack for avenging Japanese aircrew. Whenever the Japanese bombardiers aimed short of the Mokmer strip, their payloads tore into the beach or the camp itself. It was hardly an ideal homecoming for Wynne and Smoky.

The Mokmer airstrip had been seized by US forces at dawn on 7 June 1944. Surprisingly they'd faced little resistance. In truth, they'd been lured into a carefully set trap. At 9.45 a.m. the Japanese guns – concealed in caves and bunkers on ridgelines overlooking the strip – had opened fire, unleashing a savage barrage. For four hours the shells had rained down on the airbase. The US forces had held out, but the airfield itself remained unusable.

So desperate was the ensuing battle that it wasn't until 22 June – two weeks later – that the Mokmer airstrip was finally able to receive its first Allied warplanes. In the intervening days US troops had resorted to pouring drums of fuel into the caves in which the Japanese were holding out, in an effort to burn them out. Where that didn't work 'satchel charges' – powerful explosives, held in a military-issue satchel – were detonated in the caves' entrances. Invariably, that would bring down an avalanche of rocks, trapping the cave's occupants inside.

Several times the besieged Japanese forces tried to break out, by battling their way through the encircling US lines. Each attempt was thwarted, but there were still thousands of Japanese soldiers holding out in the island's hinterland. Their commander, Colonel Kuzume Naoy, had vowed to fight until the last man. Hundreds of American troops had already lost their lives in brutal close-quarter battles. US casualties on Biak would eventually top three thousand killed and wounded. Ten thousand Japanese soldiers would die.

The move to Biak Island hadn't exactly been viewed with relish by the men of the 26th. Tokyo Rose broadcasts had beamed stark warnings into their Hollandia camp: American forces faced thousands of Japanese warriors who had vowed to fight to the death in the defence of Biak Island. In many ways those broadcasts weren't so far off the mark.

Once again, the squadron's gossip-mill had gone into overdrive, and the senior officers of the 26th had found themselves struggling to quash 'dangerous and damaging rumour'. The loose talk and speculation had reached such a level that punishment was even mooted: 'violators have been informed that they may be subjected to disciplinary action.'

The squadron's arrival on Biak Island hadn't been accomplished without loss, either. A pair of P-38s had been hit on the ground by enemy warplanes. Yet there was to be no let-up in the demands being placed upon the unit. The incredibly testing conditions meant that requests for photo reconnaissance flights were running at an all-time high.

The squadron flew sixty missions during the first days of June alone. On one such sortie, First Lieutenant Warner M. Buchanan had 'completed a photo run with one engine dead and the other ready to quit at any time', the squadron's monthly war diary recorded. For that daring flight Buchanan would be awarded the Silver Star, the US military's third-highest decoration for gallantry in the line of duty.

As the days progressed the pilots of the 26th would punch out as far as the Philippines, flying a mission over Mindanao, which was approaching 1,500 miles away. There they would secure vital images of the Japanese naval bases, plus their key airfields, in preparation for what had been dubbed as 'MacArthur's Return'.

Two years earlier President Roosevelt had ordered General MacArthur to abandon his spirited defence of the Philippines. On 12 March 1942, MacArthur had acceded to that order, flying out on a B17 Flying Fortress. Upon landing in Australia, he had made his famous speech: 'I shall return.' Behind him, some 11,500 Allied troops had been forced to surrender. What followed were the horrors of the 'Bataan Death March', in which thousands of Allied and Filipino prisoners were forced to cross the jungle on foot and in utterly brutal conditions. Thousands had died.

MacArthur's promise to return was in part to avenge the inhumanity of the Bataan Death March and all those who had lost their lives. But in order to make that promise a reality he desperately needed intelligence, and for that the Lightnings of the 26th had to keep running the gauntlet, time after time after time.

During August 1944 the pilots of the 26th flew ninety-six recce missions. Every time they went out, they knew they were dicing with death. During the course of one of those sorties over the Philippines, Captain John B. Brown realized that more than an hour's fuel supply had been lost due to a break in his main fuel line. He'd switched to the wing tanks, only to find they too had malfunctioned. Regardless, he'd pushed on with his mission, out-flying enemy warplanes and securing photos of key enemy installations and shipping. He was awarded the Distinguished Service Order (DSO) for 'outstanding courage and devotion to duty'.

On the same day, 20 August 1944, another of the 26th's pilots, First Lieutenant Orin C. Darling, was in action over the Philippines. In spite of his radio dying on him, Darling had pressed ahead with his mission, though he was deprived of all communications. He'd managed to shake off three enemy warplanes and secure 'photographs of great value in our operations against the enemy'. He too would be awarded the DSO.

Such derring-do in the air was mirrored on the ground on Biak Island. Though few high-valour medals were handed out to the ground crew of the 26th, it wasn't for want of heroics on their part.

Upon arrival at Biak, First Sergeant Joyce B. Howell, the renegade Texan joker of the squadron, had decided it was time to dispense with his cowboy boots. Instead, he donned some suitable jungle wear and volunteered to join an infantry patrol going after the enemy. His plan was simple: if he made it through okay, he would forge the way for others from the 26th to do likewise. Strictly speaking, of course, it wasn't the role of the 26th to send men out to fight like infantry, but that didn't stop them wanting to go.

Three days after he'd set out, 'JB', as he was known to the men, returned with six notches carved into the wooden butt of his M1 Garand semi-automatic rifle, the standard US service weapon of the Second World War. He also brought back harrowing tales of deep jungle combat. At one stage he'd been pinned behind a fallen tree for hours as he waited for the rest of his patrol to fight their way forward and rescue him.

As soon as he learned of JB's near-death experience at the hands of the enemy, First Lieutenant – now Captain – Hartwell McCullough called the men of the squadron together. Custodian of the Squadron's classified Documents, McCullough feared that he'd heard in Howell's death-defying tales a threat to the unit's future and its fortunes.

'Men, there will be no more from the 26th permitted to go on infantry patrols,' he began, in his thick Louisiana drawl. 'If we lost anyone it'd be damn difficult to explain to Headquarters . . . Besides, I'm not sure y'all are as tough as Howell is. Squadron dismissed.' McCullough had a point. The 26th were a photo recce unit, and they needed to keep focused on the utterly vital task at hand. There was danger enough involved in executing their daring missions on the ground and in the air, without going looking for trouble.

And at the centre of the squadron's heroics here would be one man and his fearless dog.

CHAPTER 10

On Biak Island Wynne and Smoky's tent was an eight-by-ten-foot affair, and thankfully their new room-mate was a far cry from their first – notoriously dog-hating – companion. It was Frank Petrilak, the fresh-faced dog-lover who'd cared for Smoky during the time that Wynne had been in hospital with dengue fever back at Nadzab. That was the good news. The bad news was the fearsome bombing.

Their tent lay some fifty feet from the squadron's photo laboratory, which here on Biak Island was an operation that was busier than ever before. They could hear the night shifts going about their business and chatting away all through the dark hours as they processed incoming rolls of film. But they had to keep one ear open for the air-raid siren warning them that another flight of Japanese warplanes was inbound across Bird of Paradise Bay.

When the siren began its eerie wail, man and dog alike would make a mad dash for the nearest caves, which the Japanese had used as air-raid shelters before them. As they crouched in the dank and fearful darkness, they could hear the hollow whump of bombs exploding outside. As the ground shook and the air inside the cave contracted horribly with the pressure of the explosions, Wynne would do his best to comfort his dog.

They'd set up camp upon a war-blasted chunk of bare white coral that roasted under a remorseless tropical sun. Temperatures regularly climbed above one-hundred degrees. In the tents it was even hotter, sometimes topping 130. Biak was a baking-hot, blinding white, dusty, unrelenting trial of a posting, but none of that alone would kill. It was the Japanese air attacks that were the real risk to life and limb. If the warplanes came during the heat of the day, by the time the men had dashed for the caves they'd be soaked in sweat.

Smoky had already proven how smart she was on Biak. In the centre of the camp lay a barrel of drinking water. Any passing soldier was welcome to pause and slake his thirst. Smoky soon learned what it was for. If Wynne wasn't around, she'd linger by the barrel. When she spied someone approaching, she'd run up to it, bark, dash over to the passerby and bark again, before skipping back to the barrel to bark some more. The guy soon got the message. He'd bend over the barrel with cupped hands, then crouch down so she could lap thirstily.

Similarly, Smoky had shown how quick-thinking she was in her efforts to get away from her master whenever she fancied doing a little exploring, though this kind of unlicensed adventure could prove fatal, especially if she were caught in the open during an air raid. Smoky would locate Wynne in a crowd by sniffing around everyone's ankles. Once she'd detected the right scent she'd dash around and around his feet, excitedly. But if she wanted to get away, she'd execute ever widening circles, waiting for the moment when her master seemed distracted by conversation. Then, when the circuit took her directly behind him, she'd make a dash for the nearest patch of bush.

Wynne had soon got wise to this. He'd pretend not to be looking, but have her pinned out of the corner of his eye. When she made a run for it he'd yell: 'Stand! Stay!' Smoky would freeze in her tracks. He'd call her back with the standard instruction: 'Smoky, come!' She'd return to his side, acting for all the world as if she'd had no intention of going anywhere in particular.

A smart dog is forever on the ball, its mind forever busy. Smoky was the epitome of that. It took a smart master to stay one step ahead of her. But here on Biak, there were times when it made perfect sense to let the little dog have her head.

Before being sent to the front line, the professional war dogs of the Second World War were given intensive training to get them accustomed to explosions and gunfire. That was one of the key lessons learned by US and British K9 units: an animal deployed without any such acclimatization could well become a liability. Of course, Smoky had had none of that. A relative veteran these days, her capacity to deal with gunfire and bombing had had to be learned on the job.

Her reaction to the blistering air raids on Biak was telling. Just as soon as the siren's first blast was heard, she'd tense up along the entire length of her body. She'd start barking in alarm, and keep up the refrain during the mad dash for the cave shelter, as boots – and paws – tore across the coral. Yet there were times when she seemed almost to start barking *before* the air-raid sirens had raised the alarm. The knack she appeared to have for sensing things – threats especially – before they became obvious to humans was uncanny, but no one on Biak was about to question her early-warning abilities.

Could a dog like Smoky really sense the presence of incoming warplanes before they became visible or audible to humans? Possibly she could. A dog's hearing is infinitely more sensitive than our own. Dogs possess eighteen separate muscles with which to raise, lower or swivel their ears, ensuring they can determine exactly from which direction a sound emanates. Tiny though Smoky was, she could twitch her ears this way and that, using them to track distant sounds, and she could pinpoint the source of such a noise in one-six-hundredth of a second – pretty much instantaneously.

But clearly her ability to detect those incoming Japanese warplanes and the threat they embodied went beyond the purely physical. Somehow, she sensed that this thunderous noise on the distant horizon equated to danger. Smoky seemed able to sense *danger itself*, and quite possibly dogs have evolved to do just that over the millennia.

All dogs, no matter what breed or size, are descended from *Canis lupus*, the grey wolf. Dogs share 99.96 per cent of the wolf's DNA. Of course, their wolf-like ancestry has been overlain with thousands of years of selective breeding, as humans and dogs have forged the most long-lived and enduring man-animal partnership of all. The dog was the first animal to be domesticated, and today they possess an ability to bond and form relationships with humans that no other creature can rival.

Prior to domestication dogs used their acute sense of hearing to track prey and predators. They are able to hear a far greater range of frequencies than humans, and they can do so over far longer distances. In fact, a dog's hearing is around ten times more efficient than our own: a sound a human might hear at ten metres they can hear at a hundred or more. Had there been a snake living on Biak's coral, Smoky would have been able to hear its slithering from a considerable distance away.

One thing was for sure on Biak Island: if Smoky started yelping her signature bark, her fine head tilted out towards Bird of Paradise Bay, it was time to run hell for leather for the shelters.

The hectic pace of operations that August 1944 rarely faltered. Breaks came only when the squadron found itself grounded due to bad weather. Whenever that happened the men of the 26th took the rare chance to unwind. Biak's white sandy beaches were undeniably glorious. In another time, this would have been the archetypal tropical paradise island. The crystal-blue waves rolled in throatily, boasting curling white crests that dashed themselves to exhaustion on the battle-scarred sands.

In time someone discovered that discarded P-38 drop-tanks made passable surfboards, and even better hulls for fashioning DIY sailing boats. With a cockpit cut into the topside, the right amount of ballast inserted, a lone mast and sail raised above the cylindrical hull, plus a rudimentary rudder, a drop-tank could accommodate two fully grown men at sea quite comfortably. But some of the 26th's crew went one better: they adapted an old generator to serve as an inboard motor on their drop-tank craft, powering a screw.

The heat was soporific and cooling off in the sea heavenly. Sergeant Gilbert J. Frankhuizen, one of the squadron mechanics, decided the beach-goers needed some chilled drinks. Taking an unused fuel tank from a B24 bomber plus an old generator, Frankhuizen – big-boned and rangy, with an open-faced honesty about him – set about building the squadron an ice machine.

More normally, Frankhuizen, a sheet-metal specialist, would

be working on the Lightnings' fuselage and cowlings, repairing stress fractures or battle damage caused by enemy fire. The ice machine, a truly ingenious feat of improvisation, provided welcome relief. With an outer skin filled with a thick layer of compressed sawdust that acted as insulation, it was able to produce eight blocks of ice per day, each about the size and shape of a concrete slab.

A net was erected, with posts lashed to old oil drums, so the men could play beach volleyball. It too provided a real boost to spirits. As the squadron's Monthly Intelligence Summaries reported, 'Individuals lured by aquatics spend leisure hours swimming and sunbathing on the beach.' Yet despite such leisurely pursuits, the war was never far away and neither was the enemy.

One day some of the squadron's more intrepid seamen were out testing their motor-powered drop-tank yacht, when they spotted a low-lying object on the far horizon. Thinking it might be a downed airman or ship's crew on a life raft, they grabbed a small rowing dinghy, lashed it to the rear of their craft and motored out to investigate. They found what they had least expected – a makeshift raft crowded with Japanese soldiers.

Mindful of the reports of Japanese troops fighting to the last man, those crewing the 'USS Drop-Tank' decided they would take no chances. Holding off a distance, they ordered the enemy to strip. Once they were sure they had no hidden grenades or pistols secreted on their persons, they motored in and took the enemy party captive. The prisoners were loaded aboard the dinghy and a course was set for land. But en route the improvised motor conked out, so everyone had to put their backs to the oars, to beat the tide back to shore.

Unsurprisingly, a crowd of onlookers had gathered. This was the closest most of them had ever got to the dreaded enemy. But the Japanese soldiers seemed cowed and subservient, not at all the fanatical die-hards most had been expecting. They were clearly half-starved. Sitting cross-legged on the bare coral, they wolfed down the stale crusts of bread they were given and downed gallons of water between them.

It turned out that these enemy troops had become isolated from their unit, and had held out in the jungle for two hellish months. Finally, they'd run out of food completely. Taking to the raft had been a last gamble to save themselves. Those emaciated Japanese soldiers quickly became the most photographed men on Biak Island. Their clothes were in rags, their faces thickly bearded, their limbs skeletal.

More than anything, the men of the 26th couldn't help but pity them. As with most forces embroiled in this terrible conflict – the enemy included – the majority of the troops were conscripts. They had been ordered to fight by their governments or rulers and they'd had little choice but to obey. Here on Biak Island – as had happened with so many of the Japanese positions – they had been told to fight to the last. This handful of Japanese troops had decided they wanted to live and they had made a desperate bid to do so.

Getting into the beach spirit, Wynne found Smoky an excellent, sheltered swimming pool. Dogs of her size needed to be careful in rough water. The powerful surf could dash a dog like Smoky on a reef, or the tide could drag her out to sea. Wynne found a novel solution to the problem: he discovered a particular bomb crater on the beach that was just right for his dog. The breakers rolled gently into it, filling it to a depth of about four feet with calm, balmy water. It was perfect.

Smoky loved it. Her favourite pastime became chasing flocks of small birds across the beach, in the direction of the swimming pool. When they took flight to cross it, she'd dive in, doggie-paddle over, and leap out the far side to resume the hunt. The birds seemed to learn that by luring their pursuer into the crater-cum-swimming-pool they could gain themselves some short respite. They took to flying back around, knowing they'd be able to dunk her in the crater time after time.

Of course, the repeated immersions in salt water, combined with the harsh, dry nature of the bare coral, weren't exactly conducive to Smoky keeping her fine coat of hair in top order. Wynne ensured she got a daily fresh-water bath. A full helmet was used to soap and to scrub her, a half to rinse her thoroughly thereafter. Somehow, Smoky seemed to master the tough, challenging conditions. She'd yet to fall sick, unlike her master.

Fortunately, the accommodation tents were pitched upon one of the few patches of grass in the area. It helped cushion the velvety-soft pads of Smoky's feet from the sharp coral, at least when she was resting. Those pads were covered in minute, fingerprint-like tracing marks, like the tiny spreading branches of a tree. They were beautiful, and delicate, and so very easy for a dog to tear, especially when moving fast over rough, dry terrain, or running from enemy warplanes.

Smoky took to sleeping right underneath Wynne's army cot. He figured she sensed an extra layer of protection there. Or maybe it was simply all down to the smell. The scent of the familiar. She might have had her own bed – the strip of khaki material that served as the cot's cover – but it wasn't a patch on where Wynne slept. Not in Smoky's eyes or, rather, not according to her nose.

A dog's nose is up to a million times more sensitive than a human's. We might poke our nose into a cup of tea to smell if it's been sweetened with a spoonful of sugar, and even then we might not be entirely sure. But a dog can detect the scent of a teaspoon of sugar in a million gallons of water – enough to fill two Olympic-sized swimming pools to the brim.

As far as Smoky was concerned, the cot cover smelled of her. By contrast, Wynne's cot itself was crammed full of the scent of her best buddy snoozing through the heat of the New Guinea night. It resonated with his smell, the one that she adored.

Like all dogs, Smoky's sense of smell represented her universe; she was a creature of the nose. For her, the world was an incredibly rich and exciting tapestry of smells. More often than not, that was how a dog experienced a new scene – via a scent carried on the breeze. We humans see the world. A dog smells it. And, somehow, Smoky seemed able to smell trouble, too.

One fine morning Frank Petrilak invited his tent buddies for a sail on the bay. There was no flying, so it would be a welcome diversion. Petrilak was no sailor, but his friend, Jack Tankersley, was. Tankersley's first name was actually Rholan, but he preferred being known simply as 'Jack'. A corporal like Wynne, he had fine-boned, delicate features and the demeanour of a scholar. He'd spent a good deal of his youth crewing yachts, and that gave the two landlubbers – three, if Smoky were included – the confidence that they could master the coming voyage.

Theirs was a drop-tank craft, but a slightly more ambitious

model than the mono-hulled vessels. By lashing two drop-tanks together, set a few feet apart, they'd managed to form a makeshift catamaran. The whole affair was topped by a wooden platform, on which the intrepid sailors could perch. Cut into each of the drop-tanks was a cockpit, in case those crewing her needed to take shelter from wind or spray. The sail that was hoisted above was fashioned from a discarded parachute, boasting a wide expanse of the US Army's finest silk.

Tankersley proposed a cruise across the bay to visit one Biak's native settlements. The Biak Islanders tended to live in so-called 'water villages' or 'floating villages', where entire neighbourhoods were constructed over the sea. The wooden huts were suspended on stilts and linked by a labyrinth of bamboo walkways. There was little flat ground upon which to build among the island's dramatic, hilly terrain, plus the water villages took full advantage of the cooling sea breeze.

Popping Smoky into one of the drop-tank cockpits, the three men pushed off. The early-morning bay was as smooth as glass, and at first each of them had to help paddle. But shortly the wind picked up a little, the sail snapped and billowed, and they began to gather speed. But all of a sudden Smoky leapt out of the drop-tank cockpit where she was riding, and with zero warning launched herself into the water. The boat was at least half a mile out by now, and Wynne had no idea what could have got into his dog.

As the tiny dog paddled for all she was worth for shore, his biggest fear was the sharks. The outer reaches of the bay were infested with them, and while they'd yet to see any V-shaped fins cutting through the surrounding water, the sharks were sure to be lurking somewhere close by. Throwing caution to the wind Wynne dived in. He caught up with Smoky when she was about twenty-five yards from the boat. Holding her up out of the water and away from any hungry jaws he side-crabbed his way back to the vessel.

Handing Smoky up to Petrilak, he heaved himself hurriedly aboard. The sea was wonderfully warm and Smoky seemed unharmed. Puzzled as Wynne was, he was relieved that no real damage had been done. After that brief and unexpected interlude, the crew set a course for the nearest floating village, which was perched on the very tip of a distant headland.

As the drop-tank catamaran ploughed onwards, those aboard began to wonder why Smoky had taken flight. It wasn't like this dog to go running scared of anything. She was always up for any adventure. Most dog lovers have at one time or another experienced the uncanny sixth sense of their canine companions. Had Smoky detected something, danger perhaps, in the bay? The sky remained clear and the sea calm, but for whatever reason she'd seemed reluctant to journey with them. In fact, she'd seemed desperate to abandon ship. What on earth could have spooked her?

A while later Tankersley steered the craft towards shore, navigating a course around the outcroppings of a coral reef. Locals waved a welcome from the nearest stilted hut and the three men and their dog were invited in. Everything in these villages seemed to be made of bamboo, which grew to a great height and breadth in thick stands in the surrounding jungle. The hut had a split bamboo floor, the walls were of split bamboo, and even the beds themselves were made out of solid bamboo frames.

As the villagers welcomed the three visitors, Smoky dashed outside to entertain the local kids, crab-chasing on the beach. She'd pounce on an unfortunate crustacean, growl menacingly, spin around a few times in a wild blur, then let the beast go. The crab, hardly believing its luck, would rise on its legs and scuttle off, whereupon Smoky would give chase again.

But after a while the sky above the bay began to darken. Out of nowhere heavy clouds appeared on the horizon. Alert to how changeable the tropical weather could be, the three adventurers decided it was time to head back to camp. They pushed the catamaran back out to sea, paddled past the reef and set a course for home. The craft picked up speed as the wind began to gust more strongly. A particularly powerful blast drove the boat forward, the conical noses of the drop-tanks digging into the waves.

Seawater sloshed into the open cockpits. The wind grew stronger, the sharp, double-prow of the craft repeatedly being driven underwater. Petrilak started bailing, as Wynne moved to the stern of the boat, in an effort to use his weight to lift the bows. The wind stiffened. The swell to left and right became ever more ominous. Tankersley began to tack back and forth, as he tried to navigate the cumbersome vessel through the rough seas. Worryingly, he announced that he'd never had to cope with anything quite like this back home in the States.

Had they been crewing a proper yacht, they would have been able to furl the sail, drop the anchor and ride out the storm. Not in their drop-tank catamaran. The open nature of the twin steel hulls meant that she was in danger of being swamped. If that happened, their weight would drag them down to the depths.

There were no air tanks or flotation aids to keep her afloat, and if she shipped too much water she'd go down like a stone.

As they fought against the conditions and bailed frantically, all of a sudden the boat's steel double-prow ploughed into a submerged obstruction. They had struck a reef lying just below the surface and they were stuck. Wedged fast, the waves kept pounding the drop-tanks against the sharp rocks, punching dents in them. More water washed inside the open cockpits and the vessel groaned alarmingly as she twisted and slewed with each wave, but still she remained trapped.

The makeshift catamaran sounded as if she was in danger of breaking up and being torn in two. Aware that they were in desperate straits, Wynne did the only thing that he could think of: he jumped overboard, floundered around until he'd found reasonably firm footing on the reef and began to shove for all he was worth.

Straining with the effort, he managed to heave the craft back into the sea. That done he dived for her twin steel hulls, and with aching muscles managed to drag himself back aboard. The wind propelled them onwards at speed now, driving all before its blast. The only option was to keep sailing and to keep bailing for all they were worth.

They would have to try to ride out the storm.

CHAPTER 11

The battle to keep the catamaran afloat lasted for two perilous hours, and for all of that time the crew were continuously bailing out the drop-tank hulls in a bid to stay afloat. When finally their exhausted, sodden party neared the beach, they could see a group of fellow soldiers standing on the shoreline, scrutinizing their every move with binoculars. Caught up in their struggle to navigate the vessel home, Wynne and his fellows had been oblivious to how dire a predicament they had been in. It had been crystal clear to the watchers ashore.

They made landfall, and Wynne's first concern now was for his dog. Smoky was soaked to the skin and had plainly swallowed a good deal of seawater. The wind howled around them still, the storm blustery, cold and dark. So powerful were the blasts that several tents had been blown down. Luckily, Wynne and Petrilak's was still standing. It was to be a long, cold night, but at least the men and their dog had come through that sea voyage alive.

As they reflected upon the day just gone, the intrepid seamen wondered about the smallest sailor among them, Smoky. One thing stuck in their minds – the moment when she had leapt overboard. Had she somehow sensed that the storm was coming, and thus taken the desperate measure of trying to jump ship and swim to shore? Had she tried to head for land before it was too late, hoping to communicate to her fellow sailors the coming danger?

They could remember occasions before when Smoky had appeared to sense an incoming storm long before it had struck. For no apparent reason she would go very quiet and sniff the air, before starting to whimper and head for her sanctuary – invariably, the space beneath Bill Wynne's cot. A while later the storm would hit. Maybe that was what had driven her actions today?

Perhaps Smoky had demonstrated one of the most unusual and extraordinary aspects of canine behaviour: 'intelligent diso-bedience', the ability to hear and understand a human's order or command, but to disobey it for the simple reason that the dog knew better. She'd known that morning that she was supposed to sail to some mystery destination, but had she also sensed the approaching storm, and done her level best to force an abandonment of the voyage?

Some animal behaviourists and scientists argue that dogs can sense a change in the weather. They claim dogs are able to detect a drop in the barometric pressure that presages a storm. They also may detect changes in the atmosphere's static electrical field, which alters at the approach of a thunderstorm. Lightning ionizes the air forming ozone, which has a sharp metallic scent, so they may even be able to smell an approach-ing storm. In a similar way dogs and other animals may sense a coming earthquake, by detecting electrical signals produced by the movements of tectonic plates beneath the earth's crust.

Whatever the truth, there was no doubt that Smoky had been utterly determined to get off the 'Good Ship Drop-Tank' that morning, risking a long swim through shark-infested waters to do so. What breed of dog possessed such refined senses, her fellow sailors wondered? What kind of pedigree produced such a seemingly extraordinary set of instincts and an innate sixth sense? As luck would have it, they were about to find out.

It was during those long hot weeks on Biak Island that a major part of the mystery surrounding Smoky would be solved. An excited Staff Sergeant Kalt – Smoky's photographer during her *Yank Mag* parachute jumps – came to seek out man and dog. He knew what breed Smoky was, Kalt declared, breathlessly.

One of the squadron had just received his April '44 issue of the *National Geographic Magazine*. (It had taken several months for it to make it out to New Guinea.) By chance, along with features entitled 'Japan and the Pacific' and 'Jungle War: Bougainville and New Caledonia', there was one called 'Toy Dogs, Pets of Kings and Commoners', and another entitled 'Dogs In Toyland'.

'They prove she's a Yorkshire Terrier,' Kalt announced, excitedly, pointing to the magazine's dog-related features.

'A what?' Wynne queried.

'A Yorkshire Terrier,' Kalt repeated. There was a photograph of one of the breed illustrating the article, he explained. It was the spitting image of Smoky.

Wynne got his hands on the magazine and flicked through the pages. There were the adverts for 'US War Savings Bonds', and Coca-Cola and one that boasted about how 'America's fighters move in with GM Diesels', plus a stunning photo of Japan's snow-capped Mount Fuji, 'an outstanding guidepost to

Allied Bombers', the magazine declared, looking ahead to the bombing of the Japanese homeland.

The article entitled 'Jungle War: Bougainville and New Caledonia' was richly illustrated with oil paintings by an official US Army war artist. They captured the grit and fire of combat in New Guinea. One was captioned, '"H" Hour of Bougainville – Marines of the First Wave Swarm into Landing Boats'. 'Jap planes attack!' read another. 'Into Empress August Bay falls a flaming Mitsubishi Dive Bomber'. Then: 'First wave! A Jap mortar shell blasts a landing boat. Casualties are heavy, but the fighting marines gain the beachhead'. A final painting showed marines standing by a thickly tangled wall of vegetation: 'At jungle's edge Marines watch for Japs and dig foxholes'.

But what Wynne hungered to see most were the articles about the toy dogs. The first, by British writer Freeman Lloyd, lay seventy pages into the magazine. The piece warned about the threat of such small dogs being stolen to order, and how no one was immune. 'Being easily caught and carried away, toy dogs have always been a special prey for professional dog thieves,' Lloyd wrote. 'Charles II expressed . . . his concern over the loss of some of his dogs, and actually begged the thieves to leave his pets alone.'

The professional dog thieves were 'shrewd rascals who kept up to the minute on breeds and values', the author wrote, describing the Sunday morning black market for such stolen dogs, in Shoreditch, east London. Lloyd was eighty-four years old, and he'd been an editor of *Field and Stream* magazine for a quarter of a century. He was pictured at a field trial for spaniels, dressed in a feathered derby (a kind of bowler hat), formal black coat, stock necktie, corduroy breeches, heavy stockings and short gaiters. That, apparently, was what any self-respecting canine expert should be seen in at such an event.

He was certainly an authority on his subject. Several pages into the article there was the first mention of the Yorkshire Terrier. It concerned the starring role that one such dog had assumed on the stage. 'The increasing popularity of the Yorkshire Terrier (Plate V) may have been heightened . . . by the appearance of one of that breed as "protector" of the leading lady in *The Enemies* – Lillie Langtry. The little dog growled or barked at the approach of the villain in the play.'

Protecting the leading lady from the bad guys – now that sounded like Smoky all right.

There were further features on the Toy Poodle, Affenpinscher, Pug, English Toy Spaniels, Chihuahua and Pekinese. The section on the Japanese Spaniel – 'the toy dog of the Orient' – drew the eye, but the description didn't sound like Smoky at all. 'The profusely haired plume or tail carried over a side of the back proclaims the Jap to be of an ancestry different from that of . . . the toy spaniels of Europe.' That was definitely *not* Smoky.

The 'Plate V' referenced by Lloyd related to the Dogs in Toyland section – a gallery of colour photos that followed the main article. There were two pictures in Plate V. The top showed a Yorkshire Terrier which – though thoroughly beribboned, primped and prettied-up – was the spitting image of Smoky. 'Silken-haired "Suprema" is a Champion Yorkshire Terrier,' announced the caption. 'Yorkshires are excellent mousers and when not on show this one gives the family cat stiff competition.'

The image was transfixing. It was a dead ringer for Smoky.

So was the description of the breed and its distinctive coat. 'A bright, golden tan, is the desired light colour that contrasts so beautifully with the bright steel-blue hair that extends from the back of the head to the root of the tail . . . The dog should have a cushion to lie upon; hay, straw or shavings may otherwise become entangled with the coat.'

A cushion to lie upon: some hopes of that here on Biak Island!

Yorkshire Terriers – known colloquially as 'Yorkies' – were bred in the 1800s, the article explained, to hunt for rats in the woollen mills of the north of England. In the 1850s weavers in Lancashire and Yorkshire had crossed Halifax Terriers with other terrier breeds – most likely the Skye Terrier, the Paisley Terrier and the Maltese. They had produced an incredibly tenacious and courageous dog.

Their small size was actually crucial to the role for which they were bred: it enabled the Yorkie to pursue vermin down drains and tunnels. Yorkshire Terriers were born hunters, which would go some way to explaining Smoky's acute territoriality, her fearlessness – the epic battle with Colonel Turbo being just one example – and her fierce protective instincts over those that she loved.

The Yorkie was a breed still practically unknown in America, which explained why Wynne and the rest of her fan club in the 26th had failed to recognize her. But wonderful though it was, discovering her breed – that she was of English ratting origin – had done little to explain how she'd come into Bill Wynne's hands.

How on earth had a dog bred to hunt vermin in Yorkshire in the 1800s ended up abandoned in a foxhole in New Guinea at the height of the war? Her presence here in New Guinea remained an enigma, and there was not much that anyone could do to solve that right now. There was, after all, a war to be fought.

General Krueger, the American commander charged with wresting Biak Island from the grip of the enemy, had his hands full clearing Japanese troops from Biak's thick jungle, labyrinthine peaks, valleys and caves. A veteran of the First World War, Krueger had turned sixty-three in January '44 and he'd believed himself too old to be given front-line command. But MacArthur had expressed himself 'particularly anxious' to have Krueger with him.

MacArthur appreciated Krueger's hard-charging attitude. He was too good and aggressive a commander to stand by and wait for a Japanese attack, even when – as at Biak Island – estimates of Japanese strengths had turned out to be way off the mark. In the protracted and bitter fighting that had followed, Krueger had gone head to head against Adachi, the Japanese general in overall command of the enemy's New Guinea campaign.

Horribly cut off, and with his own forces plagued by disease and hunger, Adachi feared it was a campaign in which the Allies had the upper hand. Even so, he would never give in. In an effort to relieve the besieged forces at Biak Island, as well as his own encircled troops, a powerful Japanese task force was ordered to set sail for New Guinea. It consisted of the Imperial Japanese Navy's foremost carrier fleet, which would launch a massive air assault against US positions. Ground offensives would follow, intended to seize back the initiative and stabilize the Japanese lines.

As it transpired, the Japanese warships were intercepted by the

US Navy's Fifth Fleet in the waters around the Mariana Islands, which lay to the north of New Guinea in the Philippine Sea. The F6F Hellcat, the US military's leading carrier-based fighter plane, had recently arrived in the Pacific. Rugged, super-efficient and deadly, boasting superior speed, armour and armaments, it could outperform and outfight the Japanese Zero.

As the two fleets converged, the Japanese carriers sent up four massive waves of aircraft, boasting 373 warplanes. Only 130 would return. The rest were intercepted by the Hellcats and blasted out of the skies. By day two of the onslaught, which became known as the 'Great Marianas Turkey Shoot', three of the Japanese carriers had been sunk and they'd lost a total of 633 planes. The American air losses were less than a sixth of that number.

In forty-eight hours the Japanese Navy had lost ninety per cent of their carrier-based aircraft, most of their highly trained pilots and three of their most valuable warships, rendering their surviving carriers largely useless. The Battle of the Philippine Sea – the largest carrier battle in history – was a blow from which the Japanese military would struggle to recover.

The Japanese task force had failed to relieve Biak Island. They had failed to link up with General Adachi's dwindling band of fighters, marooned in the New Guinea jungle to the south of Hollandia. By late August 1944 General Krueger was able to declare the Battle for Biak Island won. There were small pockets of enemy troops stubbornly holding out, deep in the island's interior, but the key areas lay in Allied hands. Though it had not been without heavy sacrifice, it constituted a huge step forward for the Allies.

Krueger's victory at Biak, and his outfighting Adachi, would lead to him being hailed as a hero at home, his photo gracing the cover of *Time Magazine*. Such defeats left the Japanese increasingly desperate, prompting their senior commanders to seize upon a wholly new means of waging warfare, one designed to slow up the American advance and to sink as many of their warships as humanly possible. It would call for the ultimate sacrifice from their remaining pilots, who would strike first in the defence of the Philippines.

Vice Admiral Takijiro Onishi, one of the most senior Japanese commanders in the region, feared that with so few aircraft and pilots remaining to call on, the battle for the Philippines could not be won. In late August 1944 he conceived of the concept of the kamikaze, which he christened *tokubetsu kogeki tai* – the 'divine wind special attack teams'. The more familiar name of kamikaze, which usually translates as 'god-wind', would come into usage in October of that year.

Under Vice Admiral Onishi's purview, land-based squadrons would be trained for kamikaze missions, in a last-ditch effort to prevent the Americans from reaching the shores of the Imperial Japanese homeland. The Japanese hoped that such suicide attacks would make the war so costly to the US, that the Allies would be forced to offer peace terms.

The concepts underpinning the kamikazes were rooted in the Japanese samurai tradition and its sense of duty and obedience, and the importance of achieving an honourable death. As part of Japanese bushido – the martial tradition dating to the Middle Ages – *giri* (obligation) meant that the true warrior should be willing to sacrifice his own life, and of his own free will, due to his beliefs and his love of homeland, which were paramount.

Onishi organized the first kamikaze flights into four units, each named after a patriotic Japanese poem: *Shikishima* (Spirit of Japan); *Yamato* (True Japan), *Yamazakura* (Mountain Cherry) and *Asahi* (Rising Sun). He decreed that a ceremony would be held to speed each kamikaze pilot on his way. Dressed in a headband adorned with the rising sun, and with a *sennibari* – a belt of one thousand stitches made by one thousand Japanese women – strung around his waist, the pilot would eat a last ball of rice and drink sake, before climbing into the cockpit of his aircraft.

The *tokkotai* – the manual drawn up for the kamikaze – exhorted those flying to their deaths never to close their eyes, not even in the moment of their own annihilation. If they did, they might miss their way and fail to strike their target. In the final few seconds they were to shout at the top of their voices *Banzai* (an ancient Japanese war cry) and *Hissatsu* (critical strike).

By late summer 1944, General MacArthur was readying his next push northwards towards the Philippines. Once the US general had, as he'd famously promised, *returned* to that war-torn archipelago, Allied forces would be able to starve Japan of oil supplies. Deprived of fuel, she would be a defeated nation in all but name. The Japanese commanders, well aware of the danger, readied the divine wind special attack teams for what was coming.

The 26th Photo Reconnaissance Squadron would sail into the heart of the coming storm, and when they did they would have a new, and wholly unexpected, addition to their number. Yet before all that could happen there was flying to be done – both for Bill Wynne and the squadron's champion mascot.

Man and dog were about to take to the skies.

CHAPTER 12

In late August Bill Wynne decided it was time that he got air-borne. He'd trained as an aerial photographer back in the US, but he'd never yet been able to indulge his craft. Of course, he couldn't do so with the 26th, for their P-38s were single-seater aircraft. The 3rd Air-Sea Rescue Squadron were also based at Biak, and they flew missions in multi-seater planes. They were eager for specialists with his kind of skill.

He and Troop Sergeant Lester E. Switzer, a fellow aerial photographer with the 26th, volunteered for air duties. Switzer, known to all as 'Les', was the 26th's camera repair chief. The device he and Wynne would be using was an Eastman-Kodak K24, which resembled a giant iron cauldron laid on its side. It was almost as big as a man's torso, and it had a pair of solid wooden shovel-like handle grips set vertically to the sides, for swinging the heavy camera around.

Wynne and Switzer had spent months working in cramped, baking-hot confines on the ground, at either the photo lab or the camera repair department. Both fancied a change of scenery and a spell in the air, but there was another powerful incentive for those who wished to get airborne. Any airman who completed 300 hours of 'combat flying' was eligible for return to the USA. In short, they could earn a permanent passage home.

Combat flying was defined as time over territory 'where enemy fire is probable and expected'. To survive *300 hours* of such high-risk operations was a tall order indeed. On average, that might equate to one hundred or more sorties, each of which pushed deep into enemy airspace. But still, it was a dream the aircrew could hold on to and nurture.

For Switzer it was a fairly easy decision to move onto flying status with the 3rd Air-Sea Rescue Squadron. For Wynne, slightly less so. Air-sea rescue patrols generally spent inordinately long stretches in the air. The very nature of the work – scouring vast tracts of jungle or ocean for downed pilots – demanded time, and Wynne worried what he was going to do with his dog during the hours that he would be airborne and away from camp.

Towards the end of the month a young lieutenant from the 3rd Air-Sea Rescue Squadron said he was keen to have a photographer accompany him on his next flight. A fighter pilot flying a P-38 had gone down behind enemy lines in the deep Biak jungle. If the 3rd Air-Sea Rescue Squadron could find and photograph his crash-site, they might be able to guide an infantry patrol to reach the downed airman. The enemy were thick on the ground, but rescue was still a possibility.

Wynne volunteered for this, his inaugural combat flight. It would take place in a Stinson L5 Sentinel, a diminutive military liaison and spotter aircraft. The Sentinel was only a little bigger than a Piper Cub, the ubiquitous single-engine light trainer that had been co-opted for wartime service. The Sentinel's simple, reliable design and good low-speed handling made it ideally suited for military purposes, including reconnaissance, message carrying and ground control.

The Sentinel's fuselage was made from steel tubing covered with cotton treated with dope, a liquid that both stiffened and waterproofed the fabric, while the wings were fashioned from wooden frames covered in the same way. Pilot and co-pilot/observer/photographer sat side-by-side in the cockpit. While the aircraft was easy enough to fly, it barely topped 150 mph at full speed and it offered zero protection from enemy fire. The prospect of passing 300 combat hours in such an aircraft wasn't exactly enticing.

Wynne gathered together his leather flight helmet and goggles, his summer flying overalls, plus his .45 calibre M1911 semi-automatic pistol – standard US military issue – grabbing a few spare magazines of rounds, including some packed with rat-shot. When armed with that type of ammunition the pistol was basically converted into a low-power shotgun. The rat-shot was ideal for taking out snakes and any other nasties that might appear at close quarters. Lastly, he strapped on his bowie knife, a large military-issue combat blade that could be put to a wide variety of uses in the jungle.

Long before he'd climbed into the Sentinel's cockpit, Wynne had made the decision to leave Smoky in the hands of some of the squadron's old faithfuls, with his tentmate, Frank Petrilak being given special responsibility. With Petrilak keeping a watchful eye, there shouldn't be a great deal of harm that could come to her. The tiny, twenty-four-foot-long aircraft bumped and rumbled its way down the airstrip and clawed its way into the hot air. Shimmering thermals rising from the coral shook and buffeted the aircraft like a kite as the pilot fought to gain altitude.

The Sentinel climbed above the ridge that lay to the rear of the airbase, levelling off at 800 feet over what was no-man's-land. This was terrain over which US and Japanese forces had fought horrendous close-quarter battles and in which hundreds had died. Here and there pockets of the enemy were holding out, stubbornly refusing to lay down their arms.

The pilot steered a course over a series of stark ridges and valleys, the high ground marked by bare expanses of glistening white coral, the valleys tight with verdant jungle. Finally, the Sentinel reached a relatively flat section of terrain lying towards the centre of the landmass, one overshadowed by the island's rugged volcanic spine. He began to lose altitude, swooping down until he was flying around fifty feet above the ground.

With the Sentinel's fixed undercarriage almost skimming the tree-tops, the pilot began to fly search transects across the terrain, eyes searching the ground for any sign of the missing warplane. Almost immediately, Wynne noticed several holes in the ground, each of around five feet across. The caverns were equipped with crude palm-thatched roofs, though most looked as if they had been torn and blasted askew.

The pilot jabbed a thumb at the nearest. 'See those damn things?' he yelled above the engine noise.

'Yeah.'

'Those're Jap foxholes.'

Wynne had sudden visions of the enemy popping their heads and their gun-barrels out of the nearest and opening fire at less than one hundred yards. With no armour to protect the Sentinel's crew, he suggested that the pilot get them out of there pronto.

The pilot grinned. There was nothing to worry about, he assured his nervous flight companion. They'd bombed the enemy out of those very positions the previous day.

'Bombed them out like how?' Wynne queried.

The pilot's smile widened. 'We flew over and dropped hand-grenades into 'em.'

They continued their low-level search until they reached an area scattered with wreckage. A crater marked what looked like the epicentre of a crash-site. A large chunk of debris lay at its centre. It was the scorched and mangled remains of a distinctive Allison V-1710 twelve-cylindre liquid-cooled engine. The only one of its kind to see service during the war, the Allison V-1710 was fitted almost exclusively to P-38 Lightnings.

There was a long and scorched skid-mark leading up to the crater. The dark scar that had been torn through the vegetation and rock suggested that it was unlikely that the plane's pilot had made anything like a safe crash-landing. The impression was heightened by the mangled fragments of the aircraft's aluminium fuselage that were scattered to either side. While the Sentinel circled the wreckage, Wynne took a series of photos with his K24 camera. It was impossible that anyone could have survived such a violent impact, but there was always the possibility that the pilot might have bailed out while still in the air.

The Sentinel's pilot jabbed a thumb over one shoulder. He'd spotted the wreckage of a second P-38 not so far away. They flew over to check it out. At first it looked as if the aircraft was more or less intact, but as the Sentinel drew closer they could make out where a low-hanging tree had ripped open the cockpit. The pilot wouldn't have stood a chance. The poor devil had been torn to pieces by the branches.

There was little point lingering above either crash-site. The Sentinel climbed to altitude and the pilot set a course for base. As they came in across the bay and began their final approach to the Mokmer airstrip, the distinctive form of an enemy fighter – a Japanese Zero – could be seen lying in the ocean shallows. It looked largely undamaged, its marking – the red sun symbol surrounded by a thin band of white – standing out clearly on the upper side of the wings.

That pilot had more than likely survived his crash-landing. Such were the vagaries of war.

Once the Sentinel was safely down and Wynne had delivered his photographs to the lab, he went to seek out his dog. After a joyful reunion with Smoky, Petrilak and some of the others gathered, eager to hear news of Wynne's first such flight. He and the Sentinel's pilot had logged barely thirty-five minutes of 'combat flying' – that was the extent of the time they'd spent over the enemy positions. It sure would take many such flight missions to clock up the required 300 hours, so as to earn him a ticket back to the USA.

After listening to his tale, the guys forming Wynne's audience seemed more interested in his dog, and what would happen to her if Wynne took a bullet on any future such sorties.

'Hey, Wynne, if you get knocked off can I have Smoky?' one piped up, eagerly.

'No way,' Petrilak countered. 'I get her. She's mine!'

Other voices chipped in, each laying a claim to the prize-winning mascot of the 26th. As they bickered over Smoky's fate, not a man among them seemed particularly worried for Bill Wynne's welfare. It stuck him that they didn't appear to be that concerned for the well-being of his dog, either. It angered and discomfited him. He ended the debate by telling them all in no uncertain terms that if the aircraft in which he was flying went down, then Smoky would go down too.

From now on, she would be flying with him.

The dangers involved in undertaking any kind of air missions were ratcheting up all the time. Now that MacArthur had his eyes firmly on the Philippines, nearly all photo-reconnaissance flights were operating over vast distances, where for the most part the threat of enemy action was very real. And wherever those airmen flew and went missing in action, the air-sea rescue aircraft had to follow.

As the summer months turned to autumn (at least in the US or UK; there were no such seasons in the tropics), the 26th would win another DFC, for a sortie flown by Captain Herbert A. Curran, over Leyte Island, General MacArthur's intended landing point on the Philippines. Curran's daring mission had involved spending nine and a half hours in the air, during which 'heavy weather en route caused an hour's delay and consumed dangerously large amounts of carefully measured fuel'. Though well aware of this perilous state of affairs, Curran had continued with his sortie, landing back at Biak with 'only ten minutes' supply of gasoline' remaining.

The 26th pushed the limits still further. Flights were executed over Balikpapan Bay, a key Japanese harbour in Borneo (part of modern-day Indonesia), through which was shipped more than eighty per cent of their war materiel. The flights to the Philippines involved a 2,200-mile round-trip; those to Borneo a total journey of well over 2,500 miles. Typically, such sorties were led by Captain Orville Counselman, who'd taken over command of the 26th.

On one such October 1944 flight to Balikpapan Bay, a P-38 made several passes over the harbour at 28,600 feet, trying to stay above the level of enemy flak, which was clawing up as high as 23,000 feet. The pilot fired off seventy-odd exposures spread across three strips of film, capturing an armada of Japanese warships lying at anchor. Those vessels included one massive 12,000-tonne merchant ship, five 'Sugar Charlies' (2,300-tonne freighters), seven 4,000-tonne fuel tankers, plus countless smaller ships.

With all of that captured so clearly on film, Balikpapan Bay represented an incredibly tempting target. But such photos alone rarely revealed everything. Even after the closest of studies by the squadron's analysts, the actual nature of the ship's cargo might still elude discovery.

Just three weeks earlier, a Japanese merchant vessel of 5,000 tonnes had been sunk by the Allies, only for it to be discovered that she had been packed full of thousands of Dutch, British, American and Australian prisoners of war, as well as locals requisitioned as slave labour.

On 18 September 1944, the *Junyo Maru* had been steaming north up the coast of Sumatra, part of present-day Indonesia. Originally the British cargo ship the SS *Ardgorm*, she'd been renamed the *Junyo Maru* after being sold to a Japanese company in 1926. On the outbreak of war the *Junyo Maru* had been converted into a so-called 'hell ship', with extra decks fitted into her hold made from bamboo, and lined with bamboo cages, for carrying thousands of Allied POWs.

In early September the *Junyo Maru* had picked up more than 6,000, many of whom had already slaved away in inhuman conditions, hacking airstrips out of the thick jungle and levelling coral runways. They were to be shipped northwards to the 'hell railroad', a railway line being forced through the impossible jungle terrain of Sumatra. The railway line was to be used to transport coal out of Sumatra, to help fuel the Japanese war effort. Thousands were to die during the utterly nightmarish months of its construction, but on that September morning many more were to perish at sea.

The *Junyo Maru* was spotted by a British submarine, the HMS *Tradewind,* off the coast of Sumatra. Her captain, Lieutenant-Commander Lynch Maydon, was unaware that she was carrying such a desperate human cargo. He fired his torpedoes. Barely six hundred would survive what followed, as the *Tradewind's* salvo slammed into the *Junyo Maru's* hull. The ship went down in a matter of minutes, thousands of Allied POWs trying to fight their way out of the bamboo cages and reach the deck above.

Even those who did manage to abandon ship by leaping into the sea were far from being saved. Armed trawlers formed the *Junyo Maru's* escort, but the Japanese sailors crewing them beat off any who tried to clamber aboard, using iron bars. Hundreds of POWs were forced to hold out for forty-eight hours in the sea, clinging onto wreckage, as one by one their fellows lost their grip and drowned, or were picked off by the sharks.

At the time, the sinking of the *Junyo Maru* – in which some 5,620 POW and local slave-labourers perished – represented the single largest loss of life in a sea disaster ever. Determining the nature of a ship's cargo via photos taken at 28,000 feet was never going to be easy, yet it was critical to do so, hence the fliers of the 26th returning again and again to locations such as Balikpapan Bay, for each set of images was sure to yield fresh clues.

That October the squadron executed 122 reconnaissance sorties, shooting 6,776 photos from which 94,707 prints would be made. The ratio of photos developed to prints made – over 10:1 – demonstrated the very high demand for such images. That month one of the squadron's top pilots would win an Air Medal with Oak Leaf Cluster for completing 200 hours of combat flying, and the CO himself, Captain Counselman, would win a Bronze Oak Leaf Cluster to his Air Medal, for executing 100 hours of sorties.

But inevitably, such extreme risk-taking and heroics would prove costly. On 24 October 1944, a pilot from the 26th would fail to return to base.

This time the loss would be deeply personal, for Bill Wynne and his dog.

CHAPTER 13

The pilot listed as MIA was First Lieutenant Clair J. Bardsley, a good buddy of Bill Wynne's. They'd forged a friendship over sport, and particularly their great rivalry over basketball.

When based at Nadzab, they'd held a hoop-shooting contest to see who was the most skilful player. One by one all of the competitors had been eliminated, until only Wynne and Bardsley – a fiercely competitive, bull-necked redhead who wore a wispy moustache below a focused, level gaze – remained. The sun was well below the horizon by the time Bardsley had shot at and missed the basketball hoop, leaving Wynne the overall winner. The two men had remained good friends ever since.

On 24 October, Bardsley had taken off from the Mokmer airstrip at 0615 hours, heading for Ceram Island in the eastern Moluccas (part of modern-day Indonesia), another significant hub for Japanese shipping. The flight ahead of him had consisted of a round trip of over 1,000 miles, during which he'd have to climb above the New Guinea landmass and head west across the Ceram Sea. The Casualty Report penned after Bardsley went missing stated the bare, bald facts: he had encountered 'extreme adverse weather conditions . . . No further information is available.'

All anyone had to go on in terms of mounting a search was the flight plan and bearings that Bardsley had logged before taking to the skies. Clearly, no Sentinel light aircraft was capable of even attempting to track and trace such a long flight. Instead, the task would fall to the workhorses of the Air-Sea Rescue squadrons – namely the Consolidated PBY-5A Catalina flying boats.

One of the most widely used seaplanes of the war, the Catalina – 'Cat' for short – was a stalwart of anti-submarine work, convoy escorts, cargo transport and air-sea rescue missions. Wide of wing and seemingly ungainly, yet somehow hugely evocative and graceful once she took to the air, the Cat was known affectionately as 'Dumbo' to the crews that flew her. Some 3,000 were serving with the US military, and they'd been particularly effective in the southwest Pacific theatre, operating over the vast stretches of ocean that lay between the myriad scattered islands.

Indeed, Cats had played a leading role in bottling up the enemy shipping discovered at Balikpapan, by laying mines across the mouth of the bay. Those missions – executed at night – had involved over twenty hours of flying, culminating in the mines being released from 200 feet above the water. The Cats had also earned a certain infamy among Japanese ground forces for carrying out 'terror bombing' at night – dropping empty bottles with razor-blades inserted into their necks, which emitted an unearthly screaming as they fell, thus terrorizing the enemy.

Bardsley had gone missing just three weeks after he'd won his promotion to first lieutenant, something that he'd long been hoping for. Wynne was determined to be the photographer on this search and rescue flight; finding the missing airman was personal. He was equally determined that Smoky was going to accompany him.

The Catalina had a crew of ten, including a pilot and co-pilot, navigator, radio operator, radar technician and four gunners. For this late-October search and rescue sortie their crew would also include an aerial photographer, plus of course one four-legged flier.

It was 0200 by the time Wynne had grabbed his flying gear and his dog, left his tent and climbed into a jeep to drive the short distance to the camp of the 3rd Air-Sea Rescue Squadron. The night was comparatively chilly, and it would be far colder at the Cat's cruise altitude of 15,000 feet. He'd made sure to wrap Smoky snugly in her special coat of many colours.

For Wynne, flying in a Catalina had the great advantage that the aircraft's 15,000-foot flight ceiling was low enough to take a dog on board without needing any oxygen.

Wynne set off keeping the jeep's lights doused, just in case there were any enemy night-fighters prowling the skies. At first he wondered if he were seeing things, for in the faint moonlight the road ahead seemed to be alive, writhing eerily. It turned out that a mass of bright-red crabs was moving across the island, heading from forest to beach in their seasonal migration.

Having made his way safely through the undulating mass of crustaceans, he arrived at the 3rd's base in time for a glorious breakfast of fried eggs and salty bacon. Smoky had to make do with eggs alone. The salt in the bacon would make her too thirsty to cope with the many hours she would spend suspended at altitude.

During the pre-mission briefing, the aircrew were reminded

of their duties and the drills. Catalinas had rescued thousands of Allied airmen and sailors during the war. Often, a lone Cat would stand off from a major air mission, waiting for a MAYDAY call, which signified that a warplane was going down. On those occasions when the Catalina had fighter cover, the pilot would put down in the sea as soon as they had located the aircrew they had been sent to rescue. If not, the Cat's aircrew would take their chances, swooping low to drop life rafts and other supplies.

US airmen had a dye dispenser attached to their life jackets. It would trigger upon contact with seawater, the dye staining the surrounding ocean a bright yellow-orange. It was supposed to serve a dual function. One, it would mark their position to friendly aircraft like the Cats. Two, it was believed to deter sharks. But by now Bardsley's dye would have dispersed long ago. What they would be scouring the seas for was most likely a lone life raft, in the hope of finding Bardsley still alive.

With a top speed of less than 200 mph the Catalina wasn't fast. It couldn't outrun the enemy – it could only rely upon its gunners to try to outfight them. If a plane were hit, the beauty of being able to land on water meant that they could ditch just about anywhere there was ocean. The downside was that not all the natives were known to be friendly. There were stories – quite possibly apocryphal – of US aircrew having survived being shot down, only to get taken captive and eaten by remote villagers.

Readying himself for the flight, Wynne slipped Smoky into his haversack, fastening down the straps with the buckles that held them tight. As she disappeared inside, the spirited dog flashed him an eager look, as if she knew they were going on their airborne adventures again. Only, of course, the diminutive dog couldn't know that this time it was going to be very different. They weren't heading to friendly Australia for some much-needed R&R; this was a flight into the teeth of the enemy.

By 0300 Wynne found himself scrambling onto a second jeep along with a bevy of fellow aircrew. There was only the one vehicle available, so they had all had to clamber aboard, laden down as they were with parachutes, personal kit, weapons and, in Wynne's case, a hidden dog. The mass of bodies meant that the driver couldn't actually see to navigate properly, so those sitting in front of him had to yell out directions.

Once safely at the aircraft, Wynne took up position in one of the gunner's 'blisters' – a man-sized bulge of clear Plexiglas that stuck out of the side of the aircraft, just aft of the wings. Each of the blisters had its own access ladder leading up from the ground, and each was crammed with a 50-calibre heavy machine gun, mounted on a pivot.

Although the 3rd was primarily a search and rescue squadron, their aircraft was painted up like any standard combat aircraft, with a bold single star and stripe running along either side of the blunt nose. The gunners doubled as medics, and it was their role to paddle a rubber raft to any downed aircrew found at sea, often dragging them into the Catalina through the side-blisters.

Wynne decided to wait until they were well and truly airborne before revealing the presence of their mystery stowaway. The pilot punched the starter buttons and there was a belch of black smoke as first one and then the other engine roared into life. The massive Catalina, with her 104-foot wingspan and two Pratt & Whitney radial engines mounted high on the wings, rumbled down the white coral runway, the surface glowing silver in the moonlight. She lifted off, clambering ponderously into the skies.

As they climbed to altitude, Wynne reached inside the haversack and eased Smoky into the open. She pricked up her ears and gazed all around the strange new environment that she found herself in. She was suspended in a see-through blister surrounded by the expanse of the dark but starlit heavens, and with the faint glow of the sea far below.

It wasn't long before the medics-cum-gunners discovered they had a surprise crew member aboard, riding shotgun. Once Wynne had explained why he'd felt compelled to bring Smoky along, they seemed to find the whole thing hugely amusing. The idea of having a flying dog join their crew as a gunner was just fine and dandy as far as they were concerned. They hung Smoky's haversack over a nearby bunk-like stretcher, making sure she was nicely settled.

If any enemy warplanes did appear, the gun turrets would soon be spewing hot brass, as the gunners met fire with fire, at which point Smoky would be right in the thick of it. But she was a veteran and had rarely shown herself fazed by anything. Wynne reckoned she should do just fine.

It was fortunate that Smoky had experienced a few training parachute jumps, back at Nadzab. If the Catalina did get badly hit, Wynne wasn't about to leave his beloved dog in the stricken aircraft. As he'd vowed to Petrilak and the others: 'We'll go down together.' He would fasten Smoky's haversack around his waist, and bale out with her strapped to his person. Then he'd pull the 'chute, hoping to ride the thermals and find his dog a safe landing.

The Catalina powered onwards through the night, the steady

beat of her twin radial engines allowing those inside into a comparative calm. Bardsley's last known position was just east of Ceram Island. He'd completed his recce flights and had turned for home by the time the storm had hit.

As dawn broke, the sun clawing above a horizon of burnished copper and gold, the pilot began to lose altitude. He dropped to a couple of thousand feet, throttling back to ninety miles per hour. As the Cat idled along Wynne found himself scanning the rumpled folds of the ocean below him with intense focus. Bardsley had been a good friend and he was determined to play his part in locating the missing airman.

The Catalina droned onwards. The sun rose higher, the light becoming flatter as the sea became awash with a fierce tropical glare. Downed airmen carried mirrors attached to their life-jackets. They were trained to point those mirrors at a passing friendly aircraft, to signal their whereabouts in the sea. Ten pairs of eyes scanned the waves for the slightest sign of any human presence.

There was none.

Indeed, there wasn't the barest suggestion of movement any-where on the entire expanse of water. They were flying over the Ceram Sea, a 12,000-square-kilometre stretch of ocean sandwiched between the islands of modern-day Indonesia. The war might have been raging all around them, but here there was nothing, not a single vessel of any description. Indeed, it was to be another thing altogether that drew the aircrews' gaze.

As if from nowhere a long bank of black cloud seemed to roll across the horizon, darkening all. The storm swept in towards the Cat, massive and menacing. The roiling bank of cloud towered above them, reaching thousands of feet into the skies. There was no way to fly around it: their base at Biak Island lay on the far side of the vast weather front. They couldn't race ahead of it, either: they didn't have the fuel to do so.

This was similar to what must have happened to their missing airman and friend: as the Casualty Report on Bardsley had concluded, he'd hit 'extreme adverse weather' over the Ceram Sea.

The Catalina was dwarfed by the on-rushing storm. There was no option but to abandon the search. The Cat turned for home, the pilot trying to climb above the darkening tempest. As the seaplane struggled to gain altitude, its airframe shook and juddered with the impact of the first squalls. The Cat reached 12,000 feet, Smoky's haversack swinging wildly as the aircraft was thrown about by intense gusts, but still there was no way over the storm.

The pilot was forced put the Cat into a dive. They dropped to around 100 feet of altitude, all the time searching for a break in the fearsome wall of cloud. It extended from sea level to the upmost reaches of the heavens – dark, boiling and angry, and lit here and there by flashes of lighting. There was no choice: they would have to try to fly right through the heart of the cyclone, for that way lay home.

This storm was a true monster: very closely packed cells of cumulonimbus – dense, towering, vertical columns of cloud – punched upwards to great heights. Hidden within those cloud cells were massive updrafts and downdrafts. An aircraft flying into those could get its wings ripped asunder, or the fuselage twisted and warped catastrophically.

They were swallowed into the storm. It felt as if a giant was smacking the top and bottom of the Catalina with a massive sledgehammer, powerful gusts slamming into the wings and fuselage. The aircrew had to try to blank their minds to the terrible noise. Using the Cat's radar reading, the pilot had to try to steer his way through the storm cells. The radar painted a picture of where the heaviest rainfall might be, and where the most powerful up- and downdrafts were to be located. If they could avoid the points of most intense activity then they might just stand a chance of making it through.

In a tropical storm such as this, one cell of air might be descending at 5,000 feet a minute, while the one adjacent to it was rising at the same speed. If the Catalina blundered into the border between the two, it could prove catastrophic. If one wing so much as strayed across the divide, it would be like placing it into a giant guillotine. And if that happened, there would be no grabbing Smoky in her haversack and bailing out with her strapped to anyone's person.

The crew and their stowaway dog would be vomited into the howling void of the storm.

CHAPTER 14

Wynne reached out to touch the haversack in which Smoky was riding. He had to resist the urge to reach in and retrieve her, for the wildly pitching warplane was no safe place for an unsecured dog. She was better off in her bag-cum-hammock, which served to cushion the Catalina's vicious lurches and rolls. Even so, he couldn't help but marvel at how she could retain such equanimity when they were in the grip of such unrelenting violence. Possessed by a preternatural calm, the little dog had barely moved a muscle.

For what seemed like an eternity the flying boat fought her way east through the howling, wind-whipped darkness. The Catalina was thrown around like a toy in a giant's hands, the airframe groaning and shrieking with the strain. Gripped as they were in the heart of the tempest, daylight, sunlight – the air itself, it seemed – had been banished. The storm front was a thing of the night, and it dragged darkness inchoate and screaming in its wake.

Occasionally Wynne sought out the aircraft's tortured wing-tips, but they were lost in the storm, and he was blinded by the rain that drenched the Plexiglas blister. The Catalina's extremities had been swallowed by the tempest. Visibility was limited to less than a few dozen yards, which would make the job of navigating nigh-on impossible.

Somehow, after four hours entombed within that terrifying force of nature, the Catalina finally shook herself free. Achieving something close to a miracle, the Catalina's navigator had steered them safely to New Guinea through several hundred miles of perilous skies.

As the aircraft thundered into the airspace above Biak Island, the weather before them cleared. Majestic and apparently unscathed, the Catalina touched down at Mokmer airstrip, to be welcomed by a sunlit calm. It was as if the storm had never taken place at all, such were the vagaries of the weather in this part of the world.

For several minutes the crew sat within their trusty plane, taking stock and calming their thoughts. After the trials of being trapped in that storm for hours on end they needed a moment to get their pulse rates back to a little more like normal. Eventually, Wynne reached over and unhooked the haversack that held his dog. He ran a hand along the underside, feeling the warm bulge of a living, breathing animal.

By the regular rise and fall of Smoky's chest, he could tell that she was fine. She seemed to have weathered the storm better than most of them. He shouldered the bag and clambered down the ladder, giving thanks that they'd come through alive. Sadly, they'd found no sign of his friend, Bardsley, but at least eleven other lives hadn't been lost while searching for the missing airman.

Four days after Bardsley disappeared another of the squadron's fliers was listed as MIA. First Lieutenant Lee G. Smith – the pilot who'd executed the abortive recce mission over Cape Gloucester, at the time of Smoky's discovery in the foxhole – was reported lost somewhere to the south of the Talaud Islands. Lying on the border of what is now Indonesia and the Philippines, the islands were some distance north of where Bardsley had gone down.

Smith, like Bardsley, had flown into a terrible weather front. He and his wingman, Captain Carl D. Lindberg – the pilot who'd won the 26th's first DFC – had wheeled about in the face of that storm, abandoning their mission. But as they'd turned for home Lindberg had lost radio contact with Smith's aircraft. Lindberg had reported Smith as missing and a Catalina had taken to the air, but their search – like so many others – had come to nothing.

In late October 1944 the weather appeared more dangerous to the men of the 26th than enemy warplanes or ground fire. As if to prove the point, by early November the searches for Smith and Bardsley were finally called off. It was a measure of how unforgiving was this conflict that a man of Smith's stature and popularity was to leave only a fleeting memory in the squadron. There was little time or space for sentiment. On 4 November 1944 an order was issued 'to inventory and dispose of the effects of First Lieutenant Lee G. Smith, 0743523, 26 Photo Rcn Sq, missing in action'.

Yet still the grim reaper wasn't satisfied. First Lieutenant Samuel Dunaway had been deployed with the 26th from their earliest days in New Guinea. Much admired for his 'skilful and intrepid flying' and well-liked due to his modesty and good spirits, Dunaway had been executing a sortie near Biak when he dived to investigate something at sea, misjudged the distance slightly, and his wing tip had hit the water. The P-38 crashed, killing Dunaway on impact.

At times like these the men of the squadron were in sore need of something – anything - to lift their spirits. Wynne figured that Smoky might just fit the bill, but he and his dog would need to develop something truly spectacular, if they were to deliver the morale boost that all hungered for. With this in mind, Wynne decided that they would embark upon their most ambitious training exercise yet, one inspired by something that he'd witnessed during his childhood, and which had always stuck in his mind.

He was eleven years old when he'd seen a show in a local Cleveland shopping mall. A department store had sought to draw in the crowds at Christmas by having a showman and his dog perform. That dog was able to walk a double-wire tightrope, blindfolded. The young Wynne had watched the performance transfixed. He'd tried to teach the dog he owned a similar trick, but with little success.

He wondered if he might have more luck with Smoky here on war-torn Biak Island. Just as with their parachute training at Nadzab, he reckoned he'd need a talented and enthusiastic support team. First he recruited Frankhuizen – the squadron's ice-machine wizard – to weld together a T-shaped metal bar. That done, Frankhuizen torch-cut two six-inch-square plates from a discarded steel drum. These were then mounted as platforms upon the narrow ends of the Ts, the cross-strokes serving as stands upon the ground.

The inverted Ts were wedged firmly into the coral rock. A pair of old aircraft control cables were stretched between the platforms, about three inches apart, and anchored at the far ends to spikes driven into the ground, like guy-ropes. The cables were further tightened using aircraft turnbuckles – stretching screws that resembled the kind that are commonly used to tighten the ropes of a boxing ring – attached to the uprights at each of the four corners.

The tightrope walk was built within reach of the photo lab, for ease of access. That way, Wynne, Smoky and the rest of the lab crew could do some training during breaks from shifts. For Smoky's first session, Wynne found he had a ready audience. Lab Chief Irv Green watched with tender concern as he set Smoky on the course for the first time. He began by placing her four paws on the wires, and allowing her to get a feel for her balance.

Once she'd got the hang of that, he urged her to walk slowly across from one side to the other, with one hand on her lead to guide her, and the other resting lightly on her back. Slowly, under his steadying hands she seemed to gain confidence, her tiny paws becoming accustomed to the unfamiliar feel of the wires. The second day he repeated the routine, finishing with Smoky completing a full lap off the lead and with no hands to steady her at all. She navigated the strange apparatus with real assurance. But then she had always possessed an uncanny knack for learning new tricks; it seemed that there was nothing she couldn't take in her stride.

On day three of the high-wire training Wynne decided it was time to try out the blindfold. He wrapped a length of cloth around Smoky's head, binding her trusting eyes, and set her upon the wires once more. Smoky put her front down low, so her nose was between the wires, and for a moment it looked as if she was too disorientated to continue. But after a few encouraging words from her master she began to inch ahead, and she felt her way to the far side. She seemed to master the feat of being a blindfold wire-walker with ease.

Frankhuizen made a ladder with inch-wide steps, and Smoky learned to climb that. She could sit atop her perch as the blindfold was applied, before shuffling across to the far side. She was ready to deliver a staggeringly accomplished performance, but learning it had been hard and physically challenging work. Wynne decided they would refine and polish her technique during the cooler hours of the evening.

To augment the tightrope walk, he decided Smoky should also learn to trot atop a barrel. Together, the two acts would be a showstopper. They practised with an empty fifty-five-gallon steel drum that had until recently held photo chemicals. Wynne pushed the drum onto its side, then perched Smoky on top of it. Next, with her lead gripped tight he began to roll it gently using his foot, encouraging Smoky to move her feet in unison. She was such a fast learner that in no time she could jump on and off the drum at the beginning and end of the trick.

Wynne reckoned they were almost ready for the big performance. To make the show go with a real bang they needed to cut the barrel down to size and to paint it in bright 'circus' colours. Although Wynne had a team help him prepare the show's accoutrements, he conducted the training strictly by himself. Smoky wasn't kept in purdah – during a rare movie night, he'd generally allow the entire gathering to pet and to cuddle his dog – but he knew that when it came to teaching her tricks or obedience lessons, she could only have one instructor, or she would be left confused.

He decided to give the barrel roll a few final turns, once the barrel had been cut down to Smoky's size, and they'd be ready. But oddly, she seemed reluctant to engage. Instead, she lay down and rolled onto her back, refusing to get moving. Again and again Wynne tried, but Smoky kept lolling onto her side. Wynne couldn't understand what was wrong with her. This was a dog who loved to learn and to perform. What on earth could be the matter?

Maybe it was the evening heat? He took her back to their tent for some rest, laying the tiny dog on his cot. She did not seem herself at all. As he studied her carefully, wondering if maybe she was sick, from out of nowhere she produced a tiny little ball of damp black fluff. For a moment Wynne stared at it in astonishment, before he realized with a shock what it was. Their Hollandia pigeons had finally come home to roost.

'Holy cats!' he declared in astonishment. 'It's a puppy!'

Petrilak and the others within earshot came running. By now Smoky was licking the puppy all over, cleaning it up so that it would be presentable for the gathering audience. Like any good mother she seemed proud as punch at what she had produced. Wynne darted outside. It occurred to him that she might have dropped another pup or two while on the barrel and without anyone noticing.

He searched the area but couldn't find a thing. He returned to discover the tent buzzing. The general consensus was that Smoky had just lost her good conduct medal. It would need to be removed from her coat, until she'd put in a spell of the kind of chaste behaviour that would earn her the right to wear it again. There was little doubt as to the identity of the father of the pup. John Hembury, one of Wynne's good friends in the

26th, had adopted a mixed-breed terrier that was a native of Nadzab. Duke was a dark-haired, cheeky-faced devil of a dog, and it was pretty obvious that it was Duke who'd managed to work his magic on Smoky.

Word of the new arrival spread like wildfire. From all over the base GIs congregated to see the puppy that had been born in some kind of miracle birth, from a dog which herself weighed only six pounds or so. One of those visitors was a very special guest for Bill Wynne. It was Jim Craig, the guy who'd occupied the bed next to Wynne at the Nadzab field hospital. Craig seemed to have shaken off his combat fatigue and he gave a good impression of being back to his old self.

He was overjoyed to meet Smoky's surprise offspring. The puppy was so tiny that you could lay him along your two forefingers and he wouldn't even reach the palm of your hand. As Craig held her puppy, Smoky gazed at it adoringly. Wynne invited Craig to the squadron's Enlisted Men's Club – a grand name for a bamboo-framed tin-sheet hut set to the rear-side of the beach.

There was one major draw to the Club, apart from the company. The 'barman' had acquired a quantity of Coca-Cola syrup – a paste which when mixed with water plus a burst of gas transformed itself into the popular drink. Its arrival on Biak Island was ingenuity itself. A handful of B25 Mitchell bombers had been stripped of all armour and guns, so pilots could practise flying on instruments only – navigating through darkness or minimal visibility – and those practice flights had often ended up doubling as supply runs.

The B25s were loaded up with cases of booze, crates of fresh meat and barrels of the much-coveted Coca-Cola syrup. In fact so much was crammed into the bomb bays that the bomb doors often couldn't be closed properly, and the aircraft flew with the cargo hanging out of their guts. This gave rise to an affectionate nickname for the planes: the 'Fat Cats'. On one such flight the aircrew had stuffed aboard a real taste of home – 550 crates of beer, all of which had been brewed in Minneapolis, Minnesota.

The Enlisted Men's Club had been founded so the squadron could hold the odd party there. Those shindigs gave 'the men something to look forwards to', the squadron's Monthly Intelligence Summary concluded. In the autumn of 1944 they'd had a major knees-up to celebrate the first anniversary of the unit's deployment. A Fat Cat had smuggled in a consignment of liquor and the partying had ended in a wild beach brawl. Come morning, other than their pounding headaches, no one seemed particularly the worse for wear and the punch-up was already long forgotten.

Behind the makeshift bar of the Club were mounted a couple of compressed-air bottles, like conventional beer pumps. When combined with some of Frankhuizen's crushed ice, and a burst of air to lend fizz, the Club's chilled cokes were a rare kind of treat in a place like Biak. Craig and Wynne toasted the squadron's new arrival with round after round of drinks. Smoky had come with them, of course, and at the first mention of her name – 'To Smoky!' – she'd issued a sharp little bark.

The puppy had been promised to Frank Petrilak, who seemed by far the most deserving candidate to be custodian of the newest member of the squadron. They'd decided to name the unexpected offspring 'Topper'. Smoky's performance giving birth from out of the blue had topped just about anything they'd seen from her so far. In the aftermath of the birth, Smoky's new repertoire of tricks were shelved. She had maternal duties to attend to and had earned a short reprieve.

As October bled into November 1944, the 26th was about to receive its greatest accolade yet, in the form of a Presidential Unit Citation from Franklin D. Roosevelt himself. The high-prestige award recognized the squadron's ground-breaking work flying over the Philippines, where the 26th had captured any number of images that were of critical import to the war. It was a story of success in which one small dog had played an unarguable part.

When Bill Wynne had lost his beloved Pal as a kid back in Cleveland, the trauma had been so great that he'd vowed never to get that close again to a dog. Smoky had torn those vows to shreds. She'd shared his dangers and hardships, both on the ground and in the air. She'd made Wynne and his buddies laugh and forget. She'd learned to respond to his every command, she'd earned his true friendship, and she – plus Topper too – had furnished him with a much-needed diversion from the dark realities of war.

They'd stayed safe so far, but Wynne knew that further dangerous missions lay ahead. Soon the Catalina crews would be airborne again, searching for the missing. The thought that their partnership might end so suddenly troubled Wynne, and he vowed to do everything in his power to protect Smoky. Yet if the war had taught him anything, it was that danger often lurked where you least expected it.

The squadron's diary for November 1944, stamped SECRET, makes crystal clear how the weather frustrated much of that month's planned recce flying. Indeed, in many ways the thick cloud cover proved the enemy's greatest friend. But that did little to stop the spirited fliers of the 26th from trying, and that in turn meant that the air-sea rescue Catalinas had to brave the skies, searching for those lost during the storms.

It wasn't just the recce flights that were plagued by the bad weather. At 3.00 a.m. on a black November night Wynne and Smoky took to the skies once more, their lumbering Catalina labouring to gain altitude. Their mission on that night was somewhat different from those that had gone before. They were the lead flight in several waves of warplanes, all of which were making for the enemy positions located to the west of Balikpapan Bay.

The Cat left first, for it was the slowest of this mighty air armada. At 5.00 a.m. a massive flight of bombers would take to the skies, followed by their quicker fighter escorts, which would get airborne only as dawn broke across the airfield. They would form up as one over Balikpapan Bay, with the intention of launching a devastating air raid. But things didn't go quite to plan. Unbeknown to the crew manning the Catalina, a storm descended upon Biak Island shortly after their take-off. Their aircraft was the only one that had managed to get airborne, and its crew flew on in blissful ignorance, unaware that the mission had been abandoned.

Wynne had slung Smoky in her 'accustomed' place – her haversack dangling from the Catalina's bunk. Today's flight promised to be a twenty-two-hour marathon and he'd need to keep a careful eye on his dog. He couldn't keep her bagged for that long, so he'd let her run around a little on the bunk. But it was a delicate balancing act – giving her the chance to stretch her little limbs, while also making sure that she didn't get so excited that she ended up having an unfortunate 'accident'.

Smoky invariably displayed such an insatiable appetite that unless her master watched her closely, she'd eat everything she could get her paws on. He was in the habit of feeling her back and stomach daily and adjusting her meals to match her waistline, to make sure she remained healthy. On air missions such as this, Smoky had to follow a strict diet, for the enforced inactivity cooped up on board a plane meant that there was always a chance that she would end up putting on too much weight. Wynne had allowed her just a single meal, which she'd scoffed early in the morning.

They'd been welcomed with open arms by the air-sea rescue crews. Most wanted a souvenir photo with the famous dog after completing a successful mission. On previous flights Wynne had realized that whenever he allowed her out of her haversack, Smoky provided a wonderful diversion for the crews manning the Cats. She had a gift for taking their minds away from the life-threatening reality of their missions. But pooping or peeing everywhere might quickly change all that.

Undertaking that long, solo flight deep into enemy airspace was a trial even for the champion mascot of the 26th. It was bitterly cold, and after a while Wynne noticed that Smoky was shivering. He wrapped her up tight in extra woollen blankets and popped her back into her snug haversack. The drone and vibration of the engines, set to either side of their position, could play havoc with the nerves. It had to be doubly tiresome for a dog blessed with sensitive hearing. At moments Smoky looked nervous, and he noticed her panting tongue had turned a deep red. Luckily he was on hand to comfort her as only he knew how.

After a ten-and-a-half-hour flight the Catalina arrived over the target, only to discover that she was the sole aircraft to have made it into the air that morning. They were many hours into enemy airspace and if they were spotted, the lone and ponderous flying boat was a sitting duck. If a flight of Japanese Zeros came tearing up to intercept her, she would be blasted from the skies.

Many times Wynne had noticed how attuned Smoky was to his comrades' stress levels and anxieties. She was so closely in tune with her human companions that she was able to sense their worries and their trauma. But what made her truly exceptional was her ability to make the stressed and the traumatized smile, even in situations when there was so little to smile about. This was most certainly one of those.

Yet for now, they had no option but to turn tail and run like the wind.

CHAPTER 15

A few weeks previously Smoky had demonstrated most power-fully what a talisman she had become to the Catalina's aircrew. It had been another 3.00 a.m. start, with another marathon flight looming. Wynne had let his little dog off the lead to relieve herself on the grass beside the airstrip. Instead of squatting down to do her business, Smoky had made a mad dash for the bush and within seconds she was lost from sight.

The airbase was busy with airplanes and vehicles roaring hither and thither. Her sprint across the runway into the night could so easily have ended in disaster. Wynne went after her. Although it was pitch dark, he found the little dog about five hundred yards away, safe and sound. Nevertheless, he gave her a piece of his mind. He wasn't angry with her for running free, so much as he was by the thought of what might have happened to her. She could have been crushed under a taxiing aircraft's wheels, or caught in a propeller's murderous backwash. He understood that she was a dog, and that dogs love to play in the bush, but there was a time and a place for everything.

He tucked her under his arm, protectively, and carried her back to the aircraft. He climbed the ladder into the blister, and went to place Smoky in her position as haversack gunner. But as he did so, he noticed that the Catalina's crew were eyeing him and his diminutive dog in an uneasy silence. The fuselage was thick with tension and unspoken questions. Had Smoky bolted for a reason, they wondered? Had she sensed something? Had her sixth sense told her to run?

As luck would have it, the flight went ahead without the slightest incident – not even any bad weather. But Wynne and the rest of the crew had been left to wonder. Had Smoky delayed their take-off for long enough for the aircraft to avoid some hidden danger lurking in the dark skies? Had the Grim Reaper waited, poised with his scythe to cut down the aircraft and her crew, only to be frustrated by the spirited disobedience of one small dog?

Aircrew are notoriously superstitious and the men based at Biak Island were no exception. They were always on the lookout for the kind of special talisman that they believed would protect them. Some pilots flew with a pair of their sweetheart's silk stockings wrapped around their neck. Others took to the skies with crucifixes or shamrocks, or a special photograph clutched to their chests. Every man would swear blind that it was his lucky charm that kept him safe in the skies.

In time the men of the 3rd Air-Sea Rescue Squadron had begun to view their haversack gunner-dog in a similar light. If she could brave such flights unscathed, so could they – especially with their lucky charm at their side. Smoky was one of the gang and she was cherished by all with whom she flew.

Smoky's magic certainly seemed to be working when the Catalina and her crew made it back from their lonely Balikpapan mission. They touched down at Biak Island unscathed and with a huge sense of relief: those of a superstitious nature could draw their own conclusions about the presence on that flight of their talismanic flying dog.

There were of course more concrete means to keep safe in the skies. On several sorties with the 3rd Air-Sea Rescue Squadron, Wynne and Smoky were blessed with having the very best of escorts. Two of the foremost American aces in the region, P-38 pilots Major Richard Bong and Major Thomas McGuire, flew alongside them. There was a fierce rivalry between the men. Each had over three-dozen kills to his name, but Bong always seemed to be just two or three ahead of McGuire. And while the Catalina's aircrew weren't too bothered about which of the two had downed the most Japanese warplanes, they certainly appreciated the protection they provided.

By the time they flew their thirteenth mission with the 3rd, Wynne and his dog had completed over seventy hours of combat flying – nearly a quarter of the total required to earn them a ticket back to America. It was during that thirteenth mission that they were to realize they were about to leapfrog north again, heading for the Philippines, and ever closer to Japan itself.

The Catalina was returning to their base on Biak Island, when through a momentary gap in the cloud Wynne spotted a vast armada spread out far below. One of the greatest invasion fleets ever assembled was on the move, steaming northwards towards the enemy. Wynne noticed battleships, aircraft carriers, cruisers, destroyers and a plethora of smaller craft, including troopships. They seemed to stretch from horizon to horizon.

It was obvious that the armada was friendly; if not a murderous barrage of fire would have torn them out of the skies. Even so, a pair of Navy F4U Corsairs – a carrier-based fighter aircraft as potent as the Hellcat – came roaring up to intercept the lone seaplane.

Those flying the Corsairs were right to be suspicious of the lone Catalina. In February 1942 the British stronghold of Singapore had fallen to Japanese forces. Fortress Singapore had been the key British base in southeast Asia and the cornerstone of her defences in the region. The battle had lasted a little more than a week, with 80,000 British and Allied troops falling captive to the enemy. It was a crushing blow, one that Churchill had lamented as being the 'worst disaster' and 'largest capitulation' in British military history.

But along with the troops, the Japanese had captured a treasure trove of Allied war machines, including at least one Consolidated flying boat. They'd likewise seized scores of Allied aircraft across the islands of the southwest Pacific, including Bristol Blenheims, Hawker Hurricanes, Boeing B-17s and P-51 Mustangs.

Repainted in Japanese colours those aircraft had been press-ganged into service with the enemy, which is why the Corsairs had raced up to challenge the Catalina. In spite of the large and prominent star and stripe – the recognition flash for a USAAF aircraft – painted on her nose, the Corsair pilots remained suspicious.

Reports were beginning to reach Allied aircrew of a new and terrifying weapon: the suicide bomber, or kamikaze. There was clearly no better aircraft in which to attempt to crash into an Allied warship than one of their own models. The Catalina's pilot dipped his right wing, the recognized signal for 'friendly', repeating the manoeuvre several times before the Corsair fliers eventually seemed satisfied, and peeled away.

The Catalina flew over that giant armada for approaching thirty minutes. It stretched across sixty miles of ocean. To those aboard the flying boat it was clear the ships had to be steaming for Leyte Gulf, where MacArthur intended to mark his return to the Philippines. And wherever the combat troops went the 26th were bound to follow, just as soon as those new airbases lay in friendly hands.

With the invasion fleet steaming for Leyte Gulf, the air recce missions of the 26th assumed even greater urgency. That November a record 115 photo reconnaissance sorties were flown, resulting in 32,796 9 x 10-inch photos being printed and distributed to those in high command. Daily courier flights were shuttling in rolls of film from outlying airbases, and shuttling out with the printed images. Three shifts were required at the Biak photo lab to keep it churning around the clock.

That November the squadron's CO, Counselman, would earn a second Bronze Oak Leaf Cluster, for completing yet another hundred hours of combat flying. The citation read: 'For meritorious achievement while participating in sustained operational flight missions . . . during which hostile contact was probable and expected.' But continuously pushing the envelope would prove life threatening for some among the 26th.

On 17 November 1944, Hartwell McCullough – Custodian of Squadron Classified Documents, and the 26th's heart and soul – suffered a perilously close brush with death. Returning from a special mission, his aircraft had suffered a total failure of its hydraulics, without which he couldn't lower his landing gear. He'd made a perfect crash-landing on the aircraft's belly.

While he'd walked away with barely a scratch, his plane was ruled 'a total loss'. Others weren't to be so fortunate.

The squadron's MIAs needed to be replaced urgently. One recent newcomer was Second Lieutenant James H. Morrison, fresh out of training. Just days after Morrison had arrived in Biak he was assigned his first combat sortie. At 1.35 p.m. on 22 November he had taken off from the Mokmer strip, but only managed to get three-quarters of a mile into the air. His P-38 ploughed into the coral at the far end of the runway, killing him outright. The accident and its causes were recorded in a squadron Casualty Report: 'Pilot took off with full flaps, causing the aircraft to stall at an altitude of 300 feet.'

Morrison had been killed on his very first combat sortie, which had taken place on the day before Thanksgiving. That year the men of the squadron were treated to a traditional Thanksgiving dinner of turkey and pumpkin pie. Despite losing Morrison, they made a point of trying to celebrate, knowing full well that this would be the last partying any would enjoy for some time to come.

Their move to the Philippines was imminent. 'We were, we knew, moving in with the troops making the invasion . . .' the section of the 26th's war diary titled 'History & Legend' recorded. 'We would be put ashore shortly after the combat troops . . . and before more than a beachhead could be established. Our mood . . . was of fatalistic anxiety.'

But for one man among the 26th, there would be no advance to the Philippines. For Captain John M. Brown, the war was pretty much over. Brown had just topped his 300th hour of combat flying, spread across sixty-five separate missions. He left the squadron, bound for America and home. Having completed only thirteen missions and seventy-three hours of combat flying, Bill Wynne was still some way from earning his ticket back to the US, but he was offered some December shore leave in Australia. It was now or never. He'd have to grab it before the advance north, for there would be little chance of taking such breaks once the squadron was on the move. Once more, he slipped Smoky into her covert travel bag and climbed aboard a C47 Gooney Bird. This time they were heading for the bright lights of Sydney.

This flight was a little less tortuous than their previous sortie aboard the overloaded C47. Upon reaching Sydney, man and dog billeted themselves with an elderly lady who tried to argue that as combatants they should take the room for free. Wynne insisted he pay her. She'd already bent over backwards for them, turning a blind eye to the house rules that said that no dogs were allowed. She'd taken an instant shine to Smoky, and as long as Wynne could keep the little dog hidden she assured them they'd be okay.

He managed to smuggle Smoky out for daily exercise in a local park. On one of their outings, Wynne decided to give Smoky some experience of walking to heel on Sydney's busy streets, but doing so off the lead. All was going well until he went to check her position and realized that she was gone. They were in the middle of Sydney on a street thronged with people and she could be just about anywhere.

His eyes scanned the crowd, desperately. Suddenly he spotted the distinctive form of the rear-end of his dog, stubby tail and hind quarters sticking out from under the arm of a woman who was hurrying away as quick as her legs would carry her. Just as he'd read about in that *National Geographic* article, someone was in the process of trying to steal his dog!

Wynne was having none of it. He gave chase. He caught the woman up, whereupon he took her firmly by the elbow. 'Excuse me, ma'am, but you've got my dog.'

The woman turned on him, bold as brass. 'No, he isn't, Yank,' she countered. 'He's my Silky, he is!'

The Silky is a breed of terrier closely related to the Yorkie. Developed in Australia, there is little to tell the two breeds apart. The woman kept a firm hold of Smoky, as she tried to argue that the dog was walking past freely, so she'd claimed her as her own.

Wynne raised his voice now, drawing the attention of the crowd. Smoky had been his for many months, in New Guinea, he explained. She was an acclaimed war veteran and a unit mascot. 'You'd better give her back, right now!'

Realizing that it didn't look good stealing a war veteran's dog, the woman handed 'her Silky' back to Wynne, but with little good grace. He took her, and got a happy little lick on the face as his reward for having rescued her. With Smoky tucked firmly under one arm, they continued on their way. He vowed that was the last time he'd walk Smoky off the lead in Australia.

In fact, his little dog was far safer staying in their kindly landlady's room. Smoky seemed happy enough to remain there as long as she had some item of clothing – a shirt or a hat of her master's – to lie close to. The smell was comforting and it served as a reminder that her companion was never far away or gone for long.

A little later Wynne was on one of his solo outings when he

ran into some aircrew from the 90th Bomber Group, the 'Jolly Rogers'. Fellow US airmen, they made for natural drinking companions, especially as the 90th had flown missions all across New Guinea and at the same time as the 26th. They'd earned their distinctive nickname due to the massive skull and crossbones they had painted on the tail-planes of their Consolidated B24 Liberator bombers.

The fliers got to swopping war stories. There were tales told of the greatest near-death experiences the Jolly Rogers had suffered. Wynne's closest brush with death had occurred before he'd even been deployed to New Guinea. He'd been in Brisbane, he explained, en route to join the squadron, when a powerful storm had hit. He and four others had huddled together in a shack to shelter from the rain. A massive gust of wind had blown down a tree, which had smashed onto the roof of their shelter, crushing it.

All five were thrown to the ground. Although all the others were seriously injured, Wynne had landed on his haunches with his hands between his knees and bounced up again pretty much unharmed. It was nothing short of miraculous. When Wynne finished telling his story, one of the Jolly Rogers, a tail-gunner, fixed him with a very direct look.

'You know what you're being saved for?' he announced, jabbing a finger at Wynne's chest. 'You're being saved for a bullet!'

The comment stuck in his mind, and a part of him believed it, too. If he were destined for a bullet, Leyte Gulf was most likely where he would find it.

And if he did, what then would happen to his beloved dog?

CHAPTER 16

The Japanese commander who had been charged with stopping the Allies from taking the Philippines was General Tomoyuki Yamashita, one of the masterminds of their February 1942 victory at Singapore. For his successes there he'd earned the nickname 'The Tiger of Malaya'. Yamashita had taken command of all Japanese ground forces in the Philippines, operating from his new base in the capital city, Manila. He was determined to harass, delay and confound MacArthur, and to ensure that his conquest of the Philippines would cost him dear.

It was December 1944 by now, and General Adachi was well out of the picture. Adachi had made a stand in New Guinea, as ordered. But spirited though his defence had proved, he'd been sidestepped by the breakneck speed of MacArthur's advance. Adachi would hold on in the New Guinea jungles until the very end of the war, but by then barely 10,000 of his original force would be left alive, with most dying from malnutrition and disease.

At the end of December Wynne and Smoky flew back into Biak Island. With the squadron's advance on the Philippines looming, preparations were well underway. All around the camp there were heaps of gear being crated up for the big move.

Christmas and New Year were imminent, but it was hard to get into the festive spirit. At one point Wynne's exasperation boiled over, and he found himself uttering the frustrated phrase 'Holy Christmas!' At the mention of those words Smoky had jumped up and down, excitedly.

It made an instant impression upon Wynne. Did she understand or recognize the word 'Christmas', he wondered? Was she familiar with the festive season? If so, that had to be a clue to her missing past. Surely, that had to mean she was of English-speaking origin. He repeated the word 'Christmas!' Sure enough, Smoky leapt about, her eyes shining with excitement. He tried another tack. 'Sport!' he exclaimed. He got the very same reaction, and the same when he cried 'Rover!' So much for his Christmas hypothesis. He was none the wiser.

Just prior to Christmas Day all reconnaissance flights were halted so the men could concentrate on readying themselves for the move. This was just as well for there was still a great deal to be done. Everything the photo recce squadron owned had to be crated up, all except the aircraft: they would be flown north to their new Filipino airbases, once they had been secured.

At 0400 hours on 1 January 1945, Hartwell McCullough called the entire squadron together, to brief them. He was typically brief and to the point. They were going to be organized into twenty-one work parties, each consisting of ten men. This done they were to take down their tents and board the waiting ships. Two hulking great LSTs – Landing Ship, Tank; a giant, flat-bottomed vessel designed to disgorge heavy vehicles and troops directly onto almost any kind of beach – had pulled up on Biak's shoreline. Empty, they displaced around 3,600 tonnes. Fully loaded, they could carry approaching 2,000 tonnes of cargo.

Their giant bows, which split to enable loading, were swung aside and the ramps lowered, whereupon the men and machines of the 26th began to hustle aboard. Trucks loaded with kit were driven to the beach, backed up to the open ramps of the LSTs, and unloaded by hand, with their cargo being stacked in the shadowed bowels of the vessels. It was hot, thirsty and back-breaking work.

The dark and cavernous entrances to the ships dwarfed the convoys of Army trucks. Mounted on the bows of each 400-foot vessel was a circular gun-emplacement, boasting 40mm and 20mm anti-aircraft weapons, with similar gun-stations positioned at the rear. They served as stark reminders of the dangers of the coming voyage.

This was the first time the entire squadron had moved by ship since their arrival in New Guinea. It was decided to split the men and equipment between the two vessels – LST-927 and LST-706 – in case one of them was lost at sea. That way, there should still be enough skilled operators left aboard one of the ships to restart the squadron once they had reached the Philippines.

It turned out that the 26th weren't headed for Leyte Gulf after all. The Leyte landings had gone ahead, establishing MacArthur's foothold in the Philippines. The 26th were to head further north, making for the Lingayen Gulf, which lay some 500 miles beyond. They were to fight their way ashore and advance on Manila, spearheading MacArthur's bid to seize the nation's capital. Intelligence suggested that the Japanese believed an

amphibious landing on the Lingayen Gulf beaches was beyond
the means of US forces. The hope was that the shoreline would
be only lightly defended.

But of equal, if not greater, worry than the landings was the
1,700-mile sea voyage that lay before them. The Leyte landings had cost MacArthur dear, with the kamikaze, the newest
and most fearsome form of Japanese attack, responsible for
the greatest part of the losses. Already, the very mention of
that word struck fear into the hearts of Allied troops, and a
fatalistic mood fell upon the men as they boarded those two
waiting LSTs.

Wynne had been allotted to LST-706. As part of its hull
camouflage it had a giant 'shark's mouth' painted on the prow.
The ship exuded real power and menace, and with all who
were crammed aboard she was chock-full. In theory there was
supposed to be space below decks for 250 souls, but in practice
it seemed as if it was standing-room only. Wynne chose to sleep
topside. He figured the lack of crowding, coupled with the fresh
air and sea breeze would be better for him and his dog. But the
LST's deck was itself jammed with vehicles, and they would
have to find a place wherever there was space.

Smoky seemed very particular about their billet. Eventually,
they settled in a gap between a jeep and a ten-wheeler truck.
They were on the ship's prow, just to the rear of the circular
gun position, with its steel protective wall lying a few feet away.
Between that and their billet was an armour-plated ventilator,
which pumped air down to the decks below. It stood about
three feet high, and when he was lying prone on his cot it
pretty much formed Wynne's pillow. Nearby, a flight of steps ran

below decks, to where a good number of the 26th had chosen to billet themselves.

A typhoon had just blown through and the convoy set sail into the tail end of the bad weather. The sea was rough. Wynne could feel the prow of the ship slamming into the twenty-five-foot swells, followed by the roll of the vessel as she slid along the wave, and then the leaden thumping of the propellers as the stern lifted clear of the water. The vehicles were strapped to the deck with thick chains that were turning orange with rust. They rattled and groaned with every shudder of the vessel's hull.

To either side dozens of ships were spread out across the sea. Their ship, LST-706, was second in line in a column of vessels lying on the right flank of the convoy. They were making no more than ten knots – the speed of the slowest vessel – so were bound to be a good week or more at sea. On their right the sleek form of a destroyer kept pace, her sharp bow cleaving a line through the sullen, stormy waters. It was good to see her there, standing guard.

Notices had been posted on the ship's bulletin boards. They warned of 'the possibility of pro-Japanese civilians and the effects of loose talk' when they hit the ground in the Philippines. After nearly three years of occupation some of the locals might be in league with the enemy. The men of the 26th would have to be vigilant once they'd set foot on hostile soil. But before that moment came, there would be dangers enough at sea to occupy the minds of the troops.

The convoy would steam east through the Celebes Sea, before swinging north through the Sulu Sea, which would take them past the Japanese stronghold of Mindoro Island, and finally into the more open expanses of the South China Sea. The passage would take them up the west coast of the Philippines, which was a labyrinth of inlets, islands and bays. There were any number of places for Japanese warplanes to conceal themselves as they lay in wait, ready to attack.

Men gathered on the deck in groups that first day, playing cards, chatting and swopping nervous gossip. The word on everyone's lips was the kamikazes. Apparently, the convoy ahead of their own, which was carrying the 175,000-strong force that was to form the first assault wave, had been hit by scores of suicide strikes. Indeed, the skipper of their vessel, LST-706, had adopted a strict drill to try to lessen the dangers of kamikaze attacks.

He was happy enough for those on deck to erect DIY canvas shelters for the night, but come daybreak they had to be cleared right away. If a kamikaze hit their ship, the skipper wanted the deck kept as free as possible of anything that might burn. But that pretty much ignored the chief fire hazard, which was the scores of vehicles cramming the deck, each of which was loaded with petrol.

Wynne had more prosaic issues to deal with: how to keep his dog well fed, groomed and watered. Although he'd slipped her aboard riding in his haversack, it was no longer a secret that Smoky was there. It was inconceivable that anyone might object to the 26th's champion mascot travelling north with her unit. After all, she'd braved hostile skies with her fellow pilots, and she'd comforted the troops during the worst of their trauma. But still, Wynne wasn't expecting anyone to extend any special favours to Smoky.

Meals aboard LST-706 were strictly Army rations – canned or dehydrated food. Smoky was back to living out of tins, mostly of mutton stew or the ubiquitous bully beef. Wynne set himself a strict pooper watch: whenever Smoky had to relieve herself, he made sure her waste was bundled up and dropped overboard. When she had to pee, the rains would clean it away in no time. The main challenge was fresh water: there were limited amounts to drink, and nowhere near enough for the daily helmet-wash that Smoky was accustomed to.

That first day at sea her coat became stiff with sea salt. Worse still, where she hurried about on deck and brushed against the ship's chains, it became thick with rust. Within hours, Smoky had turned a dull orange-red, her hair sticking out in all directions like a cartoon explosion. She quickly attracted a fan base. Once the servicemen realized who she was – the famed champion mascot who could perform the most incredible tricks – she had a daily audience. Once again, her very presence on that ship kept the minds of soldiers and sailors off the darkness that was coming.

She wasn't the only animal stowaway. Frank Petrilak had Smoky's puppy, Topper, to care for and another unit had smuggled a big Dalmatian – their own mascot – aboard. The two dogs struck up an unlikely friendship and the Yorkshire Terrier–Dalmatian pairing proved hilarious. Smoky's spotted friend towered over her. He wore a life-jacked strapped around his middle in case he tumbled overboard, which only served to make the two of them look even more incongruous. Soldiers on the lookout for a memorable souvenir photo kept accosting the two mascot-dogs.

As far as Wynne was aware, it was Smoky's first time aboard a ship. Remarkably, she didn't seem to suffer any sickness. The LST was full of new and fresh experiences for her, most notably the smells. There was the heady reek of fuel oil from the ship's smoke stacks; the tang of sea salt; the iron scent of rust; the sharp bite of the disinfectant used to sluice down the decks. Plus there was the growing smell from the soldiers and sailors crammed aboard ship – unwashed uniforms, sweat . . . and the barest hint of fear.

By the time LST-706 was approaching the Sulu Sea, Smoky had very much found her sea legs and was eating like the proverbial horse. She would need all of her strength and her fortitude for what was coming.

As the convoy neared Mindoro Island, and the Japanese air bases sited there, the captain of LST-706 gave the order that no canvas shelters were permitted on deck day or night. No matter if it rained or not, the men would have to sleep out under the stars, for his priority was to keep the decks as free of fire hazards as possible.

They were entering kamikaze alley.

Those riding aboard LST-706 became ever more businesslike. Before setting sail the men of the 26th had been given a refresher course on the use of their Browning .50-calibre machine guns, their heaviest weapons. With the salt-laden sea air it was a struggle to keep the guns rust-free. More time spent cleaning them meant less time for playing cards or gassing. Figures sat cross-legged on deck with a canvas sheet spread before them, the various working parts of a disassembled weapon being wiped over lovingly with an oiled rag. Every now and then the sharp *clatch-clatch* of a carbine's working parts being ratcheted back and forth rang out across the deck.

They were several days into their voyage by the time the men of the 26th had grown accustomed to the rigours of life aboard ship: showering in salt water; the nightly blackout; frequent and seemingly ill-timed drills and alerts, at which point everyone would have to sprint for their allotted stations. They'd also managed to pick up some of the sailor's slang. The key saying appeared to be: 'Pass the word.' That phrase seemed to round off all announcements over the ship's Tannoy system.

The word being passed right now was distinctly ominous. Scores of Allied vessels in the seas ahead had been hit by kamikaze strikes, and no ship, no matter how well-defended, seemed immune to such attack. One of the first vessels to be sunk was the aircraft carrier, the USS *St Lo*, hit by a Mitsubishi A6M Zero kamikaze. She had gone down within thirty minutes of being struck, some 150 men losing their lives.

In the first week of January 1945, Allied forces had gone ashore at Leyte Gulf. In the process, the cruiser USS *Louisville* was hit by three kamikaze strikes. The first caused little damage, and the second succeeded only in knocking out one of her main gun turrets. But the third tore into the starboard side of the bridge. Rear Admiral Theodore E. Chandler, senior Allied commander of the cruiser force, was killed. He died while trying to help others escape the resulting inferno.

Overall, forty-one sailors were killed and over one hundred injured as a result of the kamikaze attack. The USS *Louisville*, though burning fiercely, was saved, and she steamed to a repair depot. Incredibly, she would be struck by further kamikaze strikes in the months to come.

At the same time as the USS *Louisville* was being targeted so too was a humble cargo vessel, the SS *John Burke*, one of the so-called 'Liberty Ships' – mass-produced freighters designed for transporting Allied war supplies. Packed full of ammunition and lying low in the water, the *John Burke* had been sailing north as part of the convoy riding ahead of the armada of warships carrying the men of the 26th.

As the fleet had steamed north through the Sulu Sea a kamikaze squadron had attacked. One suicide pilot flying an Aichi D3A – a mass-produced Japanese dive-bomber that was now hopelessly obsolete – made it through the *John Burke*'s defences. Such outdated aircraft had been reduced to training duties, or, as now, reborn in the kamikaze role.

Screaming towards the *John Burke*'s deck in a steep dive, the Aichi, though damaged, succeeded in hitting her between cargo holds, which were packed full of munitions. There was a blinding flash as the plane disintegrated on impact, the fuel she was carrying and the explosives packed into her fuselage detonating violently. For several seconds thick smoke billowed out of the impact site, before an enormous pillar of flame erupted from the hold. Instants later, the ship dissolved into a massive fireball, which engulfed her completely.

A mushroom cloud of smoke punched above the horizon, several of the ships to either side of the *John Burke* being damaged in the blast. When the resulting cloud of smoke cleared, the *John Burke* was no more. Another, smaller, ship steaming nearby had also been sunk in the cataclysmic explosion. The shockwave caused by the *John Burke* being torn apart was so violent that neighbouring vessels reported being hit by torpedoes. Though ships searched the sea, there were no survivors.

No vessel was too insignificant to escape the attention of the kamikazes, especially the workhorses of the infantry, the LSTs. LST-749 formed part of the same convoy as the *John Burke*. On 21 December, as the fleet had steamed north through the Sulu Sea, the kamikazes swept in. A wave of forty aircraft attacked, with Allied fighters chasing them and blazing away on their tails. As the kamikazes neared the convoy every gun on every vessel had opened up, and the fighters had been forced to peel away.

One kamikaze had made it through to hit LST-749, ploughing into the ship's bridge and wreaking death and carnage across her deck. The survivors had abandoned ship, leaving her a burning wreck. Another LST had been hit, but just the wing of the kamikaze struck the vessel, the body of the aircraft cartwheeling into the water. Theirs was a lucky escape.

LST-460 was next to be targeted. The kamikaze that made for her flew straight and true. The aircraft hit her like a massive arrow, tearing through the bridge and penetrating the mess deck, killing all of its officers more or less instantly. Fire flashed through the vessel. Those who managed to abandon ship found themselves in the water, as other kamikazes pushed home their attacks. One hit a liberty ship in her open hold, which was fortunately only loaded with timber. The crew managed to extinguish the fire.

But LST-460 was burning fiercely and she was doomed. She was sunk by US warships to prevent her from acting as a beacon for further attacks. The *John Burke*, and the two LSTs that had been sunk, were the fourteenth, fifteenth and sixteenth Allied vessels lost to such suicide attacks. In late December 1944 and early January 1945 dozens of warships were damaged or sent to the bottom of the sea by kamikazes.

Into the heart of that storm would sail the 26th, including one man and his brave little dog.

CHAPTER 17

In light of their early successes, the Japanese had embraced the kamikaze concept with fanatical zeal. Around 2,000 pilots were being trained for suicide strikes, and hundreds of warplanes were being made ready.

With stocks of old or obsolete aircraft beginning to run low, the Japanese rushed through designs for a one-use kamikaze aircraft – the Nakajima Ki-115 Tsurungi (Sabre). Of simple, basic construction and made largely of wood, the Ki-115 was able to jettison its undercarriage. Made of crude steel tubing, the wheel-assembly would drop after take-off. After all, nobody expected the pilots to be coming back to land again.

The Ki-115 was designed to be able to use any engine that might be in storage, including those from old 1920s or '30s aircraft. It was fitted with an 1,800-pound bomb, which when combined with the impact of the aircraft strike was powerful enough to split a warship in two. The Japanese high command planned to build 8,000 of these kamikaze warplanes every month, in workshops spread all across Japan.

News of the kamikaze strikes spread fast. The chief value of the kamikaze had become fear. There was little the average soldier could do against an enemy who was determined to sacrifice

DAMIEN LEWIS

his own life in order to claim as many of his adversaries as possible. You could blaze away all you liked with a ship's guns, but if a kamikaze was lucky enough to get through, your vessel was very likely doomed, and possibly all who sailed aboard her.

It was the first week of January 1945 when the convoy carrying the men of the 26th entered the waters of the Sulu Sea, south of Mindoro Island. Just prior to dusk the call to action stations was sounded. Aboard LST-706 Bill Wynne was playing pinochle – a trick-taking card game popular with the troops – together with three buddies from the 26th, Dom D'Angelo, Jim Everett and Donald Esmond. The four were seated on two cots facing each other, forming makeshift pews. The alarms had become so frequent by now that they were wearing their life jackets day and night.

To left and right the ship's crew dashed to their gun positions, dragging on their helmets as they ran. To starboard of the convoy, Wynne spotted a flight of in-bound warplanes. There were eight that he could count, though he could hear others crying warnings that there were as many as twelve. They were attacking from the east, powering in towards the convoy from out of a cloudy, overcast, brooding sky.

The ship's Tannoy ordered anybody who was not crewing the ship to take cover below. Boots clattered down the iron ship's ladders. Below-decks in the gloom the ship's crew ran through the hold slamming and bolting shut the bulkhead doors. The men of the 26th had been warned that it was an offence punishable by court martial to open any of those hatches once they had been sealed. If the ship were hit, keeping those hatches closed and the individual compartments air-tight might be the key to keeping her afloat.

The war diary of the 26th picks up the story of those first few minutes of the kamikaze attack: 'Enemy planes had been sighted . . . Some of us saw six, some saw twelve . . . The value of the drills was now apparent . . . we went to the stations below decks to which we had been assigned. Then the planes came over. We knew it only because the ack-ack guns had started to fire . . . we learned of the action concussion by concussion.'

As the ship reverberated to the drum-beat of the guns, keeping below decks became impossible for men who felt a burning urge to witness the unfolding battle. Many clambered top-side again. 'Flak burst into patches of black and ominous cloud above us, so thick that it seemed impossible for a plane to pass through unscathed . .' the war diary recorded. 'A plane was hit and exploded in the air, as another crashed into the sea. But . . . one did come through. In the hands of one of the famous Kamikaze pilots, one of the Jap planes dove straight and sure through the fire . .'

The lone aircraft screamed in. Spying the imminent threat Wynne grabbed Smoky, but he was momentarily frozen as to where to dash for cover. Should they make for below-decks, or was it too late? Then an urgent, irresistible impulse – one that Wynne could only say later was inspired by his dog – told him exactly where to go. He was to seek cover beside the wheel of the jeep adjacent to their sleeping quarters. He felt Smoky's presence guiding him, almost as if she had spoken the words in his ear.

Dog in his arms, he dived into the space between the armoured ventilator and the jeep's front wheel. Hitting the deck, Wynne pulled Smoky's form tight to his chest, trying to shield her as best he could, cupping one hand over her tiny ears to muffle the deafening sound of gunfire. He was utterly determined that no harm was going to come to his dog if he could help it. He'd shield her with his own body if he had to.

From just a few feet away the LST's gun-emplacement spat fire. The thick barrels of the cannons groped skywards, pumping rounds at the on-rushing aircraft. There was a 20mm gun positioned right behind Wynne and Smoky's place of hiding, and the crew kept reloading and firing repeatedly. The noise was all-consuming, and with each round Wynne could feel a judder of fear run along Smoky's entire frame.

He pulled her closer, whispering the words of reassurance that he hoped might calm her. 'It's okay, girl. It's okay. Don't worry, girl. Everything will be fine.'

Suddenly, there was the violent crash of something striking their ship. An instant later a wild cheering broke out all across the LST's deck. One of the enemy must have been shot down. Glancing skywards, Wynne saw two further aircraft making their approach, diving right out of the heavens.

One seemed to be headed directly for the guns that were belching fire next to where he and Smoky had taken cover. With Smoky tucked under one arm, Wynne began to crawl on hands and knees. His hands landed on something hot, jagged and sharp. It was shrapnel. Further slivers of razor-sharp metal were scattered over the deck. Somewhere close, LST-706 must have been hit.

Wynne clambered to his feet, trying to get his bearings. He watched transfixed as the LSTs gunners duelled with the on-coming warplanes. The sky was a mass of violent black explosions, as flak burst in the suicide pilots' path.

'Come on, get the bastards!' someone yelled. 'Get the lousy Japs!'

The cry was taken up by figures dotted all over the open deck. The dive of the nearest kamikaze aircraft seemed to veer off unnaturally, as if the pilot had lost all control. Moments later his warplane hit the sea, a geyser of white water erupting in its wake. A rousing cheer went up from the deck. That one at least had missed his target.

But the pilot of aircraft number two was not to be so easily brushed aside. He flew on, braving the murderous barrage of fire. To one side of LST-706 there sailed a liberty ship, heavily laden with cargo. The kamikaze chose her as his target. The aircraft bore down on the freighter, drawing ever closer. Finally, it slammed into her superstructure amidships. Within moments the liberty ship was billowing black smoke.

The guns on LST-706 were still firing, but gradually they petered out to nothing. In the comparative silence that followed, Wynne pulled Smoky close and tried his best to comfort her. She was shaking from nose to tail.

An eerie silence settled over the ship. Wynne noticed the two young gunners on the single-barrel 40mm cannon nearby, chewing gum and eyeing the sky, warily. They began to wind the cranks of the gun, swivelling it around, popping gum to the rhythm of the crank handles. The barrel swung across and lowered. They were tracking a distant target. Wynne followed the trajectory of the barrel and suddenly he could see it: yet another kamikaze was speeding towards them.

This one was trying a stealth approach, flying in only thirty feet above the wave crests. The nose of the approaching warplane was pointed directly at their ship. When it was about 500 yards out, the gunners opened fire. Boom! Boom! Boom! All it took were those three carefully aimed shots. The kamikaze did a half-spiral, before a wingtip ploughed into the sea, sending up another plume of white water.

A rousing cheer swept the deck of the LST.

The liberty ship that had been hit was the *Lewis L. Dyche*. Like the *John Burke* before her, she was packed full of a highly combustible cargo – bombs and fuses. The kamikaze had wreaked devastation, the plummeting aircraft breaking through to the ship's hold. The fire quickly spread. Eventually, it caught the first of her cargo of munitions. The ship disintegrated in a series of giant explosions. Debris from the blast damaged a nearby oil-tanker, plus a mine-laying ship, the 3,100-tonne USS *Monadnock*.

Like the *John Burke* before her, the *Lewis L. Dyche* was vaporized with all hands lost. The fate of that vessel, and the black pall of smoke she cast, was all too visible to those aboard LST-706. It served as a sobering reminder of how lucky they had been. Indeed, even aboard the LST there were those who had not escaped unscathed, and the injured included several of Bill Wynne's card-playing buddies.

In the aftermath of the attack, a dazed Dom D'Angelo approached Bill Wynne. He waved his bleeding hand. A shard of shrapnel had torn into it. Nearby, Norman Smith – a veteran of the squadron who'd just won his Asia-Pacific Campaign Medal and a Bronze Star for meritorious service in combat – was down and wounded.

Someone was kneeling over him and crying for a medic. Smith had taken a chunk of shrapnel to his side. Wynne's pinochle partner, Jim Everett, had also been hit, as had five others.

Incredibly, the only casualties aboard the ship had been within a ten-foot radius of Wynne and Smoky. Yet somehow, he and his little dog remained unscathed. One fragment of spinning shrapnel could have taken Smoky's head clean off, or eviscerated her. They had been so very lucky.

Smith's injuries were serious. The shrapnel had punctured his lung and he was bleeding heavily. He needed an urgent blood transfusion. His blood group was A Negative, and a call went out over the ship's Tannoy for a match. One of the 26th volunteered to give blood. That done, Smith was taken off the ship by a landing craft so he could get proper medical attention.

Smith had spent his entire war being utterly sanguine about the dangers of being hit. 'If it's going to happen, it's going to happen,' was his refrain, as he refused to dig yet another foxhole. Now it had happened.

Wynne remained curious as to how all those around him had been hurt and yet he and his dog had escaped injury. It turned out that a stray 20mm shell had hit the LST, one very likely fired by a neighbouring ship as it tried to blast one of the low-flying kamikazes out of the sky. The shell had torn across the deck and landed in the interior of the armour-plated ventilator that Wynne was in the habit of making his pillow for the night.

It had blasted a jagged, star-shaped dent in the ventilator's side, with shrapnel from the impact ripping out the top of the ventilator and scything across the deck. Anything in its path had been hit. If the shell's trajectory had been a few inches in either direction it would have missed the ventilator and torn into Wynne and Smoky's place of hiding. As it was, their taking cover where they had – guided, Wynne felt certain, by Smoky's sixth-sense – had saved them from injury or worse.

In reflecting upon all of this, Wynne felt convinced that he'd been saved from the bullet with his name on it – the one that the tail-gunner from the Jolly Rogers had warned him about back in Sydney. He also felt certain that it was Smoky's doing. She had directed him to take cover in a place that had put them both out of the line of fire.

Dusk settled over the convoy. Somehow, everyone knew the attackers weren't done yet. Their destroyer escort dropped back until she was riding directly astern of LST-706. Wynne decided to wander aft to see what the warship was up to. He put Smoky on her lead and gave her a walk along the full length of the ship. There was now an odd, unearthly stillness about everything.

For some reason Wynne was struck by Smoky's appearance: her hair, gummed up with rust and salt, stuck out in all directions. It was peculiarly fitting – like a cartoon of a dog that had been electrocuted or suffered a severe fright. And for sure, there were few scares to compare with being targeted by kamikazes.

As the light faded, extra guns were set up toward the rear of the LST. Wynne noticed that on the destroyer riding in their wake, every man had remained at action stations.

Then, from out of nowhere a lone warplane appeared. It made for a bizarre, ghostly apparition in the half-light. It was almost dark by now and the pilot had switched on his landing lights and lowered his undercarriage – though where on earth he intended to land in the middle of the ocean was anyone's guess.

The warplane seemed to glide soundlessly across the sea, lights flashing, as it drew ever closer to the rear-end of the destroyer.

The crew of the destroyer appeared mesmerized by the bizarre apparition. The scene was so curiously reminiscent of a friendly aircraft coming in to land that no one seemed able to bring themselves to open fire. And then suddenly, it was as if the spell had been broken. Beside Wynne and Smoky, one of the guns that had just been erected on the rear of LST-706 roared into action. As the whole ship woke up to the threat, every gun zeroed in on that lone kamikaze.

The warplane was almost at the rear of the destroyer, with the ship's crew staring up at it in astonished horror, when it juddered in the sky, taking multiple hits. Moments later it keeled over, fell hard and smashed into the sea. The plume of water it sent up rained down onto the aft section of the warship that it had so very nearly managed to strike. A cheer went up from those manning the vessels.

As darkness cloaked the convoy it was time to take stock. The captain of LST-706 announced that the vessel and her crew were credited with shooting down two, and possibly three kamikazes. Another massive cheer swept the ship's deck. Maybe the dreaded Japanese suicide pilots could be beaten after all.

Tellingly, the squadron war diary recorded of the kamikaze attacks: 'We had all experienced bombing at bases. An attack at sea was another story. Our squadron insignia seemed all too appropriate: we were indeed sitting ducks. We had worried about this eventuality. Now it was here . . .'

The 'sitting duck' reference was to the 26th's badge – a camera-wielding Donald Duck riding on a cloud.

CHAPTER 18

White Beach was the codename for the convoy's intended landing point at Lingayen Gulf. The town of Lingayen itself, the provincial capital, lay just beyond the beach. A fierce naval barrage had preceded the assault, lasting from 6-9 January 1945. Studying the town via binoculars from seaward, it was possible to make out a shell-shattered church spire, and the cratered ruins of the scores of civic buildings that lined the town's main square.

'Our enemy had been completely surprised,' recorded the 26th's war diary of their arrival at Lingayen Gulf, 'as he had thought it completely impossible to land ships at that place. We were inclined to agree with him, when we saw the difficulty encountered in beaching the LSTs during the high and rough tide.' Fortunately, the rugged and utilitarian flat-bottomed vessels proved able to brave the fiercest of seas.

But even here in Lingayen Gulf, the dangers of suicide attack remained acute, and not just from the skies. After the LSTs carrying the 26th had dropped anchor, awaiting orders for the troops to go ashore, the men aboard were warned to mount watch over the waters to either side. Thick, billowing smoke screens were being deployed to shield the convoy from an assault from the air, but there were few such defences at the waterline.

The Japanese were known to be sending *fukuryu* – suicide divers – to hit the convoy at anchor. The kamikaze swimmers concealed themselves beneath unremarkable-seeming flotsam, such as old wooden packing cases and crates. Once they'd paddled out to reach the hull of a warship, they'd detonate their explosive charges. Wynne and his fellows had to stand sentry at the ship's rail, carbines at the ready. All that night there were sharp cracks of rifle fire, as the watchers opened up on threats real or imagined on the bay's dark waters.

All through the following day the tension among those awaiting the call to go ashore kept rising. It was the middle of the night when the order finally came. Having won the battle for Biak Island, General Krueger had been placed in charge of the Lingayen Gulf landings. As soon as he learned that the 26th had yet to land, the frustrated general ordered the men of the photo recce squadron – his eyes in the sky – to get moving, and pronto.

The Japanese had put up only sporadic resistance along this stretch of coastline. General Yamashita had positioned the core of his forces along the spine of ridges and remote mountainous terrain lying inland, ready to fight a long war of attrition, as they had on Biak Island. General Krueger wanted the P-38s of the 26th up and running over those enemy positions, bringing back the vital images that he needed to plan the coming campaign. It was crucial that the Lightnings got airborne as soon as possible.

As the squadron's war diary makes clear, the word of General Krueger, Commanding General of the US 6th Army, the forces spearheading the landings here and the coming advance on Manila, was not to be gainsaid. 'General Krueger himself had ordered that we debark immediately, as his scheduled operations were dependent upon our aid . . . We did suddenly pull for shore, bumping a neighbouring LST in our haste.'

The order was passed around the men of the 26th in more forceful terms: 'Hit the beach!'

LST-706 had slipped her anchor shortly after midnight; it was still hours before daybreak by the time her blunt prow ploughed into White Beach – a stretch of steep sand pounded by rough seas. The bow doors swung open, the ramp dropped, and before the ship lay a roaring tumble of white water, breakers surging back and forth. To Wynne it was obvious what would happen if he lost his grip on Smoky among the dark and chaotic melee of the landing. Heroic and spirited though she might be, his little dog would be swept under in seconds and dragged out to sea.

He slung his kitbag over one shoulder, gripped his rifle in his left hand, his cot in the other, and tucked his dog firmly under one arm, where he knew she would be most protected. He headed down the ramp, squeezing her warm body closer to his chest. He could get another rifle, kit bag or cot. He could never find another Smoky. Steeling himself, he dropped off the ramp into the seething swell, trying to nudge Smoky higher and keep her out of the reach of the hungry waves.

Struggling to keep his footing, he turned for the shore, which was some forty feet away. A pair of lights mounted on poles had been planted on the sand as a rough guide. He fixed his gaze on those, getting buffeted first this way and that by the powerful breakers, and knowing that Smoky was getting torn at by the wave tops. Finally, his feet found firmer ground, and he was able to drag both himself and his dog onto dry land.

A pile of rations was heaped on the beach. Not knowing when they might be resupplied with food, he grabbed as many cans as he could carry – sustenance for him and his dog. He sat on the damp sand and levered open a can with his bowie knife, as figures milled about, awaiting orders. It was a first rule of such missions to eat whenever you got the opportunity, for you never knew when the next chance might come.

Suddenly, an alert was hissed from soldier to soldier. Enemy movement had been detected further up the beach. Wynne took cover on a darkened stretch of sand, with Smoky held close and low beside him. Man and dog waited, tense in the silence, the roar of the surf behind them, a dark wall of vegetation to their front.

Suddenly, a massive explosion erupted from further along the shore, fiery detonations tearing apart the night skies. An ammunition dump had been hit, sending plumes of flame and smoke rippling across the heavens, and lighting up the bay a ghostly orange.

Wynne, Smoky and the rest of the 26th dashed for cover among the palm trees that fringed the sands. But they could afford little delay. Tempting as it was to remain in the small patch of safety they had found, they had their orders, direct from General Krueger. As soon as the tide receded and the water level began to drop a little, they got busy unloading the trucks and jeeps from the guts of the LST. They had hit this beach around 3.00 a.m. By first light the first of the trucks had been loaded with gear and was on its way, heading inland for an airbase freshly seized from the enemy.

With dawn breaking, Wynne and his dog caught a ride atop a ten-wheeler Army truck that was loaded high with kit and supplies. It churned its way up the beach before reaching the hard-surfaced road that ran to its rear. The first sign of human habitation was the barrio, or slum, on the outskirts of Dagupan, a town lying inland of White Beach. As the truck turned right swinging west towards Lingayen town, more and more battle damage became visible.

The three-day naval bombardment that had preceded the landings had been fearsome. Church steeples and high buildings had taken the brunt of the shelling. In Lingayen itself, townspeople had raised the American and Filipino flags and paraded through the square to show their support for the liberation forces anchored offshore. As a result the Navy's shells had been directed away from that part of the coast.

Facing such a fearsome onslaught the Japanese defenders had put up little resistance on land, but at sea the Lingayen landings had cost the Allies dear. A total of twenty-four warships had been sunk and another sixty-seven damaged, all due to kamikaze strikes. Those vessels hit included the battleships the USS *Mississippi*, *New Mexico* and *Colorado*, the heavy cruiser HMAS *Australia*, plus numerous light cruisers, destroyers and cargo vessels.

Further south, in Leyte Gulf, the Japanese had launched a series of surprise counter-attacks. Paratroopers and amphibious forces had landed from the air and sea in an effort to retake the US-held airfield. The enemy had planned to use it as a base from which to mount a wave of further attacks. Savage hand-to-hand fighting had ensued, as US rear echelon units were hastily deployed. Though the counter-attack had finally been repulsed, it reflected how resilient the Japanese forces in the Philippines remained. Their spirits were far from broken.

The drive to Lingayen town was no more than ten miles, the road running through verdant rice paddies. Several times the truck had to pull over to allow the bulky forms of Sherman tanks to thunder by. At one point the truck rumbled past a prisoner of war compound – a makeshift wire enclosure with dejected-looking Japanese POWs kicking about inside.

They reached the shattered streets of Lingayen town, where here and there the odd fire still smouldered among ruined buildings. The truck carrying Wynne and Smoky nosed through streets strewn with rubble and busy with Filipinos clearing up the debris of recent fighting. As the vehicle eased past, locals stopped to stare, some waving and smiling a welcome. Pushing ahead, they made for the far side of town where the airstrip was located.

After almost three years of Japanese occupation the people here looked to be in a sorry state. Stick-thin figures thronged the streets. Japanese troops had carried out periodic raids, seizing the local staples of rice, chicken and pigs from wherever they could find them. The villagers had been driven to the brink of starvation, and to Wynne their plight appeared utterly desperate. Men, women and children looked as if they had been ravaged by malnutrition.

The truck reached the airbase, which was already a hive of activity. Bulldozers shunted back and forth, as combat engineers worked feverishly to get the airstrip serviceable again. For the moment their activity centred on laying down steel matting, which represented the quickest way to repair bombed-out stretches of runway. Known as Marston Mat, it consisted of interlocking lengths of perforated steel, which were used for the rapid repair of landing strips. Each steel sheet was pegged down with iron stakes to give it added stability. Aircraft taking off made a noise not unlike tyres on a motorway's rumble strips, but it was perfectly serviceable.

The number one priority for Bill Wynne and the rest of his team was to get the photo lab up and running, so they could start to process images just as soon as the P-38s took to the skies. They set up billets in a cluster of palm-thatched buildings adjacent to the runway. The local Filipinos had been asked to temporarily vacate those huts, in return for rent paid by the US Army. Time was so tight that if the laborious effort involved in pitching camp could be avoided, so much the better.

The huts weren't exactly a home from home. Traditionally, the long, feathery leaves of the nipa palm were used to roof over the wooden-framed stilted buildings common to coastal settlements. With roof and sides made of overlapping strips of palm leaves, the huts provided basic shelter from the elements. Movable palm panels could be slid aside, to offer ventilation during drier spells. The floor was of split bamboo, which was flattened out to form rudimentary boards.

Wynne climbed the bamboo ladder to enter the hut that he'd been assigned. He surveyed his and Smoky's new home. The bamboo platform shook and creaked when anyone moved. The bamboo 'floorboards' had half-inch gaps between them. Beneath them, chickens and pigs foraged for discarded food. The smell left something to be desired, and no one was about to venture below in a hurry for anything they might have dropped, but Wynne's chief concern right now was for the well-being of his dog.

His biggest worry was the hut's floor. Smoky's paws – delicate, and small enough to caress between thumb and forefinger – could easily slip through the cracks and get trapped. Despite its size and strength, bamboo is a grass with a hollow stem. When cut, the sides can be left sharp as a razor's edge, and minutely serrated to form a saw-like blade. Wynne couldn't bear to think how much Smoky might suffer if she got a paw jammed between those bamboo floorboards.

Retrieving a wooden plank from one of the trucks, Wynne slid that beneath his cot, forming a solid base for Smoky in the space that she always claimed as her own. Her sanctuary. As long as she stuck to that while in the hut she should be reasonably safe from injury.

The plight of the locals was so desperate that a decision was taken to employ those who were capable of doing any work. One party was detailed to dig a trash-pit and latrines. Another was put on pot-washing duty, and another was made responsible for hauling in the squadron's supplies. They stopped short of allowing the Filipinos to cook, because the squadron medic, having run checks, discovered that the locals were riddled with gut parasites.

Once that first garbage pit had been dug and the first waste thrown into it, Wynne was shocked to see locals scavenging for anything that might be vaguely edible. His heart went out to them. It was a powerful reminder of how much they had suffered under the Japanese. Wynne was struck by the Filipino women in particular: they had retained an extraordinary dignity and poise, in spite of the privations they had suffered. They had been brutalized, and the chance to earn a little money, or a little food in lieu of cash, was a real godsend.

The airstrip lay to the rear of White Beach, running just behind the sand dunes, with wild breakers rolling in from beyond. It was flat, open, windswept terrain, with little cover anywhere apart from a scattering of palm trees. Both the airbase itself and the makeshift hut accommodation were wide open to enemy air attacks. That first night the men of the 26th were serenaded by the familiar, hollow thud of explosions and the roar of gunfire, as Japanese warplanes screamed out of the night in a frenzied counter-attack.

The trauma of running kamikaze alley had stayed with Smoky, and she was no longer able to hide her nerves. At the first sound of distant explosions she started spinning in circles, like a tiny whirling dervish. The violence of the blasts was getting to her, fear starting to take an iron hold. In an effort to block out the worst of the noise Wynne took to cupping the little dog's ears with his hands whenever there was an air-attack. There was one comforting thought: at least here on land they were immune to the terrible kamikaze strikes.

Dogs can suffer from a canine equivalent of post-traumatic stress disorder. Most commonly, animals exposed repeatedly to combat become over-active and hyper-sensitive, losing their ability to focus or to stay on task. They might shy away from places in which they were once comfortable, but where they have experienced repeated trauma. Some become overly clingy or aggressive. Smoky wasn't at that level yet. She still sought out sanctuary beneath Wynne's cot. But she seemed increasingly nervous and anxious, and Wynne worried that if he let her go during one of the raids she might bolt in fear.

There was to be little peace at Lingayen. That first morning Wynne and Smoky were woken by the thunderous clatter of a column of heavy tanks moving along the road that lay adjacent to their hut. Dust billowed thickly from the tracks and exhaust fumes clouded the air. The column's commander was jammed in the turret of his tank, a thick cigar gripped between his teeth, his head bare to the wind. He yelled out triumphantly to the men of the 26th that they sure were winning this war.

The town of Lingayen lay around eighty miles away from Manila, across fertile rice-growing plains. With US armour and troops advancing on the capital city, the focus of the ground battle had already begun to shift in that direction. General Yamashita had ordered that Manila should be evacuated and yielded to the Allies, judging his forces too weak to make a stand there. He'd ordered all available men to take up defensive positions in the high ground that ringed the city.

But some 10,000 elite Japanese marines, under Rear Admiral Sanji Iwabuchi, had refused to obey Yamashita's orders. They remained in Manila, determined to hold it or die in the process. As the Allies closed in on the city, the besieged forces gave their most bestial instincts free rein – carrying out mass rapes, horrific torture and massacres. They targeted schools, hospitals, convents and churches for the worst of their war crimes. In one instance, Rear Admiral Iwabuchi's marines rounded up 3,000 men and killed them all.

Surrounded, trapped and facing annihilation, Iwabuchi's

forces retreated to the historic, centuries-old Intramuros area of Manila, a quarter-square-mile district made up of twisting alleyways, grand buildings and thick stone-built walls. Anxious to avoid causing civilian casualties, MacArthur had resisted using air strikes and artillery in the battle for Manila. But with die-hard Japanese marines holed up in such a concentrated area as the Intramuros, he feared a ground assault without air support or artillery would prove hugely costly.

The Japanese defenders had taken thousands of Filipinos – men, women and children alike – hostage, and were holding them as human shields. Many died in the bombardment and subsequent battles that followed, as the walled city was cleared in bitter street-to-street fighting. Over a thousand US soldiers lost their lives, with five times that number wounded. Anything up to a quarter of a million Filipinos would die during the battle for Manila, mostly due to Japanese atrocities. Facing death or capture, Rear Admiral Iwabuchi and his senior officers committed *seppuku* – ritual suicide.

The siege of Manila was the most significant and devastating episode of urban warfare in the entire southwest Pacific campaign. Few cities in Europe had witnessed the kind of brutal street-to-street fighting that took place in that city, which many likened to the horrors of Stalingrad. The bestial acts of the Japanese troops earned untold infamy, becoming known as the 'Manila Massacre'. But even when all of Manila finally lay in Allied hands, the wider battle for the city was far from won. General Yamashita had established his fortified positions in the surrounding hills, and in doing so he had seized control of Manila's water supplies.

Even as he had gone about liberating Manila, MacArthur had half his mind on the next great challenge: keeping the surviving inhabitants of this war-blasted metropolis alive. He figured there were around ten days' water supplies remaining in the city. Normally, Manila's reservoirs would be topped up from the lakes in the highlands, the flow from which was controlled by a series of dams. But now, those lakes and dams lay in Japanese hands, which meant that General Yamashita could deprive the city of vital drinking water.

Having witnessed the dark horrors that Japanese commanders and their troops had visited on the citizens of Manila, few doubted that the enemy would wage their resistance across the rest of the Philippines with any less savagery. Depriving the citizens of Manila of water was quite within their capabilities. What MacArthur needed above all else were photographs of those highland reservoirs, so he could plan how best to wrestle them from enemy hands and before Yamashita was able to dynamite the dams.

The battle for Manila had been launched in the first week of February 1945. Just days earlier, the first Lightnings of the 26th had flown into Lingayen Airbase, which had just been declared fully operational. Within twenty-four hours the squadron was busier than it had ever been, the pace of operations proving relentless and punishing. In just eight days seventy-one photo reconnaissance missions were flown – which would have accounted for a month of missions back at Nadzab. From those eight days of flights 44,174 prints were processed.

Despite the daily air raids, and the need to dig new shelters in the soft sand, the crew at the photo lab – Smoky included –

were tireless in their endeavours, churning out images day and night. In one forty-eight-hour period the lab was asked to process 19,000 prints, with 7,000 of them listed as top priority. They pulled it off, even though they ran short of the fresh water the lab needed to continue processing film.

Reconnaissance flights over mountainous terrain were plagued by navigational issues: rich deposits of iron ore in the hills caused the P-38's compasses to go haywire, 'resulting in flight lines being flown in error'. And yet still the photo recce missions continued. General Krueger demanded a record number of reconnaissance sorties be flown in support of 6th Army operations. A Piper Cub light aircraft was kept on standby at the Lingayen airstrip, ready to rush those prints to senior front-line commanders just as soon as they were dry.

As the days progressed the 26th kept up the furious pace. The men of the squadron – the photo lab teams especially – came in for fulsome praise. A pair of 6th Army captains was transferred to the 26th, as permanent liaison officers. Their role was to work with the squadron to coordinate requests for photo recce missions, to brief the pilots, and to keep aircrew informed of the rapidly changing situation on the ground, ensuring the photos got to the right commanders as quickly as possible. Under their watch, prints were rushed direct into the hands of General MacArthur, at his command post, and to Admiral Nimitz, the US Naval commander, as well as to their senior officers.

Time after time, the 26th kept delivering. When MacArthur had needed detailed images to plan his final assault on the Intramuros district of Manila, he'd turned to the pilots of the

26th. On 15 February 1945 he got the photos he'd requested, and as the result of an outstandingly brave flight mission. It was none other than Lieutenant William Bishop who had been tasked to shoot the images – the pilot who had flown Smoky to Hollandia some eight months earlier, to save her from the long sea voyage from Nadzab.

Bishop had been sent into the skies to capture the labyrinthine terrain of the Intramuros in as much detail as possible. It involved executing a high-speed dash across the city's rooftops, capturing the last redoubt of Iwabuchi's marines on film. It was a miracle that he hadn't been shot down as he skimmed through the fiercely contested airspace.

Despite the intense workload, spirits remained high. The men of the 26th felt they were at the heart of something – a campaign of major significance and maybe even a turning point in this internecine war. As their war diary recorded, 'The opportunity to work in close support of the ground troops and to observe the successful results obtained . . . served not only as an incentive for greater production but as a valuable asset in maintaining good morale.'

By the third week of February, MacArthur's overriding focus had become the battle for Manila's fresh water supply. As US troops endeavoured to drive the Japanese from the jungle-clad highlands, General Krueger threw all available forces into the savage fighting. The crucial battleground had become the valleys of the Ipo Dam, the key fresh-water reservoir serving the nation's capital.

MacArthur and Krueger hungered after the kind of highly detailed images of the Ipo Dam and surrounding terrain that would enable them to plan their final assault, mapping out the enemy's cave positions and bunkers. But in the battle for the Ipo Dam, the pilots of the photo reconnaissance squadron would be forced to make their greatest sacrifices yet.

And so too would a small dog who would prove to have the world's biggest heart.

CHAPTER 19

As the pace of operations accelerated throughout January 1945, Counselman, freshly promoted to major, was relieved of his command, and moved into a headquarters role. He too had fallen victim to the furious demands of flying duties coupled with command. Captain George B. Gathers Jr took over as the fourth commanding officer of the 26th Photo Reconnaissance Squadron in three years.

With his jet-black hair, dark eyes, strong Roman nose and classic good looks, Gathers had the typical air of a dashing and daring recce flier. Formerly the pilot of a B24 Liberator serving with a combat-mapping squadron – one tasked to draw up detailed maps of war zones based upon aerial photography – he was a hugely experienced aviator. He, like his predecessors, seemed fearless, and before long he had entered into the same punishing flight regime, which he tried to juggle with the pressures of command.

Gathers encountered his first major challenge in the skies above the Ipo Dam. The enemy were so craftily hidden among the sheer-cut ravines and caves burrowed deep into mountain passes, that General Krueger wanted images of a much higher resolution than could ever be captured from 28,000 feet, the height at which they were now generally forced to fly, to avoid ground fire.

To provide such detailed images the 26th would have to execute a series of what were known as 'low-level oblique' photo runs over the Ipo Dam area. Filmed with a K22 camera positioned to shoot out the port side of the P-38's nosecone, the pilot would have to bring his aircraft down almost to roof-top height. The engine and propellers of the aircraft would be clearly visible in the shots, framing each of the photos so captured.

A technique first perfected by British photo reconnaissance pilots, it took a rare combination of bravery, consummate flying skills and cool focus under fire. But the risks were matched by the rewards: successful 'low-level oblique' photo runs could provide unparalleled battle intelligence.

The craft of low-level recce flying had been developed during the summer of 1940, when cloud cover over the Channel had prevented the RAF from photographing the invasion fleet then being assembled by Hitler. The answer was obvious: if the recce pilots flew at a very low altitude, they would be able to sneak in below the clouds. The trouble was this put their aircraft in range of enemy flak and also made them easier targets for fighters. Survival depended on split-second timing, lightning-fast reactions and not a small degree of luck. Appropriately enough, the pilots had nicknamed these flights 'dicing' – as in 'dicing with death'.

Once it had been established that this type of low-level sortie was able to capture terrain in minute detail, the focus turned to another key enemy target. For many months there had been fierce debate about whether the Germans possessed radar technology, and if they did, whether it had reached the same level of sophistication as its British counterpart.

The majority of those involved had concluded that the Germans didn't yet have radar, but there were a handful of top scientists who disagreed. They argued that the enemy had developed a highly accurate, short-wave system. There were references in decoded German signals to a mysterious device known as the 'Würzburg'. In November 1941 a mystery object had been spotted on a reconnaissance photo filmed at high altitude over the French coast. It showed a tiny pinprick set atop the cliffs at Le Havre, with paths converging upon it. Positioned adjacent to the village of Bruneval, some believed this might be the mysterious Würzburg apparatus.

RAF Medmenham, an RAF station based at the grand country manor of Danesfield House, in rural Buckinghamshire, had become the centre of wartime British photo reconnaissance analysis. It was also where increasing numbers of US photo recce teams were being trained. The mysterious Bruneval pinprick was scrutinized by the analysts at Medmenham. One, Claude Wavell, suspected it was actually a paraboloid – a shape that resembled a large dish turned on its side.

Wavell, who'd previously worked for an air survey company in Brazil, had a reputation for brilliance. But what he needed was a low-level oblique photograph of the mystery pinprick, so revealing it in far greater detail. A day or so later, Tony Hill, a flight commander and a veteran recce pilot, was sent out to see if he could secure one. Skimming along at 300 mph and at no more than fifty feet, he had to somehow fly at the same level and to the right of the pinprick, firing off his photos as it passed beneath his wing.

That first mission failed. Undaunted, Hill returned the following day, taking one of the most iconic shots of the entire war. The image he captured revealed a clifftop manor house with a path leading from it to a bowl-like structure that pointed out to sea. Though the Würzburg apparatus was no more than ten feet in diameter, Hill had nevertheless found it and captured it on film.

At Medmenham a photo montage of the target was put together, along with a highly detailed scale model. On the night of 27 February 1942 Major John Frost led 150 paratroopers on a raid on the Bruneval station. Dropped just inland they took the small German garrison by surprise, and a British radar expert was able to begin dismantling the key components of the Würzburg bowl. While he was doing so German reinforcements arrived, but Frost and his men kept them at bay for long enough for the top-secret Würzburg radar circuitry to be snatched, along with a German radar technician as a bonus.

This allowed British scientists to study the Würzburg apparatus and establish just how it worked. Not only did this mean that they could decide whether they wanted to replicate the technology for use by the Allies, it also gave them a chance to develop the means to block and scramble the Würzburg signals. This would be key to winning what was known as the 'Radar War', most notably playing a vital role during the D-Day landings.

It was this kind of breakthrough that was needed now, to break the impasse over the Ipo Dam. Only here, a whole series of photographs was required. As the battle for the terrain around the dam became ever more grinding, bitter and murderous, the demands for pinpoint intelligence became ever more urgent. Yamashita had committed the 80,000 men of his Shimbu – *martial spirit* – force to defend the dam. They were well dug-in among rugged high terrain, cut through with sheer cliffs, knife-cut gorges and plunging river valleys.

Krueger faced a gargantuan task if he was to seize this terrain in the timescale demanded by MacArthur. His advance was frustrated by rough ground and poor roads, and once again the Allies had badly underestimated the numbers and strength of the enemy. The Japanese troops had fortified the ridges with mortars, machine guns, anti-aircraft defences, anti-tank guns and 105 and 155mm howitzers. They also boasted 447mm rocket batteries, the warheads of which were charged with picric acid, more commonly known as 'Explosive D' or Dunnite – a highly combustible form of the chemical.

Their ridge-top defences were honeycombed with caves. Some had dozens of well-defended entrances. The American forces had one significant advantage: a relatively new invention called napalm – gasoline thickened with soap. Low-flying aircraft attempted to lob fiery napalm bombs directly into cave entrances, in an effort to burn the Japanese soldiers out. But it still took boots on the ground to clear and to seal off the caves. Flamethrowers and bazookas were employed to blast and scour the entrances, after which they were dynamited shut.

Such horrific close-quarter action was a painstaking process, and MacArthur warned General Krueger that time was running out. The water shortage in Manila was acute. 'Cutting daily consumption in Manila,' he informed Krueger, urging him to greater efforts. 'Outbreak of disease of real magnitude might well prove great military disaster . . . Capture of Ipo Dam would provide definitive solution.'

A total of 250,000 gallons of napalm had been dropped on Japanese positions around the Ipo Dam, the largest amount used anywhere in the southwest Pacific up to this point. And yet still the enemy held out. After months of sustained combat, Krueger's forces were overstretched, demoralized and exhausted. Early rains turned the few existing roads into quagmires. Daily advances were less than a thousand yards, and it took twenty hours to carry wounded from the front line to the nearest medical stations.

Canine warriors were also seeing action in the battle for the dams – with war dogs being sent forward to scout enemy positions and help clear the caves. And in Lingayen, the 26th's own diminutive K9 was about to prove how she, too, could make a major contribution to ensure victory.

Several attempts had already been made by the fliers of the 26th to capture those elusive low-level oblique shots of the terrain around the Ipo Dam – ones which would enable Allied air-power to identify and blast apart the enemy's hidden defences. But those heroic efforts had ended in tragic failure.

On the morning of 19 February 1945, Lieutenant Karl M. Booth had set out to capture the Ipo Dam on film. A veteran flier, Booth had been with the 26th almost since the day of its foundation. But on this day his Lightning had failed to return to the squadron's Lingayen airbase. Typically, the new CO, Captain Gathers, took to the skies to search for him, but he had no luck. Booth joined the unit's ever growing list of MIAs.

'Two days later,' the squadron recorded, 'Lieutenant Madison E. Gillespey was reported missing in action while attempting the same minimum altitude mission in the same area.' The balding Gillespey, who always seemed a little more mature than his comrades, was another major loss for the 26th. But despite two deaths in as many days, further volunteers stepped forward to attempt the Ipo Dam reconnaissance mission, one that truly was dicing with death. It was at this vital juncture that Smoky was called upon to save the squadron's air operations from serious disruption, or worse.

If for any reason the Lingayen airbase were to be deprived of the ability to send and receive messages, it would be rendered next to useless. The squadron relied upon its ability to communicate with headquarters units almost-instantly, something usually achieved by teleprinter, a very early form of typed communication similar to texting.

The teleprinter was an electromechanical typewriter that enabled short messages, pages of text or even basic black-and-white images to be transmitted via phone lines or radio signal. Teleprinters represented the squadron's quickest means of disseminating the intelligence they had gleaned from flights. A light aircraft could then follow this up, shuttling the photographs themselves into the hands of the key commanders. The nerve centre of operations at Lingayen was the communications suite, which consisted of a radio station, switchboard and a room packed with ranks of teleprinters.

Because they were invariably handling sensitive information, nearly all of the squadron's messages were sent in code. Cryptographers worked side by side with teleprinter mechanics/typists, radio technicians and switchboard operators. Messages coming in from pilots had to be decoded, and assessed for their significance, before a newly encoded message was sent on to headquarters. The communications centre also raised the alarm if an air raid was expected. It was a highly complex and fraught operation, and keeping it running smoothly was no mean feat.

Sergeant Bob Gapp was one of the main people in charge. He worked at the switchboard, but also had responsibility for stringing the teleprinter wires from the communications centre to all relevant departments. Gapp, thickset and athletic, was accustomed to shinning up telegraph poles and palm trunks to make sure that the messages kept flowing. The signals sergeant had joined the 26th on 14 July 1943, and he'd faced all kinds of challenges since then, but the problem he'd just discovered had foxed even him. That was why he had come looking for Smoky.

By now the men of the 26th had moved into their tented accommodation. Some had even started to build their own native-style nipa palm huts-on-stilts, so taken were they with the breezy local style of living. Gapp sought out Bill Wynne and Smoky, and Wynne could tell straight away that the signals sergeant was worried. A real man's man, Gapp shifted about uneasily and hemmed and hawed a little, before giving voice to what was on his mind.

'Say, Bill, we have a problem down at the airstrip,' he began.

The enemy onslaught had taken a heavy toll on the airbase's communications systems, Gapp explained. He needed to run a telephone line through a culvert – an underground drainage channel – to enable him to establish direct communications with three separate squadrons, something that was vital to the continuance of rapid and effective air operations. The problem was that the culvert lay directly under one of the airstrip's main taxiways. He couldn't string the wires across on poles for obvious reasons – aircraft zipping about would very likely blunder into them.

The only way to lay the cable manually was to dig up the culvert, which meant removing the steel matting that had been laid to form the taxiway, excavating a channel beneath, inserting the wire, then reversing the entire process. That would involve several days, during all of which time the dozens of men and the machines involved would be working in the open and at the mercy of enemy air attacks. It would also seriously hamper air operations, putting part of the airbase out of action for days at a crucial period.

The culvert ran for seventy feet below the taxiway, Gapp explained. Now he reached the delicate part. He'd once seen a news report about a similar challenge they'd faced in Alaska. Those involved had tied a length of string to a cat's collar, placed him in the pipe and then proceeded to frighten him through with bursts of compressed air from behind. The string could then be used to drag the line through. Not exactly the kindest way of doing things, but it had proved mightily effective.

The taxiway enabled the squadron's own P-38s, plus P-51 Mustangs and P-61 Black Widow night-fighters to get airborne, all of which were in very high demand at this time. It would take at least three days and cause untold disruption if a body of men were to lay the cable by digging up the culvert; Smoky might be able to perform the task in a matter of minutes.

Gapp glanced from Smoky to Wynne, his embarrassment plain to see. 'Seems to me Smoky is a very smart dog and, you know, maybe we could coax her through,' he ventured.

'Can you see daylight through the pipe?' Wynne asked.

'Yeah, but only in the upper part.' The rest was clogged with silt, sand and other debris.

Wynne explained that he was willing to consider it on one condition. If Smoky got stuck halfway, Gapp's men would dig down from directly above her, excavating a hole through which the little dog could be plucked to safety. Gapp readily agreed. Right now, he had few other options.

They hopped into Gapp's weapons carrier – a three-and-a-half tonne Dodge light truck – and raced for the airstrip. En route, Gapp suggested they might try a similar technique to one the guys had employed with the moggie in Alaska. He'd clearly thought about this long and hard. They'd tie an extremely lightweight string to Smoky's collar. Should it snag on anything inside the culvert it would sever itself, allowing her to break free and escape.

Wynne figured he needed to see the culvert for himself, before he could green light any such a plan. They reached the location at the same time as a number of P-38s were getting their engines revved up and tested by the squadron's mechanics. As with just about everything they did at the 26th, aircraft maintenance was a round-the-clock business. Wynne winced at the thunderous roar of the Allison V12 engines. They'd need to choose a quiet moment if they were to coax Smoky through the culvert, that was for sure.

Wynne crouched down at the entrance to the passageway. There were three drainage pipes, set side by side, each about eight inches across and boxed in with wooden shuttering. Each consisted of a length of galvanized steel tubing about five feet long, the individual sections of which were pushed into the next to form a series of rough overlapping joints. At those junctures sand and debris had worked their way into the pipes, forming a series of ridges that stretched for the entire length of the culvert.

Shining his flashlight along the central of the three pipes, Wynne decided it was the least obstructed. As best he could tell, the regular sandy ridges left some three to four inches of free space, providing just enough room for Smoky to squeeze through. With his flashlight extinguished, he could actually see a dim glow of light filtering in from the far side. By contrast, the two flanking culverts showed little if any illumination bleeding through from the distant end of the tunnel.

Just then a P-51 Mustang – a fighter aircraft that was fresh into theatre – taxied over the steel matting that ran above the culvert. The noise was deafening. It sounded as if a thousand dragon's teeth were being scraped over a tank's armoured hull, the noise reverberating horribly down the galvanized steel channels.

One thing was for certain: all traffic would have to cease while Smoky ran the gauntlet of the tunnel. The little dog was still shaking from the effects of her close encounter with a P-51, and if an aircraft passed right overhead while she was in the depths of the pipe, the sound would be magnified many times over.

'We'll wait until it quietens down,' Gapp suggested, stating the obvious.

'For sure,' Wynne replied. He eyed the signals sergeant for a long second, searchingly. 'You promise you'll dig her out, if we need to.'

'Absolutely.'

'Okay, here's what we'll do. Bob, you'll have Smoky here, at this central opening. I'll be over on the far side. When we're ready, I'll call her through the pipe.'

Wynne reckoned it was the sound of her master's voice that was most likely to get Smoky through the task that lay ahead of her – just in the same way that messenger dogs would carry a signal across a thousand yards of the battlefield, so as to reach their handler waiting on the far side.

Sergeant Gapp's right-hand-man, Sergeant Casalino, another expert cable-layer, was also on hand. He began to pay out the lightweight string across the taxiway, making sure it was long enough to see Smoky the entire way across. That done, the cord was wound back onto its spool and one end was tied securely to Smoky's leather-belt collar.

Wynne settled his dog as best he could by the open end of the culvert. The entrance to the central pipe loomed before her, an empty circle of black shadow as high as her head. Smoky crouched in the bright sunlight, gazing up at Wynne, questioningly. Nobody had the faintest idea what might actually be lurking inside the dark recesses of that pipe. It was daunting.

But finally Wynne could delay no longer. Gapp had got the revving of the P-38s, engines under control and the taxiway was cleared of all traffic. It was time for Wynne to dash across to the far side; time to see how strong the bond between man and dog really was. Over the last few months Smoky had met every challenge that he'd thrown in front of her, proving that inside her tiny frame beat a heart bigger than anyone could ever have imagined – but now she was going to be put to the test as never before.

'All set?' Wynne cried, once he'd reached the far side.

'Yeah! She's ready!' Gapp yelled back. 'Good to go!'

Wynne got his face down as close to the exit of the pipe as possible, worming onto his belly as if he was about to try to squeeze through himself. 'Come, Smoky, come!' he cried.

Peering inside he could just make out a tiny little head silhouetted against the distant light. 'Come, Smoky, come!' he yelled again.

He saw her hesitate for a few seconds at the tunnel entrance, as Gapp tried to coax her inside. Wynne repeated his exhortations, and finally the tiny little dog began to inch her way into the dark pool of shadow. The pipes acted as a drainage system for a small creek, which ran alongside the airstrip. The men just had to hope that no giant centipedes, no scorpions or venomous snakes had chosen to make it their home.

'Is she coming?' Wynne yelled into the enclosed space.

'Yeah!' Gapp's voice drifted back to him, sounding strangely muted and muffled. 'I'm feeding the line!'

The seconds ticked by. Was there the sound of a distant scrabbling, as a tiny dog fought her way across, scrambling over sandbanks and wriggling through the gaps? Everyone thought so. But all of a sudden the spool of string stopped unwinding. Gapp tried feeding Smoky some more line, but she wasn't dragging it forward any more.

He gazed into the pipe. He could see a tiny little face turned back towards him, the expression on Smoky's features seeming to say: *what's holding us up here?*

'*She's caught!* She's snagged on something!'

'Smoky! Stand, stay!' Wynne yelled in response.

If the line truly was trapped somewhere, the last thing he wanted was Smoky to keep struggling forward, straining at her bonds. He peered into the depths of the shadows, desperate for a sign of his dog, but the entire expanse of air inside the pipe seemed clogged with a shifting miasma of fine, drifting dirt. Struggling to free herself, Smoky's tiny, scrabbling paws had kicked up a dust storm.

She was nowhere to be seen.

CHAPTER 20

Again and again Wynne called to Smoky. He cried out words of reassurance. He hoped that his voice would carry across to her even though he couldn't see her any more. He just had to trust that his little dog, ensnared by the cord in the depths of the tunnel and blinded by thick dust, would trust him enough to stay calm and focused and to find a way through.

At the far end of the culvert Sergeant Gapp wiggled and jiggled the line, trying desperately to loosen it.

Finally, Wynne heard the burly sergeant's voice drifting through to him. 'Okay! Okay! She's free!'

His heart leapt. 'Come, Smoky, come!' he urged her. 'Come on, baby, you can do this!'

His eyes strained to cut through the gloom, yet he still couldn't make out a damn thing. He had no idea if she was heading his way, or if she had turned back to Gapp and his companion.

'Is she still moving?' Wynne yelled. 'My way?'

'Yeah!' Gapp's voice echoed back. 'I'm still feeding out the line . . .'

'Come on, baby, you can do it!' Wynne repeated, breathlessly. With all the tension the sweat was dripping down his neck and shoulders. 'Come on! Come on!'

He gazed into the murky depths of the pipe. He figured he caught a blur of movement. Sure enough, a pair of shining amber eyes seemed to dance among the gloom, piercing the haze. Smoky was about fifteen feet away from him, her forepaws scrabbling at the floor of the pipe as she struggled to drag her dust-enshrouded form through, tugging the line after.

'Atta girl! Atta girl!' Wynne yelled in relief. 'She's coming! She's almost here!'

Spurred on by the sound of his voice and the sight of his features, Smoky broke into a run. She bounded down the final sections of the pipe, her hair sticking out in dusty tufts in all directions as she vaulted over the last of the sandy barriers. Moments later, she'd leapt into Bill Wynne's outstretched arms in a puff of sand.

Wynne stood up so that Gapp could see that the little hero of a dog had made it through. The signals sergeant broke into a wild laugh. Cheers rang out across the taxiway. Gapp dashed across to join them. He reached down, grabbed the line and dragged several more feet through, before cutting Smoky, the valiant cord-puller, free.

'Boy-oh-boy,' he declared, breathlessly, his voice thick with relief. He gestured at the thin line gripped in his hand, then at the dog cradled in Wynne's arms. 'She deserves a great big steak! I'll get the mess hall to sort it!'

Somehow, Smoky knew she had accomplished something truly special. She responded to all the smiles and the praise in typical fashion. With her entire back end waggling back and forth excitedly, she kept boxing Wynne's ankles with her forepaws, her eyes shining up at him as if to say: 'Look what I've done! Look what I've done!'

Under the War Dog Programme, big, powerful hounds had been trained as line-laying dogs. They were taught to follow a strict route while a reel attached to their hindquarters played out the cable behind them. Of course, Smoky had had no such specialist instruction. All she'd benefited from was the training that she and Wynne had managed to squeeze in between the relentless photo-lab shifts, air-sea rescue sorties, enemy bombing raids and kamikaze attacks.

She had executed the cable-laying mission almost without a hitch – testament to the extraordinary bonds forged between man and dog. While sergeants Gapp and Casalino worked at the culvert – attaching a thicker cord to the line before pulling that through, and eventually getting three thick communication cables run through the pipe – word of Smoky's heroic endeavours spread throughout the camp.

A big steak for a seven-inch-tall dog was about the size of a small burger. In short order it was served up for the 26th's heroic little mascot. In fact, Smoky was no longer just the squadron's mascot any more. After the cable-laying mission – which had saved as many as two hundred and fifty servicemen and forty aircraft from being targeted by enemy warplanes – in the minds of the men she had graduated to the role of Squadron War Dog.

With Smoky's coming of age, the 26th could forge ahead with the task at hand – capturing the Ipo Dam on film. It was late February by the time the recce mission fliers were finally able to bring back the first precious rolls of film shot at low level over the target area. As soon as the planes touched down the photo lab team rushed the negatives through the development process. Now was the moment of truth: had those daring 'dicing' sorties captured what MacArthur and Krueger so hungered to see?

The images had been filmed at such low altitude that entire frames were filled with precipitous mountainsides, thick jungle and clearly defined ridgelines. So detailed were those images that individual footpaths could be traced through the trees, like white scars twisting this way and that and cutting through the thick shadows. Individual soldiers could be seen moving on those tracks; even small animals. The images were perfect for identifying the enemy's hidden defences, so they could be hit by airstrikes and ground assaults.

'A number of requests for low obliques were completed,' the squadron's war diary recorded, stressing 'the dangerously low altitude and difficult terrain over which these missions were flown'. This was something of an understatement. In fact, from 14-21 February the squadron completed a staggering 246 photo recce sorties. Not only that, but as much as seventy-five per cent of the photos secured were judged as being of 'excellent' quality.

Some 4,800 negatives were developed, from which 44,000 prints were made. Not all were low-level obliques, of course, but so overworked were the laboratory staff that power plants and driers suffered repeated breakdowns. The squadron's technicians and mechanics were forced to work miracles in order to get the machinery up and running again. That February the 26th received a special Letter of Commendation, praising the squadron for its incredible achievements.

The photo lab came in for special mention. 'I wish to commend the officers and enlisted men responsible for the operation of the photographic laboratory, the Letter announced. 'The commendable performance of all who made this outstanding accomplishment possible has contributed much to the success of the Philippines Campaign and reflects great credit on your organization as a whole.' Among all those who had made this possible there was, of course, one small but very heroic dog of war.

It wasn't simply those operating on the front lines of war who were dicing with death. The sheer, simple mortality of all – from the lowliest trooper to the senior commanders – was about to be brought home most powerfully to all in Lingayen. At the end of the second week of April 1945 a notice was posted on the squadron's bulletin board, one that was as unexpected as it was shocking. The President of the United States, Franklin D. Roosevelt, had passed away.

Months previously, most of the GIs – Bill Wynne included – had sent in absentee ballots, to re-elect Roosevelt for an unprecedented fourth term, which had begun that March 1945. But Roosevelt had long suffered from a paralytic illness, and his health had been declining throughout the war: upon reflection, his death from a massive haemorrhage struck many as being tragic but inevitable. March was also the month of Wynne's twenty-first birthday. His girlfriend, Margie – since July 1943 also his fiancée – had written to him from the States, stressing how ill Roosevelt had seemed. He had steered the nation through the long years of war and brought it so close to the end. But here in the Philippines the fighting would have to go on without their revered Commander-in-Chief at the helm.

On the ground around the Ipo Dam troops were sent in for

the final push. Krueger and MacArthur's chief fear was that the Japanese would blow the dam to pieces before it could be captured, and every effort had to be made to prevent that from happening. On 13 May 1945, a small patrol of Filipino guerrillas reached the dam itself, under the cover of darkness. Unable to seize it, they were still able to report back vital news: the dam wall remained intact. It had been rigged with explosive charges, but General Yamashita was clearly holding on until the last moment before ordering its detonation.

P-38s and P-47 Thunderclaps – a fighter-bomber and ground attack aircraft – flew repeated sorties to hit the patch of terrain surrounding the dam that was still held by the enemy. They saturated a five-square-mile box with napalm, dropping down to one hundred feet and skipping the bombs onto their targets, leaving trails of fiery devastation in their wakes. Over 100,000 tonnes of napalm was unleashed in forty-eight hours, P-51 Mustangs following up to strafe those enemy troops trying to escape the carnage.

On 16 May ground troops moved in, using bamboo scaling-ladders to climb the fortified cliffs around the dam and root out the last of the Japanese defenders. The saturation bombing with napalm seemed to have done its task, burning most of the enemy out. The dam was taken, just as a party of Japanese soldiers prepared to detonate hundreds of pounds of TNT. They were shot dead even as they twisted the wires and raised the levers to trigger the explosives.

The remaining defenders launched a series of banzai suicide charges in a desperate attempt to re-take the dam and destroy it, but each was repulsed. By 21 May all organized Japanese resistance was over. The failure to destroy the dam was put down to a communication problem. General Yamashita had almost certainly issued the order, but the message had failed to make it through quickly enough for the men on the ground to act.

By the time the battle of the dams was won, Yamashita had lost almost half of his entire force in the area. The survivors were scattered and exhausted, plagued by disease and hunger. They were reported to be resorting to cannibalism in an effort to stay alive. Yet still there were few who chose to surrender. Japanese soldiers believed the longer they held out, the longer the military would have to ready their homeland to repulse the coming American invasion, which in turn would safeguard their families. In that belief they held on tenaciously, fought with suicidal ferocity, and died.

But American losses had also been severe. Few other campaigns had suffered such high casualty rates, which were exacerbated by the diseases and the hellish conditions in which the troops were forced to operate. Many of these units had been operating for three years of unbroken service. While MacArthur's return to the Philippines was a significant victory, it had been won at tremendous cost.

As with most units in theatre, the fliers of the 26th had lost comrades: five had been killed flying missions over the Philippines, but the squadron's work continued. By now, a US Army major had been assigned as permanent liaison to the 26th Photo Reconnaissance Squadron. He flew a light aircraft that shuttled fresh images directly to MacArthur's headquarters as soon as those photos were dry. He was immediately taken with Smoky, charmed by her role in the lab, and also by the tugs-of-war she had with the lab workers during their rare moments of downtime, in which a sock was still her favourite 'tug toy'.

The major fell into conversation with Bill Wynne. Naturally, the chat turned to dogs. Before the war he had loved to hunt waterfowl on Chesapeake Bay, a vast estuary lying on the east coast of the US. He'd been accompanied on those trips by his beloved Chesapeake Bay Retriever – a breed that looks similar to a Labrador, and which originated around the choppy waters of the estuary.

One day man and dog had sallied forth when the wind was high and the bay unusually rough. The dog had put to flight a flock of ducks and the major had brought one down with his shotgun. As the downed bird was carried away from shore on the waves, his dog went after it. He'd battled wind and surf, heading further and further away from shore. The major was forced to watch, horrified, as his powerful retriever slipped from view.

He'd waited for over an hour, but still there was no sign of the missing animal. Eventually, he'd had to turn for home, believing that he'd lost his dog to the chilly, storm-lashed waters. He lived several miles away, and he was saddened beyond words on the journey home. Several hours after his return he'd heard an odd noise outside his door. He'd opened it, only to find his Chesapeake Bay Retriever standing there wagging his tail, the duck held softly in his jaws.

The major's retriever had executed his courageous acts at sea and at a time of peace; Smoky's recent heroics had taken place underground and at a time of war. But both demonstrated a similar kind of canine dedication and endurance, not to mention the extraordinary bonds these dogs had formed with their masters. Plus for the major and Bill Wynne their love of dogs was the bridge: the passion they shared in common had enabled them to open up to each other.

By late May, there were only isolated pockets of enemy resistance remaining, and the pace of operations for the 26th began to abate somewhat. After supper each night, Wynne took to having a stroll with his dog, enjoying the balmy air of the evening. In the peace and quiet on the palm-fringed streets and on the pristine beaches, he found the time and space to reflect on all that had come to pass in this war.

With the Japanese having been driven out, local life was reverting to something like normal. Evening was such a peaceful, scenic time of day here. In the fields behind the beach, locals tended to their livestock, small boys riding atop hulking great water buffalo as they ploughed and tilled the ground. In the rice paddies, farmers knee-deep in water waved, acknowledging the presence of one of their liberators. In truth, of course, there were two: Smoky, too, had played her part.

As they strolled along the beautiful stretches of sand, with the tropical sun going down over the sea, Wynne took the opportunity to refresh some of Smoky's obedience training. There had been little chance to do so in recent months. Wherever she might have hailed from originally, Smoky seemed to be maturing. She'd stopped chasing after most fowl, as she'd liked to do in the jungle of New Guinea. A while back she'd dashed after a mother hen with chicks, but the bird had turned on her in a rage, stomping all over the little dog. She now gave all such flocks of feathered avengers a wide berth.

On another occasion Smoky had made a heedless dash across

a dirt road. She must have felt she had good excuse: she'd spotted a dog on the far side. What she hadn't seen was the GMC two-and-a-half tonne Army truck bowling along right in front of her. Fortunately, Wynne was alert to the danger. As Smoky had darted forward he'd yelled out: *'Stand! Stay!'* The tiny dog froze in her tracks just as the GMC truck had thundered past, the massive wheels a bare six inches from the tip of her tiny nose.

That was just one of many times when the training had saved Smoky's life. As they strolled along the Lingayen Gulf sands, Wynne wondered whether there were other lives they might save via Smoky's training, right here and now. Many of the GIs serving on the front line had been fighting for years. Some had seen thirty-six months of brutal back-to-back combat, with precious little leave. The trauma levels were reaching gargantuan proportions, not to mention the numbers of sick and physically injured.

The needs for the kind of therapy that Smoky could deliver had to be acute, and he wondered how they might up the entertainment factor by expanding their repertoire of tricks. Costume had to be one way. The local women were skilled in needlework, and Wynne was impressed with their beauty and their dignified poise. He contacted one and asked her to embellish Smoky's coat of many colours, so as to make it fit for what he had in mind.

She embroidered onto it by hand: 'SMOKY – Champion Yank Mascot SWPA 1944.' SWPA stood for the southwest Pacific area of operations. The seamstress was inventive and she was able to add more to Smoky's 'circus' wardrobe. She fashioned a pair of clown suits, one in bright yellow and one in verdant green, using salvaged pieces of parachute silk. The zips, designed as they were for fully-grown males, were enormous in comparison to Smoky's size, but they were all that came to hand. As a final flourish the seamstress embroidered a bar of music and assorted notes onto the suits, lending them a suitably theatrical air.

Next Wynne sought out a local man who could build Smoky a slide. He found a Filipino carpenter who spoke good English, which meant he could explain exactly what he wanted. The slide should be six inches wide, to accommodate his diminutive dog, and be a good eight feet long, with a graceful arch in the middle, so she'd accelerate quickly but slow at the end as the slide levelled off. It also needed a ladder for her to climb, plus a platform for her to sit on before launching herself into motion.

He asked how much it would cost. The carpenter grinned, a little self-consciously. He didn't want money, he explained. Instead, he wanted a camera. In the war-torn Philippines cameras were like gold dust. Luckily, Wynne happened to possess a simple box camera which came with a primitive, plug-in flash unit. He showed it to the carpenter, who seemed more than happy with the trade.

Three days later he presented Wynne with the slide. It was an astonishing piece of work, expertly crafted from glistening Filipino mahogany, a rich tropical hardwood. Kitting Smoky out in such a way and with such equipment served another purpose, too. It helped inject some liquidity into the economy, which had imploded under the long years of Japanese occupation.

Indeed, the local Filipinos were working everywhere that the US troops could find them gainful employment. Large workgroups had been organized to load and unload cases of food and other supplies, to sweep the bases clean and to launder uniforms. The local men, often skilled craftsmen, were employed wherever possible as carpenters and painters. The villagers traded chickens, fruit and other fresh food with the GIs.

War had thrown together these two very different populations – Filipino villagers and US troops. In Lingayen, as in much of the Philippines, they had become close neighbours and sometime work colleagues. The relationship seemed to work well on both side. Friendships had been forged, and after the dark predations of the years of Japanese occupation, it felt good.

After their evening stroll on the beaches man and dog would make their way back to their accommodation tent. They had new room-mates here in Lingayen. Alan Kuzmicki was a camera repair technician and a former lecturer in art at the University of Georgia (in the southeastern USA). John Barnard was a fellow photo-lab technician and a former art student from sunny California. Of course, Barnard was also an old Smoky hand: he'd held one side of the landing-blanket, during Smoky's parachute training back at Nadzab. Jack Tankersley, a native of Oklahoma, was another lab technician, and the seasoned sailor who'd helped steer their drop-tank catamaran on its near-fateful voyage. Last was John Graham, a Michigan native and the squadron's mail clerk.

One of their first tasks had been to dig a bomb shelter in the soft sand adjacent to their tent. It had to be large enough to accommodate five men and one dog, and sturdy enough to survive a near-hit from a Japanese 551-pound bomb. It was roofed over with thick coconut palm trunks and covered by a layer of nipa palm leaves, which supported the twelve inches of sand they piled on top. When finished, it was solid and substantial, and it had become a decidedly popular hangout during the air raids.

One evening Wynne and his buddies had been busy writing letters home, when the comparative peace was torn apart by the wail of the air-raid siren. Grabbing Smoky, Wynne and the others had dashed for the shelter. It was pitch dark beneath the coconut-log roof, and the five were all but bowled over when a sixth companion dived in to join them.

Once they'd lit some candles, the newcomer was instantly recognizable. It was Norman Smith, the man who'd been wounded aboard LST-706 during the kamikaze strikes as they steamed north to Lingayen Gulf. Smith had long poo-pooed taking cover during air raids. He'd argued that if a bullet had your number on it, then there was little you could do about it. But it seemed he'd changed his mind. As the enemy warplanes rained down bombs on the Lingayen airstrip, Smith had become a foremost believer in the virtues of such sturdily-built shelters.

When not under attack, one of the alternatives to an evening's letter-writing was a quick burst of Radio Tokyo. The various Tokyo Roses were still cranking out their propaganda, but in light of recent Allied victories it was sounding increasingly desperate. The men tuned in more to see how the enemy was trying to spin things, as the fortunes of the war turned against the Japanese.

The squadron's monthly Intelligence Summary (No. 12) reflected this. 'Entertainment emanating from Radio Tokyo has a new significance. Curious individuals tune in on the enemy version of current requests for amusement . . . They are curious to hear what pretext . . . the Japanese Government has to offer for its latest defeats.' Despite Radio Tokyo's best attempts to paint losses somehow as victories, their efforts proved hollow. 'The morale has been very good during the period covered by this report.'

The Lingayen movie theatre was making a great contribution to squadron morale. Built by the GIs working in tandem with locals, and made mostly from bamboo, it was managing a thrice-weekly showing, something that had been impossible back on war-torn New Guinea, due to the challenges of getting movies flown in. Not only that, but it was able to screen newsreel reports showcasing the progress the Allies were making in all theatres of the war.

As a bonus for Smoky, movie nights were when the squadron's war dog was on ultimate downtime. Wynne allowed anyone who wanted to pet and to play with his dog. She was excellent company and she loved the attention. But he wouldn't allow anyone to try out any of her tricks. As far as he was concerned the trainer–trainee relationship they had formed was sacrosanct. Wynne and Smoky were a close-knit, unbeatable team, and he couldn't allow any confusion or uncertainty to get in the way of that.

At around this time – May 1945 – a large rat began interrupting the movie nights. It took to scaling a coconut tree and climbing out along a phone wire that ran above the outdoor screen. It was bizarre – almost as if the rat sought a ringside seat. The wire lay between projector and movie screen, and once the rat was halfway across he would be silhouetted by the flickering light. Generally, he'd stop there, his tail flicking back and forth as he eyed the scenes, before trotting across to the far side, and then coming back a little later for a repeat performance.

One of the squadron's more talented artists sketched an evocative black-and-white cartoon of Ratty on the move. 'Each show night the rat would walk the wire ... about fifteen minutes after the show started,' the squadron captioned the sketch, in a moment of rare levity. 'Then, just before the show ended he would travel back. No one knows whether he was going to see his girlfriend or to get a better view of the show.'

One night a GI scaled the rat's coconut tree and got a hand on the wire. When Ratty was in position he pulled the wire down like a bowstring and let rip. Ratty flew into the air, his shadow shooting across the movie screen, before disappearing from view with a thud. Needless to say, the audience were in hysterics. Ratty clearly didn't appreciate the joke. He never put in an appearance after that.

Spirits were high in the squadron, but in a sense this was the calm before the coming storm. The Philippines had been taken, and MacArthur was turning his attention to the next steps in the march towards Japan. The 26th was about to be called upon to reach further than it had ever done before, flying reconnaissance missions over distant China, where the Japanese military had some of their last major foreign bases. If those could be captured, or at least rendered unusable, the passage to the Japanese homeland lay open to the Allies.

Yet as all were painfully aware, the entire Japanese nation had vowed to fight to the last in the defence of their emperor. Preparations were underway for a devastating final stand. Alongside the thousands of Nakajima *Tsurungi* – sabre – kamikaze aircraft and pilots that had been readied, the Japanese military had developed the *Kaiten* – 'return to heaven' – a fast kamikaze submarine-torpedo fitted with a 1,550-kg warhead. But perhaps most worrying was the development of the Yokosuka MXY-7 *Ohka* – 'cherry blossom' – a kamikaze rocket-bomb.

The *Ohka* was similar in appearance to a V1 doodlebug, but with a pilot's cockpit set amidships. Designed to be carried slung beneath a bomber, the *Ohka* was released when still miles distant from its target. From there it would glide until close enough for the pilot to trigger its solid propellant rocket motors, by which time it would be all but unstoppable. Under full thrust the *Ohka* was capable of speeds in excess of 650 mph, which meant that no aircraft the Allies possessed could come close to catching it, and it packed a devastating 1,200-kg warhead.

Between the Philippines and Japan lay the coastal islands and landmass of China. Japanese bases there would have to be identified and photographed by the high-level recce fliers, before they could be mapped and finally neutralized. Once that was accomplished, an invasion fleet could sail for Japan. The massed warships and landing craft would hit the western fringes of the Japanese homeland first, including the islands of Iwo Jima and Okinawa, with the 26th doubtless riding in the vanguard.

The Japanese had vowed to rain down kamikazes upon the Allied invasion forces, from land, sea and air. It was a daunting proposition, and the fear of what was coming loomed large. To die in what had to be the last months of the war would be the ultimate, and some might argue a senseless, sacrifice.

No one was immune to death, and as all knew, the kamikazes – thousands of them – lay in wait.

CHAPTER 21

In the first weeks of May rumour and counter-rumour swirled around the Lingayen base concerning the squadron's forthcoming move and the grim prospect of the action to come. Victory in Europe was already secured. VE Day – 8 May 1945 – had marked the moment Nazi Germany formally surrendered to the Allies. But it had proved a bittersweet experience for those serving at Lingayen, who knew plenty more fighting must lie ahead.

On 17 May an Army propaganda film was shown in the Lingayen movie theatre, entitled 'Two Down and One To Go'. It talked about how Hitler's Nazi Germany and Mussolini's Fascist Italy had been defeated, which left Japan the only remaining Axis power. Yet if the battle for the Philippines had been defined by savagery, this would surely pale into insignificance when compared with the bloody struggle that taking the Japanese homeland would involve.

At one point there was talk of how a thousand die-hard and suicidal Japanese soldiers had infiltrated the Lingayen area, filtering down from the mountains disguised as Filipino civilians. The rumour had reached the squadron by means of the 'grapevine method', according to the monthly Intelligence Summaries, which suggested that the idea was both 'absurd and impracticable'. There were precious few Japanese troops remaining in the Philippines, let alone many with the ammunition, weaponry, energy or the will to fight.

Indeed, the Japanese military had drawn back its claws, rallying all who were able to the defence of the Empire of the Rising Sun. In response, MacArthur would need to further extend his grasp, and at the vanguard of that effort would be the pilots of the 26th.

From the Lingayen airstrip a pair of P-38s took to the skies. At the controls of one sat Lieutenant Oliver, and in the cockpit of the other was Captain Gathers, the squadron's commanding officer. Their target lay over 800 miles away, on Hainan Island, which was situated on the southern coast of China. Practically the entire flight would be executed over the open expanse of the South China Sea.

Taking off at 0840 Philippines time, the 1,600-mile round trip would last seven hours in total. Their destination was the port of Sanya, on the southern tip of Hainan. In 1941 the Japanese military had seized the area and changed its name to Samah. The port had become the base of the Second Fleet of the Imperial Japanese Navy, and it was from there that they had orchestrated the invasion of Malaya (present-day Malaysia), Thailand, and subsequently Burma (Myanmar) and Singapore.

Between 1140 and 1225 the two pilots fired off 165 photos, tearing through the skies above Sanya harbour at 26,000 feet. This was one of the first ever recce flights executed over China, and Gathers summed it up with typical taut understatement in his Final Mission Report: 'SUCCESSFUL'. The squadron would go on to complete dozens more missions over China, capturing on film those enemy bases that might menace MacArthur's coming thrust towards Japan. Indeed, as much as eighty per cent of all wartime intelligence regarding China was secured from such flights.

These daring sorties were executed at enormous risk to those flying them. The Japanese nation was like a cornered rat, and those probing recce flights met with ferocious resistance. The Final Mission Report of Lieutenants Cahall and Brown, who flew over Chinese territory just days after Oliver and Gathers, was somewhat more forthcoming. It recorded how they had experienced 'Intense, heavy, accurate to inaccurate ack-ack . . . at 25,000 feet.'

That anti-aircraft fire was now reaching as high as 25,000 feet provided a stark warning that even sticking to altitude was no longer any guarantee of safety. The China sorties spurred a new rumour – that the 26th was poised to deploy to China, which at least should save them from the hell of the coming invasion of Japan. But the loss of another of the 26th's pilots – Lieutenant Clarence E. Cook – reminded all of the ever-present dangers of the war, no matter where it might be fought.

The loss of that young but talented flier – Cook had only just won his commission – drove home the sense of impending danger. The savagery involved in the battle for the remote island of Iwo Jima reinforced this impression. Iwo Jima is positioned between the Philippines and the main Japanese landmass. Lying some 750 miles south of Tokyo, it is part of Japan itself. The island was an obvious stepping stone for MacArthur, and it was heavily garrisoned by Japanese troops.

The taking of Iwo Jima had come at great cost. Despite enjoying complete air superiority, the total American casualties had exceeded those of the enemy. The island's defenders had fought as the Japanese Emperor had pledged they would – with suicidal ferocity and very nearly until the last man. Of the 21,000 enemy troops garrisoning the island, only 216 were taken prisoner, and many of those only because they had been knocked unconscious by explosions, or otherwise incapacitated.

Injured GIs had been brought back to hospitals in the Philippines in their thousands. Manila was overflowing with wounded, and where there were traumatized and injured soldiers, Bill Wynne felt certain that he and Smoky might well be called to serve. Despite the febrile atmosphere at their Lingayen base, or perhaps even because of it, this was something that he was determined to prepare for.

The Lingayen movie house doubled as a theatre – it came complete with conical-shaped stage lights crafted out of old tin, plus a bamboo stage. But Wynne craved a better, more controlled and private environment in which he and Smoky could rehearse and train. There was another incentive, as well, to do so: by intensifying the obedience training, Wynne hoped to hone Smoky's discipline so as to better the chances of keeping her safe for the remaining months of the war.

The answer was to find a bespoke training house, and Wynne set about doing so. He asked First Sergeant Joyce Howell, the hard-charging Texan cowhand who was prone to wearing cowboy boots around camp, if he could requisition a nipa palm hut solely for the purposes of training. Howell was one of Smoky's many devoted fans in the unit, so was delighted to help.

He selected a hut, clambered up the ladder, took a perfunctory look inside and told Wynne to go right ahead.

'It's all yours,' he enthused. The squadron's supplies were at Wynne and Smoky's disposal, Howell added. 'And if you need anything else, y'all just give a holler.'

Next, Wynne solicited the help of the photo lab chief, Irv Green, to convert the stilted hut into a bespoke training facility. Green secured a load of plywood lumber with which to plank-over the rickety bamboo floor. When bent into shape, discarded cardboard boxes that had once held photo paper made for excellent hurdles. Henry Wickham, the squadron's painter, decorated them with the 26th's iconic insignia – Donald Duck riding on his cloud, camera at the ready.

The plywood flooring was sturdy and smooth, and it made a great surface upon which to mount Smoky's show kit – her mahogany slide, her tightrope walk, her rolling drum, as well as a tiny little scooter that Wynne had had made for her. In their designer training house, Wynne and Smoky began to polish their skills. He even taught Smoky to leap through a bamboo hoop that he'd scavenged from an old fishing net.

Smoky was such a fast learner that Wynne figured maybe they could develop an act where the little dog actually spelled out her name. He'd never seen it done before, but he reckoned she was smart enough to grasp what he intended. He grabbed some old photo-paper boxes and cut five letters, each fourteen inches high, which together spelled 'S-M-O-K-Y'. Braced with strips of cardboard set at right angles to the backs, the letters were self-standing.

With the letters lined up on the floor, Wynne carried Smoky

over to the start, tracing the 'S' with her head repeatedly and each time pronouncing a firm and clear 'S' out loud. The following day he repeated the process with the 'M', then together they revised the first two letters. Over the next few days they completed the final three. With the 'O' he even put Smoky's little head inside the circle of the letter each time, to better impress it upon her memory.

Finally, he figured they were ready to give it a whirl. He started with the letters in their proper order, and with Smoky sitting in front of them. 'Smoky, spell your name,' he announced. She didn't so much as budge. He tried calling out the letters in order – 'S-M-O-K-Y'. Still she seemed none the wiser. He tried mixing the letters up, to see if that would trigger her interest. Still, she barely moved a muscle when he told her to spell her name.

He tried standing behind the letters, so he was facing her, to coax her into action. No joy. He tried starting early in the morning, before the heat began to build. It made no noticeable difference. He tried rainy days, which made for ideal training days – for the air was cool and most often the recce flights were grounded. Still she didn't get it. After two months of trying to master the 'spell your name' trick, Wynne gave up. For some reason it just hadn't clicked with Smoky at all.

On one level Wynne was surprised. She was normally so clever and quick, not to mention eager to learn and to please. But this time it was as if she just hadn't engaged. Almost as if she just didn't care whether she got it or not, or won any praise as a result. Almost as if she was jaded from all the training that had gone before and didn't very much give a damn. Smoky seemed to know something about the spelling trick that Wynne didn't, but as matters transpired there was no time to winkle that out right now.

A new and frightening disease swept through Lingayen. It was to be the animals who were the foremost victims of the deadly but mysterious plague. Chickens were the first to be hit. From out of the blue they began to keel over in their droves. One moment they were fine, the next they dropped dead. And just as the troops were trying to work out what the killer illness might be, it began to assail the canine population too.

As soon as Wynne got word about the mystery plague he put Smoky into isolation. Within days at least thirty dogs in the area had been wiped out. The squadron's fortunate survivors – Smoky, Topper, Duke, plus an Irish Setter freshly arrived with the men, and a little, sickly puppy adopted by a soldier called Zeitlin – were some of the few left alive. Still the mystery illness lurked and festered.

One night Wynne spotted some highly unusual goings-on. He was working the graveyard shift at the photo lab when he noticed a group of shadowy figures about fifty feet away, gathered beneath some palm trees. They appeared to be digging a hole. It was 0300 hours, a very odd time to be excavating anything. He went to investigate. To his dismay he found that his buddy, Frank Petrilak, and some others had formed a burial party for a fresh canine victim, and this time it was to be one of the squadron's own.

On the sand lay the body of Smoky's six-month-old puppy, Topper. Topper had inherited his mother's spirit, with bright eyes and perky, pricked-up ears. He'd already grown as big as her, and he'd been blessed with a beautiful black-and-tan coat of shortish, rufty-tufty hair. He'd braved six months of war. Losing him to the killer plague was heartbreaking. It was clear that no dog was safe from the scourge.

Wynne became even more protective over Smoky. Heaven forbid that he lost her now, in the final act of the war. Amid the mounting tension of the coming invasion of Japan, and with sickness ravaging the camp's animal inhabitants, there were to be other challenges, too. Chief among them was the fate of Colonel Turbo, the notorious macaque. Maybe it was due to all the cumulative stress and strain, or perhaps Turbo himself was growing shell-shocked after the years at war – but either way he truly overstepped the mark, when he turned on and badly mauled his keeper.

There were various species of macaque native to the Philippines, but Turbo possessed few survival skills and he had no experience of living in the wild; he could not simply be set free. And yet at the same time he'd become a real liability around camp. So it was that a firing squad was formed, and Colonel Turbo was read his service record, his final orders and his last rites. With that he was dispatched with a volley of rifle fire.

Eventually, the mystery disease that had ravaged the animal population of Lingayen faded away. In its aftermath a variety show featuring a mostly Filipino cast was planned, in an effort to lift the spirits of those serving at the base. The line-up of singing, dancing Filipino girls was to be one of the undoubted highlights, but so too was the moment that Bill Wynne and Smoky would step into the limelight.

At first Wynne had hesitated when asked if they would

perform. He was used to hospital audiences of a few dozen war-wounded – not the hundreds of boisterous GIs that were bound to attend a show such as this. He was no professional performer and he'd never had to face a mass audience before. But at the same time this was a perfect opportunity for him and Smoky to shine and to serve, and he didn't feel that he could say no.

He figured they needed to deliver an absolute showstopper, and for that he would need support. Henry Shacklette, one of the squadron's electricians, possessed a working Solovox – then a state-of-the-art electronic organ, incorporating a keyboard, amplifier and speaker – and he was a talented musician. Together, they worked on a repertoire of tunes to which Wynne and Smoky might take to the stage. Come show night, having musical accompaniment should help settle their nerves.

They intended to walk onto the stage performing the 'through the legs' routine, to the tune of 'Pretty Baby', singer and pianist Tony Jackson's lively music hall classic. They'd switch to the dead dog act, with Shacklette playing Chopin's haunting Funeral March. Smoky would miraculously come alive and switch to hurdle-jumping next, accompanied by 'Oh Where Oh Where Has My Little Dog Gone', the popular nursery rhyme.

'Beer Barrel Polka', one of the war's biggest pop hits, would usher in Smoky's barrel roll, while Shacklette would belt out 'The Daring Young Man on the Flying Trapeze' – the timeless circus classic – for Smoky's grand finale, as she walked the tightrope wires, after which, with blindfold removed, she would ride down the slide to finish with a flourish. It was a fine act. A dead cert of a winner. But sadly it was not to be, at least not this time.

A few days before show night, Wynne sought out the show's director, Sergeant Krog, and told him they were pulling out. Wynne's excuse was Smoky. He claimed the diminutive canine performer just wasn't ready. But the truth was quite different. It was him: he wasn't ready. The thought of facing an audience of hundreds of fellow GIs had thrown Wynne completely. In his head he knew the truth: at the eleventh hour he'd chickened out.

The director was apoplectic. He told Wynne to go to hell. Wynne was truly shaken. He went and found the guy the next day and tried to argue that he'd changed his mind. But the director was having none of it. He couldn't risk building a show around the two of them, only to have them succumb to stage fright at the last minute. And that was final.

The show went ahead to a packed audience. The fresh-faced Filipino dancehall girls – resplendent in their grass skirts and with bright flowers in their hair – took to the stage to a suitably raucous reception, serenaded by male singers in smart suits. But the night was sadly bereft of the squadron's own – Bill Wynne and their famed mascot-cum-war dog, Smoky.

Shortly after this bruising failure to perform, Wynne received a letter from Barbara Wood Smith, the Red Cross nurse who had persuaded him to do the rounds with Smoky on the Brisbane hospital wards. Wood Smith asked if he might bring their act to the Santo Tomas University in Manila. During the Japanese occupation, the university had been transformed into a prison camp, with some 3,500 prisoners, mostly Americans, being held there. On 5 February 1945 a 1st Cavalry Division tank had rolled up to the main gates and blasted them off their hinges, liberating the POWs.

Shortly thereafter, Santo Tomas University had undergone another makeover, being transformed into a vast General Army Hospital. It was June 1945 by the time Wynne had received his invitation to perform there, and the hospital was packed with casualties from across the Philippines, and from Iwo Jima and further afield.

In response to Wood Smith's request Wynne boarded a truck bound for Manila, with Smoky at his side. Apart from the small bamboo hoop, they took little of their show kit with them. Instead, they would revert to the simpler, less fraught acts that had been so popular in Brisbane.

Or so Wynne hoped – that was if he found the courage to perform at all.

CHAPTER 22

As it turned out, Bill Wynne and Smoky's tour of the Manila wards proved as much of a hit as they had in Australia. As an addition to their regular act, Wynne had decided they'd perform their own version of the Jitterbug. He and Smoky began by facing each other, each lifting an opposing foot/paw several times, before spinning around in unison in opposite directions and coming face-to-face again. That seemed to bring the house down.

Wynne and Smoky performed in fifteen wards, without a single misstep or mishap, or even the slightest hint of stage fright. The other major hit in Manila was Smoky's crooning. One injured GI asked if he might take the little dog to serenade the patients in another ward, and a Red Cross photographer fired off some snaps of them in action.

Once they were done, Wynne carried Smoky to the lawn outside, where he popped her into a GI helmet, to recreate the winning *Yank Magazine* image for the Red Cross photographer. But Smoky's tongue was hanging out exhaustedly, and it struck Wynne that she looked more like a dog-tired, war-bitten soldier, than what she had been back then – namely, the gift that never stopped giving.

Here on the Manila hospital wards man and dog had brought the house down. In light of their unreserved success, Wynne felt even more regretful about the stage fright he had succumbed to in Lingayen. That bout of nerves continued to trouble him. When Barbara Wood Smith asked if they'd like to feature on the weekly Red Cross radio show, which broadcast right across the US, he jumped at the chance. Anything to help bury the memory of that vexing failure of his to perform; to measure up to his dog; to serve.

In a downtown Manila recording studio he was interviewed about Smoky winning the *Yank Mag* contest, plus her legendary exploits running the wire beneath the Lingayen airstrip, and her subsequent performances for the injured servicemen in Santo Tomas hospital. Wynne was able to alert both his mother, and his fiancée Margie, to the forthcoming broadcast, which would go out on Cleveland's Mutual Network radio, together with dozens more such stations across the US.

At the same time ACME Newspictures, then one of the world's leading press agencies, syndicated the story of the tiny dog with the big heart who acted as a miraculous entertainer for wounded GIs. It was illustrated with the picture taken on the Santo Tomas lawn, with Smoky sprawled in the helmet. It was an instant hit. Once they were back at their Lingayen base, Wynne came across scores of fellow soldiers who'd received letters and news clippings from home, showcasing the squadron's 'wonder dog' that had made thousands happy, if only for a moment, so they could forget.

Those were the highs of their return to Lingayen. The low was the news that two more of the squadron's fliers had lost their lives. Lieutenants Henry R. Willis and James L. Wilson had been through flight training together and they'd come to the 26th as young officers. Inseparable ever since, they'd been tasked to fly a low-level recce mission over Kiangan, a mountainous wilderness in the Philippines where General Yamashita himself was believed to have made his final redoubt.

Willis and Wilson never returned from that mission. Both aircraft were shot down, crashing in a remote mountain valley practically side by side. Just days after Willis and Wilson's fateful sortie, the Japanese general would walk out of the battle-scarred hills with a small retinue of staff, and surrender to the US 32nd Infantry Division.

By June 1945 the squadron's rumour mill was practically in meltdown. All talk was of Okinawa, Okinawa. The island of Okinawa lies roughly 400 miles south of the rest of Japan, and at the time it was populated by approximately 300,000 civilians. After Iwo Jima, it was the next obvious stepping-stone for MacArthur. Once conquered, the plan was to use Okinawa as a launchpad for bombing raids over Japan's major cities, and for the final invasion of the Japanese mainland.

In the largest amphibious assault of the entire Pacific campaign, US Marines and infantry units had fought their way onto the first of the Okinawa beachheads. But the fighting would rage for almost three, terrible months. Christened *tetsu no bofu* – the violent wind of steel – by the Japanese, the name embodied the sheer ferocity of their defence, which was being spearheaded by the legions of the kamikazes.

Repeated waves of suicide attackers had swept in on the US invasion fleet. Among the vessels attacked was USS *Louisville*, the cruiser that had been struck three times by kamikazes during the Leyte Gulf landings. Hit by anti-aircraft fire and in flames, the kamikaze pilot targeting the cruiser still managed to strike home, the impact ripping the ship's seaplane off her deck, crushing a smoke stack, and killing eight sailors and injuring forty-five.

Ohka rocket-planes were also in the vanguard of the attack. Mounted aboard flights of Mitsubishi G4M twin-engine bombers, they were launched in waves. On 12 April 1945, nine G4M bombers had unleashed their rocket-borne kamikazes against the US fleet steaming off Okinawa. One had hit the destroyer USS *Mannert L. Abele*, closely followed by a second. Suffering catastrophic damage, the vessel broke in two, with her midships obliterated and her bow and stern sections sinking quickly.

This was the first US warship to be sunk by one of the rocket-powered kamikazes. Throughout May and June, more rocket-planes broke through the fleet's defences, damaging and sinking a number of other warships. In one attack, an Ohka passed clean through the hull of the destroyer USS *Stanly*, exploding beside her in the sea. It was a narrow escape, but another destroyer wasn't so fortunate. USS *Hugh W. Hadley* was hit by a speeding Ohka, causing massive damage that left her beyond hope of repair.

Yet, Okinawa was as nothing, compared to the coming defence of mainland Japan – and into this violent wind of steel would sail the 26th.

Towards the end of July Captain Gathers called the men of the squadron together. The Philippines party was over, he told them. The move to Okinawa was now. And beyond that, they were destined to join the battle for Japan.

'We must strip ourselves of personal property,' Gathers informed the assembled men, his voice sombre. Anything remotely big or bulky would need to be left behind. That meant that all of Wynne and Smoky's lovingly crafted performing kit – mahogany slide, painted drum, tightrope walk and more – would have to be abandoned. While man and dog hadn't got to use the equipment much, still they lived in hope. But there was worse.

'No animals will be permitted to go,' Gathers added, ominously. Wynne felt his heart skip a beat: leaving Smoky behind was simply unthinkable. As if reading his mind, Gathers' eyes seemed to seek him out among the crowd of anxious faces. 'All except for Smoky,' he added. 'Smoky – she's been with us forever, she's the squadron mascot and she doesn't take up any space.'

Gather's surprise announcement raised a ragged cheer from his audience.

The men began to dispose of their possessions among the locals, though those who owned dogs vowed defiantly that they would take them with them, whatever Gathers might have ordered. Of course Topper, Smoky's only offspring, would sadly remain in his Lingayen grave. Filipino friends watched morosely as tents were taken down and requisitioned huts returned as much as possible to how they had been, before the 26th had moved in. Despite the air raids and the losses of their brothers in arms, the men had been happy here.

As trucks were loaded with gear a dark and funereal atmosphere descended upon the men. Finally, the long column of vehicles rolled slowly out of a place that had been home for approaching six months. Figures perched atop the heavily laden trucks waved goodbye and forced a smile. Most knew they were never going to return; that friendships made here would never be rekindled.

'When our trucks pulled out, the roads were lined with "the neighbours" and their expressions of sorrow at our departure indicated that we had helped implement the American "good neighbour" policy in a small way,' the squadron's war diary recorded, trying to sound an upbeat note. It was not one shared by the rest of the men.

At the docks they were greeted with a wearingly familiar sight: heavily laden figures shuffled aboard an old and rusting LST, in preparation for a crowded and uncomfortable passage into the unknown. The dark and potent form of a US attack submarine lay alongside. She would be sailing with them on the coming voyage. The convoy formed up. All knew their final destination lay beyond Okinawa. The massive seaborne force was heading far beyond the battle-blasted island, for the landings on mainland Japan.

The convoy set sail. As they ploughed across the South China Sea, there was more disturbing news. The famed war reporter Ernie Pyle had been killed at the height of the battle for Okinawa. Along with President Roosevelt, Pyle had been a towering figure to the GIs, earning widespread renown for his eyewitness accounts of the rank and file of US soldiers at war.

Pyle had been killed on Ie Shima – present-day Iejima – a small island lying just to the northwest of Okinawa itself. Embedded with the US Army's 305th Infantry Regiment, Pyle had been pinned down by an enemy machine-gunner, taking cover in a ditch with other troops. When he'd risked a swift glance to check out the lie of the land, he had been shot in the head and killed instantly.

The new US President, Harry S. Truman, would praise Pyle, declaring that: 'No man in this war has so well told the story of the American fighting man as the American fighting man wanted it told.' Bill Wynne was shaken by the news. Pyle had shared the soldiers' front-line privations and their darkest fears. He had understood them. Now he, too, was gone. If a man of Pyle's stature could perish among this stretch of war-blasted sea and islands, so could anyone.

So too could any dog.

By the time the convoy had steamed into the seas around Okinawa it was the first days of August 1945. The LST ran ashore, its bow-doors opened and the men of the squadron began a repeat performance of their arrival, months earlier, at Lingayen Gulf. Inland they could see a camp surrounded by mines and barbed wire, which had been constructed by some of the first troops to land here. The fence was lined with tin cans half-filled with gravel, which would rattle if anyone so much as touched the wire, giving advance warning if any enemy tried to sneak up under cover of darkness. Hand-grenades were rigged to the wire, with the intention of blowing any would-be attackers to pieces – testament to the ferocity of recent fighting and the fear that it had left in its wake.

When that first day's unloading was complete, Bill Wynne and his fellows joined the exhausted chow line. This would be their last meal aboard the hulking great LST, and few were lamenting the fact. The voyage had been irksome, the 'hardships of crowding, lack of showers, and the rest following the old pattern', the squadron's diary noted. And the food had been little better.

Men were lining up with their mess-tins when a long piece of yellow teleprinter paper was unceremoniously tacked to the ship's bulletin board. Most thought little of it, until the murmur of the few who'd gathered to read it bled into a stunned silence. It was the quiet that only ever descends on a crowd when gripped by utter shock and disbelief.

Wynne joined those gathered at the board. The teleprinter message announced the use of the world's first-ever atomic bomb. It was 6 August and the 'Enola Gay', a US B-29 Super-fortress, had dropped the Little Boy uranium bomb on the Japanese city of Hiroshima. The initial explosion, and the resulting cataclysmic firestorm that had engulfed the city, had killed in excess of 100,000 people. Many more would die from radiation poisoning.

Wynne and his fellows read the news in a state of dazed disbelief. That one aircraft dropping one bomb could unleash the power to level a city seemed impossible, but surely the teletype didn't lie. Their reactions ranged from a great regret at the massive loss of civilian life, to a quiet elation that here surely was promise the war might be over soon. President Truman called for Japan to surrender, or it should expect a 'rain of ruin from the air, the like of which has never been seen on this earth. Behind this air attack will follow sea and land forces in such numbers and power as they have not yet seen . . .' Yet still Japan gave little hint that it was even considering capitulation.

With every hour further teletyped reports were pinned to that bulletin board. Hiroshima was a legitimate target, they declared:

it had been garrisoned by some 40,000 Japanese troops, and it had provided the headquarters to many of the regiments tasked with the defence of the Japanese mainland. A port city, it had also served as a key trans-shipment point for military supplies and personnel.

In the run-up to the bombing, the 300,000 citizens of Hiroshima had been warned to evacuate their homes, in leaflets dropped by overflying US aircraft. Those warnings had been largely ignored. A day after the blast, Japanese experts inspected the ruins of Hiroshima and confirmed that an atom bomb had caused its destruction. But the Japanese war cabinet argued that the Allies could possess only 'one or two' more such nuclear devices, and so their resistance should continue.

Two days later there would be further shocking news, which would result in the work on constructing the squadron's new photo lab being put permanently on hold. A second atom bomb had been unleashed. This one, codenamed "Fat Man", was a plutonium-based implosion-type device, and it had been dropped over the port city of Nagasaki, causing even greater devastation.

Realizing that the US possessed further such devices, Japanese Emperor Hirohito finally mooted surrender, but upon one condition: on no account was his sovereign rule to be threatened. With this agreed, on 12 August 1945 Hirohito announced to the disbelieving Japanese people that the nation was to lay down its arms. In his speech he stressed how 'the enemy now possesses a new and terrible weapon with the power to destroy many innocent lives . . . Should we continue to fight . . . it would result in the ultimate collapse and obliteration of the Japanese nation.'

A Japanese delegation was to fly into Ie Shima – the island

lying adjacent to Okinawa on which Ernie Pyle had lost his life – en route to the battleship USS *Missouri*, anchored off Manila, where the peace accords would be signed. The Ie Shima landing strip was in full view of the squadron's new camp. On the morning of the delegation's scheduled arrival, Bill Wynne found himself standing with several of his expectant fellows on the bonnet of a jeep, with a ringside view, and with Smoky at his side.

They'd tuned their radio into the air-to-ground traffic, to monitor the progress of the Japanese aircraft carrying the peace party – a pair of Mitsubishi G4M bombers. At the orders of the US military they had been stripped of their weapons and painted white, and both displayed large green crosses. A phalanx of six P-38s escorted the Japanese peace party and Wynne could hear the countdown as the flight of aircraft neared the island.

The air traffic controller on Ie Shima came on the air, requesting the two Japanese aircraft identify themselves with their agreed call-signs – Bataan I and Bataan II, a clear reference to the reviled 'Bataan death march' on which so many Allied and Filipino troops had lost their lives. The American radio operator sounded tense as he demanded they come up on air.

'Bataan I and Bataan II, come in. Repeat, Bataan I and Bataan II, come in.'

After a short delay there was a halting and heavily accented response. 'Sorry, cannot hear you. Cannot hear you.'

'Come on, you son of a bitch, or we'll knock you out of the skies!' a second voice butted in over the radio.

'I hear you!' the Japanese pilot answered, nervously. 'I hear you.' Then, with clear reluctance: 'Bataan I and Bataan II, in-bound.'

Moments later, the two Japanese warplanes hove into view, flying over the northeastern shoreline of the bay.

'It's over!' someone yelled.

'DAMN! It's OVER!' another voice echoed.

'That it is,' Wynne confirmed, laughing with relief and joy that he and his death-defying war dog had made it through alive. Finally, impossibly, the war was over.

But on Okinawa, the trials and tribulations of one man and his dog were only just beginning.

CHAPTER 23

News of the surrender was greeted by those assembled on Okinawa with unreserved jubilation. At the 26th squadron's camp they unhooked the grenades and the tin-can rattles from the wire. With the war finally over, news spread that the famed war dog Smoky had arrived on the island. Wynne was approached to perform his and Smoky's act, at a servicemen's hall run by the Red Cross.

This time there were to be no stage nerves. As matters transpired, Wynne had managed to smuggle most of Smoky's performing paraphernalia onto the LST, so they could attempt something close to their full act. Shacklette still had his Solovox with him, so there could be musical accompaniment too. A big ten-wheeler truck loaded up all of their kit, plus those members of the squadron who wanted to go see the show.

Staff Sergeant Howard Kalt – Smoky's official photographer during the Nadzab parachuting stunt – was something of an amateur magician, and he came along to help compère the evening's entertainment. When Bill and Smoky's turn came, they hustled onto stage together with Shacklette, dragging all of their kit into position. As he eyed the audience, Wynne couldn't deny that he was nervous.

'And now . . .' Kalt announced, with suitable theatricality, 'Corporal Bill Wynne and Corporal Smoky!'

The show opened exactly as they had rehearsed it so exhaustively back at their Lingayen base. The music was superbly timed, switching tunes to provide the perfect soundtrack to each of their subsequent acts. Once Smoky had completed the tightrope walk, Wynne removed the blindfold and she slid down the mahogany slide with a flourish. That done, Wynne gave a quick bow and scurried off stage. Shacklette gave a final fanfare on the Solovox, but it was drowned out by the cheering and applause.

Here on Okinawa their show had proved to be the hit that Wynne had always believed it would. Here on Okinawa – on Japanese soil – man and dog had slain the ghost of their stage fright, which had haunted them in the Philippines. They had done so on the land of the former enemy, but in a time of peace. Maybe that was what had made the crucial difference: the lack of wartime tension and nerves had freed them up to perform and to shine.

Altogether, the squadron's casualties were the heaviest of any recce squadron serving with the 5th Air Force Group. The 26th had suffered thirteen dead and ten wounded. But their losses were thankfully light compared to some of the front-line infantry and marine units. Had the invasion of Japan gone ahead – had the atomic bombs not precluded that necessary evil – millions more would have died. The men of the 26th were fortunate, and they were slated to be returning home any day now.

Via a stopover in Korea, the squadron was to sail back to the USA, the country whose shores they had left almost three long years ago. A handful of men volunteered to remain on Okinawa, so as to avoid the sea voyage to Korea, and to wind down the squadron's affairs on the island. Bill Wynne was one of them. He didn't feel he should subject Smoky to long days at sea. Instead, they'd catch a flight, just as soon as a transport became available. In the interim, their duties would be to dispose of what remained of the paraphernalia of a photo reconnaissance squadron at war.

They bulldozed the photo supplies, and whatever else they could dispose of. But in the process of demolishing the camp Smoky fell ill. She developed a sinus infection, her nasal passages becoming blocked. She was constantly coughing and sneezing. Within days it had worsened so that her nose was permanently clogged with thick mucus. Though she wagged her tail and seemed energetic and in good spirits, Wynne grew increasingly worried. What a bitter irony it would be to lose her now.

The 4th Marine Regiment's War Dog Platoon was camped not so far away. These were the famed 'Devil Dogs' – patrol, message and tracker K9s that had served on the front lines and beyond, operating side by side with their handlers. Wynne walked to their camp, hoping to find a veterinarian. He was directed to the tent of a medic whose role it was to care for the dogs. To every side German Shepherds and Dobermans were barking wildly and straining at their leashes.

Wynne found the medic in his tent seated at a desk. He explained what was wrong with Smoky. The medic said that he had nothing with which to treat the dog's sinus infection, but suggested that if Wynne fed her a mixture of raw eggs and fresh milk it should clear up. He escorted Wynne off the War

Dog Platoon's camp, giving him a quick tour of some of the more famous inhabitants.

He pointed to one, a grizzled German Shepherd. 'That one saved his patrol twice,' he announced, simply.

Another dog was barking wildly. 'He's a one-man dog,' the medic explained. His handler had been killed in a foxhole and the traumatized dog wouldn't let anyone near the body. Eventually, another handler had wooed the dog in his own, inimitable way. That handler was the only guy the dog would let near him now. Fiercely loyal and protective beyond reckoning, the dog had had an uncanny ability to alert patrols to danger long before any of the other canine warriors seemed able to sense it.

There were other dogs who'd been cited for their brave actions, and still more who were recovering from the wounds they'd suffered in combat. For Wynne, it was a humbling and sobering experience. These dogs – they were yet more canine heroes of this war.

Back at camp all he could find in the mess hall were some dried milk and powdered egg. He whisked them together with water, and set the bowl for Smoky. She wolfed down the thick, gloopy liquid. The next morning she seemed a little better. He began to feed her the mixture morning, noon and night. Within three days the sinus infection seemed to have gone.

But Zeitlin's sickly puppy had caught the bug real bad. No matter what anyone might try, he just went from bad to worse. Eventually, it was clear that they would need to put the sad little fellow out of his misery. He was constantly wracked by fits and shakes and he was suffering horribly. No one had any experience of how to do this, so they formed a support party to help Zeitlin through what was coming.

They decided to dig a shallow hole and place the sickly puppy in the bottom of it. Zeitlin insisted on carrying out the mercy-killing himself. He took his carbine and ended his beloved dog's life with one bullet. He was utterly devastated, and everyone around him felt terrible as they threw soil into the tiny animal's makeshift grave.

There wasn't long to dwell on the loss. A warning came in that a typhoon was on its way. Okinawa, like most of Japan, is subject to a typhoon season from May to November. Powerful tropical cyclones blow northwards from the Philippines, gathering power and force over the South China Sea and sucking up water in their wake. On average, a dozen such storms hit Japan and its surrounding seas in a year. August just happened to be the peak of the season.

Tellingly, the local Okinawans had laughed when they'd seen the men of the 26th erecting a tented camp, and nailing corrugated iron to the roofs of the mess hall. They'd explained about the 'big winds' that regularly hit the island. The locals lived in tiny houses with massive walls. There was no glass in the windows and thick red tiles lay heavy on the roofs. Taking heed, Wynne and his fellows had weighed down the corner of tents with sand bags, but other than that there hadn't been a great deal more they could do.

Now, with the majority of the squadron already departed for Korea a typhoon was poised to hit. US military forecasters warned that Okinawa was slap-bang in its path. Wynne and his few fellows prepared as best they could. Using leftovers scavenged from the remains of the photo lab, they build plywood walls to shield their twenty-by-twenty-foot tent. Lashing the plywood to the uprights, they hoped they were ready for the storm.

At 2300 hours that August night it struck. The first blasts of almost horizontal rain slammed into the plywood 'walls' and . . . they held. Wynne and the others who shared the tent felt reassured. They drifted off to sleep, relieved that their defences seemed up to the task. Four hours later they awoke to utter silence and stillness. Had the storm passed? They sat on their cots chatting about what this unnerving calm might signify, but eventually they dozed off again.

At 0500 hours Wynne was jolted violently from his sleep. There was an almighty crash, and a stupendous gust of wind simply tore their tent out of the ground and whisked it away into the dark and howling heavens, like a giant kite. The calm had been the eye of the storm and the typhoon was back with a real vengeance.

Soaked to the skin, Wynne grabbed his blanket, slung Smoky on his cot, and with that gripped firmly in his grasp he dashed for the nearby mess hall, which was still standing. All of a sudden a massive gust caught the cot, ripped it from his hands and spun it into the air. Gripped by fear, he watched as it rose higher, turning two cartwheels in mid-air, Smoky somehow managing to hold on resolutely to the material.

All around torn sheets of corrugated iron were hurtling through the air, like giant, jagged-edged arrows. If one of those struck Smoky, she was a goner. Wynne sprinted after the cot, eyes skywards, as it continued to perform its aerial acrobatics

and Smoky clung on. Maybe it was due to all her circus training – the drum-roll, the slide, the scooter, the high wire – but
for whatever reason, Smoky seemed able to ride that demented
rollercoaster of a flying carpet with miraculous ease.

For fifty feet or more she held on, before the cot dropped
low enough for Wynne to lunge and catch hold. He dragged cot
and dog to earth. With the little dog jammed tightly under one
arm and the cot pointed dead ahead like a spear, he sprinted
the last few remaining yards to the mess hall. The building was
ruined. The roof had been ripped clean off and it was open to
the howling sky. Even the heavy sandbags had been taken by
the storm. But the rain wasn't coming in that way. Driven by
winds of nearly 150 mph, it was hammering in horizontally,
blasting through what remained of the plywood walls.

Wynne placed his cot against what appeared to be the least
damaged section of wall and set Smoky on top of it. For two days
and two nights they huddled in utter misery, eating whatever
cold canned food came to hand, as the wind howled and the rain
lashed relentlessly. Finally, the wind settled to something like
half of its peak. Battling seventy mph gusts the small, bedraggled
band of survivors struggled across to an adjacent building: the
mess hall of the Army Air Force's 6th Group headquarters, it
was a somewhat more substantial, sturdy building.

There they were served their first decent hot meal in three,
storm-lashed days. But the news was far from encouraging. A
second typhoon, believed to be just as powerful as the first, was
headed in their direction. It hit that night, and once again the
rain and wind found its way through every defence, soaking
man – and dog – to the skin.

Wynne decided enough was enough. Extreme measures were called for. He'd heard that there were caves burrowed into the nearby hillsides, which the locals used as tombs. Deciding to brave the spirits of the dead, he grabbed Smoky and dashed for the nearest dark opening. He crawled inside, only to discover a line of ornate ceramic pots secreted deep in the shadows, no doubt packed full of the bones of deceased Okinawans.

In the local Buddhist tradition, the locals would lay the body of a dead family member in such a cave, waiting for the natural process of decomposition to take its course. Some years later they would return to it, gather up the bones and clean them in a ceremony called *senkotsu lit* – washing bones. After that they'd put them in one of the clay or stone pots arranged next to their deceased relations: their final resting place. The tombs – known as *hafu baka*, or roofed graves – doubled as the family shrine.

The *hafu baka* in which Bill Wynne and Smoky had taken refuge was only about four feet high, but it was deep. Wynne set the pots outside to make room for himself and his dog. It was a decidedly eerie place of refuge, but at least it was dry and they were safe from the storm, which thundered and raged outside. Trying his best to rest, an exhausted Wynne woke several times in the night to find Smoky growling, her gaze fixed accusingly on the darkest recesses of the cave.

It was unnerving. Wynne had brought a candle with him. He struck a match and lit it, peering about anxiously. Deep in the guts of the cave a row of eyes gleamed in the light like ghostly coals. Thankfully, it turned out that this was not the enraged spirits of deceased Okinawans, fearing they had been summarily ejected from their place of eternal rest. It was instead a flock of goats, who, like man and dog, had found the only safe refuge from the storm in the house of the dead.

One night of this was about all that Wynne could stomach. With the storm abating, the following morning he returned to what remained of the mess hall. There, he found Duke's owner, John Hembury, together with his plucky little terrier. Together, the two men gathered up what remained of their sodden belongings and hitch-hiked a ride to the airport. Five GIs had been killed in the storms; they didn't want to risk joining their number.

At the airbase the moorings of the Curtis C46 Commando cargo-planes had been torn loose. Wingtips were battered and broken, and any number of rudders had been ripped clean off. Not an airframe among them was still serviceable. As the winds died down, replacement aircraft were flown in. Wynne and Hembury persuaded one of those pilots to fly two men and two little dogs away from the path of the typhoons.

They wanted out of Okinawa, and they weren't too picky about how they managed it.

CHAPTER 24

After a largely uneventful flight, they landed at Kimpo Airport – known today as Gimpo Airport – to the far west of Seoul, the South Korean capital, from where they caught a ride to the squadron's new base, situated in a farming area on the outskirts of Inchon Harbour – now known as Incheon – Seoul's main port. Quartered in an abandoned Japanese military barracks, after the hell of Okinawa at the height of the typhoon season this seemed to them like sheer luxury.

There were four men to each room, each of which boasted a pair of pot-bellied kerosene stoves set dead centre, to keep it toasty. At night those sleeping closest to the burners roasted. Periodically, the stoves' pot bellies would issue deep booms, belching forth clouds of black soot-balls, which would cover everything, sleeping man and dog included. Neither Wynne nor Smoky minded particularly. The rooms were warm and free of wind, and they were dry.

Their existence in Korea became a waiting game. Every day, the men of the squadron expected to receive orders to board a waiting transport at Inchon docks. Every day, no such order came. It was frustrating. Some of the squadron's fliers began taking to the skies again, this time executing air recce missions over Korea.

'In September we moved to Korea,' the squadron's war diary recorded, 'and during a period of uncertainty and waiting, mapped US occupied Korea, and pinpointed airfields, ports and major cities.'

With the end of the war the world was changing. New alliances were forming, new enmities raising their ugly heads. It was good to be ready, especially as Korea would become such a flashpoint for American-Soviet rivalry. In the coming Cold War, Korea would be divided in two nations (present day North and South Korea).

Understandably, those Korean recce flights were a low-key and secretive affair that involved only a handful of men. Most were stuck in their quarters with precious little to do. A highlight was the moment when trucks pulled up at the barracks, distributing Japanese military paraphernalia. Wynne grabbed a rifle and a bayonet from the heap, which included several officer's swords. They would serve as souvenirs of all that had gone before, and all that might have been, had the battle for Japan not been halted by the dropping of the atom bombs.

Wynne kept packing and repacking his kit, restlessly, in preparation for the journey home. One day he emptied out his barracks bag, a kit sack that had gone on ahead of him by sea. Near the bottom he discovered the cardboard letters that he'd cut out at their Lingayen base, when he'd tried – unsuccessfully – to teach Smoky to spell her own name. What had he kept those for, he wondered?

There was little else to do, so he figured he'd try them on Smoky one last time. Intrigued, bored, kicking their heels, a crowd of fellow soldiers gathered. They watched curiously as

Wynne set the letters up near the entrance to their dorm. He decided to start with a real mix-it-up. He arranged the letters so they spelled 'M-K-O-S-Y'.

Gazing at them, he told his little dog: 'Smoky, go spell your name.'

With barely a moment's hesitation Smoky trotted over to the fourth letter in line, which stood twice as tall as her, and plonked herself down, facing it. It had to be a coincidence, Wynne told himself. It simply had to be.

'Next,' he ordered.

Smoky got up, stepped across three letters and sat down opposite the 'M'.

'Good lord,' Wynne muttered. Surely, there couldn't be two such coincidences in a row.

'Next,' he commanded.

Smoky shuffled right two letters, coming to a halt facing the 'O'. Incredible.

'Next.'

Without hesitation she moved left one, to the 'K'. Wynne didn't doubt it any more. Smoky knew this. She'd known it all along. For some reason she just hadn't wanted to show him she did, when they'd trained for it so relentlessly back at their Lingayen base. Here, in the relaxed and relatively peaceful atmosphere of the abandoned Japanese barracks, she'd decided to let him know.

'Next,' he commanded.

Sure enough, Smoky moved sharply right three, and came to a halt facing the last letter of her name: 'Y'.

'Well, I'll be . . .' Wynne exclaimed, under his breath.

The room exploded into applause. Wynne grabbed his dog

and gave her an almighty great hug, praising her for being so clever. Then he got her to do it all over again, just to be absolutely certain. It was quite simply amazing. Their greatest show yet.

He turned to his audience and explained how he'd tried to get her to learn to do this trick back in the Philippines, but no matter what he'd tried his dog had refused to play ball. As he spoke, it dawned upon him what he had been doing wrong. He'd been force-training her. He'd been forcing it and she'd hated it. Smoky had wanted to show him a better way – that she would learn when she was good and ready.

Wynne knew well how at times even top athletes needed a break from the relentless pace of training, to re-ignite their enthusiasm for and dedication to their craft. Smoky was no different. In addition to which, he had been trying to force the trick upon her in the midst of the trials and tribulations of war. Smoky had known all along what he was trying to achieve. Refusing to be taught and to perform had been Smoky's rebellion.

One of the guys seemed to take umbrage at the story Wynne had just related. 'That poor dog can't defecate unless you say so!' he objected. 'What the hell d'you think you're training her *for*?'

Wynne felt chastened. After all, Smoky was the mascot of the squadron. Every man in the 26th felt as if he owned a tiny little part of her. In a way, her well-being was the responsibility of every single one of them.

He shrugged. 'I don't know. I'm not sure. Maybe we can do some shows when we get home.'

The guy glared. 'You know something? You get a wife, she's gonna hate that dog!'

Wynne didn't reply. Clearly, at one time or another he had

pushed Smoky too hard. He'd not been aware of it back then. He'd felt as if he was doing the right thing for all the right reasons, first and foremost of which was to protect her. But here in Korea, Smoky had found a way to let him know that he'd gone too far. At times.

Yet even so, he *had* got her through this war unscathed. At least, so far.

One last hurdle – and it was a major one – lay before them: the homecoming. Orders had already been posted, making it clear that 'No dog or mascot will go back to the US on a War Department ship.' Wynne had feared that such orders were in the offing. He'd heard horror stories of dogs being removed from such vessels, or worse still, thrown overboard. In truth, he was scared, but he was equally determined that Smoky was going home with him, come what may.

He got hold of an oxygen mask case, of the kind that pilots use to carry this vital piece of kit to their aircraft. It was made of a soft green canvas and was fitted with lots of zippered pockets and buttoned flaps. He cut a hole in the bottom of it, just the right size for a Yorkie to sneak inside, and attached a flap to seal it closed.

Just as they had with the haversack that he'd used to smuggle Smoky into Australia, they practised repeatedly with the gasmask bag. Wynne had Smoky crawl in through the bespoke opening, and spend long periods lying absolutely quiet and still. It was pliable and adjusted well to her movements. If she stood, the bag stood with her. If she chose to lie down, it crumpled and creased to suit. Once she was settled, she tended to stay settled in there for long periods of time.

Wynne decided to put the gas-mask hideout to the test. He got Smoky to crawl inside, placing some personal items, including toiletries and a few pairs of socks, on top. Thus armed, he strolled across to the mess hall, setting the bag on one of the tables. Cooks bustled about and the odd soldier paused to chat as Wynne proceeded to unload the bag's contents, as if searching for something deep inside.

Then, on the command of 'Okay!', Smoky wriggled out of her secret door, and as if by magic she appeared.

They'd drawn a small crowd. People laughed and applauded. All understood exactly what Wynne was preparing for, and one or two remarked on what an ingenious set-up it was.

'No one will ever know she's there!'

Wynne figured they were right. If his buddies in the squadron hadn't even realized what was in the bag until Smoky had emerged, surely those policing the ships against canine stowaways wouldn't stand a chance. He taught Smoky to sleep in the bag. She grew fond of her place of hiding. Upon reflection, the delay in their setting sail for home had been a good thing. They'd needed time in which to train and to prepare for perhaps the greatest threat yet, which sadly emanated from their own side.

On 1 November 1945, a notice was posted declaring that everyone from the squadron would be departing the Inchon base the following morning. Embarkation time was 0700 hours, on the USS *General W H Gordon*, a grey-hulled troop transport sporting two enormous, black-rimmed funnels.

That night, as Wynne cuddled up to Smoky for their final night in the barracks dorm, he let his mind drift to thoughts of home: of his mother, and of his fiancée, Margie. After years away, he wanted to surprise her, stepping off a bus or a tram and walking in through her front door to give her a massive hug.

Following a pre-dawn breakfast of pancakes, bacon and coffee, the men boarded a convoy of waiting trucks. Wynne had Smoky safely cocooned in her gas-mask sanctuary. His buddy, Hembury, had had to give Duke to a fellow GI, for he didn't have a place to keep the terrier at home in the US. Needless to say, he was devastated at having to do so. Another soldier carried a pet monkey with him, secreted in an ammo box. Sod the rules.

Despite her cunning place of concealment, Wynne was worried sick about Smoky. He had the letter that Barbara Wood Smith had written him, commending Smoky on her performance with the wounded. He had photos of the little dog at work on those hospital wards. But would that mean anything to those who had been ordered to police the military's draconian rules? Smoky meant so much to those who knew her. But to those who did not? It didn't bear thinking about.

Upon arrival at Inchon Harbour they caught a barge to the waiting ship. Wynne saw figures mount the gangplank. One was Shorty Randall, the guy to whom Hembury had chosen to give Duke. The terrier was too big and boisterous to be carried concealed. Randall had him gripped in his arms. At the top of the gangplank a ship's officer started shouting and gesticulating at the dog. Randall barged past, waving a sheet of paper in the face of the officer.

Wynne stepped up to the gangplank. It was narrow and steep. At the last moment he'd exchanged the gas-mask bag for a heavy kit bag owned by a buddy of his. Ed Piwarski had hurt his back and was in need of the help. Wynne kept his eyes glued to Piwarski, as he stomped up the gangway ahead of him, the still form of Smoky slung in the gas-mask sack over his shoulder.

Ten yards short of the inspecting officer, Wynne felt one of the heavy bags he was carrying slip. It jammed at his feet. Angry voices yelled from below: 'Hurry up! Hurry it up!' The inspecting officer fought his way down to Wynne. He grabbed one of the heavy bags, wrestling it out of Wynne's struggling grasp.

'My buddy's injured!' Wynne exclaimed, by way of explanation, nodding towards the figure of Piwarski, nearing the top of the gangplank. 'I gotta carry his bag too!'

The officer didn't seem to give a damn. He just wanted everyone to hurry up and board. Moments later Piwarski had made the top of the gangway. So, too, had Smoky.

Wynne hurried after them, being reunited with his dog when safely below decks. He chose a top bunk set far into one corner, away from prying eyes. He placed Smoky on the mattress, still in her pack, and settled back to wait. The ship could carry 5,000 troops and it would take all night before she was fully boarded. But just prior to setting sail, the loudspeaker crackled and there was an announcement as unexpected as it was unwelcome.

'Will the man who brought the dog aboard report to the troop office. Will the man who brought the dog aboard report to the troop office.'

Wynne's heart nearly stopped. Surely, the message couldn't refer to Smoky? No one had even seen her come aboard. The guys all around glanced at him, anxiously, but he raised a pair of crossed fingers. He told himself that he was going nowhere. A worried-looking Randall headed top-deck. Shortly, he was back. He'd been called before the ship's Transport Commander and ordered to take his dog Duke ashore.

As he'd exited the guy's office, one of the ship's crew had dragged him to one side. He could hide Duke, the sailor had told him, but only deep in the bowels of the ship. He had two other dogs down there already. So it was that Duke was sent to the depths of the *General W H Gordon*'s hold. He would have to ride out the coming voyage secreted there.

The ship weighed anchor and set sail. As soon as they were out of the harbour the sea became rough and Wynne fell victim to seasickness. He felt so bad he couldn't even leave his bunk for meals. A group of fellow soldiers from the 26th, seeing that her master was out of action, volunteered to serve as Smoky's protectors. They took her top-deck for fresh air and walks, screening her with the mass of their bodies.

Despite their best efforts, come day four of their voyage the Tannoy barked again: 'All men who have brought aboard either dogs or monkeys, report to the ship's office, immediately!'

A sickly Wynne was gripped by horror. He had visions of Smoky's tiny form being hurled over the ship's rail. Surely, no one could know that she was aboard. Though he was barely able to walk, he made his way to the ship's office, staggering and reeling drunkenly as he went. He might as well see what all the fuss was about.

Five men were there ahead of him. The Troop Commander was yelling at them, his face puce with anger. 'No dogs and especially no monkeys travel back on this ship!'

'But sir,' one of the soldiers pleaded, 'these are war dogs. I have a letter from the Colonel—'

'I don't care if you've got a letter from MacArthur himself!' the Troop Commander roared. 'No dogs go back on my ship!'

Wynne felt too sick to even try to join in the heated debate.

'Do you have any idea what it will cost to bring a dog into the States?' the Troop Commander demanded. 'A thousand dollars – that's what customs will charge you!'

The soldier drew himself to his full height. 'But sir, I have a thousand dollars and I'm quite happy . . .'

Wynne wasn't listening any more. He felt so sick he had to return to his bunk. To hell with it. He decided to keep absolutely schtum about Smoky. If the Troop Commander didn't get to hear of her presence or see her, he could hardly object or do anything about it, could he? The men of the squadron offered to lend Wynne whatever cash they had to cover the $1,000 quarantine fees that the Troop Commander was banging on about.

On day seven of the journey a group of ship's officers began to search the decks for stowaways. A pair of GIs had been scheduled to leave the vessel in Inchon, but they had reportedly hidden themselves aboard so as to secure an early ride back to the US. The search party didn't find the two fugitives. But one of them, a Navy lieutenant, did spot Smoky.

'Whose dog is that?' he demanded, accusingly. All eyes turned on a sickly Bill Wynne. 'Is the dog registered on the ship?' the lieutenant challenged.

Wynne shook his head. 'No, sir.'

'Didn't you hear it piped on the PA system?'

'Yes, sir. But I've been too sick to move. I haven't even made it to chow but two times since we set sail.'

Wynne was telling the truth about his failure to make any

meals and he must have looked sick as a dog, for the lieutenant believed him. Nevertheless, he was told to report to the ship's office in quick order.

An hour later Wynne found himself standing unsteadily before the ship's captain. He was warned that he might have to pay a bond if he was determined not to give up his dog. Wynne said that he would gladly do so. He was made to swear an oath, raising his right hand and averring that he was telling the 'whole truth, so help me God'. That done, he signed a paper that exonerated the captain and crew of USS *General W H Gordon* from any responsibility for 'One dog'.

With that paper grasped in hand, Wynne made his unsteady way back below decks. He showed the paper around Smoky's support crew, triumphantly. It seemed that for now at least their worries were over.

The USS *General W H Gordon* had been sent to Korea to join the invasion of Japan, carrying troops for the landings. The captain was determined to break his own record for the journey home. Steaming at thirty knots he had fast rounded Japan, headed past the Aleutian Islands, before proceeding south along the western Canadian seaboard.

On day ten out of Inchon seagulls swarmed around the ship's deck. Wynne was feeling a little recovered and he'd taken Smoky for a stroll in the fresh air. The little dog barked furiously each time a gull swooped in close and low. Smoky and Wynne proceeded to perform one or two of their tricks, as sailors and soldiers laughed and cheered. He noticed the ship's captain watching from the bridge and smiling, indulgently.

At dawn on day twelve, the ship steamed past the islands

of Puget Sound, an estuary on the northwestern coast of the USA, in Washington State. A little harbour boat headed out to intercept the troopship. It was packed full of young women in gaily coloured clothes. A band began to play, as the girls danced and sang a well-rehearsed homecoming routine. They waved placards reading: 'WELL DONE' and 'WELCOME HOME'. The guys lining the deck of the *General W H Gordon* went wild.

The troopship steamed into Washington Harbour, in the city of Tacoma, lying within the heart of Puget Sound. Wynne put Smoky into her gas-mask hideaway and stowed his Japanese rifle and bayonet in his barracks bag. The vessel dropped anchor and the gangplank was lowered. As he stepped off the gangway onto American soil, he spied a customs inspector lined up with the other top brass to form the reception party.

For a moment he stiffened, drawing Smoky tighter, but all those figures did was smile and salute at the homecoming troops marching past. As the crowds cheered and waved, there wasn't the barest hint of any searches or inspections. A convoy of trucks was waiting to whisk the men of the 26th Photo Reconnaissance squadron away to a smart army barracks, in the nearby base of Fort Lewis.

There, an absolute treat was laid out: fresh milk, fresh salad, huge T-bone steaks, and real ice-cream. It was the kind of food that for approaching three years the men had only tasted in their dreams. Smoky enjoyed some milk and a slice of steak, before curling up on Bill Wynne's cot. She was safely home – or at least, she had arrived in what was to be her new home: America.

Of course, no one was any the wiser as to where the small dog with the world's biggest heart had originated from. Regardless, after the long years at war Smoky had made it through safe and sound. If Smoky's past was filled with mystery, then her future, with her companion Bill Wynne at her side, was one full of promise.

And that, really, should be the end of the story.

'That should end the story,' concluded the History & Legend of the 26th Photo Reconnaissance Squadron. 'Only it doesn't. Just as the old saying tells us that "old soldiers never die", so it is true that old squadrons never die. Those of our buddies who are numbered amongst the fallen, for us will never die. They will achieve immortality in our memories and will be alive as long as any of us are alive to remember them and cherish their memories.

'The Australians, on the anniversary of the deaths of sons or brothers or comrades, insert "In Memoriam" notices in their newspapers, usually starting with the phrase "In proud and loving memory." It was a phrase that many of us admired. It would be a phrase that would be appropriate to borrow now. In thinking of the friends we have lost by death or separation, in thinking of the days of our brotherhood and camaraderie, of the hardships, grief, work and fun we shared, we shall always be one in holding them "In proud and loving memory".'

In proud and loving memory.

EPILOGUE

At the end of the Second World War, General Hatazo Adachi, who had spearheaded the Japanese resistance in New Guinea, surrendered to Australian troops. By then, only 13,000 of his original army were left alive. He was subsequently tried as a war criminal by the Allies and sentenced to life imprisonment. He testified in defence of every officer under his command who was likewise tried as a war criminal.

On the morning of 10 September 1947 Adachi used a knife to commit suicide in his cell. He had written a letter to those men and officers of his command who had survived. It read:

Notwithstanding the fact that my officers and men did their best in exceptional circumstances, surmounting all difficulties ... the hoped-for end was not attained, because of my inability. Thus I paved the way for my country to be driven into the present predicament. The crime deserves death.

During the past three years of operations more than 100,000 youthful and promising officers and men were lost and most of them died of malnutrition. When I think of this, I know not what apologies to make to His Majesty the Emperor and I feel that I myself am overwhelmed with shame ... I have demanded perseverance far exceeding the limits of man's endurance of my officers and men, who were exhausted and emaciated as a result of successive campaigns and for want of supplies.

At war's end General Tomoyuki Yamashita, who master-minded Japanese resistance in the Philippines, was also tried for war crimes. Yamashita was found guilty and sentenced to death, even though his defence argued that in many cases he was not aware of the atrocities committed by troops and had not approved them. In some cases the soldiers in question had not even been under his command. The ruling established the legal precedent known as the 'Yamashita standard', by which a commanding officer can be held legally accountable for atrocities committed by those under his command, even if he was not aware of them and did not support such actions. On 23 February 1946 Yamashita was hanged in a Manila prison camp.

In early 1946 the 26th Photo Reconnaissance Squadron was disbanded, although it would be reformed as a reserve unit from 1947–9. It was reformed once more, in 1955, as a unit operating Boeing B-47 Stratojets, a long-range high-altitude jet-powered aircraft then known as the 'fastest bomber in the world'. The reconnaissance version flew top-secret and danger-ous missions over the Soviet Union, carrying state-of-the-art radar and camera equipment. The unit was renamed the 681st Bombardment Squadron in late 1961 and converted to bomb-ing duties only, before being permanently disbanded in 1962 (although see note on its successor, below).

At the end of the war, RAF Medmenham's work as the centre of photo reconnaissance skill and excellence – for both the British and their American allies – was kept a strict secret, as the Cold War loomed large. The skills developed for spying on Nazi-occupied Europe – or the jungles of Japanese-occupied New Guinea – were far too of-the-moment and sensitive to be made public. It was not until Constance Babington Smith published a book about Medmenham's work, entitled *Evidence In Camera*, in 1957, that the secrets started to come out.

By then, of course, high-altitude US spy planes were flying missions over the Soviet Union, their fuselages packed with sensitive electronic eavesdropping equipment and state-of-the-art camera systems. The U2 flights in particular were so sensitive that each required Presidential approval and all were under the overall command of the CIA, not the Air Force. The then Soviet leader, Nikita Khrushchev, said of those flights that they 'spat in the face of the Soviet people'.

But as with the sorties flown by the pilots of the 26th over the southwest Pacific during the Second World War, even those U2 flights weren't immune to danger. In May 1960 a new long-range Soviet missile succeeded in shooting down a U2 piloted by Francis Gary Powers, who bailed out and survived. He was captured and the Soviets retrieved cameras and other sensitive equipment from the wreckage. The Americans tried to claim the U2 aircraft had got lost on a high-altitude weather-testing mission. The story did not wash, and the temperature of the Cold War lurched another few degrees lower.

*

After their triumphant November 1945 homecoming, Bill Wynne and Smoky's story was covered widely in the US media. They became a sensation. Wynne had been unable to get most of their performing kit out of storm-swept Okinawa, so he had to re-create much of the same equipment in Cleveland, to meet the demand for him and his dog to appear on radio and news shows, and for photo calls in the printed media. They were also in high demand to perform before live audiences, all of whom were fascinated to see this famous war dog in action.

Wynne quickly saw that Smoky loved to play up to the crowd. Clever and smart, she knew she could get away with things when performing that he would never allow during practice. They had an act where she would jump through three hoops in a row. But when live on stage, she'd often dodge the second hoop, skirting around it, which invariably drew a chorus of wild cheers and laughter from the audience. Realizing how much they seemed to appreciate the famous war dog's cheeky wilfulness, Wynne worked such 'disobedience' into their regular acts.

As they had done when in the field, they began to act as a therapy man-and-dog team in the local hospital, which was full of those injured and traumatized in the war. On one occasion they performed before a group of wheelchair-bound soldiers. One began gurgling excitedly and holding out his arms to Smoky. One of the nurses asked if he might get to hold the dog. He took her in his arms, and smiling widely began to swing her back and forth, gently. The nurses were in tears. It turned out the soldier had been catatonic for two years, barely moving or displaying any emotions. Smoky had broken through all of that.

Wynne was contacted by a travelling circus. They asked if

they might book him and Smoky for eight live shows, for which they'd pay him a fee of $200. Wynne agreed. He contacted good friends, needing a carpenter to help him re-create Smoky's high-wire apparatus. They managed it in time, but on the night of the first performance the clown took to the stage, to the thundering of some circus cannons. At the sound of the blasts Smoky started to spin on the spot nervously, just like she had done during the air raids on Biak Island.

Wynne had no option but to take Smoky outside, to shield her from the blasts. It was February in Cleveland and bitterly cold, but there they were forced to stay until the firing was finished. They were to be the final act, the grand finale to round off the show. Previously, the circus owner had booked a rodeo act and it had been a disaster. The stakes were high. But by the time Smoky and Wynne took to the stage, the audience had mostly left. Just a few dozen remained. The previous acts had gone on too long and drained the audience away.

Those who remained loved the show, but it wasn't enough. After their fourth night, the circus owners called Wynne into their office. They were cancelling his act, and they offered him a compromise fee of $100. Wynne objected that he'd signed a contract for $200. The owners pointed out that he might have signed the contract, but they never had. It was a take-it-or-leave-it offer. Wynne was disgusted, and he vowed never to agree to such a performance again.

In any case, other requests were flooding in. There was a call from a local Kennel Club. Would Wynne and Smoky do their act immediately prior to the Best in Show competition? Wynne had never been to a dog show before, but the act went down a storm. Wynne was contacted by several Yorkie owners. One, Goldie Stone, was a Yorkie breeder from Columbus, Ohio. She praised Smoky for her fine lines and asked Wynne if he and his dog might be willing to visit.

They travelled to Ohio by train, together with Margie. Goldie Stone was hugely impressed with Smoky. She told Wynne that Smoky was a fantastic specimen of such a dog and that she could have sold her for $250 as a puppy. She wondered what her ancestry was, and the subject of how on earth Smoky had got to New Guinea came up. Wynne had to confess that he had absolutely no idea.

In the spring of 1946 Wynne began work on a book telling his and Smoky's story. He wrote in long hand, and found it a blessing to unburden himself of his wartime memories. Together, his mother and Margie typed and edited the manuscript. In between the writing, man and dog toured a number of hospitals. In Chicago, they were met by the Red Cross, accompanied by a phalanx of press reporters. Chicago's *Daily News*, *Sun* and *Herald* all covered their story. One reporter wrote: 'Smoky looks like the business end of your wife's favorite mop dyed in tobacco juice.' But it was all good publicity.

Wynne and Smoky did their act for GIs dying with cancer and for others who'd lost their minds during the war. They helped raise the profile of animal shelters, shooting promotional films with them. Wynne used some of his contacts to reach out to *Life Magazine*, to see if the publishers might also be interested in his and Smoky's book. The word came back that they had covered the story of several Second World War mascots, and felt that another might well be overkill.

Wynne reckoned people were tiring of the war. They'd lived its horrors and privations and losses: they wanted to get on with living the future. He shelved the idea of publishing the book that he had written. He carried on doing live shows, even returning to the Parmadale orphanage where he'd spent two years as a young child.

Wynne married Margie, his Cleveland fiancée, in September 1946. She had a good job with a veteran's association, but then Wynne spotted an advert for a trainer, to prepare dogs to act in motion pictures. The job seemed tailor-made for him. He applied and was asked to go to California, to try it out. He and Margie decided to move to California and give Hollywood a whirl. They arrived with Smoky, and Wynne signed up as a trainer on a trial basis. He was soon schooling dogs through film, and meeting some of the most famous master trainers, who worked on big budget movies.

He joined the Hollywood Animal Handlers and Trainers Association. He and Smoky performed at the Hollywood Canteen, a hangout for war veterans. The night of their first show Smoky went crazy. Instead of responding to the first acts as normal, she started racing in between the stage curtains and ignoring Wynne's every command. Every time he found her, she darted off in another direction and the audience was starting to howl with laughter.

When he dashed behind the curtain to grab her, she went out centre stage, playing to the audience. Wynne eventually managed to get her under control again and they were able to finish the act as he'd intended. The odd thing was, the entire performance – Smoky's craziness included – seemed to have gone down a storm. They were invited to do a private show for a big Hollywood producer. Other big shots began to show real interest in him plus his diminutive, but hugely spirited little dog.

The trouble was Margie. From her well-paid job in Cleveland she'd been reduced to sitting at home all day long while Wynne and Smoky were out at work, and the days were perilously long. Hollywood producers tended to save money by pushing shoots through to ten o'clock at night, rather than scheduling extra days. She was sick, she wasn't eating well and she certainly wasn't enjoying Hollywood.

Her job was still waiting for her back in Cleveland, so after just three months of marriage they decided to part ways temporarily. She'd head back to Cleveland, and Wynne would give it a while longer, hoping to break through. Days later Wynne received a letter from Margie telling him that she was pregnant. Now her sickness made a great deal more sense. She'd moved back in with her parents and things weren't so bad. They could brave the separation for a while longer.

Wynne was contracted to be a handler in a Warner Brothers movie starring Ronald Reagan – the future US president - entitled *Night Unto Night*. The dog he was handling was a mongrel named Butch. One evening Wynne returned to his car in the parking lot, and Smoky was standing on the back of the driver's seat, waiting for him. The wife of the movie's producer had spotted her, and she called her husband over. Together they admired Smoky, and Wynne got her to run through a few tricks as he explained her wartime career.

The producer's wife begged her husband to let Smoky appear in *Night Unto Night*. The producer objected she was too good to play a bit-part. He'd make her the star of his next movie, he proclaimed. He was dead serious, as well. Wynne sensed this might be the turning point in his and his dog's Hollywood career.

But at around that time Margie got in contact to inform him that Cleveland NACA (the forerunner to the present-day NASA) had been in contact, offering him a job as a flight photographer. They could hold the job for one week only and it paid $3-5,000 per year. Wynne would need to be in Cleveland by 28 January 1947 and ready to start work if he wanted to make the job his.

Wynne was all but broke in Hollywood. He'd survived on scraps of work, but there was never enough. His mother called, urging him to return home. His wife was pregnant, he had no firm prospects in Hollywood and the offer of a job with NACA was too good to turn down. Wynne's buddies in the film business learned that he was on the verge of leaving. Many urged him to stay. They made promises, but what he needed was a firm, bulletproof commitment to money and work.

Nothing was forthcoming, so Wynne and Smoky left Hollywood and headed home. Starting work at Cleveland NACA Flight Propulsion Center was pretty much like returning to the 26th Photo Reconnaissance Squadron. Nearly everyone was former military. They were flying former USAAF B-24 Liberators and B-25 Mitchell bombers, testing groundbreaking de-icing kit at altitude and in the often freezing conditions over Cleveland's Great Lakes region.

A device like a mini-furnace blew hot air through ducts, playing it over the leading edges of the bombers' wings. The sheer power of the heat it produced could melt off almost any ice that formed. The icing test flights weren't without danger, but at least there was no risk of being targeted by ack-ack or enemy fighters, being hit by tropical cyclones or of having to bail out over hostile jungle.

In between the flight work Wynne and Smoky continued to perform. A booking agent got them shows at ice hockey matches, boxing bouts, night clubs and theatres. They were always a smash hit and the audiences brought the roof down with their applause. But it still wasn't Hollywood. One of the main Hollywood handlers called. He offered Wynne a full-time job as a trainer in his kennels. But when Wynne demanded a legally binding contract and guaranteed wages, he went silent.

Wynne called Goldie, the Yorkie breeder, and asked if he might buy a male dog to mate with Smoky. She sent him a puppy from a prize stud male, one whose coat had the strong steel blue and brilliant gold hues that are prized by breeders. That puppy earned the name 'Mr Terrific', or Terry for short. Two weeks later Smoky came into season and she and Terry fell very much in love. Smoky became pregnant, and in the excitement of the moment Terry was put out in the yard and went missing.

No one had a clue what could have happened to him. Wynne and family and friends searched high and low. They nailed up lost-dog posters everywhere. But no matter what they tried there was no further sign of Terry. Wynne understood then what it must have been like for Smoky's original owners to lose her in the New Guinea jungles, as they had done.

On 27 June 1947 Smoky gave birth to one little puppy, her second after Topper (who'd died during the mystery Lingayen plague). The very next day Margie gave birth to a daughter,

Joanne Marie. When Smoky's pup was four months old they gave her to Margie's sister, Helen. Though family life was getting very busy, Smoky and Wynne continued to perform their shows.

By 1949 Wynne and Margie had several young children to care for (they would end up raising nine). Having never known his father, Wynne was determined that his own family would never suffer from such a similarly absent parent. He had to balance the demands of travelling on show business with spending time at home with his wife and children, and to that end he was determined to stick to local 'day-jobs' to ensure he might do so. The best were those like the NACA contract, which took the skills he had learned in the 26th and put them to civilian use.

Wynne and Smoky were booked to do a regular children's slot on a local TV station. They had to leave the NACA lab early every Friday and rush over to make their appearance on Cleveland's Channel 9. In October 1953 Wynne was approached by a local paper, the *Cleveland Plain Dealer*, to take a job as a photographer with them. The money was better than he was making at NACA and with six children by now it was tempting. He spoke to his boss at NACA and was told there was no way they could match the newspaper's offer. He took the job.

The following year the Sunday paper carried the story that Smoky the famous war dog was retiring from her show business career. Smoky, who had to be a good ten years old by now, was still in fine form, but Wynne decided it was better to quit when they were still ahead.

Not long after this he was invited to take a regular Sunday morning TV slot. As Smoky was retired, she'd only be asked to do one trick, and most of the show would involve Wynne training other dogs and interviewing guests. He reckoned that was doable, and so they began to appear on the regular slot: 'How to Train Your Dog, with Bill Wynne and Smoky.' The show ran for thirty weeks and was a big hit, but eventually Smoky really did have to retire for good.

On 21 February 1957 Wynne came home from work and found Smoky apparently sleeping soundly. In truth, she'd passed away. Not a man to cry easily, this time Wynne gave vent to his grief freely. As they were about to move house and they didn't want to lose Smoky's gravesite, they decided to bury her in the Cleveland Metroparks, known as the 'Emerald Necklace', a beautiful stretch of woodland, cliffs and rivers surrounding the city.

They found a special tree where Wynne and Margie had once carved a heart and their names, as sweethearts, and dug Smoky a grave beneath it. Smoky's body had been carried there in a shoe box. As Wynne went to lower the body into the grave, his seven-year-old daughter, Susan, asked: 'But Daddy, how is Smoky going to breathe?'

Caught unprepared, he couldn't ignore her bright blue tearful gaze. 'She doesn't need to breathe any more,' he answered. 'She's in dog heaven.' He did his best to hide from her his own tears, because fathers are supposed to be strong at such times.

Wynne's employer, the *Cleveland Plain Dealer*, printed an obituary, which told the entire story of the famous war dog and her subsequent show business career. The day it was published Margie took a phone call from Grace Guderian, who had been a lieutenant nurse assigned to a field hospital during the war. She explained how she had lost a female Yorkie in New Guinea in early 1944. Her then fiancé, also serving in the military, had bought her the dog from a Brisbane dealer as a Christmas gift. Grace Guderian had named the dog Christmas.

A while later she'd deployed to Dobodora, in New Guinea, which is where the little dog had gone missing. Bill Wynne and his wife could only conclude that Christmas and Smoky were one and the same animal. Wynne remembered the time on Biak Island when Smoky had reacted with such excitement to the word Christmas. He hadn't made much of it at the time. It made perfect sense now. The breeder who had sold Grace Guderian the puppy had made a great show of the pedigree and class of the Yorkie. There could not have been two such dogs in circulation in Nadzab at around that time.

There was one mystery. How had Smoky got from Dobodora, where she'd gone missing, to Nadzab, where they had found her, a distance of some 180 miles? It turned out that Grace Guderian had taken Smoky to a show being performed at the Dobodora base by Bob Hope, then a popular comedian, actor and singer. Christmas had disappeared during the show. Bob Hope was touring bases and very likely flew on to others, including Nadzab. Somehow, Christmas must have made that journey as part of his retinue, or on one of countless other flights shuttling between the various bases.

That was all that Wynne could imagine. At Nadzab, she'd run off again, only for a die-hard dog-hater, Ed Downey, to discover her abandoned in the foxhole. Wynne could think of no other scenario to explain how the little dog had made it into his life as she had. To make a full circle of the amazing series of coincidences in Smoky and Bill Wynne's incredible – fated? – coming together, it turned out that Grace Guderian and her husband lived not a few blocks from the Wynnes' house in Cleveland.

Smoky's first owners were able to give Wynne some photos of her as she was when they had her, in which she looked about five months old. He calculated that she had to have been born sometime around the middle of 1943.

Since her death Smoky has been formally honoured in many different ways. In 2005, on America's annual Veterans Day, 11 November, a bronze life-size sculpture of Smoky sitting in a GI helmet atop a two-tonne granite block was unveiled at the Cleveland Metroparks, sited above the very spot where Smoky is buried. It is dedicated thus: 'Smoky, the Yorkie Doodle Dandy and the Dog of All Wars'.

The American Kennel Club Museum of the Dog in St Louis, Missouri, has a permanent display dedicated to Smoky. The 26th Air Space Intelligence Squadron, the successor to the 26th Photo Reconnaissance Squadron, has a memorial dedicated to Smoky at their Hickam Air Force Base, on Hawaii. The Ohio Veterinary Medicine Association has a memorial dedicated to Smoky, the 'No. 1 Dog Hero', in its Columbus, Ohio, Animal Hall of Fame. There are other such memorials across the US.

Smoky was also awarded the People's Dispensary for Sick Animals (PDSA) Certificate for Animal Bravery or Devotion in April 2011, in Britain. In May 2014 the *Animal Planet* TV show – a Discovery Communications broadcast – concluded that when Smoky did the rounds of the wards in the Nadzab hospital, she became the world's first ever therapy dog of record;

in other words, she was the first dog ever recorded to have carried out such therapeutic duties.

There is a permanent memorial and statue of Smoky at the Royal Brisbane Women's Hospital, unveiled in December 2012, to recognize her Australian roots and the role she served as a therapy dog in Australian hospitals. In July 2013 she was also awarded the Australian Defence Force Trackers and War Dog Association's War Dog Operational Medal, and in December 2015 she was given the Australian RSPCA's Purple Cross Award. The award recognizes the deeds of animals who have demonstrated exceptional courage, risking their own safety to save a person's life.

In 1996, Bill Wynne's rendition of his and Smoky's story, entitled *Yorkie Doodle Dandy: Or, the Other Woman Was a Real Dog*, was published by Wynnesome Press. For any reader whose wider interest may have been piqued by this book, it remains in print, now published by Top Dog Enterprises.

Author Damien Lewis supports the pioneering and exceptional work of the following two canine charities. He is proud to be a patron of Bravehound and in 2018 he received a Canine Partners retiree dog named Moxie, who has become a beloved member of the Lewis household. Please do join in supporting their work in whatever way you can.

Dogs can help heal invisible wounds:
A profile of Bravehound

Veterans with Post Traumatic Stress Disorder and other mental health conditions can become isolated and find it difficult to relate to other people, and to adjust to life as a civilian. Bravehound partners veterans with dogs, giving them twenty-four hour companionship and a structure to their day.

We provide training and support – and of course the dogs themselves – for the lifetime of each Bravehound.

Do please get in touch if you would like to hear more about Bravehound and how you might support our work.

www.bravehound.co.uk
hello@bravehound.co.uk
+ 44 7980631110

BRAVEHOUND

Amazing dogs. Transforming lives:
A profile of Canine Partners

Canine Partners is a registered charity that trains assistance dogs for people with physical disabilities including civilians and members of HM Armed Forces.

Our dogs are trained to help with everyday tasks such as opening and closing doors, unloading the washing machine, picking up dropped items, pressing buttons and switches and getting help in an emergency. They also increase independence, confidence, self-esteem, a sense of security and bring companionship and increased social interaction.

Canine Partners receives no government funding and relies solely on public donations.

For further information visit caninepartners.org.uk or call 08456 580 480.

Amazing dogs. Transforming lives.

caninepartners.org.uk

Registered Charity No: 803680
(England and Wales) and SC039050 (Scotland)